HOW LAW WORKS

How Law Works

The Machinery and Impact of Civil Justice

ROSS CRANSTON

OXFORD

UNIVERSITY PRESS

OXFORD
UNIVERSITY PRESS

Great Clarendon Street, Oxford OX2 6DP

Oxford University Press is a department of the University of Oxford.
It furthers the University's objective of excellence in research, scholarship,
and education by publishing worldwide in

Oxford New York

Auckland Cape Town Dar es Salaam Hong Kong Karachi
Kuala Lumpur Madrid Melbourne Mexico City Nairobi
New Delhi Shanghai Taipei Toronto

With offices in

Argentina Austria Brazil Chile Czech Republic France Greece
Guatemala Hungary Italy Japan Poland Portugal Singapore
South Korea Switzerland Thailand Turkey Ukraine Vietnam

Oxford is a registered trade mark of Oxford University Press
in the UK and in certain other countries

Published in the United States
by Oxford University Press Inc., New York

British Library Cataloguing in Publication Data

Data available

Library of Congress Cataloging in Publication Data

Cranston, Ross.
How law works : the machinery and impact of civil justice / Ross Cranston.
   p. cm.
Includes index.
ISBN 0–19–929207–8 (hardback : alk.paper)   1. Justice.   2. Civil rights.
3. Justice, Administration of.   I. Title.
K240.C73 2006
347—dc22

2005027910

Typeset by Newgen Imaging Systems (P) Ltd., Chennai, India
Printed in Great Britain
on acid-free paper by
Biddles Ltd., King's Lynn

ISBN 0–19–929207–8   978–0–19–929207–3

1 3 5 7 9 10 8 6 4 2

Preface

How Law Works is a study of the civil justice system. It cannot pretend to be exhaustive about so vast a topic, especially across a number of jurisdictions. The discussion is fleshed out along a number of dimensions. First is the characterization of some aspects of the subject as being about the machinery of the law, and others about the law's impact. Included in the machinery of justice chapters is an examination of who gets access to justice and how; the institutions of the law (the courts and other bodies which resolve disputes); and the personnel of the law (mainly lawyers, but also judges, public officials, and paralegals). As to the chapters on the impact of the law various issues are addressed: the gap between the aspiration of law and the reality; that in some situations law can be destructive of social patterns; the relationship between law and economic development; and whether law can be transplanted from one society to another.

Next are the threads which run through the book and which are collected together in the concluding chapter. One of these concerns fundamental values of the law such as access to justice, equality before the law and the rule of law. In exceptional cases these spin off enforceable legal rights but in the main found public policy arguments for how the civil justice system should work. Procedure, another thread, is central to the functioning of the civil justice system. Too often it is overlooked in favour of the substantive law. In this book procedure extends beyond the rules of court to the administration and organization of the justice system as a whole. Running until the end of the book is a further thread, that understanding how law works demands a knowledge of both law and law's context. Context is the social, economic, and political backdrop to the law. That context is best explored in studies which are firmly based on empirical evidence. Empirical evidence does not provide unequivocal answers to normative questions, but it certainly offers a firm base for their consideration. Throughout the book there is reference to the findings of social research. Unfortunately not a great deal of social research has been done on the civil justice system or its impact compared with the enormous volume of criminological research.

Finally, there are the specific arguments of the book about the working of the civil justice system. It is not the function of this preface to anticipate these. Attention here needs only to be drawn to a number of points. To begin, the opening chapter offers an analytical overview for the book. It is neither high theory nor simple description. Rather it sets out various models for understanding. These are both frameworks for thinking about issues and occasionally what social scientists call 'theories of the middle range'. Secondly, while the book is grounded in the British experience, its horizon is comparative and extends not only across the Atlantic but to south and south-east Asia. Although that part of the world contains the world's largest common law jurisdiction, the region is little studied by European lawyers. That presents its own difficulties for anything like a complete understanding. Thirdly, the book has little about the machinery of legislation. Partly that is because legislation was the subject of a previous book, also published by Oxford University Press, *Law, Government and Public Policy* (Melbourne, 1987). The second part of this book, on the impact of law, includes, however, the impact of legislation. Fourthly, while not at the forefront, various policy prescriptions emerge from the discussion. Thus the book is both descriptive and prescriptive. While some of the proposals for reform are reasonably self-evident, others will not be especially fashionable among those closely involved in the working of the civil justice system.

At the time I was completing this book the National Gallery in London held a further exhibition in its 'Art in the Making' series. This time it was about the artist Edgar Degas. With his oil painting, Degas employed the conventional pattern of notebook drawings, followed by oil sketches of details, pastel studies of the whole scene and then the final canvas. *Miss La La at the Cirque Fenando*, 1879, in the National Gallery, is illustrative. A skilled draftsman, Degas outlined forms, trying different positions for limbs, heads or backgrounds until the final location of each was decided. He would revisit paintings, often dating back many years, to rework them, as with *Young Spartans Exercising*, 1860, also in the Gallery. Work in pastel was coupled with a highly unconventional use of tracing paper, which among other things enabled Degas to replicate the same figure in any number of future works, sometimes by tracing the image in reverse (see D. Bromford *et al.*, *Art in the Making. Degas* (London, 2004), 21–2, 24, 30).

This book imitates Degas' techniques of developing a complete work over a period, revisiting earlier pieces to rework them, and replicating particular aspects in different contexts (although there are no cases, as far as I can tell, of reversing these: my arguments still face the same way, although there is occasionally some realignment). So I confess to having plundered previous books and articles. All have been updated and revised, sometimes mercilessly, to fit within the framework of *How Law Works*. Originally Chapter 3 was a paper delivered at a British Council seminar, published in J. Faundez (ed.), *Good Government and Law* (London, 1997). It has been retouched with subsequent developments. The following chapter on courts has had various exhibitions, first at (1986) 5 *CJQ* 123. While the basic structure remains, the content has been varied considerably. In its published form in A. Zuckerman & R. Cranston (eds), *Reform of Civil Procedure* (Oxford, 1995), ch. 5 was a truncated version of a background report I prepared as Lord Woolf's academic consultant for his Access to Justice inquiry. Since it appeared before the final report of the inquiry, it has had to be very substantially rewritten to take this, and the new Civil Procedure Rules, into the picture. For Chapter 6 I have updated and tightened my presidential address to what is now the Society of Legal Scholars (then the Society of Public Teachers of Law), published in R. Cranston (ed.), *Legal Ethics and Professional Responsibility* (Oxford, 1995). The following two chapters are revisions of much older works. Chapter 7 appeared in different parts of my *Legal Foundations of the Welfare State* (London, 1985), although in this form (although not substance) in C. Samford & D. Galligan (eds), *Law, Rights and the Welfare State* (London, 1986). (Several paragraphs from the former have also strayed into Chapter 2 as well.) The core of Chapter 8 was published in (1973) 8 *U Qld LJ* 60. Chapter 9 is barely recognizable as the report I produced as rapporteur for a World Bank/Asian Development Bank seminar in Manila in 1992, and published in [1995] 39 *St Louis ULJ* 759. Chapter 10 is an updated version of an essay in honour of Professor Jacob Ziegel, from (1991) 19 *Can.Bus. LJ* 296.

In preparing this book, and its component parts, I have incurred many debts over a long period. I list my creditors without handles: Sonali Abeyratne, Michael Anderson, Nony Ardill, William Blair, Hugh Collins, Guy Dehn, Edward Elliott, Hazel Genn, Mohan Gopal, Christopher Greenwood, Roy Goode, Andrew Harding, John McCorquodale, Richard Moorhead, Anthony Ogus, Sylvia Vir Singh, David Sugarman, Rachel Mulheron, Robert Turner, Roger Smith, Philip Wood, Robert Worthington, Reeza Hameed, Christos Hadjiemmanuil, and Basil Markesinis. Officials at what was then the Lord Chancellor's Department, now the Department for Constitutional Affairs, assisted at various points. In my last years as a Member of Parliament I learnt much from my membership of the Constitutional Affairs Select Committee. As mentioned, I was fortunate to serve as the academic consultant to Lord Woolf's Access to Justice inquiry. For the sake of completeness, I also draw attention to my involvement in some of the events described in Chapter 10 (see p. 303, n. 62). Susan Hunt expertly typed the whole manuscript and the Law Department of the London School of Economics and Political Science has provided a home for its completion.

Summary of Contents

Contents

1

Introduction

Ali v Keith Hudson t/a Hudson Freeman Berg[1] involved a claim by Mr Ali for damages against the solicitor who had acted in the sale of his restaurant business. Previously Mr Ali had failed in an application to the Chancery Division for specific performance of a purported agreement for the sale. The county court struck out the action against the solicitor as disclosing no cause of action and as being frivolous and vexatious, and ordered Mr Ali to pay the defendant's costs, later quantified as £14,592.64. Subsequently that court held that, given the delay, it would not be in conformity with the Overriding Objective of the Civil Procedure Rules (CPR) to put the defendant to the expense of an appeal until Mr Ali paid that amount plus interest. The judge held that his power to do this was in accordance with the case management powers in the CPR. Mr Ali said that he could neither pay nor raise any money so that the effect was that he could not proceed. When the case came to the Court of Appeal Clarke LJ (with whom Ward and Potter LJJ agreed) held that it would only be in an exceptional case (if ever) that a court would order security for costs if the order would stifle a claim or an appeal. In any event an order should not ordinarily be made until the party concerned could be shown to be regularly flouting proper court procedures or otherwise to be demonstrating a lack of will to litigate as economically and expeditiously as reasonably possible. The weakness of a party's case would ordinarily be relevant only where it had no real prospect of succeeding.

There is nothing out of the ordinary in *Ali's* case. It is one of the hundreds of cases decided each year by the Court of Appeal which lie not officially reported. Yet a little patience uncovers several features of note. First, in reaching his conclusion, Clarke LJ referred to 'the fundamental importance of access to the Courts'. It was unnecessary to rely on the Article 6 jurisprudence under the European Convention on Human Rights, he held, because cases prior and subsequent to the CPR recognized the fundamental value that individuals are generally entitled to untrammelled access to the courts, subject only to the sanction that they are in peril of an adverse costs order if unsuccessful.[2] Next, there were the obvious procedural aspects to the case. As with the rules of court which it replaces, the

---

[1] [2003] EWCA Civ 1793; [2004] CP Rep 15.

[2] *Abraham v Thompson* [1997] EWCA Civ 2179; [1997] 4 All ER 362, 374; *Hamilton v Al Fayed* [2002] EWCA Civ 665; [2003] QB 1175, paras 47, 63–65.

CPR forbids a court to order security for costs on the ground of an individual claimant's inability to pay, unless resident in some specified overseas jurisdictions. It goes further than its predecessors in extending that principle to appeals.[3] However, the case management power, CPR r 3, confers a wide power to stay cases, or to make case management orders with conditions attached such as the payment of security for costs. As we have seen Clarke LJ reconciled these different provisions and held that the courts have the jurisdiction to make such orders, but the discretion to do so could not be unlimited in the light of the principles governing access to the courts. Finally, there was the context of the case. Mr Ali had come to Britain from Bangladesh, built up a business, only to be hit by economic troubles. His legal aid having long since been withdrawn, Mr Ali was tenaciously pursuing a legal remedy for his business losses. He did this as a litigant in person up to and including the permission stage for the Court of Appeal hearing. At that point I enter the scene having been asked by the Pro Bono Unit of the Bar to argue the appeal.

These three features of *Ali's case*—values, procedure, and social context—run as threads through this book. Access to justice is clearly a fundamental value directly relevant to the working of the law, along with others like equality before the law and the rule of law. In a post-modern, secular age it has become standard practice to deconstruct values, thereby underplaying their impact. Certainly the merit, meaning, and application of particular values are contestable. The enforceable legal rights spun off from these fundamental values may fall short in practice. Yet these values can still affect legal behaviour on a daily basis and give coherence to legal systems and legal reform. Thus access to justice has driven the public funding of legal services and the reform of procedure. Equality before the law has acted as some restraint on the excesses of power. The idea of the rule of law underpins the UK legal system and has been behind important legal changes in emerging market economies. These are just examples.

A pervasive set of values for legal ordering is that related to the professional conduct of lawyers. The system of legal ethics comprises the basic rules for lawyers in their day-to-day work in the law. Not only is their own behaviour affected but that of others, since lawyers are guardians of the way their clients carry out transactions, ensuring they comply with the law. In this and other ways—in protecting clients, for example, from the untrammelled force of the law–lawyers act as a social group, mediating between state and society. The system of legal ethics also contains the ideals which impel lawyers to make real in the working of the law values such as access to justice and equality before the law.

Procedure—the second thread—makes law work by enabling individuals and groups to vindicate their rights and to resolve their disputes in an orderly manner, thereby making manifest the values of the law but also serving larger purposes, such as facilitating social harmony and oiling the wheels of commerce. Yet many

---

[3] CPR rr 25.13(2), 25.15(1).

are denied access to justice. Without publicly funded legal services, substantial parts of society would not be able to obtain it. The present-day challenge is to use public moneys in innovative ways, to tap new sources of funding and to harness the altruism of the profession. Moreover, procedural change and renewal are as vital as public subsidy in making law work effectively for all sections of society. That encompasses reform in the procedure and administration of the courts but also steps such as providing effective internal review mechanisms in public and private bureaucracies, and fostering alternative dispute mechanisms (ombudsmen, arbitration, and mediation) and collective action. We underrate procedural issues in these broad senses at our peril.

The final thread to the book is an underlying conception of law in and of society. One facet of law's context is its historical and social setting. Another is the law's purpose. Law can be used instrumentally—to give an official stamp to certain outcomes, to settle disputes and for social engineering. A third facet is that law has a societal impact, it has social consequences. Their working practices orient many lawyers to concentrate on process and immediate results, rather than on social functions or consequences. Legislators are very aware of the social functions of law. But in their struggle about the enactment of a law and in quickly passing on to the next, they have little appetite or machinery to evaluate in detail the social consequence of past laws. Setting, purposes, and impact are but three facets of a law's social context.

This chapter attempts an analytical overview of the book. Broadly it follows the subjects of the chapters in the book. But it is not a summary; rather it annotates the chapters within the broader context of their subject matter. The first part of this chapter therefore explores access to justice. Access to justice, the argument runs, is more than access to the courts. Nor need it necessarily involve lawyers. How law can work to further access to justice needs to take both these points to heart. Given the centrality of the courts and lawyers to the working of the legal system, the next part of the chapter explores how courts can be understood institutionally and how lawyers' behaviour can be located within the working of the law. Then the chapter turns to law as social engineering: what is law's role in furthering values and social goals, why might it fall short in this task, and what of the sometimes dramatic, if unintended, consequences which law produces? The chapter looks finally at law working instrumentally to further economic development, in particular in emerging market economies. This discussion is intertwined with the issue of whether the laws of one country can be successfully transplanted elsewhere.

Access to Justice

Professor Lawrence Friedman has observed that when people talk about 'access to justice' they mean many different things, but 'every discussion assumes a goal called "justice", and assumes further that some group or type of person living in a society finds the door closed. . . .'[4] The European Commission considered the meaning of access to justice within the context of its Green Paper on Access to Justice for Consumers. It saw the problem of access to justice as the gap between the law and the reality of individuals seeking to vindicate rights.

> If the rights recognised by the legal order thus created are infringed through a breach of one of these norms, a procedure (judicial or administrative) must exist in order to 'render justice' . . . If such a procedure did not exist or was not 'accessible' to the holders of the interest protected by the legal order, there would clearly be a gap between the legislator's designs and the reality experienced by citizens. The problem summarised here under the rubric 'access to justice' is nothing other than that of this gap between law and reality.[5]

The Green Paper goes on to describe the need for access to justice if cases of non-performance of contractual rights are not to proliferate, since the existence of a working justice machinery encourages the spontaneous performance of obligations.[6] We return to this issue at various points. It is enough to say here that as well as enabling individuals and groups to vindicate rights, and have their disputes resolved, access to justice is beneficial because it affirms people's faith in the system. Access, not least in public law, can also act as a brake on powerful interests. This is especially important in a society with an authoritarian regime but no less essential in a liberal democracy.[7] The role of access to justice in facilitating economic activity, in particular in relation to financial transactions, should not be overlooked and features in a number of the following chapters.[8]

If access to justice is to be achieved individuals and groups must be aware that their legal rights are affected, know of sources of advice and assistance, and be able expeditiously to access those of an appropriate quality, at a price within reach. Ultimately access to justice means being able to have one's case resolved by a body which is impartial, non-corrupt, and fair. Whether lawyers and courts are always necessary to this is a large issue. There is a plausible argument which questions whether enhancing access to legal procedures rather than, say, improving regulation or establishing a compensation scheme might not be the better way of making certain rights effective.[9] Moreover, were public and private bureaucracies to minimize errors in the first place, to correct those which occur quickly and effectively, and to feed problems back for correction in the future—such properly constructed internal procedures would bring a significant improvement. There is also much to the argument that rights may be as effectively vindicated through

[4] 'Access to Justice: Social and Historical Context', in M. Cappelletti & J. Weisner (eds), *Access to Justice* (1978), vol. 2, 3, 5. See also M. Galanter, 'Access to Justice as a Moving Frontier', in J. Bass, W. Bogart, F. Zemans, *Access to Justice for a New Century. The Way Forward* (Toronto, 2005).

[5] Commission of the European Communities, *Green Paper. Access of Consumers to Justice and the Settlement of Consumer Disputes in the Single Market*, COM (93) 576, 1993, 15.   [6] *ibid.*, 7.

[7] See C. Harlow, 'Access to Justice as a Human Right', in P. Alston (ed.), *The EU and Human Rights* (Oxford, 1999); J. McBride, 'Access to Justice and Human Rights Treaties' (1998) 17 CJQ 235.

[8] 100–5; Chapters 9, 10 below.

[9] I. Ramsay, 'Consumer Redress and Access to Justice', in C. Rickett & T. Telfer (eds), *International Perspectives on Consumers' Access to Justice* (Cambridge, 2003), 38–40.

self-help, alternative dispute resolution, and collective procedures as through courts and tribunals. Many individuals have relatively low-level disputes with businesses which have supplied faulty goods or services, with neighbours, or with bureaucracies like a hospital, a social agency, the police or local government. Their primary aim is to have these disputes authoritatively and satisfactorily resolved, but cheaply and expeditiously. Lawyers and courts are not generally seen as conducive to this; even as a long stop there is a great deal of apprehension about the cost, bother, and stress of an entanglement with lawyers and litigation.

It is not an issue of high constitutional principle if as a matter of public policy encouragement is given to dispute resolution procedures other than courts.[10] Alternative dispute resolution is one of the priorities of the European Union in the field of civil justice. What matters is access to justice and the quality of the machinery to achieve it. Some of these non-curial procedures are described in the next two chapters, but also in Chapters 9 and 10, where self-help comes into its own. In practice the working of the law is a plural world and the courts and other dispute resolution machinery operate side by side.[11] The balance may favour the orthodox where it is important to expose issues publicly, to rely on or create precedent, or to invoke the full weight of public enforcement. Accessibility, speed, and cost may point, on the other hand, to self-help, a tribunal, or a form of alternative dispute resolution.[12] It does not make sense in some countries to place lawyers and courts centre stage if the concern is the empowerment and material advancement of the poorer sections of society. Lawyers are in the cities and towns catering to the middle class and the courts may be riddled with inefficiencies, delays and, worst of all, corruption.[13] As well as training paralegals for the rural areas, attention in these countries may need to be given for the time being to administrative agencies, local government, informal justice systems, and other institutions and processes which can immediately advance legal rights and resolve disputes.

In 'fitting the forum to the fuss' much turns on a detailed consideration of the circumstances. An example is the concern in Britain over litigation for medical negligence. Most of those who suffer medical errors do not pursue a claim. The bulk of clinical claims which have been litigated have failed, many at considerable

[10] cf. A. Le Sueur, 'Access to Justice in the United Kingdom' [2000] EHRLR 457, 458, 474.

[11] Department for Constitutional Affairs, *Transforming Public Services: Complaints Redress and Tribunals*, Cm 6243 (London, 2004). See Y. Dezalay, 'The Forum Should Fit the Fuss: The Economics and Politics of Negotiated Justice', in M. Cain & C. Harrington (eds), *Lawyers in a Postmodern World* (Maidenhead, 1994).

[12] On the cost advantages of certain forms of alternative dispute resolution: A. Brown, A. Barclay, R. Simmons & S. Eley, *The Role of Mediation in Tackling Neighbour Disputes and Anti-Social Behaviour* (Scottish Executive, Edinburgh, 2003), ch. 7; J. Dignan, A. Sorsby & J. Hibbert, *Neighbour Disputes: Comparing the Cost-Effectiveness of Mediation and Alternative Approaches* (University of Sheffield, Centre for Criminological and Legal Research, 1996).

[13] S. Golub, *Beyond Rule of Law Orthodoxy: The Legal Empowerment Alternative*, Carnegie Endowment for International Peace, Democracy and Rule of Law Project, Paper No. 41, October 2003; Department for International Development, *Justice and Poverty Reduction* (London, 2000), 13–15; Department for International Development, *Safety, Security and Accessible Justice* (London, 2002), 35–44.

expense to the legal aid fund. Nonetheless, the potential exposure of the National Health Service to medical negligence claims is still considerable.[14] As well as its expense and the time taken, litigation inhibits, it is said, a culture of openness whereby medical mistakes by doctors and others are reported and lessons learnt.[15] With these factors as background, the Chief Medical Officer has proposed a new NHS Redress Scheme (rejecting a non-fault compensation scheme in the process). In brief outline, a new body would handle relatively low value claims (up to £30,000) and cases involving severely neurological impaired babies. Individuals would not be precluded from pursuing a claim in the courts unless they had accepted a redress package, which could couple compensation and treatment.[16] Given the complexity of the issue, it is not surprising that the proposal is still being debated.[17]

So access to justice need not mean full engagement in the formal legal process although it must always be there as a backstop. One intended aspect of an efficiently functioning court system is to promote the processes of private bargaining and settlement—a point taken up in Chapters 4 and 5. There is also the possibility of self-help and other dispute resolution machinery. There is no magic in these non-curial procedures. Thus a properly constructed small claims court may have the same advantages of accessibility, speed, and affordability as some alternative dispute procedures. It is also useful to be reminded that some forms of alternative dispute resolution like commercial arbitration have become costly and as dependent on lawyers as the courts.[18] And it is certainly unacceptable for business and public bureaucracies effectively to force a private dispute resolution procedure on those who complain about them, where there is no public scrutiny or accountability.[19] Quite apart from the public policy considerations, redress to the courts in some form needs to remain an option as a matter of common law and the European Convention on Human Rights.[20]

If there is access to the formal legal process, contact can be with a range of courts, not of equal standing. If cases are forced to go to a lower level court, such as

---

[14] e.g. National Audit Office, *Handling Clinical Negligence Claims in England*, HC 403 (London, 2001); Lord Woolf, *Access to Justice. Final Report*, (London, 1996) 3, 170–96; H. Genn, 'Access to Just Settlement: The Case of Medical Negligence', in A. Zuckerman & R. Cranston (eds), *Reform of Civil Procedure* (Oxford, 1995).

[15] *Learning from Bristol. The Report of the Public Inquiry into Children's Heart Surgery at the Bristol Royal Infirmary 1984–1995*, Cm 5207 (London, 2001), 366–71; A. Merry & A. McCall Smith, *Errors, Medicine and the Law* (Cambridge, 2001).

[16] Department of Health, *Making Amends. A Report by the Chief Medical Officer* (London, 2003). See also L. Mulchany et al., *Mediating Medical Negligence Claims. An Option for the Future?* (London, 1999).

[17] cf. the new NHS complaints system: National Health Service (Complaints) Regulations 2004, SI 2004/1768.

[18] P. Brooker, 'The "Juridification" of Alternative Dispute Resolution' (1999) 28 *Anglo-Amer.LR* 1.

[19] Arbitration Act 1996, ss 89–91. See C. Scott & J. Black, *Cranston's Consumers and the Law* (London, 2000), 87.

[20] House of Lords, House of Commons, *Joint Committee on Human Rights*, 5th Report, Session 2003–4, HL 35/HC304, paras 57–76.

the small claims court, it is necessary to justify the 'rougher' justice that may result.[21] Why, to put it another way, should large commercial cases or public law issues be in the highest courts, while ordinary individuals are confined to vindicating many of their rights lower in the system? History will often be the explanation for the allocation of cases to different levels of court. Comparison with how matters are handled in comparable jurisdictions is one test as to whether that holds water as a justification. Less expensive and elaborate procedures may also be justified because that is a proportionate response or, as one writer puts it, the moral harm is less.[22] Calibrating moral harm involves contestible judgments as to the importance of the substantive right involved and an evaluation of the extent to which that right has been violated. The level of the financial loss is typically used as a proxy for this.

Resources are a third justification. As Adrian Zuckerman so rightly observes:

> A country can no more maintain an absolute commitment to reaching the truth in civil litigation than it can maintain an unlimited commitment to the best possible health system, regardless of cost, or to the most efficient transport system. The provision of adjudication, like the provision of any other amenity, must be subject to what the country can afford and necessitates compromises.[23]

Zuckerman also points to the fair allocation of court resources, including to those who are not yet or only just in the queue: unless court resources are rationed these may never get access to justice, or if they do may be subject to such inexcusable delay as to destroy in effect the value of a right (for example, a decision comes too late to put things right).[24] In practice, the justification for particular institutional arrangements is often pragmatic. A combination of the way things have been done in the past, judgments about worth, importance and complexity, and importantly what can be afforded are all brought to bear. Sometimes it will be as crude as concluding that rough justice is better than no justice at all. Certainly the social research evidence is that the majority of small claims litigants in England and Wales accept without much question the relatively simple and unpolished methods adopted by district judges.[25] That public acceptance underpins the more theoretical arguments for the small claims system.

---

[21] Similarly with the 'rougher justice' of non-curial procedures.

[22] M. Bayles, 'Principles for Legal Procedure' (1986) 5 *Law and Philosophy* 33.

[23] A. Zuckerman, 'Reform in the Shadow of Lawyers' Interests', in A.A.S. Zuckerman & R. Cranston (eds), *Reform of Civil Procedure* (Oxford, 1995), 74. See also J. Jolowicz, *On Civil Procedure* (Cambridge, 2000), ch. 1.

[24] A. Zuckerman, *Civil Procedure* (London, 2003), 10–11, 33. Delay may be a breach of the fair trial guarantees in Article 6(1) of the European Convention on Human Rights: e.g. *Brazil v Brazil* [2002] EWCA Civ 1135; *The Times*, October 18, 2002, CA; *Mitchell v United Kingdom* (2003) EHRR 52; 14 BHRC 431.

[25] J. Baldwin, 'Litigants' Experiences of Adjudication in the County Courts' (1999) 18 *CJQ* 12, 18. See also T. Tyler, 'Citizen Discontent with Legal Procedures: A Social Science Perspective on Civil Procedure Reform' (1997) 45 *Amer.J.Comp.L* 871.

Pragmatism, however, has its limits. Even rough justice must meet certain minimum standards to be acceptable. One touchstone is efficiency: the aim should be to avoid error and do justice while at the same time minimizing cost.[26] The difficulty is to identify what this entails. Is there room for values such as fairness in procedure or the dignity of those involved? For example, debt recovery could be carried out efficiently by a court, at little cost to creditors, but it would not be fair if the debtor's side of the case could never be heard. Professor Michael Zander has suggested that the fundamental question in evaluating a civil justice system is whether it holds the balance fairly between the parties, as far as practicable trying to have a level playing field between the two sides. This has to be weighed 'in the light of the need for due economy and efficiency'.[27] Zander's approach has an attractive simplicity. There are more elaborate approaches than Zander's to whether a system accords access to justice. Thus one approach is to ask whether it is fair and seen to be so (equality of access, a full opportunity to participate, consistency of treatment); it makes efficient use of resources; its procedures and costs are proportionate to the nature of the issues involved; it is just in the results it delivers; it processes complaints with reasonable speed; it provides reasonable certainty; it is understandable to those who use it and responsible to their needs; and its process is effective in terms of being adequately resourced and organized to meet these principles.[28] As an ideal these criteria seem thoroughly desirable. Without some attempt to prioritize, however, they are either an unattainable counsel of perfection or a jumble of goals which may conflict in practice.

Deciding on the overriding goals for a system of justice depends on its nature and setting. One author has gathered together six clusters of quality statements for the social goals to be achieved in the handling of disputes:

(1) they leave disputing parties feeling that their individual desires, as defined by themselves, have been satisfied in terms of the experience and the outcome of the process (Individual Satisfaction); or

(2) they strengthen the capacity of and increase the opportunity for disputing parties to resolve their own problems without being dependent on external institutions, public or private (Individual Autonomy); or

(3) they facilitate or strengthen the control of public and private institutions, and the interests they represent, over exploitable groups and over possible sources of social change or unrest (Social Control); or

(4) they ameliorate, neutralize, or at least do not exacerbate existing inequalities in the societal distribution of material wealth and power (Social Justice); or

(5) they provide common values, referents, or 'texts' for individuals and groups in a pluralistic society, and thereby increase social solidarity among these individuals and groups (Social Solidarity); or

---

[26] cf. R. Posner, 'An Economic Approach to Legal Procedure and Judicial Administration' (1973) 2 *J.Leg.Stud.* 399.   [27] M. Zander, *The State of Justice* (London, 2000), 5.
[28] D. Lovett & A. Westmacott, *Human Rights Review. A Background Paper* (Ministry of Attorney General, British Columbia, Victoria, 2001), 136.

(6) they provide opportunities for and encourage individual disputants to experience personal change and growth, particularly in terms of becoming less self-centred and more responsible to others (Personal Transformation).[29]

For England and Wales, the Court Service has a set of objectives which echo several of these: the satisfaction of users and ensuring disputes are resolved quickly, effectively and in a manner proportionate to the issues at stake, without compromising access.[30] Concern with those getting access, and their satisfaction with the process, have been more to the fore since the Civil Justice Review.[31] As to the other Court Service objectives, these echo the Overriding Objective of the Civil Procedure Rules, first set out in Lord Woolf's report on Access to Justice. The Overriding Objective emphasizes doing substantive justice, but within a reasonable time and using no more than proportionate resources. As we shall see in Chapter 5, it was Lord Woolf's report which gave a boost to managing court resources more effectively, and using proportionate procedures, to further access to justice.[32]

The barriers to access to justice are many and we return to them at various points in the book. There is the substantive law itself. It is a regular criticism that the substantive law is too complex and inaccessible. There is an argument—with little, if any empirical support—that the social cost of this is an increasing ignorance of the law and a growing disrespect for the law and those who administer it. Then there are the cultural, psychological, geographical, and other barriers which mean that many with legal problems do not seek legal redress. Apart from these issues of personal capability there is also the cost. Publicly funded legal services to overcome problems of personal capability and financial capacity are taken up in the next two chapters. Structural barriers include procedures, since they can make access difficult and disproportionately costly. Reforming civil procedure to further access to justice is discussed, as already indicated, in Chapter 5. As with other types of social reform referred to in the book individuals acting rationally may make adjustments in the light of reforms which then act to thwart their purpose.

Where does all this leave the notion of a compensation culture in which claiming has become too easy, with adverse consequences such as defensive medicine (more tests and procedures), activities of public benefit being abandoned through fear of crippling litigation (for example, volunteering; school trips), and a possible sapping of personal responsibility?[33] It is important that the issue be considered

---

29 R.A. Baruch Bush, 'Defining Quality in Dispute Resolution' (1989) 66 *Denver ULR* 335, 347–8.

30 Her Majesty's Court Service, *Annual Report and Accounts 2003–2004*, HC 788, 2004, 9.

31 Civil Justice Review, *Report of the Review Body on Civil Justice*, Cm 394 (1988). See R. Thomas, 'Civil Justice Review—Treating Litigants as Consumers' (1990) 9 *CJQ* 51, 51–2.

32 149–52 below.

33 F. Furedi, *Courting Mistrust. The Hidden Growth of a Culture of Litigation in Britain* (Centre for Policy Studies, London, 1999). See also E. Lee, J. Peysner, T. Brown, I. Walker & D. Lloyd, *Compensation Crazy. Do We Blame and Claim Too Much?* (London, 2002). The US literature is enormous: e.g. M. Galanter, 'Real World Torts: An Antidote to Anecdote' (1996) 55 *Maryland LR* 1093; R. Marcus, 'Malaise of the Litigation Superpower', in A. Zuckerman (ed.), *Civil Justice in Crisis* (Oxford, 1999).

dispassionately, in the light of systematic evidence, without distortion by anecdote or urban myth. Too often the debate is built on the back of the selective reporting of bizarre claims and surveys of business feeling (instead of their actual experiences). Various points can be made. First, the adversarial legalism of the United States is not in prospect for Britain given the differences in institutional arrangements—for example, civil juries are routine in the United States as is an overall heavier reliance on courts as instruments of social policy.[34] Secondly, we see in Chapter 4 that in important areas rather than overclaiming there is underclaiming because those with legitimate grievances do not pursue them.[35] Thirdly, the judicial statistics put paid to any suggestion of a litigation explosion. Overall in the High Court the claiming rate has been decreasing in recent years, so too in the county court.[36] There have been increases in certain types of claim, for example liability claims against public bodies and education authorities. Partly this may be because of a greater consciousness of rights, a less deferential attitude towards those in authority, and scientific advances making it easier to demonstrate causation. Despite the cost to the public purse, this is not of itself undesirable and may induce beneficial changes such as improved safety procedures in public bureaucracies.

There are also the claims generated by new rights and liabilities recognized in the common law (for example, psychological injury) and statute (for example, employment rights). To an extent a publicly expressed concern about the compensation culture may mask an opposition to some of these changes in substantive law. Elsewhere the debate about tort law has led to a legislative truncation of personal injury damages.[37] There is an issue about the cost of weak claims, settled for their nuisance value. The role of litigation funding arrangements, claims management companies, and the legal ethics behind this is examined below.[38] A hardy perennial is the high transaction cost of court-related processes in settling claims. In the main that cost reflects the inevitable cost of lawyers in investigating claims and then bargaining with the other side. One estimate is that about a third of the cost of compensation payable under insurance or by public bureaucracies like the health service, the police and local authorities is attributable to the legal and administrative costs; for cases with small settlement values it will be much greater.[39] Compensation schemes are sometimes posited as a way of achieving the goal of satisfying such claims at a much lower transaction cost per case.[40] In so far

---

[34] e.g. R. Kagan, 'Should Europe Worry About Adversarial Legalism?' (1997) 17 *OxJLS* 165; T. Burke, *Lawyers, Lawsuits and Legal Rights* (Berkeley, CA, 2002).   [35] 108–12 below.
[36] Department for Constitutional Affairs, *Judicial Statistics 2003* (London, 2004), 23, 30, 41, 51.
[37] Civil Liability Act 2002 (New South Wales). See Commonwealth of Australia, *Review of the Law of Negligence Final Report* (Canberra, 2002).   [38] 51, 67, 197 below.
[39] Institute of Actuaries, *The Cost of Compensation Culture* (London, 2002), para. 4.2. See also Lord Woolf, *Access to Justice. Final Report*, (London, 1996) Annex 3, 'Survey of Litigation Costs' (by Professor Hazel Genn), Table 4; C. Silver, 'Does Civil Justice Cost Too Much' (2002) 80 *Tex.LR* 2073.
[40] e.g. Lord Chancellor's Department, *Compensation for Road Accidents. A Consultation Paper* (London, 1991) (a no-fault scheme for claims up to £2,500). This scheme would still have covered most claims issued in 2003.

as these schemes are no-fault, there will inevitably be more claims and hence a greater overall cost. Unless this is less than the legal and administrative costs saved, compensation levels may have to be reduced unless the budget is expanded. No-fault schemes may also dilute safety incentives for public and private bodies. Cutting out lawyers also lies behind more modest proposals, such as expanding the jurisdiction of small claims courts to handle personal injury cases.[41] Here the danger is that unrepresented claimants would struggle to formulate their case since they would not be on an even playing field with larger organizations like insurance companies.

Courts, Procedure, and Lawyers

Access to justice, then, is far from an exact fit with access to the courts. The machinery of justice has a horizon extending to a range of other dispute-resolution machinery such as ombudsmen, arbitration, and mediation. Courts, though, are quintessentially associated with the machinery of justice: it is right to give them specific attention. Yet how best are courts to be understood if the focus is the working of the law, in particular, its more effective working? How might courts be appropriately conceptualized if the concern is to further values such as access to justice or to understand their impact? An institutional analysis offers important insights into the working of the courts. It can be pursued along a number of lines.

At the basic, yet crucial, level of management an institutional approach takes form in the objectives of the Court Service for England and Wales to improve the delivery of justice in the civil courts.[42] In its strategic document *Modernising the Civil and Family Courts*,[43] the Court Service sets out a programme of institutional change to meet these objectives including internal reorganization (for example, separating 'back office' administration and hearing centres), greater use of technology by users, officials, and judges, and being more responsive to users in the way contact can be made with the courts, claims issued and judgments enforced. As with other parts of the public sector courts now have performance indicators measuring matters such as delay and the level of satisfaction of users.[44] Performance indicators are not confined to British courts: the World Bank has used a wide range of performance indicators to compare the efficiency and effectiveness of courts across jurisdictions.[45] Compensation is now payable to court

---

[41] Better Regulation Task Force, *Better Routes to Redress* (London, 2004), 25–6.

[42] 9 above.

[43] (London, 2002). See also Lord Chancellor's Department, *Modernising the Civil Courts. A Consultation Paper* (London, 2001); Lord Chancellor's Department, *Civil Justice 2000* (London, 2000). [44] Her Majesty's Court Service, *op.cit.*, 84–7.

[45] e.g. E. Buscaglia & M. Dakolias, *Comparative International Study of Court Performance Indicators* (Washington, DC, 1999); M. Dakolias, *Court Performance Around the World* (Washington, DC, 1999).

users for breach of the Courts Charter. Such measures reflect modern management techniques, although in areas such as procedural reform, for example case management, these take their own particular path in the courts. In addition, there is now a recognition that courts are one among a number of institutions involved in the resolution of civil disputes. Parties are encouraged to use these other institutions first under the Overriding Objective of the Civil Procedure Rules.

Unless sensitively handled, managerial goals like expedition and the monitoring of performance have the potential to sap the values which are the foundation of the court's operation—judicial independence, fair process, and fidelity to law. Chief Justice Spigleman of New South Wales has written that quantitative measurement sometimes conceals important value judgments in that not everything can be counted, for example the quality of judicial decision making, the justice of outcomes, and the fairness of procedures.[46] Without institutional renewal, however, the goals which the legal system proclaim may not be achievable. 'Justice delayed is justice denied' is a commonplace truism, but still a strong reason to streamline litigation and a powerful indictment of legal systems where parties may wait more than a decade for judgment. As well as delay, the cost of litigation can not only be a source of inefficiency but an affront to the values of access to justice and equality before the law. Despite the public value of court judgments, if the cost to the parties of litigating are substantial when compared with the value in dispute, the system itself comes into question.

The Civil Procedure Rules constitute a new procedural code designed to make the courts work better, in particular by grappling with these hardy perennials of cost and delay and in doing so to facilitate access to justice. As mentioned, the rules grew out of Lord Woolf's report *Access to Justice*. The broad outline of the Woolf proposals—updating the rules of civil procedure, case management, facilitating settlement and alternative dispute resolution, and using proportionate procedures—derived to an extent from experience in the United States although much of the detail was original (for example, the pre-action protocols are especially noteworthy).[47] The Woolf proposals are now replicated in reform agendas elsewhere.[48] Thus, for India, case management and expanding mechanisms for alternative dispute resolution have strong advocates as a means of restoring public trust and confidence in the civil courts, bedevilled as they have been by delays and backlogs.[49] The English experience is different from that elsewhere, however, in that procedural reform was successfully introduced by a big bang, rather than incremental change. One reason behind the success of big bang was that reform

---

[46] J. Spigleman, 'The "New Public Management" and the Courts' (2001) 75 *ALJ* 748. See also A. Le Sueur, 'Developing Mechanisms for Judicial Accountability in the UK' (2004) 24 *LS* 73.

[47] R. Marcus, ' "Déjà vu All Over Again"? An American Reaction to the Woolf Report', in A. Zuckerman & R. Cranston (eds), *Reform of Civil Procedure* (Oxford, 1995). On the protocols: 150 below.   [48] 283ff. below.

[49] H. Chodosh *et al.*, 'Civil Justice Reform: Limitation and Preservation of the Adversarial System' (1998) 30 *NYU Int'l L&P* 1; 85 below; 281 below. For elsewhere in the Commonwealth see 148 below, n. 13.

was enthusiastically embraced by the judges.[50] In the light of this, we need to pour a considerable amount of cold water on the theory that judicial concern with procedural rules is likely to follow the self-interest of the judges, rather than the public interest.[51]

At a more theoretical level, another institutional approach to the workings of the courts examines them as one of the institutions of the state, not impervious to the same type of analysis used for these. Illustrative of the insights such an institutional analysis can bring is Professor John Bell's paper 'The Judge as Bureaucrat'.[52] In brief summary, Bell considers that the judge's subordination to law, independence of politics and partial interest, and authority derived from the application of the law, fit well with Weber's bureaucratic ideal. So too does the notion of judges performing a public service, which reinforces the values of impartiality and neutrality. Bell concludes, however, that especially in the common law system, judicial and bureaucratic functions differ so much that the characterization of the former as bureaucratic is inadequate. Judges are instruments not so much of the will of other law-makers, as are bureaucrats, but of general legal values which they have a hand in creating and which 'they often have to defend against interpretations placed on them by other organs of government and power-holders in society'.[53]

Much of the literature treating the courts as similar to other organs of the state is north American, and driven by the key role which the US Supreme Court plays in the body politic.[54] While that means that some of it is not directly applicable to jurisdictions which do not have a constitutional court, the insights offered by treating courts as one of the organs of the state should not be neglected. Questions addressed include the extent to which courts are involved in making policy, about how interest groups conceive of the courts as another avenue for advancing their view of the public interest, and about how far judicial decisions reflect underlying attitudes or, in appellate courts, the influences of leadership and group dynamics. These questions about courts arise, to a greater or lesser extent, in all jurisdictions.[55]

The institutional perspective adopted in Chapter 4 is yet another approach, treating courts as a system. In rough outline, there are inputs to any system and the transformation of these to outputs. Applying a systems approach to courts

---

[50] See J. Plotnikoff & R. Woolfson, *Judges' Case Management Perspectives: The Views of Opinion Formers and Case Managers*, Lord Chancellor's Department Research Series 3/2002 (London, 2002).

[51] J. Macey, 'Judicial Preferences, Public Choice and the Rules of Procedure' (1994) 23 *J.Leg.Stud.* 627.

[52] In J. Eekelaar & J. Bell (eds), *Oxford Essays in Jurisprudence* (Oxford, 1987). See also M. Damaska, *The Faces of Justice and State Authority* (New Haven, 1986).

[53] In J. Eekelaar & J. Bell (eds), *op. cit.*, 55.

[54] M. Shapiro, *Courts* (Chicago, 1981) is the seminal study. See also H. Jacob *et al.*, *Courts, Law and Politics in Comparative Perspective* (New Haven, 1996); M. Shapiro & A. Stone Sweet, *On Law, Politics and Judicialization* (Oxford, 2002); H. Kritzer, 'Martin Shapiro: Anticipating the New Institutionalism', in N. Maveety (ed.), *Pioneers of Judicial Behaviour* (Ann Arbor, 2002).

[55] e.g. D. Robertson, *Judicial Discretion in the House of Lords* (Oxford 1998); J.A.G. Griffith, *The Politics of the Judiciary*, 5th edn (London, 1997).

throws light, first, on the barriers to access to justice, the type of parties able to surmount them, the subject matter of the cases they bring and whether the 'haves' come out ahead in litigation. It also highlights that many cases entering the system are subject to routine processing: 'Most of the undefended work of the civil courts requires little or no judicial intervention'.[56] There is also the attrition of cases as settlements occur—a trend encouraged in England and Wales by the Woolf reforms[57]—so that in terms of the bulk of cases entering the system adjudication is atypical. Another feature of a systems approach is that the work of the courts is seen against the backdrop of society as a whole. Social and economic issues must be transformable into legal terms if they are to be addressed by courts. The upshot may be that the underlying issue is disguised in legal terms for the purposes of litigation. On the other side of the coin, the court process exhausts itself with a judgment on a discrete issue or issues and its enforcement. This might not resolve the underlying social or economic issue: other avenues might subsequently be sought by the litigants or those they represent. This is but one aspect of the limited impact which court decisions may have.

While an institutional analysis uncovers much of how the courts work, it fails if it neglects their distinctive features. One of these is that although the courts are reactive, they must generally hear the cases which are brought to them. Thus those with a plausible legal argument, and resources, will generally obtain a hearing, even if they cannot get an issue onto the political agenda. Especially important is that courts are impartial and act independently of the other organs of the state. Indeed courts will sometimes stand in opposition to other such organs, especially the executive. In Britain this will typically result in statutory or judicial review of administrative action or in a court considering whether legislation is compatible with the European Convention on Human Rights. Coupled with this is the courts' distinctive feature of reasoned decision making, at its most creative adapting doctrine to new situations. Reasoned decision making adds to the legitimacy of the courts, persuading parties to accept adverse rulings and generally underpinning judicial standing in the community. Reasoned decision making also provides a road map for others as to the outcome of future cases, the so-called radiating effects of court decisions. Except for the parties, who wins and loses may not be as important as what the court says. Providing a guide to the future the court enables cases to be settled without the occasion of litigation. Social and economic arrangements can be made with reasonable confidence as to their legality. Thus courts are not simply working to resolve disputes but are helping to constitute law for society. Internal dispute resolution within private or public bureaucracies, and techniques of alternative dispute resolution such as mediation or arbitration, do not share these characteristics. This is the public benefit in judgments, in creating precedents which are used to settle other disputes. Of course many cases are

---

[56] Lord Chancellor's Department, *Modernising the Civil Courts. A Consultation Paper*, (London, 2001) 27.   [57] S. Roberts, 'Settlement as Civil Justice' (2000) 63 *MLR* 739, 745.

essentially private disputes, with judgments not being published (although they may be available electronically as in *Ali's* case) because they involve the application of established principle rather than the creation of new precedent. Even here, however, there may be an advantage to know that the courts are continuing to operate along relatively fixed lines so that settlements can continue on that basis.

To suggest, however, that courts are primarily there to give concrete meaning and expression to public values is too grand a conception of the judicial function in Britain.[58] The position with courts such as the United States or Indian Supreme Courts is different; they are entrusted with having the last word in expounding for each generation the meaning of constitutional values. In Britain the task is more circumscribed but nonetheless important. There are a limited number of public values inherent in the common law both in relation to the operation of the courts themselves and discoverable in various branches of substantive law.[59] These are not trivial values. That is already evident in the discussion of access to justice.[60] Another common law value is equality before the law, albeit that this can take various forms such as formal equality (treating like cases alike) or the principle of only discriminating in substantive law provisions, when this is properly justified. Chapter 7 examines why equality before the law as a value might fall short in liberal democracies. We see another example of its application in Chapter 8: on occasion the colonial courts in Australia invoked a notion of equality before the law to shield Aboriginals from some of the worst excesses of the white settlers.[61]

As well as such values in the common law, legislation may confer a mandate on courts to give meaning to identified public values. The notable, but not exclusive, example in Britain is the Human Rights Act 1998, which entrusts courts with the difficult task of giving meaning to the values in the European Convention. For courts to go further with values other than what is already there in the common law or legislation would be dangerous. Quite apart from the potential damage to their legitimacy, courts are in no position institutionally to divine public values when these are not already given expression in the law. When they have attempted it they have appeared to many to be out of touch and to have had conceptions of public values not in keeping with the popular mood or general legal principle.[62] Better that politicians perform the difficult task of identifying and giving expression to new public values.

---

[58] e.g. O. Fiss, *The Law As It Could Be* (New York, 2003), chs 1–2.

[59] e.g. R. Goode, *Commercial Law in the Next Millenium* (London, 1997), 12 ff.; D. Feldman, 'Public Law Values in the House of Lords' (1990) 106 *LQR* 246; J. Stapleton, 'The Golden Thread at the Heart of Tort Law: Protection of the Vulnerable', in P. Cane (ed.), *Centenary Essays for the High Court of Australia* (Sydney, 2004); J. Doyle, 'Common Law Rights and Democratic Rights', in P. Finn, *Essays on Law and Government* (Sydney, 1995), Vol. 1.

[60] 4 above; 35–9 below. See *R (Daly) v Secretary of State for the Home Department* [2001] UKHL 26; [2001] 2 AC 532, 537H–538A, *per* Lord Bingham and 548G–H, *per* Lord Cooke of Thorndon.

[61] 242, 243 below.

[62] e.g A. Ashworth, *Principles of Criminal Law*, 4th edn (Oxford, 2003), 70–5.

Making law work in the courts is a range of persons from judges through court clerks to ushers. Other dispute settlement involves arbitrators and mediators. The wider sphere of the law encompasses those as varied as legislators and regulators. Most of these roles do not need to be occupied by lawyers. That even applies to a large part of the judiciary in England and Wales, because the majority of cases on the criminal side are disposed of by the lay magistracy (although magistrates have access to legal advice and receive some legal training). In practice, however, lawyers are essential to the working of a modern legal system, because of their expertise in the making and application of the law and in the operation of its machinery. Chapter 6 is therefore given over to the role lawyers play in the working of the law.

At one level it is relatively straightforward to paint a picture of the legal profession. Annual statistical reports from the Law Society show the dramatic increase in recruitment, with occasional variations in the upward trend associated with external events such as economic downturn. The figures demonstrate the changing gender composition: whereas over the decade from 1993 the total number of practising solicitors grew by 50 per cent, the total number of women practising solicitors more than doubled. In 2003 more than one half of new admissions were women, and women comprised some 40 per cent of all practising solicitors. However, there was not the same representation at partnership level and there is an obvious leaching of talent.[63] (The same trends are evident in those with a known black or other minority ethnic background. In 2003 they accounted for some one in six new admissions and some 8 per cent of all practising solicitors.) The transformation in the structure of law firms is also evident. At one end of the profession the sole or very small practice has often grown, amalgamated, or disappeared.[64] At the other end of the profession the law firms devoted to corporate work have hundreds, and in some instances, thousands of lawyers and a global reach.[65]

Making sense of this broad picture can proceed along various avenues. The first takes the fractured nature of the profession as given and lifts the veil on its different parts. Given their economic significance, it is not surprising that the large law firm has had its share of attention. Its internal dynamic is said to be driven by the promotion to partnership tournament and by a restructuring to meet the needs of international corporations.[66] The historic experience in England was of a legal

---

[63] B. Cole, *Trends in the Solicitors' Profession: Annual Statistical Report 2003* (London, 2004), 11, 13, 18, 47–8. See also C. McGlynn, 'The Status of Women Lawyers in the United Kingdom', in U. Schultz & G. Shaw (eds), *Women in the World's Legal Professions* (Oxford, 2003). In 2003, just over half of new barristers were women making 32 per cent of all barristers. (One in ten practising barristers were from an ethnic minority: Bar Council, *Annual Report 2003* (London, 2004)).

[64] B. Cole, *op.cit.*, 24. In 2003 there were 6,153 sole practitioners and 15,811 solicitors in partnerships of two to four persons, out of a total of 72,545 practitioners (*ibid.*, 27).

[65] J. Lewis & J. Keegan, *Defining Legal Business: Understanding the Work of the Largest Law Firms*, RPPU Research Study 27, Law Society (London, 1997).

[66] M. Galanter & T. Palay, *Tournament of Lawyers: The Transformation of the Big Law Firm* (Chicago, 1991); J. Flood, 'Megalawyering in the Global Order: The Cultural, Social and Economic Transformation of Global Legal Practice' (1996) 3 *Int'l J.L. Prof.* 169.

profession complacent in its conveyancing monopoly and largely indifferent to developing a market for its services.[67] Now the profession is highly sensitive to competitive pressures. In particular the large law firm employs the full range of marketing techniques, including lobbying and use of the media.[68] In terms of its legal work, Professor John Flood has provided us with sociological accounts of the large law firm engaged in the capital markets, corporate restructuring, and commercial arbitration.[69]

Along the spectrum from the large law firm are those firms engaged in personal injury work. Concentration of this work in specialist, high volume hands has occurred in Britain on the claimant side consequent on the administration of legal aid funding and now its replacement with conditional fee agreements. Professor Hazel Genn's detailed work on personal injury lawyers found that as a result of their expertise specialist firms were more effective than generalist firms in obtaining damages. Specialist firms reduce risk to themselves and their clients by rejecting weak cases early on and concentrating effort on those with a good chance of success.[70] Personal injury lawyers get their cases through referrals, the membership of panels constituted by organizations like trade unions and insurance companies and some direct marketing.[71]

Towards the other end of the spectrum are the 'cause' lawyers—those taking human rights cases, acting for non-government organizations (NGOs) or pursuing social issues through public interest litigation.[72] Cause lawyers may be in private practice or working for organizations. The causes they advance can be as varied as individual liberty, the environment and 'pro-life'. There is no incompatibility between cause lawyering and professional and financial success.

[67] M. Burrage, 'From a Gentlemen's to a Public Profession: Status and Politics in the History of English Solicitors' (1996) 3 *Int'l J.L. Prof.* 46–7; D. Sugarman, 'Who Colonized Whom? Historical Reflections on the Intersection Between Law, Lawyers and Accountants in England', in Y. Dezalay & D. Sugarman (eds), *Professional Competition and Professional Power* (London, 1995), 230–3.

[68] G. Hanlon, *Lawyers, the State and the Market* (Basingstoke, 1999), 123 ff.

[69] J. Flood 'Capital Markets, Globalisation and Global Elites', in M. Likosky (ed.), *Transnational Legal Processes—Globalisation and Power Disparities* (London, 2002); 'The Vultures Fly East: The Creation and Globalisation of the Distressed Debt Market', in D. Nelken, J. Feest (ed.), *Adapting Legal Cultures* (Oxford, 2001); J. Flood & A. Caiger, 'Lawyers and Arbitration: The Juridification of Construction Disputes' (1993) 56 *MLR* 412. See also Y. Dezalay & B. Garth, *Dealing in Virtue. International Commercial Arbitration and the Construction of a Transnational Legal Order* (Chicago, 1996).

[70] H. Genn, *Hard Bargaining: Out of Court Settlement in Personal Injury Actions* (Oxford, 1988). See also H. Kritzer, 'The Fracturing Legal Profession: The Case of Plaintiffs' Personal Injury Lawyers' (2001) 8 *Int'l J.L Prof.* 225, 234, 239–42.

[71] cf. S. Daniels & J. Martin, ' "It's Darwinism—Survival of the Fittest": How Markets and Reputations Shape the Ways in Which Plaintiffs' Lawyers Obtain Clients' (1999) 21 *L. & Policy* 377.

[72] e.g. G. Chambers, *Practising Human Rights: UK Lawyers and the European Convention on Human Rights*, RPPU Research Study Law Society (London, 1998); M. Elvy, M. Alexander & T. Keevil, 'Tobacco Litigation: 1992–1999', in C. Hodges (ed.), *Multi-Party Actions* (Oxford, 2001). For cause lawyering elsewhere, see A. Sarat & S. Sheingold (eds), *Cause Lawyering* (Oxford, 1998); L. Trubek & J. Cooper (eds), *Educating for Justice Around the World* (Aldershot, 1999); A. Sarat & S. Scheingold (eds), *Cause Lawyering and the State in a Global Era* (Oxford, 2001); L. Trubek, 'Public Interest Lawyers and New Governance Advocating for Healthcare' [2002] *Wisc LR* 575.

Although they may not match the resources of their adversaries, cause lawyers can enjoy the advantages of being repeat players and of a sympathetic media. In different jurisdictions their work is facilitated by the substantive law (notably, the possibility of constitutional or human rights challenges), public funding (in Britain primarily through legal aid), procedural reform (for example, the introduction of multiparty or class actions) and the receptivity of the courts.

Even if public policy is not its immediate concern, social research into particular types of lawyering may assist in its formulation. Illustrative is a study of some forty solicitors practising family law in England.[73] The findings belie the popular perception of a legal process which is in the main wastefully expensive and harmful to the resolution of family disputes. Control by the Legal Services Commission of legally aided family work, the study found, generally ensured quality and value for money. (That the money is recoverable by a statutory charge on any family property may have been an added incentive to cost control.) The concentration of family work in specialist hands meant that there was no great incentive to escalate unnecessarily the effort on individual cases since staying in business depended rather on the high and efficient turnover of cases.[74] There was no evidence of work done to increase costs; rather the reverse as clients were advised to fill out forms themselves (to avoid disputes about household possessions) and if possible to sort out questions about the children between themselves (to minimize costs).[75] The exception was that lawyers with wealthier clients were more inclined to respond to their wish to pursue unreasonable expectations. As for fostering conflict, lawyers in the study were reluctant to litigate matters although the court process was used as a means to take negotiations forward. There was a pride in reaching agreement, courtesy, and support for people under stress or whose lives were in disarray, and skilful financial advice followed by action.[76] As members of law firms the solicitors thought of themselves as running a business, but in dealing with individual clients they saw themselves as professionals, offering the best possible service to each client.[77]

It is this idea of professionalism which provides a second avenue for exploring lawyers' work. One model of professionalism accords with this view among professionals, that they are not simply in business but following a vocation. It emphasizes their social functions as a profession such as standing between state and citizen, and accepts as distinctively professional traits those such as taking the public interest into account.[78] Because in this view a profession acts in the public interest, self-regulation and some restrictions on competitive forces are justified. That model of professionalism is rejected as hopelessly naive by a second account which emphasizes the collective advancement of a profession's interests through

---

[73] J. Eekelaar, M. Maclean S. Beinart, *Family Lawyers* (Oxford, 2000). See also R. Hunter, 'Adversarial Mythologies. Policy Assumptions and Research Evidence in Family Law' (2003) 30 *JL&Soc* 156.   [74] J. Eeekelaar, M. Maclean & S. Beinart, *op.cit.*, 177–8, 190–6.
[75] *ibid.*, 76, 112–3.   [76] *ibid.*, 78, 81–8, 103–8.   [77] *ibid.*, 182, 195.
[78] e.g. G. Millerson, *The Qualifying Associations. A Study in Professionalisation* (London, 1964).

market control and status gains.[79] Adam Smith's conspiracy against the public by traders to raise prices becomes, in this context, the neo-corporatist project of maintaining restrictions against competition in the provision of professional services coupled with the protection of a profession's independence and standing and the social homogeneity of its members. A third model of professionalism conceives of an implied contract between the professions, the state, and consumers. In return for its status, its protection from unrestricted competition and limited government regulation, a profession in turn guarantees the state and consumers a high level of service from its members, a service ethic, strong moral standards and protection when things go wrong (indemnity insurance, compensation funds and so on).[80]

While suggestive, each of these models of professionalism is lacking. It may be that the first is too inclined to accept the professions' own claims at face value. Yet the second goes overboard in debunking those claims. Specific practices of the past, such as the conveyancing monopoly for English solicitors, or some of the restrictive practices of barristers, may have lent it some support.[81] On the whole, however, it has not been backed by extensive inquiry into the workings of lawyers.[82] The research that there is has found that a neo-corporatist model does not capture adequately the complexity of legal life.[83] As to the third model, the 'implied contract' model of professionalism, it comes into question given the growth of state intervention in the workings of the legal profession. Its proponents rationalize this as a renegotiation of the contract to match governmental and consumer concerns about access to legal services and the standard of service on offer.

Whatever models of professionalism, if any, one might want to invoke there is no doubt that the legal profession is under strain as '[t]he practice of law has become more commercialised . . .'.[84] Professional associations like the Law Society have found it increasingly difficult to perform their historical role in representing an increasingly fractured profession.[85] Government action has intruded

[79] R. Abel, *The Legal Profession of England and Wales* (Oxford, 1988), 4–30; M. Larson, *The Rise of Professionalism* (Berkeley, 1977), xvi.

[80] A. Paterson, L. Farmer, F. Stephen & J. Love, 'Competition and the Market for Legal Services' (1988) 15 *JL&Soc* 361; A. Paterson, 'Professionalism and the Legal Services Market' (1996) 3 *Int'l J.L. Prof.* 137.

[81] M. Zander, *Lawyers and the Public Interest* (London, 1968) is a classic account. See D. Sugarman, 'Bourgeois Collectivism, Professional Power and the Boundaries of the State: The Private and Public Life of the Law Society, 1825–1914' (1996) 3 *Int'l J.L. Prof.* 81 for some historical examples. See Administration of Justice Act 1985, s 11 (end of conveyancing monopoly); Courts and Legal Services Act 1990, s 55.

[82] M. Berends, 'An Elusive Profession?' (1992) 26 *L&Soc.R.* 161, 167; D. Sugarman & W. Pue, 'Introduction', in D. Sugarman & W. Pue (eds), *Lawyers and Vampires. Cultural Histories of Legal Professions* (Oxford, 2003), 6, 22.

[83] T. Halliday, *Beyond Monopoly. Lawyers, State Crises and Professional Empowerment* (Chicago, 1987).

[84] *Arthur J.S. Hall & Co. v Simmons* [2000] UKHL 38; [2002] 1 AC 615, 682E, *per* Lord Steyn. See G. Hanlon, 'A Profession in Transition' (1997) 60 *MLR* 798; H. Kritzer, 'The Professions are Dead, Long Live the Professions' (1999) 33 *L&Soc.R.* 713.

[85] A. Francis, 'Out of Touch and Out of Time' (2004) 24 *LS* 322.

onto the notion of an autonomous, self-governing profession, although the extent to which this has been ideologically driven is sometimes overstated.[86] No doubt some government proposals are inspired by a naive economic analysis, which assumes that important professional rules which restrict competition are automatically to be condemned, without adequate regard to their public interest benefit in maintaining professional standards.[87] But there has been a genuine concern: thus the Law Society had the responsibility for administering legal aid removed because of concerns about the administration and cost.[88] The handling of client complaints about solicitors has been a running sore with the government and consumer groups, and in this area has led to a gradual erosion of self-regulation.[89] And the fashion for the purgative quality of competitive forces provides the backdrop for proposals to permit outside ownership of law practices and multi-disciplinary practices, despite the dangers to law as a profession and the greater potential for conflicts of interest (or worse).[90]

That leads to the third avenue for examining lawyers' role in making law work, the ethical rules which govern their behaviour. It is the subject matter of Chapter 6 but recurs throughout the book.[91] The link with the law's fundamental values and with procedure has already been made. Thus lawyers as a social group are uniquely placed to constitute access to justice.[92] At an individual level that obliges activities such as *pro bono* advice and assistance. More fundamentally the legal profession can contribute to advancing values such as access to justice and equality before the law through their role in the administration and reform of the law. The more lawyers are exposed to access to justice problems and procedural deficiencies through *pro bono* work the stronger the platform for change. Legal institutions relate to ethical values in other ways. Thus how courts work depends on, and can only be understood, in the light of, assumptions about the ethics of the profession.[93] In some countries freeing the justice system of corruption is a necessary condition if the human rights and the contract and property rights of all are to be protected.

So examining lawyers through the lens of legal ethics blends well with other themes of the book. But there is more to the focus on legal ethics than that. First, as Professor Martin Partington suggests, the failure of other theoretical

---

[86] M. Burrage, 'Mrs Thatcher Against the Little Republics', in T. Halliday & L. Karpik, *Lawyers and the Rise of Western Political Liberalism* (Oxford, 1997).

[87] Office of Fair Trading, *Competition in Professions* (London, 2001). For the government response: Lord Chancellor's Department, *In the Public Interest?* (London, 2002).

[88] 47 below.   [89] 182 below.

[90] Sir David Clementi, *Review of the Regulatory Framework for Legal Services in England and Wales. Final Report* (London, 2004), 115–28, 133–9; H. McVea, 'Predators and the Public Interest—The "Big Four" and Multi-disciplinary Practices' (2002) 65 *MLR* 811; H. McVea, 'Legal Disciplinary Practices—Who Needs Them?' (2004) 31 *JLS* 563; D. Fischel, 'Multidisciplinary Practice' (2000) 55 *BusLR* 951; L. Fox, 'MDPs Done Gone: The Silver Lining in a Very Black Enron Cloud' (2002) 44 *Arizona LR* 547.   [91] 54, 150, 286 below.

[92] C. Parker, *Just Lawyers: Regulation and Access to Justice* (Oxford, 1999).

[93] R. O'Dair, *Legal Ethics* (London, 2001), 9.

approaches to analysing law may mean that now legal ethics is the preferred alternative approach to raising issues relating to the role of law in society.[94] Secondly, concern within the legal profession about its future has been especially acute in recent times in the light of the economic pressures on lawyers to be more businesslike, the destructive force of competition policies on traditional methods of practice, and the way a less deferential society and more cynical media combine to undermine the notion of law as a profession. None of this is to suggest that competition does not have a role, that existing ways of doing things should be sacrosanct or that the profession has never been the author of its own misfortune and never fallen short of its responsibilities.[95] Law, however, is still a profession of ideals and idealism. One has only to compare the legal profession with many other professions to see how highly lawyers prize their integrity and the pains they take to preserve it.[96] Lawyers and the public need to be reminded of this but lawyers need also constantly to revisit their ethical obligations.

Finally, the system of legal ethics has an important explanatory power in how lawyers work. The rules, codes and norms which comprise the standards of professional conduct are a collective statement of how to behave as a lawyer. They can be used to evaluate particular practices such as charging practices by identifying their ethical failings.[97] In addition to this internal function for the profession, legal ethics also have an external prospect of signalling to the public what they can expect of lawyers.[98] In everyday legal life lawyers are influenced to act ethically in a variety of formal and informal ways. Formally, there is public exposure—of what lawyers do in court and of other matters such as the conflicts of interest facing large law firms. Informally, there are the myriad ways that ethical standards are articulated on a daily basis. As Professor Veronica Taylor puts it:

Lawyers remind each other constantly about how they should behave. They gossip about who is an ethical, competent lawyer and who is not—and this gossip can have a direct consequence on the profits or business opportunities of their colleagues. . . . [C]lient expectations also encourage lawyers to behave ethically.[99]

Law's Impact

Legal values such as access to justice are valuable in themselves. They represent what a society and its legal system stand for. So, too, with the detailed legal rights set out in common and statutory law. But legal values and rights without delivery

---

[94] M. Partington, 'Book Review' (1999) 2 *Legal Ethics* 217, 221.

[95] See e.g. A. Kronman, *The Lost Lawyer. Failing Ideals of the Legal Profession* (Cambridge, MA., 1993); D. Rhode, *In the Interests of Justice* (New York, 2000).

[96] S. Shapiro, *Tangled Loyalties. Conflicts of Interest in Legal Practice* (Ann Arbor, 2002), 450–1.

[97] e.g. H. Kritzer, 'Lawyers Fees and Lawyer Behaviour in Litigation' (2001) 80 *Tex.LR* 1943, 1979.

[98] D. Nicolson & J. Webb, *Professional Legal Ethics* (Oxford, 1999).

[99] V. Taylor, 'Anti-Corruption and Asian Legal Professions', in T. Lindsey & H. Dick (eds), *Corruption in Asia* (Sydney, 2002).

are a delusion and can breed cynicism or worse. Understanding how legal values and rights work in practice helps in the trimming and tacking so they can become a reality. There is also the more general aim of making accountable those propounding a law, those responsible for its implementation and those operating law's machinery. If, say, new legislation is proposed to improve the position of communities it is only right that that claim be evaluated. After all, public moneys are probably involved and other choices can be made for their spending. Open government demands that people know how well public policy, and law as an avenue for its expression, are being delivered and law-makers and others need to be held to account.[100]

Evaluating law's impacts is not, however, straightforward. Consider the reaction of a 40-year-old Bangladesh widow, Taheranessa, to a government supported scheme for making credit available to the poor:

A weaver with a young son, she is unable to go to market to sell her cloth herself because she is female. The social organization of the weaving market is such that she and her son are profoundly disadvantaged and must sell cloth and buy supplies through middlemen traders who extract a margin for their services. Despite the apparent opportunity of a government development programme targeted at poor weaving households, Taheranessa chose not to apply for a loan because she reasoned that trying to meet repayments would only generate further difficulties until her son was old enough to take the cloth to market himself.[101]

Here credit was available to Taheranessa but for understandable reasons she decided not to take advantage of it. The loan was from the Grameen Bank, so that if she had not been able to make the repayments she would have faced great pressure from fellow group members whose future access to credit was dependent on all keeping up their payments.[102] Then there would have been the need to take an informal loan, which would likely have led to even greater indebtedness. So it requires detailed inquiry into the social, cultural, and economic circumstances which determine the fate of development policies like this, and legal and public policy interventions. Too often in assessing how law works lawyers, 'have been lazy about subjecting their hunches—which in honesty we should admit are often little better than prejudices—to systematic empirical testing'.[103]

At the outset are the goals of a law and how it is given expression. Knowledge of the interest groups behind a proposal is often revealing. It may never have been intended that the law was to match fully its ostensible ends. The purpose may

[100] House of Commons, Public Administration Select Committee, *On Target? Government by Measurement*, HC 26 (London, 2003), para. 99.

[101] A. McGregor, 'Routes out of Poverty—Understanding Why the World's Poor Stay Poor', *The Edge* [Economic and Social Research Council], Issue 12, March 2003, 25. See also his 'Village Credit and the Reproduction of Poverty in Rural Bangladesh', in J. Acheson (ed.), *Economic Anthropology and the New Institutional Economics* (Washington, DC, 1994); and www.welldev.org.uk.

[102] See 289 below.

[103] R. Posner, 'The Summary Jury Trial and Other Methods of Alternative Dispute Resolution: Some Cautionary Observations' (1986) 53 *Uni.Chi.LR* 366, 367.

have been more to mark a symbolic gain than to produce immediate, real-world results. Driven by the electoral cycle or media demand, claims of quick results may prove illusory. Technical defects in a law's preparation may be obvious on its face or on further examination of the practical application of its provisions. Then there is the issue of technique and whether the legal and administrative regime for the law's implementation is the most appropriate. Success will often turn on consistent political will, clear policy, and strong agencies with expertise and resources. The reaction of those to whom a law is directed is also crucial. Conceptually this turns on a range of factors: what does a law mean for behaviour? is this contrary to self-interest? how is that coloured by a disposition in general to comply with the law? how real is the threat of sanctions for failing to comply? Not surprisingly laws may have unanticipated consequences, although in some analyses this is put as highly as an impact which is 'precisely opposite to the one intended. . . .'[104] Such claims of 'legal backfire' need close scrutiny for they are often used as rhetoric by opponents of a law without evidence in support.

Measuring the impact of a law is a task of considerable difficulty. Take framework legislation for an expansion in education, the health services, or the civil justice system. The inputs will be measurable and, after a while, it will be possible to identify outputs such as new or refurbished schools, hospitals or courts buildings, or the appointment of additional teachers, medical workers, or judges. Outcomes, not outputs, may be crucial, however, to the aims of the law—improvements in the education and health of the population or greater access to justice. Uncovering these is more difficult. Proxy measures may be possible, but there are immediate problems. Does improved access to justice, say, turn on the number of cases handled, the cost and speed of resolving them, or the degree of satisfaction of users? And will any of this be relevant to the lives of people? Professor Hans Micklitz noted that there were some 10,000 decisions under the German Unfair Contract Terms Act but none knew whether and to what extent the situation of the individual had improved.[105] Then causation raises intractable issues. The percentage of patients in a hospital who get better may say more about their personal habits and self-care than what the hospital does; the level of school results, more about the encouragement parents give their children; and the number of litigants and the speed with which they press their cases, more about the situation in the economy.[106] As to law, 'it is difficult to isolate the effects of law as opposed to other factors such as education, a changing job market, shifts in population, and alterations in public attitudes. . . .'[107]

---

[104] C. Sunstein, 'Paradoxes of the Regulatory State' (1990) 57 *U.Chi.LR* 407, 407. See R. Hillman, 'The Rhetoric of Legal Backfire' (2002) 43 *Boston CLR* 819.

[105] H. Micklitz, 'Privatisation of Access to Justice and Soft Law—Lessons from the European Community', in T. Wilhelmsson & S. Hurri (eds), *From Dissonance to Sense: Welfare State Expectations, Privatisation and Private Law* (Aldershot, 1999), 565.

[106] J. Wilson, 'The Problem of Defining Agency Success', *Performance Measures for the Criminal Justice System*, Bureau of Justice Statistics, US Department of Justice (Washington, DC, 1993) 158.

[107] W. Bogart, *Consequences. The Impact of Law and Its Complexity* (Toronto, 2002), 309.

Within government, assessing the impact of law takes place in various guises. It is now standard practice to prepare a regulatory impact assessment for new laws and regulations, which compares various options for dealing with an issue and lays out their benefits and costs.[108] Once adopted it is common to set performance indicators or targets with the aim of measuring success.[109] There are now performance indicators for courts.[110] An aspect of performance is public satisfaction with a service, as with the regular survey of court users' views.[111] Then there is the evaluation by the various official inspectorates of whether performance indicators and targets have been met.[112] For example, legislation enables the government to set standards which health and care bodies must use in discharging their obligations and establishes a Commission for Healthcare Audit and Inspection, and a Commission for Social Care Inspection to monitor performance against these.[113] They publish ratings of the agencies they inspect drawing on evidence from performance indicators, inspections and other sources. Evaluating performance in this manner has proved controversial. Critics claim that targets can impair morale, encourage evasion and produce perverse incentives. Proponents contend that they drive achievement by agencies of their legislatively entrusted goals.[114] A balanced assessment in Britain is that targets are necessary both on accountability grounds and as a tool for improving standards, but that they need to be fewer, there must be more local input in their setting, tiered measures are preferable to snapshots and there has to be adequate evidence to support assessments.[115]

Concern with the impact of law recurs throughout this book. Whether changes in legal aid and the use of alternative dispute resolution have had a beneficial impact on access to justice is explored in Chapters 2 and 3. Chapter 4 has a discussion of the social ramifications of court decisions. However significant in doctrinal terms a decision may lack force for third parties, not least because the courts do not have executive machinery to channel behaviour.[116] In Chapter 5 the implications of the Woolf reforms for settlements, a less adversarial culture and the cost of litigation, are explored. Then the second part of the book turns to the impact of law in earnest. Chapter 7 examines whether legal and social rights translate into practice. While rights are to some extent self-enforcing, the role of state agencies

---

[108] Cabinet Office, *Regulatory Impact Assessment Guidance* (London, 2005).

[109] N. Carter, R. Klein & P. Day, *How Organisations Measure Success: The Use of Performance Indicators in Government* (London, 1992). [110] 12 above.

[111] e.g. S. Ho, 'Magistrates' Courts Waiting Times on the Day and User Reaction Surveys: 2004', Department for Constitutional Affairs, *Statistics on Magistrates' Courts* (London, 2005). See H. Kritzer & J. Voelker, 'Familiarity Breeds Respect: How Wisconsin Citizens View Their Courts' (1998) 82 *Judicature* 58.

[112] e.g. C. Hood, O. James, C. Scott, G. Jones & T. Travers, *Regulation Inside Government* (Oxford, 1999); P. Day & R. Klein, *Auditing the Auditors* (London, 2001); C. Hood, O. James, B. Peters & C. Scott, *Controlling Modern Government: Variety, Commonality and Change* (Cheltenham, 2004).

[113] Health and Social Care (Community Health and Standards) Act 2003, ss 41–42.

[114] See P. Collins, 'The Reinventing Government Scorecard'; M. Bichard, 'Mission-Driven Government', both in P. Collins & L. Byrne (eds), *Reinventing Government Again* (London, 2004); D. Marquand, *Decline of the Public* (Oxford, 2004).

[115] House of Commons, Public Administration Select Committee, *op.cit.* [116] 139 below.

in the delivery of rights is scrutinized. Particularly underlined is the importance of those in charge feeding good practice into routine procedures for frontline staff, whether they be the police, regulators, or social welfare officials. Chapter 8 takes as a case study the destructive impact of European law on the lives of Aboriginals in Australia. Here there was a definite disjuncture between the rights for Aboriginals and the reality of public policy, contained in a panoply of legislation controlling their lives. Chapters 9 and 10 are about the impact of law on economic development. That issue deserves to be seen in context.

Law, Economic Development, and Legal Transplants

In recent decades a conventional wisdom has evolved linking for developing countries the rule of law with economic growth, sustainable development and poverty alleviation.[117] Multilateral financial institutions like the World Bank, regional development banks and some non-governmental organizations advocate for emerging and developing countries good governance, one aspect of which is a legal system of a type associated with states operating under the rule of law.[118] In modern accounts, the rule of law has both formal and substantive aspects—a legal system with an independent, impartial, and non-corrupt judiciary, laws that are clear, publicly available and in accordance with the constitution and human rights, and a court system which is accessible and efficient, protects contractual, property and human rights and provides for judicial review of government action.[119] Some like Professor Amartya Sen would contend that rule of law reform along these lines must be valued in itself as part of the process of development, not just for the way it may aid economic or any other type of development.[120] Another line of argument is that rule of law reforms, by themselves, are only part of the story. What is also needed is legal empowerment of the disadvantaged, which will benefit them in a broad array of development fields that may not have a strict legal dimension such as education, public health promotion, and agriculture.[121] Both glosses on the basic argument have great force. Nonetheless, the concern here is with the policy prescription, that along with a transparent and democratic political system, efficient bureaucracies and developed public institutions, rule of law reforms will encourage investment,

---

[117] There is a growing literature about economic growth which is 'pro-poor': M. Ravallion, 'Pro-Poor Growth: A Primer', *World Bank Policy Research Working Paper*, 3242 (Washington, DC, 2004).

[118] e.g. I. Shihata, 'Democracy and Development' (1997) 46 *ICLQ* 635; T. Carothers, 'The Rule of Law Revival' (1998) 77 *Foreign Affairs* 95; *Promoting the Rule of Law Abroad*, Carnegie Endowment, Democracy and Rule of Law Project No. 34, 2003.

[119] e.g. P. Craig, 'Formal, and Substantive Conceptions of the Rule of Law' [1997] *PL* 467; T. Allan, *Constitutional* Justice (Oxford, 2001). cf. W. Whitford, 'The Rule of Law' [2000] *Wisc LR* 723.

[120] A. Sen, *Development as Freedom* (New York, 1999), 37.

[121] Asian Development Bank, *Legal Empowerment. Advancing Good Governance and Poverty Reduction*, (Manila, 2001), 27.

reduce corruption and cronyism, and generally contribute to social and economic development.[122] Law, in other words, matters.

There is historical evidence of a link between law and economic development.[123] Over the last decade there have also been a number of large, cross-country studies which, by using proxies for rule of law measures such as the quality of legal institutions, lend support to the thesis.[124] Yet the relationship between rule of law reform and economic development is complex; as ever real-world contingency must be taken into account. It may be that in some respects it is economic development which facilitates a better functioning legal system, or that factors such as investment or political change move both economic development and legal reform in the same direction.[125] Another difficulty with causation in the thesis is identifying the relevant factors in the relationship. Is the key to economic growth the symbolic value of new law on the books, or is the effectiveness of legal institutions in practice more significant?[126] Is governmental accountability, not least through the courts, a necessary element of the rule of law and, if so, how do we explain the East Asian model of economic development, best exemplified these days by China?[127] Further there is the puzzle of foreign investors, who are important in bridging the gap between investment and savings. While they say that they want a legal system which has a clear framework for contracting, which protects property, including intellectual property, rights, and which provides for the timely resolution of disputes, in practice the existence of business opportunities means that they may invest heavily in countries where these basic features of the rule of law are absent.[128]

[122] On the earlier law and development movement see D. Trubek & M. Galanter, 'Scholars in Self-Estrangement: Some Reflections on the Crisis in Law and Development' [1974] *Wisc LR* 1062; B. Tamanaha, 'The Lessons of Law and Development Studies' (1995) 89 *Amer.J.Int'l.L.* 470; J. Faundez, 'Legal Technical Assistance', in J. Faundez (ed), *Good Government and Law* (London, 1997).

[123] e.g., P. Atiyah, *The Rise and Fall of Freedom of Contract* (Oxford, 1979); D. North, *Institutions, Institutional Change and Economic Performance* (Cambridge, 1990) J. Getzler, *A History of Water Rights at Common Law* (Oxford, 2004), 4 ff. critically reviews the literature. Especially relevant to the essays in this book is K. Pistor & P. Wellons, *The Role of Law and Legal Institutions in Asian Economic Development 1960–1995* (Oxford, 1999), esp. 5–7, 19, 35–6, 47–55, 89–90, 107–11, 154–7.

[124] A. Brunetti et al., 'Credibility of Rules and Economic Growth: Evidence from a Worldwide Survey of the Private Sector' (1998) 12 *World Bank Economic Review* 353; R. La Porta, F. Lopez-de-Silanes, A. Shleifer & R.W. Vishny, 'Legal Determinants of External Finance' (1997) 52 *Journal of Finance*, 1131; R. La Porta, F. Lopez-de-Silanes, A. Shleifer & R.W. Vishny, 'Law and Finance' (1998) 106 *Journal of Political Economy* 1113. See also R. Levine, 'The Legal Environment, Banks, and Long-Run Economic Growth' (1998) 30 *Journal of Money, Credit, and Banking*, 596.

[125] R. Messick, 'Judicial Reform and Economic Development: A Survey of the Issues' (1999) 14 *World Bank Resource Observer* 117, 122.

[126] K. Pistor, M. Raiser & S. Gelfer, *Law and Finance in Transition Economies*, Centre for International Development, Harvard University, Working Paper No. 49, 2000.

[127] F. Upham, *Mythmaking in the Rule of Law Orthodoxy*, Carnegie Endowment for International Peace, Rule of Law Series, No. 30, 2002; C. Jones, 'Capitalism, Globalization, Rule of Law' (1994) 3 *Soc. & Leg. Studies* 195.

[128] A. Perry-Kessaris, 'Finding and Facing Facts About Legal Systems and Foreign Direct Investment in South Asia' (2003) 23 *LS* 649; V. Taylor, 'The Transformation of Indonesian Commercial Contracts

In theory law can have an impact on development by facilitating economic activity through encouraging savings and assisting in the allocation of capital. It can do this by having predictable, transparent and enforceable rules which ensure well-functioning markets, appropriate business forms, and efficient methods for dealing with default and insolvency.[129] Government subject to law is part of the equation, to guarantee that insiders cannot use state power arbitrarily to trump property and contractual rights recognized by law. Yet law's contribution to development in practice is a long-term and tortuous process. As a matter of public policy it demands a sensitivity to its inherent limits, the context in which it operates and the force of other social and economic factors.[130] There is always the potential for unintended consequences. A neat illustration pertinent to the issue of credit and security law is provided by the colonial courts in India, which were superimposed on a system where informal sanctions operated in rural areas to guarantee the repayment of credit, but which also encouraged moneylenders to carry debtors in difficult times. In one account new creditors, with access to the enforcement mechanisms of the colonial courts, entered the market, forced down margins, which reduced the capacity of local moneylenders to accommodate debtors in difficulty.[131]

Once again how the law actually operates is at least as important as the law in the books. Using law for utilitarian ends means acknowledging, for example, the importance of non-state norms such as commercial custom, informal methods of social control and alternative mechanisms of dispute resolution. As well, it should not be forgotten that law's outcomes are not value-free and that law can be part of the struggle for power in society. Protecting contractual and property rights may simply shield what a powerful, and possibly corrupt, elite has seized under the cover of state power. Even more benign societies recognize the need for statutory control and well-oiled regulatory agencies to curb the abuses of free contracting and markets. Apart from equity concerns, the state must police markets to curb corrupt and predatory practices which undermine their very integrity.[132] Nor does creating a system which works for private economic interests mean overlooking values such as equality before the law, the wider public interest and the more vulnerable in society.[133]

---

and Legal Advisers', and G. Goodpaster, 'The Rule of Law, Economic Development and Indonesia', both in T. Lindsey (ed), *Indonesia. Law and Society* (Sydney, 1999), 281, 286, 287.

[129] R. Posner, 'Creating a Legal Framework for Economic Development', *World Bank Research Observer*, vol.13, February. 1998, 1.

[130] P. McAuslan, 'Path Dependency, Law and Development' (2001) 1 *J.Commonwealth L.& Leg.Ed.* 51, 58.

[131] R. Kranton & A. Swamy, 'The Hazards of Piecemeal Reform: British Civil Courts and the Credit Market in Colonial India' (1999) 58 *J.Develop.Econ* 1.

[132] G. Roland & T. Verdier, *Law Enforcement and Transition*, CEPR Discussion Paper No. 2501 (London, 2000).

[133] See, e.g., C. Dias & J. Paul, 'Lawyers, Legal Resources and Alternative Approaches to Development', in C. Dias *et al.* (eds), *Lawyers in the Third World: Comparative and Development Perspectives* (Uppsala, 1981).

All of this militates against a notion that economic development follows from a blind transplant of Western legal models to developing and emerging economies. It cannot be assumed that their introduction will automatically occasion sophisticated economic transactions, foster the establishment of complex enterprises or further the resolution of legal disputes. This is quite apart from the adverse reaction which could follow because transplanting Western law might be interpreted as a form of neo-colonial domination. Ideally, what is wanted is an incremental approach, drawing on theory and international best practice, and over time melding this to local conditions in the light of accumulated experience.[134] In many cases copying Western models is unavoidable because of pressure of time, the lack of expertise and the demands of outside interests for immediate action.[135] It might also be that a window of opportunity for fundamental reform presents itself; the ideal in these circumstances is a counsel of perfection and will miss the boat.

At the level of theory Montesquieu argued that it was unlikely that the laws of one nation would suit another, given the variety of environmental factors making up 'the spirit of the law'.[136] In a more modern account, Professor Otto Kahn-Freund thought it possible to transplant law but emphasized the very great difficulties. Factors which in his account are especially important are political institutions, ideologies, and the power structure.[137] Professor Alan Watson's contrary thesis is that transplants can readily be made. Law has a strong autonomy from societal forces, law representing the culture of the legal elite.

[Law] is above all and primarily the culture of the lawyers and especially of the law-makers, that is, of those lawyers who, whether as legislators, jurists, or judges, have control of the accepted mechanisms of legal change . . . Law is largely autonomous and not shaped by societal needs; though legal institutions will not exist without corresponding social institutions, law evolves from the legal tradition.[138]

Lending support to Watson's view are his own speciality, Roman law, and other major episodes of legal transplantation: Napoleon carried his code to other parts of Europe; in the nineteenth and first part of the twentieth century, imperial powers like Britain and France took their laws to other continents; and in recent decades international financial institutions like the World Bank have marketed their models to developing and emerging economies.

So at a purely formal level law can be transplanted. The obvious issue is does a transplanted law become living law, and if so, how? There are no easy answers.

---

[134] A. Seidman & R. Seidman, 'Using Reason and Experience to Draft Country-Specific Laws', in A. Seidman, R. Seidman & T. Wälde (eds), *Making Development Work* (London, 1999).

[135] T. Wälde & J. Gunderson, 'Legislative Reform in Transition Economies: Western Transplants: A Short-cut to Social Market Economy Status?' in *ibid.*, 92–5.

[136] See J. Allison, *A Continental Distinction in the Common Law* (Oxford, 1996), 12–13.

[137] O. Kahn-Freund, 'On Uses and Misuses of Comparative Law' (1974) 37 *MLR* 1. See also A. Rosser, 'The Political Economy of Institutional Reform in Indonesia', in K. Jayasuriya (ed), *Law, Capitalism and Power in Asia. The Rule of Law and Legal Institutions* (London, 1999).

[138] A. Watson, *The Evolution of Law* (Baltimore, 1985), 119. See also his *Society and Legal Change*, 2nd edn (Philadelphia, 2001), 98–111.

Taxonomies in which certain families of law transplant efficiently and others ineffectively are not especially convincing;[139] fashionable taxonomies, even less so.[140] Nor are some of the massive empirical studies which give them some support. What can be said is that a transplanted law is changed in use: it will be transformed through interpretation and application, and even be amended to take in local conditions. Secondly, whatever the law, transplanted or otherwise, commercial activity goes on. Thus in England and the United States informal norms, as with commercial customs, have always been part of the working of the law.[141] In some situations transplanted law may have a greater chance in the commercial area, in particular the investment and financial sectors, because there is a need, especially among foreign investors.[142] But commercial laws which trench on rights in the wider community are likely to be resisted. Security and insolvency laws fall into this category, if they threaten employees' continued employment in a jurisdiction which has no social security system.[143] On the other hand, criminal and family laws have been successfully transplanted, even laws which were forced, initially, onto a jurisdiction.[144] Such transplants have had a catalytic effect. It seems that the positive attitude of local elites, including legal elites, cannot be underestimated.[145] It is all a very mixed picture, but context cannot be underestimated.

In this book these issues of the role of law in economic development, and legal transplantation, are discussed in Chapters 9 and 10. They take as a case study the provision of credit, in particular the role of security (collateral) in facilitating this. Closely related are other areas such as insolvency and corporate governance.[146] In broad outline secured transactions law gives creditors and investors a priority claim against the debtor's property (the collateral) should it be unable or unwilling to pay in accordance with the credit or investment contract. The importance of an effective security law for an economy is recognized in World Bank Guidelines in this way:

A modern credit-based economy requires predictable, transparent and affordable enforcement of both unsecured and secured credit claims by efficient mechanisms outside of insolvency, as well as a sound insolvency system . . .

---

[139] D. Berkowitz, K. Pistor, J-F. Richard, 'Economic Development, Legality and the Transplant Effect' (2003) *Eur.Econ.R.* 165. cf. R. La Porta, F. D.Lopez-de-Silanes, A. Shliefer, & R. W. Vishny, 'Law and Finance' (1998) 106 *Journal of Political Economy* 1113.

[140] U. Mattei, 'Efficiency in Legal Transplants: An Essay in Comparative Law and Economics' (1994) 14 *Int'l R.L. & Econ* 3; 'Three Patterns of Law: Taxonomy and Change in the World's Legal Systems' (1997) 45 *Am.J.Comp.L.* 5. See M. Smith, 'Comparative Law and Legal Culture' (2003) 15 *Bond LR* 20, 24–5.

[141] R. Cranston, 'Commercial Law and Commercial Lore', in J. Lowry & L. Mistelis (eds), *Commercial Law: Perspectives and Practice* (London, 2005).

[142] F. Shaver, 'The Politics and Incentives of Legal Transplantation', CID [Harvard University] Working Paper No. 44, April 2000, 9–11.   [143] 270 below.

[144] A. Harding, 'Global Doctrine and Local Knowledge: Law in South-East Asia' (2002) 51 *ICLQ* 35, 44–5.   [145] F. Cross, 'Law and Economic Growth' (2002) 80 *Tex.LR* 1737, 1774.

[146] e.g. B. Kamarul & R. Tomasic, 'The Rule of Law and Corporate Insolvency in Six Asian Legal Systems', in K. Jayasuriya (ed.), *Law, Capitalism and Power in Asia* (London, 1999); G. Walker & T. Reid, 'Upgrading Corporate Governance in East Asia' [2002] *JBL* 59.

The legal framework should provide for the creation, recognition, and enforcement of security interests in movable and immovable (real) property, arising by agreement or operation of law. The law should provide for the following features:

- Security interests in all types of assets, movable and immovable, tangible and intangible, including inventory, receivables, and proceeds; future or after-acquired property, and on a global basis; and based on both possessory and non-possessory interests;

  . . .

- Methods of notice that will sufficiently publicize the existence of security interests to creditors, purchasers, and the public generally at the lowest possible cost;
- Clear rules of priority governing competing claims or interests in the same assets . . .

  . . .

- Enforcement procedures should provide for prompt realization of the rights obtained in secured assets, ensuring the maximum possible recovery of asset values based on market values. Both nonjudicial and judicial enforcement methods should be considered.[147]

All this has considerable intuitive appeal. That security rights under credit and investment agreements are readily enforceable means that lenders and investors can more accurately manage and control the risk of default. It encourages discipline on the part of debtors. Disputes are more readily resolvable in the shadow of the law. By contrast, if enforcement of a credit or investment contract is doubtful, creditors and investors cannot price the risk of default accurately. A premium needs to be extracted to compensate for the uncertainty or for the risk of non-performance. In some cases the confidence of creditors and investors may be so eroded that credit is altogether unavailable.[148]

Security law is as important for the poor as for others. In his *The Mystery of Capital*, Professor Hernando de Soto observes that in developing countries, although the poor may have capital such as growing crops or possibly land, it is 'dead' economically—it lacks adequate legal protection and, crucially, cannot be used as collateral for credit. Access to ready finance is the preserve of the elite.[149] Similarly, a recent study of the Asian Development Bank underlines the importance of small and medium-sized enterprises to sustainable economic growth. It argues that the key to their success is access to readily available, cheap and long-term credit that turns on a legal framework enabling small borrowers to give security over their movable property, since unlike larger enterprises they are less likely to be able to offer land and buildings as security.[150] What Chapter 9 does is

---

[147] World Bank, *Principles and Guidelines for Effective Insolvency and Creditor Rights Regimes*, excerpts in (2003) 1 *World Bank Leg* Review 627, Principles 1, 3, 5. See also UNCITRAL, *Security Interests. Draft Legislative Guide on Secured Transactions*, www.unictral.org

[148] B. Adler, 'Secured Credit Contracts', *New Palgrave Dictionary of Economics and the Law* (London, 1998), vol. 3, 405.

[149] H. de Soto, *The Mystery of Capital* (New York, 2000), 6–7 90–2, 156–63.

[150] Asian Development Bank, *op.cit.*

to examine the reality of credit and security law in the region covered by the Bank. Chapter 10 then goes on to one country in Asia, Sri Lanka, to tell the story from colonial times to the present day of the transplant into that jurisdiction of credit and security law. The overriding theme of the two chapters is that there are no easy answers.[151]

[151] C. Walsh, 'The "Law" in Law and Development', *Law in Transition*, Autumn 2000, 7.

PART I

THE MACHINERY OF JUSTICE

2

Access to Justice: I

Anatole France's observation about equality before the law is well known: '[T]he majestic equality of the law, which forbids rich and poor alike to sleep under the bridges, to beg in the streets, and to steal their bread.' It appeared in his *Les Lys Rouge* (1894),[1] what to modern eyes is an otherwise turgid love story, from the mouth of the eccentric bore Choulette. It is nonetheless priceless. Its essential truth has application to access to justice in the aphorism that, in England, justice is open to all like the Ritz hotel.[2] How law can work in this exclusionary way takes acute form in *The Trial*. Franz Kafka's K is told of a man from the country, waiting for years before the law, who thinks that all should be able to go inside, at all times. The door-keeper says that access may be possible, in the future. After years of brief, impersonal conversation with the man, and after taking his possessions, the door-keeper finally shuts the door in the man's face with the cruel jibe that the door was intended for the man alone.[3] Yet access to justice surfaces only occasionally in popular consciousness. Perhaps it is regarded as too mundane and unimportant. John Grisham's thriller *The Street Lawyer*[4] should give the lie to this, as he follows Michael Brock from his successful anti-trust (competitive law) practice as an associate in a large Washington law firm to a public interest practice with the homeless as its clients.[5]

The importance of access to justice has already been touched on in Chapter 1, admittedly in less riveting form than offered by Grisham.[6] Both there and elsewhere in this book we explore the obstacles to individuals getting access to justice, both in developed and developing countries.[7] The most obvious obstacle to access to the formal justice system is cost, for courts and private lawyers do not come cheap. The upshot is that without compensating mechanisms, large sections of the population will be effectively excluded from access to the formal justice system. This chapter is about those compensating mechanisms and how they work to further access to justice. One is public funding, although a preliminary

---

[1] Trans. as *The Red Lily*, Bodley Head edn (London, 1927), 95.
[2] R. Megarry, *Miscellany-at-Law* (London, 1955), 254.
[3] F. Kafka, *The Trial*, definitive edn (London, 1956), 238–40.   [4] (New York, 1998).
[5] Grisham touches on public interest law in some of his other novels: Rudy Baylor tumbles over his insurance fraud while providing free legal advice to senior citizens (*The Rainmaker*, 1995) and Clay Carter comes across his crucial murder as a public defender (*The King of Torts*, 2003).
[6] 3–11 above.   [7] 112–6, 223–4 below.

issue discussed in the first part of the chapter is how publicly funded legal services can be justified given the many other calls on the public purse. Public funding takes various forms. The next part of the chapter examines one of these, traditional legal aid, sometimes called judicare, where public funding goes to paying private lawyers who take on clients largely as if they were fee-paying. Traditional legal aid has been the preferred mechanism for publicly funded legal services in Britain. As the legal aid budget has come under pressure, however, other structures for public funding to further access to justice have become increasingly important. Some of these are examined in the third part of the chapter. The following parts of the chapter move away from public funding. The penultimate part considers whether it is possible to stimulate private provision of legal services to close some of the gaps in access to justice. The final part explores alternative dispute mechanisms to deal with people's legal disputes. These are especially important since they are a viable way for many to achieve justice. Professor Hugh Collins goes as far as suggesting that 'the distributive outcomes for poorer litigants such as consumers is likely to be superior to the alternative of improving access to courts and the vindication of contractual rights'.[8]

Justifying Publicly Funded Legal Services

Equality before the law, legal rights, unmet legal needs, and social exclusion— these provide four bases for justifying publicly funded legal services. The first justification is that equality before the law—mainly in its procedural sense—cannot exist without publicly subsidized legal services, for otherwise many cannot assert their rights. Equal access to justice means that disputes are determined by the intrinsic merits of the arguments of the parties, not by inequalities of wealth or power.[9] The Overriding Objective of the Civil Procedure Rules—dealing with cases justly—recognizes this by defining that to include 'ensuring that parties are on an equal footing'. If, as claimants and defendants, people are before a judicial body without adequate legal assistance, the integrity of the process is threatened since it is based on the assumption that both parties can properly prove facts and present legal argument. More fundamentally, a system of civil justice must be judged by the way it treats those at the bottom of society. In other words the concern must be not simply with access to justice but with equal access to justice. In practice equality before the law as a justification for publicly funded legal services needs some refinement in its practical application. One reason is the issue of resources, and the need to decide between priorities, to which we return. Another is the reality that if everyone had the same ready access to law as, say, the

---

   [8] H. Collins, *Regulating Contracts* (Oxford, 1999), 323.
   [9] Legal Action Group, *A Strategy for Justice* (London, 1992), 112. cf. R. Smith, *Justice: Redressing the Balance* (London, 1997), 3–11. See 216, 310 below.

government or large corporations, society might be racked by conflict and the legal system might be strained to the point of collapse.[10] Nonetheless, equality before the law is the touchstone against which access to justice, and the system of publicly funded legal services, must be measured.

Protecting rights, especially fundamental and human rights, is the second justification for publicly funded legal services. A crucial aspect of this, and essential to the rule of law, is keeping the executive power in check. Individuals and institutions have rights conferred by the state but must sometimes assert rights against the state. Underlying this second justification is the notion that law is an integral part of society and that access to legal services is essential for individuals to pursue and defend their legal rights. Sometimes access to justice is put in terms of the key to rights of citizenship,[11] although as with asylum seekers citizenship should not be a prerequisite. The rights argument sits comfortably with an ethical model of the lawyer who single-mindedly pursues the legal rights of individual clients, even though this conflicts with powerful individuals and institutions and perhaps with prevailing values in society.[12] The public interest is furthered by the enforcement of legal rights which would otherwise go by default. The proper functioning of the modern state demands the protection of certain basic civil and social rights affecting liberty, housing, social welfare, and employment. This can only be achieved if—in addition to the effective operation of public agencies— legal services are available to people, irrespective of means, to enforce these basic legal rights.

The rights argument has some support in law. Access to justice has been held by the courts to be a fundamental right at common law, which means that it cannot be overridden by general or ambiguous words in legislation.[13] Not only is access to justice a fundamental right in itself but it is a prerequisite to the exercise of other fundamental rights. Yet neither under the European Convention on Human Rights nor the United States constitution is there a firm guarantee of publicly funded legal assistance in civil cases. Time will tell whether Article II-107 of the Charter of Fundamental Rights of the European Union takes the matter further: 'Legal aid shall be made available to those who lack sufficient resources insofar as such aid is necessary to ensure effective access to justice'. As Professor Conor Gearty puts it, a human right to civil legal aid is at one of those frontier points where 'the rhetoric of enforceable human rights is confronted with its own limitations in a society committed to the retention of unequal levels of resources as between its members'.[14] Under the European Convention on Human Rights only in exceptional circumstances can such a right be invoked by virtue of

---

[10] D. Rhode, *Access to Justice* (New York, 2004), 6.

[11] The National Consumer Council and Citizens Advice refer to the 'fourth right' of citizenship.

[12] 191 below.

[13] *R v Lord Chancellor, ex p Witham* [1998] QB 575, 585–6; *R (Daly) v Secretary of State for the Home Department* [2001] AC 532, 537H–538A; *R v Secretary of State for the Home Department, ex p Simms* [2000] 2 AC 115, 131F.

[14] C. Gearty, *Principles of Human Rights Adjudication* (Oxford, 2004), 137.

Article 6(1)—where the withholding of legal aid would make the assertion of a civil claim practically impossible or where it would lead to an obvious unfairness of the proceedings.[15] Complexity of procedure and law, the applicant's lack of capacity to represent himself or herself, and the importance of what is at stake might all point to exceptional circumstances under the Convention, but such broad indicia are of little assistance in ranking specific claims. Identifying fundamental rights which demand publicly funded legal services for their enforcement might be a more helpful approach, although there would still be problems of classification and ranking. Is access to justice to defend the right to freedom of expression in Article 10 of the European Convention more important than access to justice in relation to the environment recognized in Article 9 of the Aarhus Convention?[16] Is a claim by an elderly residential landlord classifiable as a right to livelihood, and does it rank equally with the claim to housing of her lodger when she threatens him with eviction for non-payment of rent and bad behaviour?

Meeting legal needs is a third justification for publicly funded legal services. In more recent times the concept of relative need has emerged as a means of targeting scarce resources. That has been coupled with notions of effectiveness, so that when the benefit of allocating resources is low, need may have to go unaddressed.[17] A systemic approach to need has developed from social research into whether the legal needs of ordinary people are being met by existing institutions. People are interviewed about problems faced in the recent past (which are not revealed to them as being necessarily legal problems), about what action they took, and more generally about the nature of services available in their community which provide legal assistance. The problems are chosen because in the expert judgment of the researchers they raise important legal issues. Usually the respondents are asked, or the researchers decide, if the problems experienced are serious. The findings of this research enable unmet legal need in the community to be mapped.[18]

There are difficulties in the concept of legal need and, indeed, in its measurement. What, for example, is a legal need? It cannot simply be a problem that is taken to lawyers, because a hypothesis is that certain types of legal problem are not taken to lawyers. Neither can it be a problem which professional opinion defines as a legal need. For example, it seems accepted that many lawyers have

---

[15] *Airey v Republic of Ireland* (1979) 2 EHRR 305 is the leading case. See also *Steel & Morris v United Kingdom* [2005] EMLR 15; *McVicar v United Kingdom* (2002) 35 EHRR 22; *P, C and S v United Kingdom* [2002] 3 FCR 1, ECHR; *Aerts v Belgium* (1998) 29 EHRR 50; *Re Perotti* [2003] EWCA Civ 1521; *The Times*, November 27, 2003. The leading US case is *Lassiter v Department of Social Services*, 452 US 18 (1981). See also J. McBride, 'Access to Justice and Human Rights Treaties' (1998) 17 *ICLQ* 235. C. Harlow, 'Access to Justice as a Human Right: The European Convention and the European Union', in P. Alston, M. Bustelo & J. Heenan (eds), *The EU and Human Rights* (Oxford, 1999).

[16] Convention on Access to Information, Public Participation in Decision-Making and Access to Justice in Environmental Matters, done at Aarhus, 25 June 1998, [2005] OJ L124/4, 17 June 2005.

[17] R. Moorhead & P. Pleasence, 'Access to Justice After Universalism' (2003) 30 *JL&Soc* 1, 2, 10.

[18] 109–10 below.

not appreciated until relatively recently that there are complicated legal issues associated with matters like social welfare benefits. In one somewhat dated study social workers did not refer cases to lawyers partly through ignorance of the law, the operation of publicly funded legal services and what lawyers did, but partly also because in their judgment lawyers fostered conflict, put profit first if in private practice, and were generally unhelpful.[19] These latter considerations were part of their definition of legal need but would almost certainly not be part of a lawyer's definition. On the other hand, it cannot be said that a legal need arises wherever legal rules apply, since legal rules permeate everyday existence. Similarly, demand is no definite measure of need, since demand is historically determined and can be and is orchestrated, not least by entrepreneurial or campaigning lawyers. As indicated a further consideration is that need cannot be separated from the cost of meeting it.[20]

A fourth view is to justify publicly funded legal services because of what may be achieved through them in the way of improving the social and economic position of the more deprived sections of society. In a significant document the Law Society has expressed the belief that the timely provision of legal aid services can prevent people becoming socially excluded or rescue those who have become excluded.[21] With publicly funded legal services the Legal Services Commission has as a priority directing more civil law resources into 'work tackling social exclusion'.[22] For these purposes social exclusion is shorthand for what happens when people or areas suffer from a combination of linked problems such as the lack of access to services, unemployment, low skills and incomes, inadequate housing, crime, poor health, and family breakdown.[23] At one level the social exclusion justification is based on the evidence that people are more likely to achieve a resolution of their case when they receive advice from a lawyer or from a skilled non-lawyer providing active assistance (for example, negotiation with the other side, representation at hearings).[24] Therefore, the justification runs, programmes

---

[19] A. Phillips, 'Social Work and the Delivery of Legal Services' (1979) 42 *MLR* 29.

[20] H. Wray, 'Legal Needs Research in a Local Community' (2000) 19 *CJQ* 386. See also R. Moorhead, *Pioneers in Practice. The Community Legal Service Pioneer Project Research Report*, Lord Chancellor's Department (London, 2000), ch. 8; J. Johnson, 'Studies of Legal Needs and Legal Aid in a Market Context', in F. Regan, A. Paterson, T. Goriely & D. Fleming (eds), *The Transformation of Legal Aid* (Oxford, 1999).

[21] Law Society, *Protecting Rights and Tackling Social Exclusion* (London, 2004), 5 (hereafter *Protecting Rights*).

[22] Legal Services Commission, *Corporate Plan 2004/05–2006/07* (London, 2004), 11. See also Secretary of State for Work and Pensions, *Opportunity for All*, Cm 6239 (London, 2004), 79–80.

[23] Social Exclusion Unit, *Breaking the Cycle* (London, 2004), 13.

[24] H. Genn, 'Tribunals and Informal Justice' (1993) 56 *MLR* 393, summarizing H. Genn & Y. Genn, *The Effectiveness of Representation at Tribunals*, Lord Chancellor's Department (London, 1989), ch. 3. cf. R. Young, 'The Effectiveness of Representation at Tribunals' (1990) 9 *CJQ* 16, 23. For US studies: C. Seron *et al.*, 'The Impact of Legal Counsel on Outcomes for Poor Tenants in New York City's Housing Court' (2001) 35 *Law & Soc.Rev.* 419; K. Monsma & R. Lempert, 'The Value of Counsel: 20 Years of Representation Before a Public Housing Eviction Board' (1992) 26 *Law & Soc.Rev.* 627; T. Eisenberg, 'Negotiation, Lawyering and Adjudication' (1994) 19 *Law and Soc.Inq.* 275, 281 ff. cf. Erratum for 'Grievances, Claims and Disputes: Assessing the Adversary Culture', in

designed to reduce social inequality, or to mitigate its effects (for example, tax credits or social welfare benefits), will not achieve their goals unless there are adequate legal and related services to guarantee their implementation.[25]

At another level the social exclusion justification refers to the cumulative effect of unresolved social problems. Anecdotally it is possible to see how addressing one problem can stifle the emergence of other problems: ensuring that social welfare benefits are paid can avoid housing eviction and uncontrollable debt; compelling an education authority to provide support to a child with severe dyslexia can prevent a cycle of decline in her own life and that of her family; and addressing domestic violence in its early stages can ward off a range of consequences from family breakup to physical and psychological injury.[26] There is some empirical support that in certain circumstances problems are additive and end up in social exclusion. Professor Hazel Genn's *Paths to Justice* found that certain types of situation had a cascade effect, in that a bundle of problems might flow from certain justiciable problems which a person experienced.[27] This was confirmed in a more recent national survey in England and Wales, drawn from a random selection of 3,348 residential households. It found that certain problem types were associated with an increased risk of additional problems being experienced. For example, domestic violence, divorce and relationship breakdown appeared more likely to trigger additional problems: the causal link to difficulties with housing, debt, and social welfare benefits is easily imagined.[28] Of those experiencing civil justice problems, some 46 per cent reported multiple problems, the four principal problem clusters being family (domestic violence, divorce/separation, children); homelessness (rented housing, unfair police treatment, being the subject of a legal action); health and welfare (clinical negligence, welfare benefits, mental illness, immigration); and economic circumstances (consumer, employment, money/debt, neighbours).

So public funding of legal services can be justified. But public funds are finite. Not all legal rights can be vindicated or every legal need met. There must be some balance struck between rights and needs on the one hand and resources on the other.[29] There are at least two dimensions to this. The first is that the case for publicly funded legal services must be made vis-à-vis other public services such as health and education. When budgets are imposed for public expenditure on

---

D. Trubek *et al.*, *Civil Litigation Research Project Final Report*, Law School, University of Wisconsin-Madison, 1983, Part B, III–170.

[25] e.g. Social Exclusion Unit, *Young Runaways* (London, 2002), 74, 78; Department for Transport, Local Government and the Regions, *More Than a Roof. A Report into Tackling Homelessness* (London, 2002), 16.

[26] Lord Chancellor's Department and Law Centres Federation, *Legal and Advice Services. A Pathway Out of Social Exclusion* (London, 2001).

[27] H. Genn, *Paths to Justice* (Oxford, 1999), 35–6. See 109 below.

[28] P. Pleasence *et al.*, *Causes of Action: Civil Law and Social Justice* (London, 2004), 47–8. See 109 below.

[29] cf. the balance struck in the CPR between the demand by some for court resources and the need for a fair allocation: 150 below.

these other services, it is simply not realistic to expect spending on legal services to be uncapped and demand led. In terms of achieving a more just society, the claims of the health and education budgets may rank equally, if not higher. Goriely and Paterson put this point well:

. . . a just society is much more likely to depend on the fair allocation of jobs, education, housing, and income than on anything a legal aid scheme can deliver. Once one accepts that justice involves issues of substantive rather than purely formal equality, then legal services no longer have a first call on society's resources, but must take their place alongside other welfare expenditure programmes.[30]

What is therefore required is that more attention be given to a calculation of the benefits from publicly funded legal services and whether they match that from an equal allocation of public resources to education or health.

Various benefits from publicly funded legal services can be identified to enter that calculation. One is to further the rule of law. Access to justice is necessary for equality before the law, which is part of the rule of law and enhances the legitimacy of the state. 'Equality before the law, like universal suffrage, holds a privileged place in our political system, and in theory inequality before the law delegitimises that system.'[31] Legal services are a component of access to justice, and recourse to public funding is necessary if many in the population are to have at least a minimum degree of legal advice and assistance. To deny such advice and assistance to those without wealth and power not only disadvantages them when they are faced with claims against them, but also means that unlike others they cannot capture the benefits which legal action may confer. Examples of these benefits are compensation following an accident, protection against domestic violence, a better environment in which to live, and an ordered distribution of what they own on death. The legitimacy of the state can also involve more basic calculations. A benefit of publicly funded legal services is to assist in resolving conflicts and thus to assuage dissatisfaction with the operation of society and the despair, cynicism, and conflict which may otherwise arise. Unresolved social disputes can prolong or exacerbate social conflict, hardship, and mental and physical harm and distress.[32] Elsewhere in the book we also see that enforcing legal rights and duties can be functional for economic development.[33] These radiating effects of publicly funded legal assistance are difficult to measure but nonetheless real.

These larger benefits merge into the more mundane ones of ensuring the civil justice works smoothly, making public policy effective and preventing social problems arising. The first of these points can be illustrated by the common observation that if litigants in person were represented the courts could operate

---

[30] T. Goriely & A. Paterson, 'Introduction', in A. Paterson & T. Goriely (eds), *Resourcing Civil Justice* (Oxford, 1996), 7.

[31] D. Luban, *Lawyers and Justice. An Ethical Study* (Princeton, 1988), 264.

[32] H. Genn, 'Unmet Legal Need', unpublished paper, November 1999, 3.   [33] 25–7 above.

more efficiently. As to the second, the effectiveness of a public policy programme turns in part on the ability of its beneficiaries to enforce their rights under it.[34] In practice this will often not involve legal action, or even the taking of legal advice. However, it does presuppose that the beneficiaries know about their entitlements and have the confidence and skills to pursue or defend them, and that if they face significant obstacles they can invoke assistance of a legal character if this is appropriate to overcoming them. It has been said that although the British welfare state was originally collectivist, it matured in a more individual age so that its beneficiaries are expected to enforce many of their entitlements, ultimately through courts and tribunals.[35] The benefits of preventing social problems arising have already been mentioned. Because problems appear in clusters—for example, those unfairly dismissed may lose their housing, which in turn may lead to family breakup—resolution of the first problem may avoid a cascade effect. Not only is that a benefit to the individual but there may also be a benefit to the state in costs avoided. To continue with this example there would be the direct costs in welfare benefits not paid and the indirect costs in anti-social behaviour dampened as children remain in a stable environment.

The second dimension to budgeted public funding is that choices must be made about how the moneys available for legal services are to be allocated. For many years in Britain this was done largely implicitly, and without strategic vision. Criminal defendants obviously required assistance, but on the civil side priorities were demand led by the existing patterns of professional practice. Thus a common criticism was that much of the civil legal aid moneys went on matters such as matrimonial work but not on debt or social welfare. Cost savings were effected through whatever means would meet minimum political resistance: the scope of the legal aid scheme was limited by excluding certain categories of help (for example, tribunal representation), tightening the means test for those in the population eligible for assistance, and restraining the remuneration payable to lawyers for cases undertaken. More recently the policy has been to transfer some public moneys from lawyers in private practice to the non-profit sector, to privatize legal assistance where this is possible, and to simplify and promote alternative procedures so as to reduce the costs of individual assistance. Each of these approaches may have positive benefits; they are examined later in the chapter.

If public funding for legal services must be prioritized, how is that to be done? One way of approaching the question is to address the process by which it is to be carried out. At a general level one could say that it should be done transparently, in a reflective manner, and so as to take into account changing circumstances.

---

[34] Another factor is whether those delivering it can get on with the job: e.g. the benefits in time saved in a busy health centre by having a part-time lawyer or paralegal deal with law-related inquiries may well justify the cost.

[35] T. Goriely, 'Making the Welfare State Work: Changing Conceptions of Legal Remedies within the British Welfare State', in F. Regan, A. Paterson, T. Goriely & D. Fleming (eds), *op.cit.* See 225–35 below.

More specifically, one could focus on the mechanics.[36] For less serious civil matters, as with some compensation claims, queuing may be used, as it is in the national health service, so that all claims are treated equally. Unless particular categories of case are separated out, however, queuing is not appropriate: for example, where a person's liberty, livelihood, or housing is under threat, immediate assistance is generally required. Steering people towards other avenues of redress—conditional fees, self-help, or alternative dispute resolution—is also possible. If prioritizing is to be express, criteria must be developed as to which type of case to fund. To what extent the public or representatives of the public are involved with government and the legal profession in developing these criteria must also be considered.

Another dimension to prioritizing is to identify criteria for ranking claims. That can be done by the type of case. Assistance for criminal cases is treated as central in all systems. That has a constitutional foundation in some jurisdictions and under the European Convention on Human Rights.[37] The justification is that a person must be in a position to mount an effective defence when confronting the exercise of state power, especially when that can result in a loss of liberty or reputation. The difficulty is in drawing boundaries: should publicly funded legal assistance be available for only 'serious' crimes, where imprisonment will inevitably follow a conviction; should it be confined to the trial of a defendant or should it be accessible at an earlier stage, for example arrest; and should the quality of assistance be in some way guaranteed, so that it at least matches that of the prosecution? The analysis is even more difficult on the civil side. Should family work get priority over housing? Within housing should assistance be confined to tenants or include landlords? If it is confined to tenants, should it be extended to those who have a history of anti-social behaviour and are being threatened with eviction because of it? Should test case or group litigation be supported, or is the more effective weapon funding lobbying or campaign work? Ranking claims presents intractable issues, although that is no reason for not attempting it.

In practice publicly funded legal services have been shaped by a variety of factors. Comparing legal aid schemes across different jurisdiction fails to identify any one determinative factor across all societies.[38] As we have already seen in considering the justifications for publicly funded legal services, the importance of ideas should not be overlooked. There is no better illustration of their impact in this regard than the vicissitudes of federal government funding for legal services in the United States. Reginald Heber Smith's *Justice and the Poor*, published in 1919,

---

[36] R. Dingwall, P. Fenn & J. Tuck, *Rationing and Cost-Containment in Legal Services* (Lord Chancellor's Department Research Services No. 1/98, London, 1998), 6–8, 10–11.

[37] A. Ashworth, 'Legal Aid, Human Rights and Criminal Justice', in R. Young & D. Wall (eds), *Access to Criminal Justice* (London, 1995).

[38] e.g. F. Regan, 'Why Do Legal Aid Services Vary Between Societies? Re-examining the Impact of Welfare States and Legal Families', in F. Regan, A. Paterson, T. Goriely & D. Fleming (eds), *op.cit.*

challenged the legal profession in the United States at an ethical level to further access to justice for everyone, regardless of their ability to pay.[39] Partly in response bar associations and law schools supported legal aid programmes, which were sometimes also funded by municipalities and social agencies. From the 1960s, as part of a broader 'war on poverty', this patchwork of legal aid for individuals had superimposed on it the federally funded legal services programme of the Office of Economic Opportunity. Public funding was now available for community-based legal services programmes, which went beyond legal aid for individuals to embrace lobbying campaigns and public interest litigation before the courts and administrative agencies, designed to change public policy.

The following decades saw a reaction, both at a political level and the level of ideas. It began in California, where the then governor, Ronald Reagan, attempted to veto a grant to the rural legal assistance programme, which had successfully mobilized against some of his policies. The Legal Services Corporation Act, passed in 1974 under President Nixon, was a compromise: community-based legal services programmes continued, with some restrictions on their campaigning and test-case activity and a requirement to explore other models of delivering publicly funded legal services, such as through lawyers in private practice (the judicare model). Federal funding was severely cut under President Reagan, although this was partly offset as local programmes accessed funds from foundations, state and local governments, and other sources. Then in 1996 Congress passed legislation restricting programmes funded by the Legal Services Corporation from involvement in political lobbying and certain types of public interest litigation, for example class actions and challenges to welfare reform measures.[40]

The 1996 legislation reflected in good part the analysis in Charles Rowley's *The Right to Justice*,[41] published in 1992. Writing from the viewpoint of the Virginia school of political economy, Rowley argued that the programmes funded by the Legal Services Corporation were hijacked by special interest groups to promote their own collectivist law reform.[42] In economic terms consumer preferences were playing little role in determining the allocation of public resources to publicly funded legal services. Instead of providing client services on mundane matters such as divorce and credit, Rowley contended that lawyers and social activists were furthering their own goals of social and political change through such devices as public interest litigation. To impose control on these tendencies, Rowley's preferred solution was that favourite recipe of the Virginia school, a voucher system.[43]

In Britain, the dominant idea behind publicly funded legal services is said to be the social administration approach.[44] That approach has been criticized as too

---

[39] (New York, 1919).

[40] J. Kilwein, 'The Decline of the Legal Services Corporation', in F. Regan, A. Paterson, T. Goriely & D. Fleming (eds), *op.cit.*, 61. The latter restriction was challenged successfully in *Legal Services Corporation v Velazquez*, 531 US 533 (2001).   [41] (Aldershot, 1992).

[42] C. Rowley, *The Right to Justice* (Aldershot, 1992), 315.   [43] *ibid.*, 377.

[44] M. Cousins, 'The Politics of Legal Aid—A Solution in Search of a Problem' (1994) 13 *CJQ* 111, 115.

pragmatic in its orientation, ignoring the ideological and other tensions within which policy is developed. In this analysis even policy which explicitly rejects a social administration approach has been tarred with the same brush because of the emphasis on individual citizenship and rights.[45] That is too crude an analysis and glosses over the real divisions about how publicly funded legal services in Britain should operate. Within the social administration approach, if that is how it is characterized, there have been conflicts between on the one hand an anti-lawyer tradition which prefers to rely on agencies oriented to public service to deliver programmes, and on the other a more rights-oriented approach, derived from a distrust of how such agencies operate in practice.[46] In Britain there has also been some tension over legal aid, delivered through the private profession, and salaried lawyers, whether providing publicly funded legal services to criminal defendants (a public defender system) or in more deprived neighbourhoods through law centres. None of this is to deny the role of broad structural factors in shaping publicly funded legal services, whether these be a country's state of economic development or the character of its welfare state. As well there are what are almost accidents of history, such as the elaborate method of obtaining divorce in Britain. Change to that was successfully resisted by the church and the legal profession in the years immediately after World War II, so that the only way to meet the pent-up demand for divorce by ordinary people was through legal aid provided through practitioners who could operate the complex and expensive procedures.[47]

Legal Aid

'The general rule', said Bowen LJ in 1885, 'is that poverty is no bar to a litigant, that, from time immemorial, has been the rule at common law, and also, I believe, in equity'.[48] In practice, poverty effectively barred litigants from enforcing their common law and statutory rights. There were, it is true, limited procedures under which it was theoretically possible for poor people to litigate. Statutes of 1495 (11 Hen.VII, c.12) and 1531 (23 Hen.VIII, c.15) established the *in forma pauperis* procedure, under which the poor did not have to pay for writs and could be assigned a lawyer free of charge in the common law courts.[49] In the eighteenth century the formal requirements for suing *in forma pauperis* in the common law courts became stricter. Only plaintiffs were covered, and poor litigants had to demonstrate the merits of a case beforehand by paying for counsel's opinion.

---

[45] *ibid.*, 116.

[46] T. Goriely, 'Rushcliffe Fifty Years On: The Changing Role of Civil Legal Aid Within the Welfare State' (1994) 21 *JL&Soc* 545. See Chapter 7 below.

[47] T. Goriely, 'Making the Welfare State Work: Changing Conceptions of Legal Remedies Within the British Welfare State', in F. Regan, A. Paterson, T. Goriely & D. Fleming (eds), *op.cit.*

[48] *Cowell v Taylor* (1886) 31 ChD 34, 38.

[49] e.g. J. Maguire, 'Poverty and Civil Litigation' (1923) 36 *Harv.LR* 361.

Modifications were made in England in the late nineteenth century, and then in 1914 the poor persons' procedure was formalized.[50]

Despite the obvious inadequacies of the procedure, there was little pressure to change it—from the bar because it provided training for young barristers, from the Law Society because it did not interfere too greatly with the profession, and from the government because no great demands were made on public moneys. The poor persons' procedure was very limited: it did not apply to the county courts, did not cover out-of-court work, relied on *pro bono* work by lawyers (there were many instances where cases favourably reported on could not be brought because there were no solicitors willing to take them), and worked with a strict means test, and the poor still had to find the necessary out-of-pocket expenses.[51] Although the county courts established in 1846 were portrayed as the 'poor man's courts', in fact they benefited commercial interests, and from the outset the poor appeared in them as defendant debtors. Poor plaintiffs were almost unheard of, partly because the poor persons' procedure was not available, although some country court judges may have permitted it.[52] Despite overwhelming evidence, the profession continued to believe that poor people with meritorious claims could institute county court actions. That belief was perhaps only seriously challenged in 1970, when the Consumer Council study, *Justice Out of Reach*, demonstrated empirically that ordinary people hardly ever did so.

The legal aid scheme, part of the post-World War II Labour Government's welfare state, established a framework for civil legal aid in courts and tribunals, to be available to both the poor and those of moderate means (who were to pay a contribution proportionate to income). For the first time on the civil side, lawyers were to be remunerated for work undertaken. A network of centres for legal advice was also to be established, staffed in part by salaried solicitors for those who appeared unable to afford it in the normal way. From the outset the legal aid scheme was hit by financial stringency.[53] The provision for salaried solicitors was never implemented. Nor was public funding supplemented, for example, through interest on solicitors' client accounts—a method used in north America and Australia to help fund legal aid.[54] Individuals applying for legal aid faced a means test. Generally speaking, below certain levels of income and capital no contribution was required (the free limits); between the free limits and higher levels of income and capital (the eligibility limits), persons qualified but had to make a contribution. Moreover, an applicant had to demonstrate reasonable grounds for taking, defending or being a party to proceedings, or could be refused legal aid if

---

[50] RSC, Ord 16, rr 22–31.

[51] B. Abel-Smith & R. Stevens, *Lawyers and the Courts* (London, 1967), 142–9. The dock brief system in the higher criminal courts allowed a defendant to choose a barrister from those in court, on payment of a small fee. The system was immortalized by John Mortimer in his play *The Dock Brief*, published in his *Three Plays* (London, 1958), later filmed with Peter Sellers, Richard Attenborough, and Beryl Reid (1962).   [52] *Cook v Imperial Tobacco Co.* [1922] 2 KB 158.

[53] e.g. M. Zander, *Legal Services for the Community* (London, 1978).

[54] D. Rhode, *Access to Justice* (New York, 2004), 106, 112–3.

proceedings appeared unreasonable in the particular circumstances of the case.[55] Legal assistance was never fully available in tribunal proceedings although in the British welfare state tribunals have played a more important role than the courts in the lives of tenants, social welfare claimants, and employees. The assumption has been that because of the informality of tribunals, and with the help of tribunal members, people can generally represent themselves.[56]

Change in the administration of the legal aid scheme in the 1980s was driven partly by the then government's policy of using new models for organizing public services such as contract to govern the relationship between government and the providers of services, and 'new public management' techniques involving quality assurance and the auditing of services.[57] The Legal Aid Board assumed the administration of the scheme from the profession partly in an effort to control rapidly increasing costs. Fixed fees were introduced for some work, franchising was adopted in 1994 as a method of quality assurance for legal aid lawyers, and the not-for-profit sector was for the first time allowed access to legal aid moneys if they met the quality standards. From its establishment the Legal Aid Board saw as one of its principal challenges the supplier-led nature of legal aid: this meant good coverage in areas such as family law, personal injuries, and crime, but not of social welfare law (for example, debt, welfare benefits, housing) where solicitors generally lacked the expertise or incentive. Other problems as seen by the Board were a lack of quality control within some firms where high volume work was done by non-lawyers; fraud by some practitioners; and the aggressive marketing by some solicitors of certain services, often by the systematic canvassing of housing estates, with little value to most clients.[58] Concern with the continual increase in legal aid expenditure was widely shared, in particular the growing number of applicants with complex legal problems typically associated with expensive litigation.[59] Tightening the means test, and to an extent attempting to control lawyers' remuneration, were the favoured instruments to control expenditure.

The Access to Justice Act 1999 confirmed existing trends in the administration of legal aid.[60] The Board was replaced by the Legal Services Commission. The Community Legal Service—the term 'legal aid' has been abandoned—works within a controlled budget. Entitlement (if within the statutory criteria) is replaced by a scheme of priority areas for funding. These were identified in 1998 as social welfare cases; other cases of fundamental importance to people's lives

---

[55] e.g. Legal Aid Act 1974, s 7(5).

[56] *Tribunals for Users. One System, One Service. Report of the Review of Tribunals by Sir Andrew Leggatt* (London, 2001), paras 4.21–4.23.

[57] R. Moorhead, 'Third Way Regulation? Community Legal Service Partnerships' (2001) 64 *MLR* 543, 544–50.

[58] See *R v Legal Aid Board and Lord Chancellor, ex p Duncan* [2000] EWHC Admin 294, paras 52–6; [2000] COD 159 CA; Lord Chancellor's Department, *Striking the Balance. The Future of Legal Aid in England and Wales*, Cm 3305 (London, 1996), 8–10.

[59] House of Commons, Public Accounts Committee, *Civil Legal Aid Means Testing*, 25th Report, Session 1995–96, HC 314 (London, 1996), para. 7.

[60] See R. Abel, *English Lawyers Between Market and State* (Oxford, 2003), 293 ff.

(principally, care and adoption of children and cases of domestic violence); and cases involving a wider public interest (principally, those producing substantial benefits for a significant number of people, those raising important and new legal issues, and those challenging the actions of public bodies or alleging abuse of power by public officials).[61] The Funding Code sets out eligibility for cases to be funded: the chances of success must be at least 50 per cent and the potential recovery must generally bear a specified minimum ratio to the anticipated costs of the case. Merits are still vetted. Community legal partnerships (CLPs), comprising suppliers of legal services, funders and community representatives, coordinate the provision of publicly funded legal services at local level.[62]

The system of franchising has been replaced by a system of contracting, which has resulted in a considerable reduction in the number of suppliers. The Legal Services Commission enters contracts with suppliers of civil legal work—which comprises legal representation and legal help—primarily private solicitors, although there is an increasing amount of legal help being given by not-for-profit agencies, primarily Citizens Advice Bureaux, law centres, Shelter (through its housing aid centres) and other advice agencies. The legal help being given by the not-for-profit sector is concentrated in debt, welfare benefits and, to an extent, housing.[63] To bid for a contract, suppliers must meet certain quality standards (recognizable by a Quality Mark) and are audited on a regular basis. They are contracted to undertake a certain number of instances ('matter starts') of legal help in specialist categories, although a supplier has a certain tolerance to assist in other areas.[64] Legal representation is contracted on an individual basis. The demands of meeting quality standards is one factor in the concentration of civil legal aid in a reduced number of larger law firms. Many smaller firms have withdrawn from publicly funded work or merged. That tendency is accentuated as the Commission moves to contracting with 'preferred suppliers', which meet the highest standards of quality. A corollary, however, is that law firms undertaking publicly funded work are less accessible geographically, which has given rise to criticism of 'advice deserts'.[65]

Public interest litigation (sometimes called structural litigation or cause lawyering) in which the courts are used to precipitate social change, has not featured prominently in Britain. That contrasts with the United States, as we have seen, and with other places like India, where there has been notable public interest litigation, especially before the Supreme Court. (Some of this is touched on in the

---

[61] Lord Chancellor's Department, *Modernising Justice*, Cm 4155 (London, 1998), 28.
[62] The experiences of CLPs is patchy: Citizens Advice, *Partnership Potential? Citizens Advice Bureau Views of the Community Legal Service* (London, 2003).
[63] Legal Services Commission, *Annual Report 2003/04* (London, 2004), 21–2.
[64] R. Moorhead & R. Harding, *Quality and Access: Specialist and Tolerance Work under Civil Contracts* (London, 2004).
[65] e.g. J. Sandbach, *Geography of Advice*, Citizens Advice (London, 2004), Appendix; Law Society, *Access Denied* (London, 2002); House of Commons, Constitutional Affairs Committee, *Civil Legal Aid. Adequacy of Provision*, HC 391 (London, 2004) (hereafter *Adequacy of Provision*).

following chapter.[66]) Largely this has been because until relatively recently legal aid was not available to fund cases with a group or community interest, although a case brought by an individual would sometimes have wider implications or be a test case. Multiparty actions have been supported by legal aid, although on the basis that each individual in the group might have a case.[67] The enormous cost to public funds of some failed multiparty actions has not enhanced the reputation of legal aid, whether or not criticism is justified.[68] Since the late 1990s, cases with a significant wider public interest have been for the first time fundable through legal aid, with lower hurdles for the merits and cost-benefit tests. There has been a raft of public law cases involving the Human Rights Act 1998. A public interest advisory panel advises the legal aid authorities whether proposed litigation raises important enough public interest issues to be funded. Outside the legal aid scheme non-governmental organizations (NGOs) such as Justice, Child Poverty Action Group, and Greenpeace, and government equality and human rights bodies, have participated in public interest litigation.[69]

A starting point in assessing legal aid in Britain is to acknowledge that it is funded more generously than other schemes.[70] For example, the Netherlands spends less than half the amount per capita, although in terms of legal aid coverage it is nearly a match for the English scheme. Direct comparisons like this are indicative only because of the different institutional arrangements: thus continental European countries have more judges, adopting a more inquisitorial approach, which may lessen the need for legal aid in litigation. Funding for civil legal aid has increased significantly over the last twenty years. Table 1 shows that from £71 million for non-family civil matters in 1984–5 it grew tenfold to £768 million in 2001–2. Funding then declined to just over £600 million in 2003–4, reflecting the fact that the legal aid budget was by then capped.[71] Despite this significant increase over the twenty years, the amount allocated to legal aid represents a declining proportion of what society has spent on the cost of legal services as a whole.[72]

In terms of overall eligibility, the legal aid scheme in England has also compared favourably with other jurisdictions.[73] Over the last fifteen years the proportion of

---

[66] 91–3 below.

[67] See C. Hodges, *Multi-Party Actions* (Oxford, 2001), 187–8. (Part V of the book has case studies of some of the litigation, e.g. G. Hickinbottom, 'Benzodiazepine Litigation'.)

[68] See e.g. Legal Aid Board, *When the Price is High. Reforming the Legal Aid Board's Handling of Group Actions and Other High Cost Civil Cases* (London, 1997). [69] 120–1 below.

[70] Council of Europe (European Commission for the Efficacy of Justice), *European Judicial Systems* 2002, CEPEJ (2004) 30 (Strasbourg, 2004), Tables 4–5; E. Blankenburg, 'Judicial Systems in Western Europe: Comparative Indicators of Legal Professionals, Courts, Litigation, and Budgets in the 1990s', in E. Jensen & T. Heller (eds), *Beyond Common Knowledge. Empirical Approaches to the Rule of Law* (Stanford, 2003), 83; E. Blankenburg, 'Lawyers' Lobby and the Welfare State: The Political Economy of Legal Aid', in F. Regan, A. Paterson, T. Goriely & D. Fleming (eds.), *op.cit.*

[71] *Hansard*, HC, vol. 428, 20 December 2004, c.1387w.

[72] *Hansard*, HC, vol. 430, 24 January 2005, c.138w.

[73] F. Regan, 'Why Do Legal Aid Services Vary Between Societies', in F. Regan, A. Paterson, T. Goriely & D. Fleming (eds), *op.cit.*

Table 1. Civil (non-family) Legal Aid, 1984–5 to 2003–4

		Representation		Advice and Assistance*	
	Expenditure (£m)	Bill volume†	Average cost (£)	Bill volume†	Average cost (£)
2003–04	609	47,144	7,017	540,175	515
2002–03	674	62,880	6,414	566,321	478
2001–02	768	84,044	5,974	546,684	414
2000–01	669	108,013	4,876	518,910	275
1999–00	671	115,714	4,570	804,101	176
1998–99	703	132,648	4,392	766,091	157
1997–98	692	155,737	3,764	800,591	132
1996–97	663	176,139	3,246	755,596	120
1995–96	596	182,192	2,805	737,782	115
1994–95	514	169,294	2,589	752,130	100
1993–94	455	167,115	2,267	794,602	96
1992–93	369	148,621	2,076	675,507	89
1991–92	276	129,529	1,780	544,964	83
1990–91	196	103,893	1,596	418,086	73
1989–90	163	96,894	1,425	396,068	62
1988–89	133	91,138	1,242	377,868	54
1987–88	110	83,620	1,060	411,242	51
1986–87	92	76,971	970	358,473	48
1985–86	82	73,001	904	341,312	46
1984–85	71	75,718	776	290,378	43

* Advice and assistance includes all other non-family civil legal help outside certificated representation.
† The official information available is for bills paid, not cases.

individuals eligible for civil legal aid has not fallen greatly, declining from about just over 60 per cent of the population in the 1980s to about 50 per cent today.[74] However, these general figures conceal the difficulties of obtaining assistance because they include those having to make a contribution. The trend has been to require all but the poor to pay this. Thus in 1993 the financial eligibility limits were reduced so that only those with incomes at or below the level of income support—the most basic social welfare benefit—were eligible for legal aid without payment of a contribution. For those above that income, legal aid was available with a contribution of one third of the difference between the level of income support and actual income. The effect was that in the case of the latter few contributory legal aid certificates were issued because of the inability of those on such low incomes to pay anything.[75] In 2002 changes were intended to extend financial eligibility to more low-income families although, to achieve this within a fixed budget, caps on gross income and capital were imposed. The upshot was that since the value of the house was included in the calculations of capital, increasing

[74] *Hansard*, HC, vol. 432, 21 March 2005, c.611w.
[75] Legal Aid Board, *Annual Report 1996–97*, HC 52 (London, 1997), 61–3.

numbers of homeowners on low incomes fell outside the scheme.[76] The absence of the middle classes from legal aid threatens long-term support for the scheme.

The general increase in expenditure on civil legal aid over the last twenty years funded an increase in legal aid provision. There are, nonetheless, two caveats to enter. First, as is evident from Table 1, growth in provision was certainly not proportionate to the tenfold increase in expenditure from the first part of the 1980s to the late 1990s and early 2000s. At its peak, there was little more than a doubling of the assistance provided. The reason was simple—average costs went up tenfold as well, the increase being especially acute in the last five years. Secondly, the amount of legal aid for court representation, as opposed to other legal advice and assistance, fell fairly dramatically. Partly this was because of the introduction of conditional fee agreements for personal injury claims, replacing legal aid. Partly it also reflected decisions of the Legal Services Commission to squeeze the civil legal aid budget, made against the background of escalating costs elsewhere, in particular in children cases, asylum claims, and criminal defence.[77]

Various factors may explain the steep rise in average costs of legal assistance. One is that legal matters have become more complex, sometimes the result of new legislation like the Human Rights Act 1998.[78] There seems a good case for stronger regulatory impact assessments, taking legal aid costs into account.[79] Indeed, there is an argument for the proponents of legislation, a particular government department for example, to pick up the tab. Another is the expense of meeting the quality assurance and audit requirements of the legal aid authorities. As lawyers have improved their management systems to meet these standards, they may also have been able to claim more effectively. There is also the possibility of legal aid lawyers 'cherry-picking' the most complex, and thus the most highly remunerated, matters.[80] This is a variation of the economic theory of supplier-induced demand, whereby legal aid lawyers could be seen deliberately to oversupply clients with services because others are paying.[81] Enough has been said to conclude that supplier-induced demand can be only a partial explanation.[82] That

---

[76] J. Sandbach, *op.cit.*

[77] The cost of representation and advice for asylum increased dramatically between 2000–1 and 2002–3; statutory curbs have been introduced to reduce expenditure e.g., Asylum and Immigration (Treatment of Claimants, etc) Act 2004; Constitution Affairs Committee, House of Commons, *Immigration and Asylum: The Government's Proposed Changes to Publicly Funded Immigration and Asylum Work*, HC 1171 (London, 2003); *Government Response to the Fourth Report on Immigration and Asylum*, HC 299 (London, 2004). For human rights reasons criminal legal aid (unlike civil legal aid) is not cost capped.

[78] R. Moorhead, 'Legal Aid and the Decline of Private Practice: Blue Murder or Toxic Job?' (2004) 11 *Int'l J.L. Prof.* 159, 178.   [79] 24 above.

[80] *Protecting Rights*, 18.

[81] G. Bevan, A. Holland & M. Partington, *Organising Cost-effective Access to Justice*, Social Market Foundation (London, 1994).

[82] e.g. D. Wall, 'Legal Aid, Social Policy, and the Architecture of Criminal Justice: The Supplier Induced Inflation Thesis and Legal Aid Policy' (1996) 23 *JLS* 549; A. Gray, 'The Reform of Legal Aid' (1994) 10 *Oxford Rev. of Econ. Policy* 51, 62; G. Bevan, 'Has there been Supplier-induced Demand

is not to overlook a related issue that the legal aid debate has been dominated by the powerful voices of legal aid providers, which have not always echoed the concerns of those needing publicly funded legal services.

As with all public policy the challenge for government with publicly funded legal services is to develop a strategy and to marshall a range of policy instruments to implement it effectively. Traditional legal aid still has an important role to play in that strategy. That means that legal aid lawyers must be properly remunerated. If not, they may fail to undertake work which is socially necessary but financially unattractive. For example, there is a good deal of anecdotal evidence that solicitors often turn away domestic violence cases because they involve a lot of unremunerative work and occupy scarce resources.[83] Inadequate remuneration, along with lack of job security, poor career prospects, and a feeling of being undervalued account for the lack of newly qualified solicitors being attracted to legal aid work and the retention problems with existing legal aid practitioners as they drift off to private work.[84] The Bar Council has removed the ethical obligation on barristers to take certain family work on the cab rank principle, because it does not regard it as being adequately remunerated.

The challenge for the legal profession is to recognize that the case for traditional legal aid will not be accepted automatically in a world where competition for public moneys is intense and models of service delivery are everywhere being challenged. The issue of a greater role for a salaried service in publicly funded legal services must be faced. As the Law Society has said, so long as professional independence is protected there 'can be no automatic assumption that private practice should be the dominant mode of legal aid provision'.[85] The mixed model used by insurers, of in-house staff handling cases initially and then referring some out to private lawyers on their panel, has had considerable success in terms of cost and efficiency. The extensive network of legal aid provision in the Netherlands, at much less cost to the public purse than in Britain, is attributable in part to the use of staff bureaux (*buros voor rechtshulp*), which handle routine cases. Experience in Canada and elsewhere has shown a cost advantage for employed lawyers, partly through economies of scale and partly through use of paralegals.[86] The evidence in Britain is equivocal: thus one comparison of private lawyers and not-for-profit agencies delivering legal aid concluded that the latter were more expensive per

---

for Legal Aid' (1996) 15 *CJQ* 98; T. Goriely & A. Paterson, 'Introduction', in A. Paterson & T. Goriely (eds), *Resourcing Civil Justice* (Oxford, 1996), 18–20.

[83] *Adequacy of Provision*, para. 38. See also Legal Aid Practitioners Group, *Legal Aid. Where Next?* (London, 2003), 32–5.

[84] *Adequacy of Provision*, paras 52–9, 80–86. L. Norman, *Career Choices in Law. A Survey of Law Students*, Law Society Research Study 50 (London, 2004), 41–52; L. Norman, *Career Choices in Law. A Survey of Trainee Solicitors*, Law Society Research Study 51 (London, 2004), 31–43.

[85] *Protecting Rights*, 33.

[86] T. Goriely, *Legal Aid Delivery Systems*, Lord Chancellor's Department Research Paper No. 10/97 (London, 1997); A. Currie, *Legal Aid Delivery Models in Canada*, Department of Justice, Canada (Ottawa, 1999), 24–5; *Adequacy of Provision*, paras 133–136.

case and often took longer, but provided a higher quality service and better outcomes for clients than other suppliers.[87] What is clear is that the future lies both with traditional legal aid and other models of service delivery. There will be a complex mix of approaches and structures, varying with local circumstances and experience, taking into account client need and budgeted resources.

Public Funding: Others Structures

Historically, legal aid has been the main focus of publicly funded legal services in Britain. Despite the cost disadvantage of delivering publicly funded legal services through private lawyers, a major advantage has been the pressure on government from the profession as a whole to maintain and expand the level of spending. Other countries have adopted different models. For example, employed lawyers have featured more in the delivery of publicly funded legal services in Europe and north America.[88] Without widespread professional involvement, the success of these services has sometimes fluctuated with the winds of political fortune. Yet even in Britain public moneys have sometimes been channelled in other ways than legal aid. A notable example has been the law centre movement, which has survived now for over three decades. Another important not-for-profit tool for furnishing legal assistance has been advice centres, the best known of which are Citizens Advice Bureaux. Coupled with law and advice centres is the use of techniques extending the delivery of legal services such as telephone advice lines. Moreover, the not-for-profit sector has also seen paralegals come to the fore, which raises the issue of their further deployment. Not discussed here are other models such as not-for-profit law firms, the location of employed lawyers in private law firms and community interest companies delivering legal services. All will expand in the years to come.

Community law centres

First developed in the United States in the 1960s as part of the 'war on poverty' community-based law centres have spread to other countries.[89] North Kensington law centre in London was opened in 1970 and other law centres followed. Initially, law centres sometimes faced opposition from the legal profession, which claimed that they would create social and professional divisions. For local lawyers

[87] R. Moorhead, A. Sherr & L. Webley, *Quality and Cost: Final Report on the Contracting of Civil Non-Family Advice and Assistance Pilot* (London, 2001). See also T. Goriely, 'Evaluating the Scottish Public Defence Solicitors' Office' (2003) 30 *JLS*. 84. Evaluation of the English public defender schemes is not complete at the time of writing.

[88] See T. Goriely & A. Paterson, *Access to Legal Services. A European Comparison*, Scottish Executive and Law Society (England and Wales), Research Study No. 38 (Edinburgh & London, 2000).

[89] e.g. E. Johnson, 'Justice and Reform a Quarter Century Later', in F. Regan, A. Paterson, T. Goriely & D. Fleming, *op.cit.*; J. Cooper, *Public Legal Services* (London, 1983).

the fear was that they would lose business to law centres, although some also objected to what they thought was the political stance law centres adopted. In some places the profession was able to use the rules of practice to advance these arguments, for law centres had to obtain waivers for breach of certain of the rules such as those against touting and sharing fees with non-lawyers. Political and legal action was also used.[90] The compromise eventually reached with the profession in England was that law centres would usually not engage in conveyancing, commercial matters, divorce and related work, the administration of estates, larger personal injury claims, and criminal matters involving adults—all sources of income for the profession.

Law centres are now an accepted part of the scene, although the numbers have remained fairly stable since the 1980s (about 50 in England) and they account for only a small part of the legal aid budget. Their funding may come from the Legal Services Commission (by contract as with private solicitors), the local authorities where they operate or other sources such as charities. Funding of law centres has never been especially secure or stable, an obvious threat to their survival.[91] A hallmark of law centres is that they are firmly established in local communities. Since these are typically deprived communities, law centres can rightly claim to be helping combat social exclusion.[92] There is participation by the local community through the management committee of a law centre. Community participation is useful in strengthening the commitment of the community to a law centre; it makes a law centre more responsive to local needs; it gives guidance to the staff on a community's problems and priorities; and it leads people to identify the centre as a place to turn to with their problems. Through participating in the management of law centres members of the community acquire organizing skills and a knowledge of law and the legal system.

One of the justifications for law centres has been that they have made legal services available to people who might not otherwise enjoy them through traditional legal aid. Solicitors have generally not been available for social welfare law work: law centres have gone beyond family and children cases—a major component of legal aid spending on the civil side—to the wide range of decisions affecting ordinary people made by employers, businesses, and government in areas such as debt, housing, employment, and public law. Law centres have also tried innovative working practices: they may be open out of hours, operate telephone advice lines or mobile services, or engage in outreach work in the community.[93] Some law centres have specialized in work for particular parts of the community such as young people.

---

[90] E. Johnson, *Justice and Reform: The Formative Years of the OEO Legal Services Program* (New York, 1974), 91–2; D. Rhode, *Access to Justice* (New York, 2004), 66–8.

[91] F. Zemans & A. Thomas, 'Can Community Clinics Survive?', in F. Regan, A. Paterson, T. Goriely & D. Fleming, *op.cit.*, 85.

[92] e.g. Department for Constitutional Affairs and Law Centres Federation, *Legal and Advice Services. A Pathway to Regeneration* (London, 2004).

[93] Law Centres Federation, *Annual Report 2000/1*, 7, 14, 17.

While engaging in individual casework, for which there is an obvious demand, many law centres have also worked with groups in the community (tenants, residents, social welfare claimants, and employees). Casework and such structural work are intertwined, for the former can have implications for structural work by identifying patterns of more general concern.[94] Concentrating on caseload alone runs the risk that underlying symptoms are ignored and that problems about which no one complains are neglected. Moreover, success in casework is sometimes ambiguous in that assisting particular individuals may be at the expense of other individuals, as where one client moves up the waiting list for social housing but in doing so displaces others. Structural work aims to strengthen the capacity of tenants, residents, claimants, and employees to campaign for policy changes. At a basic level this includes advising groups on the juridical form they might take, on their constitution, on how money should be held and meetings conducted, and on possible sources of funds. At another level it includes matters such as assisting in representing groups before courts, tribunals and inquiries and advising them on where and how to exert pressure on those in authority. The parallel here is with lawyers acting for government and commercial interests, who service individual legal problems but also engage in wider legal and lobbying action. As well law centre efforts at community legal education have contributed to making individuals aware of their rights and how to enforce them.

Advice centres

The range of advice centres is considerable—Citizens Advice Bureaux, independent advice centres, and housing aid, money advice, and local authority advice centres are just some. Apart from advice at the centres themselves it is also available through outreach services and telephone helplines.[95] Outreach services are located in doctors' surgeries, community centres, leisure facilities, and elsewhere.[96] A national telephone helpline, National Debtline, is for people with debt problems. The service is free and independent, albeit funded by government and financial institutions. In more rudimentary form the service has existed since 1987. The service provides self-help advice to callers, with written information to back this up. It is not primarily concerned with debt management plans, although these can follow, increasing through telephone gateways to other, more specialized debt services. A generally positive evaluation of National Debtline identifies one drawback: although the less well-off socio-economic groups are more likely to be

---

[94] Law Centres Federation, *Tackling Social Exclusion Together* (London, 2002), 1–2. See also H. Sommerlad, ' "I've Lost the Plot": An Everyday Story of Legal Aid Lawyers' (2001) 28 *JLS* 335.

[95] J. Sergeant & J. Steele, *Access to Legal Services. The Contribution of Alternative Approaches*, Policy Studies Institute (London, 1999).

[96] e.g. L. Sherr, R. Harding, S. Singh, A. Sherr & R. Moorhead, *A Stitch in Time—Accessing and Funding Welfare Rights Through Health Service Primary Care* (London, 2002); S. Abbott & L. Hobby, 'Welfare Benefits Advice in Primary Care' (2000) 114 *Public Health* 324.

in need of its money advice given their borrowing and income patterns, they are disproportionately less likely to use it.[97] The evaluation says that there is therefore a continued need for face-to-face interviews, although the pressure on existing services is enormous.[98]

Advice centres provide a range of other services in addition to proffering advice such as representation, referral, training, and the preparation of materials. With extra funding there is obvious scope for an extension of their existing services, geographically and otherwise, in furtherance of access to justice. As well as expanding existing services they might, to give just one example, adopt a greater role in education. Training sessions for litigants in person before tribunals and courts could be one aspect. We should not be surprised that the activity of advice centres can have a positive impact on dispute resolution. Clarifying the arguments with professional help means the other side can appreciate their force and also be made to realize that the matter cannot be 'brushed under the carpet'. There is thus the pressure on the other party which involvement of an adviser can bring.

Research generally suggests a correlation between advice and success. For example, in the Genns' study of tribunals this was brought out in various ways. Thus, with social security appeals tribunals, in cases where appellants had not obtained advice before their hearing, appeals were allowed in just over a quarter of cases. When appellants had obtained advice, appeals were allowed in about 46 per cent of cases.[99] Moreover, appellants who received advice were significantly more likely to attend their hearings than those who did not—and we know that attendance at a hearing generally boosts the chances of success. Clearly, as the Genns pointed out, there are two factors operating here: the one is that pre-hearing advice sifts out the hopeless case. The other is that the advice which appellants obtain in preparing their cases improves the chance of success. Importantly, the relationship between advice and success did not operate in relation to employment tribunals except that advice led to representation which in turn led to a better result. If applicants were unrepresented at the hearing, pre-hearing advice conferred no advantage.[100] Pre-hearing advice did mean, however, that an applicant was more likely to settle, and less likely to abandon, his or her case. The adversarial nature of employment tribunals—driven in that direction by the presence of lawyers—no doubt has something to do with the result, however much tribunal chairs bend over backwards to assist the unrepresented. These findings are supported elsewhere. Thus Professor Hazel Genn's national survey, *Paths to Justice*, found that cases in which no advice at all was obtained were 45 per cent

[97] HM Treasury, *Promoting Financial Inclusion* (London, 2004), 44.

[98] cf. J. Hobson & P. Jones, 'Telephone Advice Pilot' in Legal Services Commission, *Improving Access to Advice in the Community Legal Service*, (London, 2004). See also Department of Trade and Industry and Department for Work and Pensions, *Tackling Over-Indebtedness Action Plan* (London, 2004); S. Edwards, *In Too Deep. CAB Clients' Experience of Debt*, Citizens Advice (London, 2003).

[99] H. Genn & Y. Genn, *The Effectiveness of Representation at Tribunals*, Lord Chancellor's Department (London, 1989). See also 39 above.   [100] *ibid.*, 95.

less likely to be resolved than those where advice was obtained from a solicitor or law centre. Where advice was obtained from other advice sources (including from Citizens Advice Bureaux) there was a 30 per cent less chance of it being resolved than where advice had been obtained from a solicitor or law centre. However, when advice from an advice agency was coupled with active assistance, the results were not significantly different from those when advice was obtained from a solicitor or law centre.[101]

Non-lawyers in advice agencies can and do provide assistance of a legal character, especially in matters such as debt, welfare benefits, and consumer protection. And there is no reason why they cannot provide it as effectively as lawyers. Quite apart from anything else, however, only lawyers can do certain types of work. No doubt as well matters handled by advice agencies may have a legal component, which could pass unrecognized in the absence of lawyers. Despite this and the other advantages lawyers can bring, few advice agencies employ lawyers full-time.[102] However, they often enable people to obtain access to solicitors who are acting part-time on a *pro bono* basis.[103] It is fair to say that these rota schemes differ in their operation, reflecting in part the skills of those participating. Increasingly advice centres undertake work funded by the Legal Services Commission. In March 2004 some 414 not-for-profit agencies held general civil contracts with the Commission: those were mainly in the areas of welfare benefits, debt, housing, immigration, and employment. By contrast with solicitors, not-for-profit agencies did virtually nothing in areas such as family, personal injury, clinical negligence, and mental health.[104]

Referral between advice agencies and lawyers in private practice should be a two-way process. After examining the caseload of 36 Citizens Advice Bureaux, one study concluded that this did not occur wholesale. Only about one client in seven contacted a solicitor as a result of advice received from a bureau, and it seemed only about one in fifteen clients were referred direct to a solicitor. A further 2 per cent saw a solicitor through a CAB rota scheme.[105] In a detailed study of solicitors' social welfare work carried out in Cornwall, Newham (London) and Oldham, Elaine Kempson found a greater amount of referral out to law centres and advice agencies.[106] In the recent national study of justiciable problems already referred to, people seemed to have a reasonably clear idea of where to go to obtain

---

[101] H. Genn, *Paths to Justice* (London, 1999), 172. See also 96–8, 252. See also P. Pleasence *et al.*, *Causes of Action: Civil Law and Social Justice* (London, 2004) 97–8; Consumers Association, *The Community Legal Service: Access for All?* (London, 2000), 49.

[102] National Citizens Advice Bureaux, *Employment of Solicitors in Bureau* (London, 1993), 3–4.

[103] e.g. Citizens Advice, *Justice Matters* (London, 2004), 3 (200 bureaux provide access to over 1,000 specialist solicitors). 'Law Works' (www.probonogroup.org.uk/) is a partnership of the Solicitors Pro Bono Group and the Law Centres Federation matching lawyers willing to help with the need in law and advice centres.

[104] Legal Services Commission, *Annual Report 2003/04* (London, 2004), 21.

[105] J. Baldwin, 'The Role of Citizens Advice Bureaux and Law Centres in the Provision of Legal Advice and Assistance' (1989) 8 *CJQ* 24, 26.

[106] E. Kempson, *Legal Advice and Assistance*, Policy Studies Institute (London, 1989), 23.

particular types of advice and assistance—different services have different images.[107] Where those in the study successfully obtained advice, 23 per cent of advisers were in Citizens Advice Bureaux or other advice agencies (including, for example, consumer advice services and law centres). Twenty-six per cent of advisers were solicitors. Other types of organization or person accounted for more than 8 per cent of advisers.[108] While just over one half of respondents obtained advice from only one adviser, almost one third went to two advisers and 11 per cent to three advisers. The typical pattern when there was more than one adviser was passage from a generalist adviser (such as a Citizens Advice Bureau) to specialist adviser (such as a solicitor).[109] People clearly got lost in the process of referral, although persons referred from places like Citizens Advice Bureaux had a better record of getting further advice than those referred by solicitors.[110] Referral fatigue may be inevitable as some choose to 'lump' a problem. Better signposting and other relatively simple devices would ensure more people reach those to whom they are referred.[111] The general point which emerges is that it is wrong to think of solicitors as at the heart of the advice network when they are not the only or main port of call for non-family problems.[112]

Over the last decade or so a number of duty advice schemes have been established in the county courts.[113] They are court-based advice and representation schemes and mainly an offshoot of advice agencies and law centres. (By contrast duty solicitor schemes in the criminal courts are mainly staffed by private practitioners.) Reporting in 1992 the National Consumer Council found just over 30 such schemes, mainly in urban areas.[114] By 2004 Citizens Advice Bureaux helped run advice desks in 129 county courts providing advice and representation for those attending court.[115] So geographically the coverage of duty advice schemes is growing, but it is still variable. So, too, is their mode of operation: some proffer only advice; others provide representation (often to negotiate with the other side but sometimes to represent a client in court). Some schemes operate on housing possession days, others extend beyond this to debt and other matters. And some focus on the day itself, while others encourage a continuing contact and casework with the client. *Possession Action* is a report from Citizens Advice about beneficial advice at court where tenants were threatened with possession or eviction. In 41 per cent of cases the possession action or warrant was suspended; in 21 per cent

---

[107] P. Pleasence *et al.*, *op.cit.*, 62, 69–70.   [108] *ibid.*, 67.   [109] *ibid.*, 67–72, 75.
[110] *ibid.*, 77.

[111] R. Moorhead & A. Sherr, *An Anatomy of Access: Evaluating Entry, Initial Advice and Signposting Using Model Clients*, Legal Services Research Centre (London, 2003).

[112] R. Moorhead, M. Sefton & G. Douglas, *The Advice Needs of Lone Parents*, One Parent Families (Cardiff, 2004), 73.4.

[113] In the Royal Courts of Justice in London there is a permanent Citizens Advice Bureau. Freephone legal advice is available at some courts.

[114] National Consumer Council, *Court Without Advice* (London, 1992), 1. See also L. Bridges, *The Provision of Duty Advice Schemes in County Courts* (Legal Aid Board, London, 1991).

[115] Citizens Advice, *Home Remedies* (London, 2004), 4.

of cases there was an adjournment on terms; and in 21 per cent of cases more realistic repayment arrangement were made.[116]

The success of duty advice schemes depends partly on court support. Generally there is strong support from judges and court staff for duty advice schemes: they promote efficiency by helping litigants to make reasonable offers; make people less anxious and aware of the implications of the hearing; and if litigants are not receiving all the welfare benefits to which they are entitled, are generally in a position to help remedy this. Courts now provide accommodation for duty advice services, either allocating an interview room for the day or, more satisfactorily from the point of view of the schemes, a permanent place. Common sense identifies the key role of ushers, bailiffs, and other court staff in channelling people to duty advice schemes. Perhaps more importantly, with respect to court support, effective duty advice schemes turn on a court's listing practices for cases and on liaison between a court and the scheme's representatives about listing on a particular day. Especially in the less busy courts, listing to concentrate particular types of cases where advice is likely to be sought means that funders can justify an adviser being present.[117]

Paralegals

Legal assistance for individuals does not necessarily mean the provision of a lawyer. There is a long tradition of paralegals in Britain. Traditionally the law clerk—now the legal executive—was the backbone of the solicitor's office. Claims assessors have long negotiated with insurance companies on behalf of those with personal injury claims, typically charging a percentage of the recovery.[118] In Citizens Advice Bureaux, and larger law centres, non-lawyers have provided legal advice, assistance, and representation (mainly before tribunals). Now to assist those with complaints against the National Health Service there is a free independent complaints advocacy service, delivered in some regions of England by Citizens Advice.[119] While patchy, there are also independent advocacy services for those with learning and other disabilities or impairments, and for elderly and mental health groups. Increasingly there are citizen advocacy groups which involve volunteers committing themselves over a period to speaking up for and representing the interests of those with learning difficulties.[120]

---

[116] Citizens Advice, *Possession Action—A Last Resort* (London, 2003), 25. (In 51 per cent of cases the client was able to obtain continuing advice. 13 per cent found that they were entitled to more welfare benefits than they were aware.)

[117] C. Wilson, 'Housing Possession Court Duty Scheme Pilot', in Legal Services Commission, *Improving Access to Advice in the Community Legal Service* (London, 2004), 53.

[118] Department for Constitutional Affairs, *The Report of the Lord Chancellor's Committee to Investigate the Activities of Non-legally Qualified Claims Assessors and Employment Advisers* (London, 2000), paras 71–80.

[119] Health and Social Care Act 2001, s 12; National Health Service Reform and Health Care Professions Act 2002, s 16.

[120] W. Lewington & C. Clipson, *Advocating for Equality*, Independent Advocacy Campaign (London, 2003).

There is a strand of thought which values paralegals over lawyers:

> . . . they tend to be more accessible than lawyers, more capable of understanding and working with ordinary people . . . less likely to distort the informal procedures of tribunals and more capable of providing a broad and flexible range of assistance, going beyond the immediate (and possibly superficial) 'legal' problems.[121]

In some contexts skilled non-lawyers can be just as effective—indeed possibly more so—than lawyers.[122] In one British study, already mentioned, the researchers compared the way lawyers and paralegals funded by legal aid handled cases of debt, housing, welfare benefits, and employment. Overall it found that the paralegals provided the higher quality service in terms of outcomes. Although paralegals took longer, clients seemed to give them higher satisfaction scores because they listened, explained, stood up for them and treated them as if they mattered. Moreover, peer review of their case files found that not only were paralegals as equally capable as lawyers of giving substantial advice, but their files were more likely to be rated as excellent than those of lawyers (13 per cent as opposed to 3 per cent). The authors of the study identified specialization as the key: the work of the paralegals in the not-for-profit sector examined were trained in social welfare law when many law students receive no such training at law school or beyond.[123]

There are no restrictions in England, as there are in some jurisdictions, on paralegals providing legal advice and representation before tribunals. The courts are a different matter. Lay persons could always represent themselves in court, but historically lawyers have had a monopoly of representing others. There are now some exceptions. The *Civil Justice Review* saw an enhanced role for lay representatives to further access to justice.[124] Following their recommendation, s 11 of the Courts and Legal Services Act 1990 empowered the Lord Chancellor to remove the restrictions on rights of audience and rights to conduct litigation in specified proceedings in the county court. A limited order has been introduced which permits lay representatives in the small claims jurisdiction, although for some odd reason only if the client is present.[125] A second approach in the Courts and Legal Services Act 1990 is that a body whose regulations and rules on matters such as ethics, discipline, and complaints have been approved can grant rights of audience to its members. Few professional or trade bodies are in a position to surmount this

[121] Legal Action Group, *Life Without Lawyers* (London, 1978), 3–4.

[122] e.g. H. Genn & Y. Genn, *op.cit.* But context is everything: R. Abel & P. Lewis, 'Putting Law Back into the Sociology of Lawyers', in R. Abel & P. Lewis (eds), *Lawyers in Society. An Overview* (Berkeley, 1995), 200.

[123] R. Moorhead, A. Sherr, A. Patterson, 'Contesting Professionalism: Legal Aid and Nonlawyers in England and Wales' (2003) 37 *L&Soc.R.* 765, 785, 787–8, 795–7. See also R. Moorhead, A. Sherr & L. Webley, *Quality and Cost: Final Report on the Contracting of Civil Non-Family Advice and Assistance Pilot* (London, 2000).   [124] Cm 394 (London, 1988), 63–4.

[125] Lay Representatives (Rights of Audience) Order 1999, SI 1999/1225; CPR, PD 27, para. 3.2(2).

hurdle, even if they wished to do so.[126] As well, under s 27(2)(c) of the 1990 Act, a court has discretion to allow lay representation in any case. The Court of Appeal has said that the discretion to grant rights of audience and rights to conduct litigation should only exceptionally be exercised in favour of those who make a practice of seeking to represent unrepresented litigants.[127] Finally, in some cases a person may have an appropriate and reputable 'McKenzie friend'.[128] Under the ruling in that case, as subsequently explained, the friend can take notes, quietly prompt the litigant, and offer advice and assistance. In addition, as Neuberger J put it in *Izzo v Philip Ross & Co. (a firm)*,[129] a case might take three times longer if a relatively inarticulate and unknowledgeable litigant has at every turn to have matters explained by the McKenzie friend rather than the latter putting the case directly. Neuberger J said: 'Further, in these days of human rights consciousness, the court would want a good reason before it required a person to present his own case inarticulately when there was someone with relevant abilities who was ready to speak for the litigant.'[130]

Should the restrictions on paralegals assisting litigation be liberalized? There is a strong public interest in persons working in the justice system being assisted or represented by the properly trained and accredited, who are subject to ethical duties. Thus a public scandal over unscrupulous immigration advisers led to the establishment of an immigration services commissioner, who regulates non-lawyer immigration advisers in accordance with a code and rules about competence and behaviour, maintains a register of advisers, protects good practice, and handles complaints about, and prosecutes, errant advisers.[131] There are also dangers of 'professional' lay representatives exploiting litigants for financial or ideological gain and causing disruption to the court. This seems to be behind the ban on regulated immigration advisers appearing as a McKenzie friend.[132] But there is a strong argument for a presumption in favour of permitting a litigant in person to have a McKenzie friend who, in the circumstances described by Neuberger J, might also address the court. Not only is there something invidious in a court deciding that a lay litigant does not need the assistance that they themselves think they need. The empirical evidence also clearly demonstrates that it is critically important for people's satisfaction with the civil justice system, and hence their acceptance of the rule of law, that if caught up in litigation they feel treated fairly and are able to articulate their case.[133] Lay assistance may be one aspect of this.[134]

---

[126] Courts and Legal Services Act 1990, s 27(2); Institute of Legal Executives Order 1998, SI 1998/1077.

[127] *Paragon Finance plc v Noueiri* [2001] EWCA Civ 1402; [2001] 1 WLR 2357. See also *R v Bow County Court, ex p Pelling* [1997] 1 WLR 1807; [1999] 4 All ER 751.

[128] *McKenzie v McKenzie* [1971] P 33; *Re O (Children)* [2005] EWCA Civ 759; [2005] 2 FCR 563.

[129] [2001] TLR 506.   [130] *ibid.*, 507.

[131] Immigration and Asylum Act 1999, Part V.

[132] *OISC News* [Office of the Immigration Services Commissioner], Issue 12, Spring 2004, 2.

[133] R. Moorhead, 'Access or Aggravation? Litigants in Person, McKenzie Friends and Lay Representation' (2003) 22 *CJQ* 133, 153.

[134] H. Kritzer, 'Rethinking Barriers to Legal Practice' *Judicature*, vol. 81, Nov–Dec 1997, 100.

Facilitating Private Legal Provision

The halcyon days of demand-led expenditure on civil legal aid, and its generous coverage of a substantial section of the population, are well and truly behind us. In a world of competing demands on public expenditure there is no realistic prospect of recapturing that past. It is the situation facing all developed countries. What is needed are new ways of achieving the levels of access to justice associated with legal aid at its zenith. This part of the chapter begins with procedural mechanisms whereby access to the courts can be more readily financed on a private basis—contingency and conditional fees are the examples. It then turns to legal expenses insurance, which has long operated in Germany and has been actively encouraged in countries such as Sweden where, as in Britain, the welfare state is firmly entrenched but legal aid at existing levels has been sustainable no longer.[135] Finally, the possibilities of 'unbundling' legal services and 'do-it-yourself lawyering' are briefly discussed.

Introducing such measures in any particular jurisdiction may require legislative change. They certainly demand a close monitoring to ensure that access to justice and social welfare are being achieved.[136] We still await a detailed assessment of the impact of conditional fees in England. Such measures may also raise ethical issues, for example creating new conflicts of interest for lawyers. Each of them does not have an unlimited scope nor do they remove the need for publicly funded legal services. For example, while legal expenses insurance has great potential, it is only open to those who can afford the premium. Moreover, the success of these measures turns, as well, on other changes, in particular procedural reform. One example is the need for a more interventionist judiciary, as occurs at present in the small claims jurisdiction, for those representing themselves in court.

Contingency fees

For almost a century contingency fees have been widely used in the United States to fund litigation. Proponents not infrequently describe contingency fees as the 'key to the courthouse door'. While this is too glib, contingency fees provide access to justice to those otherwise unable to afford the cost of litigation and unable to access publicly funded legal services. The idea is simple: the fee a client pays is ordinarily a percentage of the amount of any recovery on the claim, whether by way of settlement, trial or alternative dispute resolution. Payment of any fee is contingent, however, on recovery: a losing claimant pays nothing. Expenses, notably for expert witnesses, are treated separately, and ordinarily

---

[135] F. Regan, 'The Swedish Legal Services Policy Remix: The Shift from Public Legal Aid to Private Legal Expense Insurance' (2003) 30 *JLS* 49.

[136] e.g. B. van Velthoven & P. van Wijck, 'Legal Cost Insurance and Social Welfare' (2001) 72 *Economic Letters* 387.

remain the obligation of the client, although the lawyer may pay them during the course of the case and then deduct them from any recovery.

The economic ramifications of contingency fees have been extensively analysed.[137] From the point of view of the client the risk of losing shifts to the lawyer, especially attractive to the risk-averse client. In tort cases, the risk aversity of the lawyer with a portfolio of cases approximates that of the insurance company, normally standing behind defendants and with its own inventory of cases.[138] In the event of a successful outcome, a client faces the risk that the deduction from the recovery may be a higher amount, indeed a much higher amount than is justified by the work the lawyer has put into the case. By defini-tion, however, the percentage fee can never exceed the recovery. The fact that the lawyer's fee turns on the outcome should provide the client with a degree of comfort, that there is a reasonable chance of success, for otherwise the lawyer would not be undertaking the risk. It should also act as an incentive to the lawyer to maximize the recovery, since the fee is generally geared to how much is obtained. By definition a contingency fee as a percentage of damages means the fee is proportionate, though whether the proportion is reasonable will obviously depend on its level. Sometimes, no doubt, contingency fees can produce a disproportionate reward for the lawyers but it seems this is not as common as is sometimes suggested. America's leading scholar on the subject, Professor Herbert Kritzer says that analyses of the returns from contingency fee practice show that in a large proportion of cases lawyers actually make substantially less, on a per hour basis, than they would from work for which they could charge prevailing hourly rates. The real profits from handling contingency fee work come from a very small segment of cases, which few lawyers can 'cherry-pick'.[139] Moreover conditional fees, to which we turn shortly, can also produce returns for the lawyer that are disproportionate to the work done and the risks run.

It is said that there are other disadvantages to contingency fees. First, they cannot easily be used in certain litigation—criminal cases, disputes over children, public law cases—where there is no monetary recovery. Perhaps more import-antly, they are not especially helpful in complex litigation against determined opponents, since the law firm will be carrying the cost of the case from its own resources—a considerable burden in this type of litigation.[140] Secondly, there may be incentives for lawyers to act contrary to the interests of their clients and the

---

[137] e.g. H. Gravelle & M. Waterson, 'No Win, No Fee: Some Economics of Contingent Legal Fees' (1993) 103 *Econ.J.* 1205; W. Emons, 'Expertise, Contingent Fees and Insufficient Attorney Effort' (2000) *20 Int'l Rev. Law & Econ.* 21.

[138] E. Inselbuch, 'Contingent Fees and Tort Reform' (2001) 64 *Law & Contemp. Problems* 175, 178.

[139] H. Kritzer, *The Justice Broker* (New York, 1990), 118–20. See also H. Kritzer, 'Seven Dogged Myths Concerning Contingency Fees' (2002) 80 *Wash. ULQ* 739; G. Marshall, 'The Economics of Speculative Fee Arrangements' (2002) 21 *CJQ* 326.

[140] M. Galanter, 'Anyone Can Fall Down a Manhole: The Contingency Fee and its Discontents' (1998) 47 *De Paul LR* 457, 475. See also J. Shapland *et al.*, *Affording Civil Justice*, Law Society RPPU Research Study No. 29 (London, 1998).

public interest, both in their pursuit of a claim and the size of the fee taken from any recovery.[141] Thus it is said that the lawyer on a contingency fee will seek a quick settlement, having put little into a case, rather than doggedly pursuing it to maximize the client's recovery. But this assertion rests partly on assumptions about the behaviour of the other parties to a case, notably a defendant's insurer. In any event, it seems no more likely to occur in the case of the lawyer retained on a contingency fee basis than, say, on an hourly rate. Here again the ethical restrains discussed in Chapter 6 come into their own in demanding that the lawyer subordinates economic self-interest to the client's interest.

It is the excesses associated with contingency fees which have attracted the most criticism. An aspect is said to be that unnecessary litigation is generated and the North American experience is invariably cited. The argument must be treated with some reserve, since lawyers working on contingency fees bear the risk. One empirical study in the United States suggested that lawyers on contingency fees actually screened out potential litigants who had no case.[142] Another aspect is the windfall fees which lawyers sometimes gain, quite disproportionate to the effort expended on a case. As already indicated, this argument must be put in context: a contingency fee is set *ex ante*, before the outcome is known, although it is fair to say that a lawyer with expertise in a particular field, for example personal injury law, will have a reasonably good chance of estimating its chances of success and perhaps, too, the range of damages. With more complex cases, however, risks increase. The percentage a lawyer takes in clinical negligence and product liability cases is generally higher than in running down cases to reflect that risk. Concern about excessive fees as a percentage of damages explains why contingency fees are still resisted in England. In the United States ethical and legislative rules purport to curb the excesses. The Model Code of Professional Responsibility of the American Bar Association prohibits contingency fees in divorce cases, for example, on the ground that they would drive lawyers to litigate whatever the chance of reconciliation.[143] Although lawyer and client are free to set the percentage fee in many cases, ever since the first ABA Code of Ethics in 1908 courts have been alert to protect clients against unjust charges by lawyers. In some states statute specifies an outer limit on the percentage of any recovery the lawyer may obtain.[144]

Contingency fees have not generally been available to fund litigation before the English courts, although they have been acceptable for tribunal claims and for pre-litigation work. As a matter of law a contingency fee agreement is potentially unenforceable because it breaches the public policy against maintenance and

[141] e.g. L. Brickman, 'ABA Regulation of Contingency Fees: Money Talks, Ethics Walk' (1996) 65 *Fordham LR* 247; *Royal Commission on Legal Services*, Cmnd 7648 (London, 1979), vol. 1, 177.

[142] H. Kritzer, 'Contingency Fee Lawyers as Gatekeepers in the Civil Justice System', *Judicature*, vol. 81, July–Aug, 1997, 22.   [143] C. Wolfram, *Modern Legal Ethics* (West, 1986), 535–41.

[144] e.g., *Gisbrecht v Barnhart*, 535 US 789 (2002). Regulation, if any, varies from state to state. In Canada, contingency fees based on a percentage of the damages are permitted in all the provinces except Ontario.

champerty. Maintenance is supporting litigation in which a person has no legitimate interest, and champerty occurs when a person maintaining another stipulates for a share of the proceeds of the litigation. Since the crimes and tort of maintenance and champerty were abolished,[145] much now turns on the court's assessment of whether in the particular case the contingency fee agreement 'might tempt the allegedly champertous maintainer, for his person gain, to inflame the damages, suppress evidence, suborn witnesses, or otherwise undermine the ends of justice'.[146] The decision in which these words appear may foreshadow a more conducive environment for contingency fee agreements, not least because of the change in public policy permitting conditional fee agreements. There is now a considerable head of steam favouring the adoption of contingency fees in England to further access to justice.[147]

Conditional fees

Conditional fees are, like contingency fees, dependent on success. It is not surprising that conditional fee agreements are known popularly as 'no win, no fee' agreements. However, conditional fees differ from contingency fees in that lawyers cannot take any part of the client's recovery as the fee. Rather conditional fees build on the English rule as to costs: whereas in the United States parties bear their own costs whatever the result, the English rule of costs is that successful parties can generally recover their costs from the other side (the 'loser pays' principle). Yet conditional fees in England go one step further than speculative fees in that the legislation enables lawyers to recover a success fee, in addition to their ordinary fee, from the losing party. The success fee is a percentage uplift on the lawyer's ordinary fee, and is supposed to compensate them for the cases they lose.

In many ways the legislative adoption of conditional fees has legitimized the practice over many years whereby some solicitors, in particular those associated with trade unions, have 'specced' personal injury cases. These solicitors would not charge a client if unsuccessful, but if successful would claim such costs as were recoverable from the other side. Such speculative fees were lawful in Scotland, although resisted by the English profession on ethical grounds. Conditional fees were permissible from 1995, once secondary legislation was put in place under s 58 of the Courts and Legal Services Act 1990. However it was the Access to Justice Act 1999, coupled with the removal of legal aid for most damages and money claims, which established conditional fees as such an

---

[145] Criminal Law Act 1967, s 124. See A. Walters & J. Peysner, 'Event-Triggered Financing of Civil Claims' (1999) 8 *Nottingham LJ* 1, 11 ff.

[146] *R (Factortame Ltd) v Secretary of State for Transport (No. 8)* [2002] EWCA Civ 932, para. 36; [2003] QB 381, 400C, CA, cf. *Awwad v Geraghty & Co.* [2001] QB 570, CA.

[147] Better Regulation Taskforce, *Better Routes to Justice* (London, 2004), 29–30. See M. Zander, 'Will the Revolution in the Funding of Civil Litigation in England Lead to Contingency Fees?' (2002) 52 *De Paul LR* 259; J. Peysner, 'What's Wrong with Contingency Fees?' (2001) 10 *Nottingham LJ* 22.

important avenue in England for access to justice. An issue is the scope for further extension of the concept.[148] The adoption of conditional fees effectively puts paid to the idea of a contingency legal aid fund whereby a successful applicant, supported by the fund, then pays part of the recovery to the benefit of the fund.[149] Under the 1999 Act conditional fees are permissible in all civil cases, including arbitrations, although not in family work if no finance or property claim is involved.[150] Collective conditional fee agreements are designed for trade unions, commercial organizations and others providing or purchasing legal services for groups.[151]

Under the legislative arrangements, an uplift of up to 100 per cent of the fee is recoverable by the successful claimant. There is no express legal obligation on lawyers to fix the uplift by reference to risk although the reasons for any particular uplift must be set out briefly in the agreement.[152] Since the uplift is recoverable from the losing side, a client has no incentive to act as a brake on its amount. The professional rules for solicitors require risk to be taken into account in setting the uplift, but other factors can also be considered.[153] Yet again the importance of ethical rules is underlined.[154] The courts eventually intervened to curb excessive success fees. The Court of Appeal held that simple cases which settle without the need to issue court proceedings and where the prospects of success are virtually 100 per cent should ordinarily attract only a 5 per cent uplift.[155] With modest and straightforward road traffic accident cases a reasonable success fee is 20 per cent, on the assumption that there are no special features threatening success.[156] Subsequently, rules of court have fixed the success fee for cases after October 2003: for motor vehicle personal injury cases settled out of court it is no more than 12.5 per cent for solicitors, rising to 100 per cent for riskier cases which conclude at trial.[157] The rules of court represent an agreement between lawyers and the insurance industry, brokered by the Civil Justice Council, and follow the introduction of fixed recoverable costs for road traffic accident claims settled

---

[148] Legal Services Commission, *A New Focus for Civil Legal Aid* (London, 2004), 36–8.

[149] D. Capper, 'The Contingency Legal Aid Fund' (2003) 30 *JLS* 66; Bar Council, *Contingency Legal Aid Fund* (London, 1989).

[150] Access to Justice Act 1999, s 27, substituting new ss. 58, 58A in the 1990 Act.

[151] Collective Conditional Fee Agreements Regulations 2000, SI 2000/2988.

[152] Conditional Fee Agreements Regulations 2000, SI 2000/692, reg 3(1)(a).

[153] Law Society, *Guide to Professional Conduct of Solicitors*, 8th edn (1999), Annex 14F, para. 17. See also Bar Council, *Guidance on Conditional Fee Agreements* (London, 2002).

[154] e.g. Society of Advanced Legal Studies, *The Ethics of Conditional Fee Arrangements* (London, 2001), esp. ch. 6; S. Yarrow & P. Abrams, 'Conditional Fees: The Challenge to Ethics' (1999) 2 *Leg.Ethics* 192.

[155] *Halloran v Delaney* [2002] EWCA Civ 1258; [2003] 1 WLR 28, CA; *Re Claims Direct Test Cases* [2003] EWCA Civ 136, para. 101; [2003] 4 All ER 508, 530; *Atack v Lee* [2004] EWCA Civ 1712; [2005] 1 WLR 2643.

[156] *Callery v Gray (Nos 1 and 2)* [2002] UKHL 28; [2002] 1 WLR 2000, HL. See M. Zander, 'Where Are we Heading with the Funding of Civil Litigation' (2003) 22 *CJQ* 23, 28–30.

[157] CPR r 45.16. See CPR rr 45.17 (counsel's fees), 45.18 (increase over 12.5 per cent); 45.20–22 (employer's liability cases).

before court proceedings are instituted.[158] They are based on a revenue neutral model which assumes that the income for lawyers obtained from a portfolio of cases funded by conditional fee agreements should be no more than that from a portfolio of cases funded without such agreements.[159]

Because of the 'loser pays' principle, an unsuccessful party will generally be saddled with the other party's costs. To obviate this as a barrier to legal action, clients can take out an 'after the event' insurance policy, providing cover against the risk as to costs. Typically these policies also include as an insurance risk both sides' disbursements. To prevent the high cost of such insurance policies threatening the adoption of conditional fee agreements, statute provides that the premium for after the event insurance cover is recoverable from the losing party.[160] As with all costs awarded under the 'loser pays' principle, the court must not allow the cost of a premium unless it has been proportionately and reasonably incurred. If there is any doubt about this, the court will resolve the issue in favour of the paying (losing) party.[161] The availability of any pre-existing—before the event— insurance cover is one of the factors specifically identified in the relevant practice direction to be taken into account in whether an after the event premium is reasonable.[162] The Court of Appeal has held that in relatively small, straightforward personal injuries claims arising from motor vehicle accidents, it is reasonable for claimants to rely on that before the event cover.[163] In that event no conditional fee agreement is necessary, and therefore no success fee or after the event premium is recoverable. The legal costs associated with the case are thus more likely to be reasonable and proportionate to the value of the claim—an overriding aim of the rules of civil procedure, as we see in Chapter 5.

As a general rule, any type of privatization must be accompanied by steps to control potential abuses in what will effectively be a less-regulated market. The story of claims management companies and no win, no fee arrangements from the late 1990s underlines the point. These companies came into their own with the introduction of conditional fees. Their modus operandi has been the recruitment of claimants by advertising and marketing. There is nothing wrong with this in principle, but in its worst manifestation it has involved targeting vulnerable people by cold-calling and encouraging fraudulent claims. (Cold-calling by those introducing business to solicitors in now prohibited.[164]) Once recruited claimants have been vetted, and if the prospects of success have been good, a case has been sent to a solicitor on the company's panel. Partly the income of the claims management companies has derived from the fees which solicitors have paid for this work. Ultimately the Court of Appeal held that these were referral fees which

---

[158] Civil Justice Council, *Annual Report 2003* (London, 2004), 21; *Annual Report 2004* (London, 2005), 20, 37.

[159] P. Fenn & N. Rickman, *Calculating 'Reasonable' Success Fees for Employers' Liability Accident Claims*, Civil Justice Council (London, 2004). [160] Access to Justice Act 1999, s. 29.

[161] CPR rr 44.4(1), (2), 44.5(1). [162] CPR, PD 44, para. 11.10.

[163] *Sarwar v Alam* [2001] EWCA Civ 1401; [2002] 1 WLR 125; [2001] 4 All ER 541, CA.

[164] *Guide to the Professional Conduct of Solicitors*, Annex 11B, Section 2A(4)(b).

until recently solicitors could not charge under their ethical rules.[165] Partly also the income of the claims management companies has come from arranging the after the event insurance to cover an adverse order of costs. The most notorious of the claims management companies arranged credit to finance the insurance premiums, which meant some claimants ended up owing money at the end of the process.[166]

The collapse of two large claims management companies in 2002–3 brought the sector into disrepute. To regain their reputation the remaining claims management companies have formed a trade association, with a code of practice to be approved by the Office of Fair Trading. Not all claims management companies are adherents and the Better Regulation Taskforce has recommended that if progress is not made in raising standards by the end of 2005, the government should act to replace self-regulation.[167] In the meanwhile existing consumer protection controls on advertising need to be enforced rigorously in relation to claims management companies, and there need to be strict guidelines on the sometimes distasteful advertising which the companies have displayed in hospitals and doctors' surgeries.[168]

Legal expenses insurance

Insurance is another way of furthering access to justice. People take out legal expenses insurance against the risk that they may need to take legal action or alternatively may become liable to a legal claim. Before the event legal expenses insurance is widely available in Britain at a low premium as an add-on to motor vehicle and house insurance policies or as part of a credit or charge card agreement. Trade unions and professional associations also offer legal expenses insurance, or its equivalent, as a benefit of membership. For individuals, stand alone legal expenses insurance is unusual in Britain, although there are commercial policies available to cover businesses for employment disputes, prosecutions, and tax investigations. In the late 1990s some 17 million people were paying premiums for some form of legal expenses insurance, typically as part of a motor vehicle or household insurance policy. Over two fifths of motor vehicle policies had legal expenses insurance attached, covering passengers as well as owners. Most claims under them are to pursue in the event of accident the policy excess or hire cost of a replacement vehicle. The add-on to household insurance may provide

---

[165] *Sharratt v London Central Bus Co. Ltd* [2004] EWCA Civ 575; [2004] 3 All ER 325 also known as *Accident Group Test Case (No. 2)*. See now *Guide to the Professional Conduct of Solicitors*, Annex 11B, Section 2A(3).

[166] *Callery v Gray (No. 2)* [2001] EWCA Civ 1264; [2002] 1 WLR 2142; [2001] 4 All ER 1. See M. Zander, 'Where Are We Now on Conditional Fees?—or Why This Emperor is Wearing Few, If Any, Clothes' (2002) 65 *MLR* 919, 927–9; J. Sandbach, *No Win, No Fee, No Chance*, Citizens Advice Bureaux (London, 2004), 17–18.

[167] Better Regulation Task Force, *Better Routes to Redress* (London, 2004), 20.

[168] *ibid.*, 23–4.

cover for employment, consumer or property disputes, personal injury claims, and motor vehicle prosecutions. Legal expenses insurance may extend to other family members. Typically it covers lawyers' and experts' fees and an opponent's costs if a case is unsuccessful, up to a specified maximum (for example, £25,000 or £50,000).[169]

Low-value claims under legal expenses insurance may be handled internally by the insurance company, but matters are often referred out to specialist law firms on the company's panel. With personal injury cases, given the high rate of success, and the commercial value of being on the panel, lawyers are unlikely to make any financial claim on the insurance company but will rely on the costs payable under the 'loser pays' principle. The contrast with conditional fee agreements under-pinned by after the event insurance is obvious: here there is no success fee for the lawyer, the premium (low though it be) is not recoverable and the lawyers, not the insurance company, bear the risk. Access to justice is facilitated further because, along with the personal injury work, the insurance company might also require panel lawyers to undertake other claims under the policies, such as consumer claims, claims not fundable under conditional fee agreements or which ordinarily they would turn away on a cost-benefit calculation. It is unclear whether the corollary in some cases is a lower quality service as work is pushed down in the law firm to paralegal staff.[170]

Legal expenses insurance has had a longer history and deeper penetration elsewhere in Europe. The concept took hold in Germany in the 1920s, once motoring became popular. German law required legal expenses insurance to be written by specialist insurers, so as to obviate the conflicts of interests thought to arise if it was added to policies principally intended to cover other risks. Now around a half of German households have cover, and a higher percentage of drivers. In such jurisdictions an important explanation for the high level of pene-tration is that legal costs and expenses tend to be fixed (and therefore predictable) and also more in proportion to the amount at stake.[171] The adoption of fixed litigation costs in England may therefore be a boost to legal expenses insurance.[172] Until recently in Germany, lawyers would always make the decision themselves whether an insured's claim should be brought under any legal expenses policy. That guaranteed the same level of service as for ordinary clients. By contrast in Britain, insurance companies make costs predictable by vetting claims, referring

[169] There is useful information in *Sawar v Alam* [2001] EWCA Civ 1401; [2002] 1 WLR 125; [2001] 4 All ER 541, CA.

[170] P. Abrams, *In Sure Hands? Funding Litigation by Legal Expenses Insurance: The Views of Insurers, Solicitors and Policyholders* (London, 2002), 9, 21.

[171] V. Prais, *Legal Expenses Insurance in Europe—An Inspiration?*, LSE Discussion Paper, May 1998; V. Prais, 'Legal Expenses Insurance' and A. Gray & N. Rickman, 'The Role of Legal Expenses Insurance in Securing Access to the Market for Legal Services', both in A. Zuckerman & R. Cranston (eds), *Reform of Civil Procedure* (Oxford, 1995); M. Kilian, 'Alternatives to Public Provision: The Role of Legal Expenses Insurance in Broadening Access to Justice: The German Experience' (2003) 30 *JLS* 31. On group legal services and legal services plans in the United States: D. Rhode, *Access to Justice* (New York, 2004) 72–3, 97–8. [172] 152 below.

those claims with a good chance of success to a specialist law firm, usually a member of their panel, and transferring much of the risk to the lawyers.

Once legal expenses insurance began to be written in Europe by mainstream insurance companies, in addition to specialist providers, there were potential conflicts of interest. The one insurance company may have written both the legal expenses insurance under which a claim is being advanced and the insurance policy under which it is being defended. Although conflicts of interest are not unusual in insurance—the one insurance company may have written all the policies invoked by the drivers or passengers in a motor vehicle accident—concern about the potential conflicts in this area led to a European Community directive in 1987.[173] Under it the legal expenses part of any general policy must be separately identified. Moreover, the insurance company must hive off the part of the business dealing with legal expenses insurance into a subsidiary with separate staff to undertake the processing and to provide legal advice. Finally, the directive enshrines the principle of the freedom to choose one's lawyer, which in practice has been interpreted to mean that insured persons may select lawyers of their choice once efforts to settle a claim by negotiation have failed and legal proceedings have to be initiated. In practice most insured use the specialist lawyers on the company's panel. The directive does not cover other potential conflicts of interest, such as the commercial pressure on lawyers to settle a case because the insurer insists its cases must be self-financing.

Empowering individuals

Delivering civil justice need not necessarily involve lawyers, or at least need not involve lawyers for the whole of a matter. A case may be capable of being 'unbundled', so that complex tasks are completed by a lawyer or expert—perhaps funded by legal aid—but the more straightforward parts undertaken by the client. The lawyer undertakes to perform specific, limited work, without taking on responsibility for the whole case.[174] Moreover, information technologies can make legal self-help sites and publications (for example, court forms, wills) readily available.[175] There is no reason why assistance for their use should not be accessible in the same way. 'Legal guidance systems' can lead users through the tasks involved in making basic decisions and presenting claims.[176] Telephone help lines and other more traditional means, such as the self-help manuals, may be more convenient for some. In the family law context the evidence suggests that self-help

---

[173] Directive 87/344/EEC on Legal Expenses Insurance [1987] OJ L185/77, 4 July 1987; Insurance Companies (Legal Expenses Insurance) Regulations 1990, SI 1990/1159, reg 6.

[174] F. Mosten, *Unbundling Legal Services* (Chicago, 2000). See also J. Giddings & M. Robertson, 'Large-scale Map or the A–Z? The Place of Self-Help Services in Legal Aid' (2003) 30 *JLS* 102.

[175] cf. those on www.tesco.com

[176] R. Susskind, *The Future of Law* (Oxford, 1998), xxiv. An example is provided by Money Claim Online, run by the Court Service, which is available to individuals and businesses wishing to make money claims: CPR, PD 7e; www.moneyclaim.gov.uk.

services are a successful substitute for legal representation in uncomplicated matters such as non-contested divorce proceedings.[177] Overall, however, self-help has its limits: those with low levels of competence in terms of education, confidence, verbal skills, and emotional fortitude are likely to need some help in resolving justiciable problems, especially so where the problem is serious and the opponent intransigent.[178] Community legal education may do something in this regard, but has a separate justification in furthering the rule of law.

Alternative Dispute Resolution

Access to the courts is not the only or even the main avenue for those seeking access to justice. Help and assistance in relation to pursuing and enforcing legal rights and responsibilities may be obtainable through other mechanisms. Some of these like ombudsmen, arbitration and mediation, now fall under the rubric of alternative dispute resolution. 'Alternative', however, hardly does justice to the pedigree and extent of these forms of dispute resolution. The Ombudsman—the first dispute resolution mechanism discussed here—is a relatively recent import to Britain. Arbitration and conciliation have been used for commercial dispute settlement for centuries.[179] The Advisory, Conciliation and Arbitration Service (ACAS) traces its history to the voluntary conciliation and arbitration service established in 1896 to settle industrial disputes. As well as continuing with this, much of ACAS's current work is with individual complaints to employment tribunals, three quarters of which are settled or withdrawn at the ACAS stage and never reach a tribunal hearing.[180] As we see in the second section of this part, the idea of conciliation and arbitration has been applied to facilitate access to justice for consumers. Unlike the small claims jurisdiction, such sector specific arbitration schemes are not subject to a financial limit. As Lord Woolf noted in his *Access to Justice* inquiry, however, the schemes are not widely used: lack of publicity and a perceived lack of openness and independence appear to be the main reasons for the relatively low take-up.[181] By contrast, community mediation, funded by social landlords and other agencies, has seen a remarkable growth.[182] Arbitration for housing disputes, which goes one step further, is now being promoted by some local authorities. Although the motivation may be to curb 'no win, no fee' housing claims, arbitration in this area could be as effective and efficient as the courts.

---

[177] L. Mather, 'Changing Patterns of Legal Representation in Divorce: From Lawyers to *Pro Se*' (2003) 30 *JLS* 137.   [178] H. Genn, *Paths to Justice* (London, 1999), 254.

[179] M. Mustill & S. Boyd, *Commercial Arbitration*, 2nd edn (London, 1989), 5.

[180] ACAS, *Annual Report and Resource Accounts 2003/04* (London, 2004), 10–13, 22.

[181] Lord Woolf, *Access to Justice. Interim Report* (London, 1995), 139.

[182] e.g. J. Gray, M. Halliday & A. Woodgate, *Responding to Community Conflict. A Review of Neighbourhood Mediation*, Joseph Rowntree Foundation (London, 2002). On family mediation: G. Davis *et al.*, 'Mediation and Legal Services—The Client Speaks' [2001] *Fam.L.* 110. See also [2001] *Fam.L.* 186, 265.

Finally there is collective justice—the third topic discussed here—the only way some individuals will ever obtain access to justice. Their social position, the disproportionate costs to them (including the opportunity costs) in relation to potential benefits, and other barriers to the machinery of dispute resolution, all militate against their taking individual action. Collective justice may provide the answer. It takes many forms, including class actions and support for civil action by public agencies.

Ombudsmen

Ombudsmen have a shorter lineage than arbitrators yet these days a more extended family tree. Since the Parliamentary Ombudsman was established in 1957, the number of ombudsmen has proliferated. For grievances against maladministration in the public sector, the Parliamentary Ombudsman has been joined by those such as the Local Government Ombudsman, the Health Service Ombudsman, the Independent Police Complaints Commission, and the Prisons and Probation Ombudsman. A review for the Cabinet Office has concluded that public sector ombudsmen need to respond to the changing nature of public service delivery.[183] As significant for the cause of civil justice there are now a considerable number of ombudsmen concerned with the private sector. While some like the Legal Services Ombudsman, the Housing Ombudsman Service and the Pensions Ombudsman may have a statutory basis,[184] others have been constituted by the relevant industry itself, no doubt in some cases to forestall legislative action. Among the private sector ombudsmen are the Estate Agents and the Telecommunications Ombudsmen.[185] The Financial Ombudsman Service, constituted under the Financial Services and Markets Act 2000,[186] absorbed some eight private ombudsman schemes including the Banking Ombudsman, the Building Societies Ombudsman, and the Investment Ombudsman.[187]

---

[183] P. Collcutt, *Review of the Pubic Sector Ombudsmen in England* (London, 2000). See e.g. M. Seneviratne, *Ombudsmen* (London, 2002); R. Gregory & P. Giddings, *The Ombudsman, The Citizen and Parliament* (London, 2002).

[184] Courts and Legal Services Act 1990, s. 21. See R. James & M. Seneviratne, 'The Legal Services Ombudsman: Form Versus Function?' (1995) 58 *MLR* 187; Housing Act 1996, Sch 2; Pensions Schemes Act 1993, Part X.

[185] Ombudsman for Estate Agents, *2003 Annual Report* (Salisbury, 2003); Office of the Telecommunications Ombudsman, *Annual Report 2004* (Warrington, 2004).

[186] Part XVI. See E. Ferran, 'Dispute Resolution Mechanisms in the UK Financial Sector' (2002) 21 *CJQ* 135; R. James & P. Morris, 'The New Financial Ombudsman Service in the United Kingdom: Has the Second Generation Got it Right?', in C. Rickett & T. Telfer, *International Perspectives on Consumers' Access to Justice* (Cambridge, 2003).

[187] On the predecessor bodies: e.g. P. Rawlings & C. Willett, 'Ombudsman Schemes in the United Kingdom's Financial Sector: the Insurance Ombudsman, the Banking Ombudsman, and the Building Societies Ombudsman' (1994) 17 *Consumer Policy* 307; P. Morris & J. Hamilton, 'The Insurance Ombudsman and PIA Ombudsman: A Critical Comparison' (1996) 47 *NILQ* 119; R. James, M. Seneviratne & C. Graham, 'Building Societies, Customer Complaints, and the Ombudsman' (1994) 23 *Anglo-Amer.LR* 214; P. Morris & G. Little, 'The Ombudsmen and Consumer Protection'. in P. Cartwright (ed.), *Consumer Protection in Financial Services* (London, 1999), ch. 2.

The volume of complaints dealt with by ombudsmen is considerable. For example, in 2003–4, the Financial Ombudsman Service referred some 97,901 complaints to its adjudicators and completed some 76,704 cases.[188] By comparison in 2003, there were 15,167 trials and 52,143 small claims hearings in the county court in England and Wales.[189] Partly the high volume of complaints to ombudsmen reflects ease of access: apart from having to have a complaint first considered by the relevant organization, there is no fee or other condition of access. Dissatisfied complainants are not bound by a decision (although the organization may be) and so can later pursue their case in the courts. With the Financial Ombudsman Service awards of up to £100,000 are possible, compared with the £5,000 limit in the small claims jurisdiction. (Like the small claims jurisdiction the ombudsman shares the advantage that there is no threat to the unsuccessful complainant of having to bear the other side's costs.) Is it any wonder that the Financial Ombudsman Service and its predecessors have denuded the civil courts of any substantial litigation over matters such as first-party insurance claims?[190] The Better Regulation Taskforce considered the need for a more general consumer ombudsman, but decided that in an already crowded ombudsmen market one more would only add to the confusion.[191] Lord Woolf applauded the role of ombudsmen in his *Access to Justice* inquiry. He thought there would be an advantage in ombudsmen having a discretion to refer complainants to the court and, where a point of law is concerned, being able to apply to the court for a ruling without requiring a complainant to start court proceedings. Courts should also be able to refer issues to an ombudsman, with the ombudsman's and the party's consent. The ombudsman's findings of fact in any subsequent proceedings would be accepted as being correct in the absence of clear evidence to the contrary.[192]

The ombudsman system has two broad functions. The first, and obvious function, is to handle individual grievances. Generally speaking, people must exhaust an organization's internal complaint procedures, but having done that can have a matter taken up by the relevant ombudsman. In this sense the ombudsmen are an alternative to the courts, although in an important respect their jurisdiction is broader in that they can proceed inquisitorially and can decide a matter on other than legal grounds. For example the Financial Ombudsman Service determines a complaint by reference to what is, in the opinion of the ombudsman, fair and reasonable in all the circumstances of the case.[193] In considering that, the ombudsman takes into account the relevant law and regulations, the regulator's rules, guidance and standards, relevant codes of practice and, where appropriate, what he considers to have been good industry practice at the relevant time.[194] The

---

[188] Financial Ombudsman Service, *Annual Review 1 April 2003–31 March 2004* (London, 2004), 19, 22. At the time of writing its jurisdiction is to extend yet further, to consumer credit complaints.
[189] *Judicial Statistics*, Cm 6251 (London, 2004), 44. See 115 below.
[190] W. Merricks, 'The Jurisprudence of the Ombudsman' [2001] *JBL* 654.
[191] Better Regulation Task Force, *Better Routes to Redress* (London, 2004), 27.
[192] Lord Woolf, *op.cit.*, 140.   [193] Financial Services and Markets Act 2000, s 228(2).
[194] Financial Services Authority Handbook, Dispute Resolution, R 3.8.1(2).

courts have held that an ombudsman has considerable scope in deciding what is
fair and reasonable, which may not coincide with the position the law would
require.[195] By the same token not all complaints about a particular body may fall
within the terms of reference of the ombudsman covering that sector. Moreover,
private sector ombudsmen have sometimes a surprisingly limited coverage. For
example, the Estate Agents Ombudsman, although well used, covers less than 50
per cent of the sector at the time of writing.

The second function of an ombudsman is to establish benchmarks of good
practice within a sector and to raise industry standards.[196] Thus the Financial
Ombudsman Service has produced a series of technical briefing notes indicating
how it expects particular issues to be dealt with by the financial sector.[197] Courts
are not generally adept in doing this, even if they wanted to: they have a general,
rather than a special, jurisdiction and as well do not always have a sufficient caseload to acquire a detailed knowledge of, or to monitor, changing practice within a
particular sector. Not only can an ombudsman give guidance to the industry, it
can also liaise with the regulators when there appears to be a systemic problem, in
addition providing input in relation to new law.

The British and Irish Ombudsman Association has identified four key criteria
before it will grant an ombudsman recognition: independence, effectiveness, fairness, and public accountability.[198] Independence turns primarily on whether the
ombudsman is independent of those subject to investigation: thus they should
constitute no more than a minority of the membership of the ombudsman council which appoints the ombudsman and to which he or she reports. In addition the
terms and conditions of an ombudsman's appointment should not undermine
independence, and the ombudsman alone should have the power to decide
whether a matter is within the jurisdiction of the scheme. Concerns have been
expressed as to whether more needs to be done to guarantee the independence of
private ombudsmen.[199]

Effectiveness depends first on coverage. In due course it is expected that all, or
virtually all, firms in an industry should participate. Secondly, the office must
be adequately staffed and funded. Accessibility is the third aspect: the right to
complain should be adequately publicized by those subject to the scheme; those
subject to complaint must have proper internal complaint procedures;[200] the
office should be directly accessible to complainants unless specified by statute;

---

[195] *R (Norwich and Peterborough Building Society) v Financial Ombudsman Service Ltd* [2002]
EWHC 2379 (Admin), para. 77; *R (IFG Financial Services Ltd), v Financial Ombudsman Service Ltd*
[2005] EWHC 1153 (Admin), *per* Stanley Burnton J.

[196] Independent Policy Commission on Public Services, Report to the National Consumer
Council, *Making Public Services Personal: A New Compact for Public Services* (London, 2004), 70.

[197] See www.financial-ombudsman.org.uk

[198] See www.bioa.org.uk Quaere: should use of the term 'ombudsman' be subject to statutory
control to prevent its devaluation in the public perception?

[199] R. James, *Private Ombudsmen and Public Law* (Aldershot, 1997), 220–1.

[200] See Financial Services Authority Handbook, Dispute Resolution: Complaints, R 1.2–1.3.

the ombudsman's procedures should be straightforward for complainants to understand and use; and those complaining should be entitled to do so free of charge. Fourthly, the criteria require that the ombudsman be entitled to investigate a complaint without the prior consent of those against whom it has been made. Except where provided by legislation, the ombudsman should be able to obtain relevant information and documents from those subject to investigation.[201] This gives access which the complainant would not have. Coupled with the inquisitorial process used by ombudsmen, this means that complainants need not compile the same degree of evidence as necessary for a court or tribunal. Finally, the ombudsman's decisions should be legally binding or—a surprising weakness—there should be at least a reasonable expectation that they will be complied with. (In cases where they are not, the ombudsman should have the power to require publication of non-compliance.)

Fairness, according to the criteria, depends on proceeding in accordance with the principles of natural justice, making reasoned decisions, explaining to complainants why a particular case is not taken up for investigation, and notifying a decision and the reasons for it in writing. Built into an ombudsman's very procedure, however, are some potential threats to fairness. Questions of fact, if not evident from the documents, must be resolved in a fairly rough and ready manner. Inferences need to be drawn from documents which are available, although the absence of information on a firm's file might be construed against it. In defence of the procedure it can be that that it accords with the purpose of ombudsmen, which is 'delivering rapid, unlegalistic justice, without cutting too many legal corners . . .'.[202] The absence of a personal hearing in the bulk of cases may give an appearance of unfairness in the eyes of some but is essential if costs are to be kept down.

Finally, there is public accountability, crucial to the rule of law. Under the criteria this depends on publication both of the jurisdiction, powers and method of appointment of an ombudsman and of his or her annual report including, if the ombudsman decides, anonymized reports of investigations. The latter enable bargaining in 'the shadow of the ombudsman' and would seem essential when, unlike the courts, decisions are taken behind closed doors and there are few oral hearings. The Office of Fair Trading has suggested that ombudsmen's annual reports should also reveal any company persistently guilty of malpractice.[203] Not only might this act as a deterrent to firms but it could also enhance the independence of an ombudsman in the eyes of the public. To further accountability, the National Consumer Council has recommended an independent body, with majority public interest and consumer representation, to monitor the various

---

[201] cf. Financial Services and Markets Act 2000, s 231.

[202] *Westminster CC v Haywood* [1998] Ch 377, 387E, *per* Robert Walker J. cf. R. Nobles, 'Keeping Ombudsmen in their Place—The Courts and the Pensions Ombudsman' [2001] *PL* 380; 'Access to Justice through Ombudsmen: The Courts' Response to the Pensions Ombudsman' (2002) 21 *CJQ* 94.   [203] Office of Fair Trading, *Consumer Redress Mechanisms* (London, 1991).

ombudsman schemes.[204] No doubt the body could also review the differences in the jurisdiction and procedure of the schemes with an eye on greater consistency.

In 1991 the Office of Fair Trading asked a sample of the general population whether they were aware of certain ombudsmen. The results were disappointing: only 27 per cent were aware of the Insurance Ombudsman, 24 per cent of the Banking Ombudsman, and 22 per cent of the Building Society ombudsman.[205] A questionnaire sent out to 565 insurance policyholders found that just 20 per cent learnt of the existence of the Insurance Ombudsman from the insurer.[206] There is evidence that members of private ombudsmen schemes have not publicized them sufficiently,[207] although there is now an onus to do so for reognition by the British and Irish Ombudsman Association. The volume of complaints going to the Financial Ombudsman Service suggests that the waves of publicity about matters such as mortgage endowment mis-selling have significantly raised its profile with the general public, compared with its predecessors.[208] Analysis of those complaining to the Financial Ombudsman Service is that users are typically older (which might reflect the nature of financial services) and, given their newspaper reading habits, from the higher socio-economic groups.[209] This confirms earlier survey evidence on those going to predecessor ombudsmen. It was found that many who complained had experience of complaining. Complainants did not have a high view of the industries' internal complaints procedure, although partly this reflected the fact that the sample was drawn from those who had exhausted internal procedures and then turned to an ombudsman. Interestingly, a not insignificant number of complainants used professional advice to prepare their claim, even though ombudsman schemes are designed to be used without it.[210]

Consumer arbitration schemes

Sector-specific conciliation and arbitration schemes are a form of industry-sponsored dispute resolution for consumers which now operate in a patchwork of industries. Typically these industries are not as tightly regulated as those giving rise to successful ombudsman schemes, which is an important explanatory factor in relative success. All that is demanded is compliance with the general standards

---

[204] National Consumer Council, *Ombudsman Services* (London, 1993), 85.

[205] Office of Fair Trading, *op.cit*. The OFT thought these figures might be an overestimate, given that the answers were prompted.

[206] J. Birds, 'Legal Access and Private Sector Ombudsmen', in J. Shapland & R. Le Grys (eds), *The Changing Shape of the Legal Profession*, Institute for the Study of the Legal Profession, University of Sheffield (Sheffield, 1994), 103.

[207] C. Graham *et al.*, 'Publicising the Bank and Building Society Ombudsman Schemes' (1993) 3 *Consumer Policy Review* 85.

[208] Of the some 98,000 new matters in the year ended March 2004, 51,917 were mortgage-related: Financial Ombudsman Service, *Annual Review 2003–4* (London, 2004).

[209] *ibid.*, 27, 39.

[210] J. Birds & P. Graham, 'Complaints against Insurance Companies' (1993) 1 *Consumer LJ* 92, 101; National Consumer Council, *Ombudsman Services* (London, 1993).

of the law of goods and services, that goods be of acceptable quality and fit for the purpose, and that services match the description and be performed with reasonable care and skill. Another factor is the lack of publicity so that consumers do not use them and retailers have no great incentive to join the schemes or to police compliance by others through the relevant trade association.[211] The schemes have been instituted, in the main, pursuant to codes of practice which trade associations in these industries have drawn up with the encouragement of the Office of Fair Trading (OFT).[212] Coverage in some sectors is low, with adherence to the code being limited. OFT criteria for approval require that every code include provision for conciliation services, if complaints are not resolvable by the code members' own internal complaints procedures. Moreover, each code must include 'the availability of a low-cost, speedy, responsive, accessible and user-friendly independent redress scheme to act as an alternative to seeking court action in the first instance'.[213] The scheme must be binding in respect of code members who must not be able to block a complainant going before the scheme. Code members are bound to accept any judgment under the scheme.

Under the codes individual adherents undertake to expedite the settlement of genuine complaints.[214] A scheme will then use its good offices to try to conciliate a complaint informally if the consumer has already taken up the matter with the business involved.[215] The aim of conciliation may be to reach a settlement without any close attention to the consumer's entitlement at law. This approach cuts both ways: on the one hand the consumer may be disadvantaged by a compromise solution, but on the other hand conciliation can be speedy and may deal with matters like dilatoriness, erroneous billing and poor service, which may not amount to a legal wrong. If conciliation fails, consumers refer a matter to adjudication or arbitration, which is provided for in almost all the codes of practice as the method of resolving the more intractable complaints.[216] Arbitration is conducted under the provisions of the Arbitration Act 1996 by an independent arbitrator, a member of the Chartered Institute of Arbitrators. Arbitrators may be assisted by experts and may obtain an independent report if necessary. Consumers may pay a fee but this is usually the limit of their liability and any fee may be refundable at the discretion of the arbitrator. The trade association bears the remaining cost of the arbitration. To reduce costs, in particular to consumers who lose, arbitration is almost invariably conducted on documents submitted by the parties, in which they present points of claim and defence, although in exceptional circumstances the arbitrator can call on them to appear in person.

---

[211] H. Collins, *Regulating Contracts* (Oxford, 1999), 353.   [212] Enterprise Act 2002, s 8.

[213] Office of Fair Trading, *Consumer Codes Approval Scheme. Core Criteria and Guidance* (London, 2004), 29. See Office of Fair Trading, *Annual Report and Resource Accounts 2003–04* (London, 2004), 44–5.

[214] Office of Fair Trading, *Consumer Codes Approval Scheme. Core Criteria and Guidance* (London, 2004), 26.   [215] *ibid.*, 28.

[216] *ibid.*, 30.

Arbitration under the codes of conduct provides a quick and relatively inexpensive means of resolving consumer complaints and also relieves the state of the burden of funding tribunals or judicial machinery. It is an alternative to the small claims procedure in the courts. However, relatively few cases are settled by arbitration under the OFT approved codes of practice. The exception is the Association of British Travel Agents (ABTA) scheme, which in 2003 dealt with nearly 17,000 complaints. Of these, 1,200 went to arbitration. For other schemes the usage is much lower, even where adequate arbitration arrangements exist and are free. While recorded complaint levels are in the thousands under these schemes, the use of arbitration is in the double digits for some schemes, and lower for many others.[217] So compared with the number of small claims in the courts, consumer arbitration is small beer indeed. Possibly this is because its credibility has suffered because it is conducted in private, in the absence of complainants, and under the auspices of the trade associations without close monitoring.[218] The new approved OFT process for recognizing consumer codes of practice attempts to address this by requiring schemes to be more transparent in their operation. Perhaps the biggest obstacle to the success of these schemes is a lack of awareness on the part of the public.[219] As a result relatively few complaints ever go there in the first place.

Collective justice

Courts, tribunals and other dispute resolution mechanisms are not wholly a middle-class preserve.[220] In the courts personal injury claims are advanced by those across the spectrum, from employees suffering industrial injuries to those in their Porsches involved in road accidents. 'By their nature, the employment and social welfare tribunals are populated by many at the lower end of the socio-economic scale.' And there is no reason to think that mediation in family or neighbour disputes is used only by those in the higher socio-economic classes. Yet we have good evidence from national surveys that those with justiciable problems in low-income occupations or of a black or minority ethnic background are less likely than average to take action to resolve them.[221] There is some evidence that those going to ombudsmen tend to be in the higher socio-economic classes.[222] And the acknowledged expert on small claims in Britain, Professor

[217] M. Doyle, K. Ritters & S. Brooker, *Seeking Resolution. The Availability and Usage of Consumer-to-Business Alternative Dispute Resolution in the United Kingdom*, Department of Trade and Industry and National Consumer Council (London, 2004), 2, 53–4.
[218] National Consumer Council, *Out of Court: A Consumer View of Three Low-cost Trade Arbitration Schemes* (London, 1991); M. Doyle, K. Ritters & S. Brooker, op.cit., 54–5.
[219] T. Goriely & T. Williams, *Resolving Civil Disputes: Choosing Between Out-of-Court Schemes and Litigation*, Lord Chancellor's Department Research Series No. 3/97 (London, 1997), 34–5; Scottish Consumer Council, *Consensus Without Court: Encouraging Mediation in Non-Family Civil Disputes in Scotland* (Glasgow, 2001).   [220] 117, 144 below.
[221] P. Pleasence et al., *Causes of Action: Civil Law and Social Justice* (London, 2004), 55–6; H. Genn, *Paths to Justice* (London, 1999), 135–6.   [222] 76 above.

John Baldwin, has noted that small claim users are typically professional people or middle class.[223]

All this supports the case for collective justice. By this is meant some sort of mechanism which advances the grievances of individuals but minimizes the extent to which they need to take the initiative. The class action is one mechanism for collecting and advancing claims, each of which may be worth a relatively small amount when compared with the cost of pursuing them in court. (Multiparty actions are the avenue for large-scale personal injury claims.[224]) A consultation about introducing a class action procedure in England and Wales through the Civil Procedure Rules attracted support, but also disagreement on individual aspects and opposition from business interests because of the potential for abusive claims.[225] Class actions still rely on the existing court system: for this reason nothing further is said here.[226] A variant of the class action is the British government's coal health compensation scheme, which is said to be the world's largest personal injury compensation scheme. Miners affected by respiratory disease or second vibration white finger, and their relatives, are paid out after a medical assessment or, where less lung damage has been suffered, a breathing test to monitor loss of function.[227]

The regulatory agency is another collective mechanism. Its focus is mainly the behaviour of the regulated and its weapons moral suasion and ultimately prosecution for the most troublesome cases.[228] Those consumers with grievances are a well-spring of regulatory action and compensation for them is sometimes a consideration. If regulators take up their customer complaints to seek individual satisfaction, that is an inexpensive alternative to litigation. There can be concern as to whether some regulators—for example, a utility regulator which sets prices and standards—will be sufficiently disinterested to resolve consumer complaints objectively.[229] Putting that to one side, regulators taking up complaints can be an effective, and inexpensive, means of bringing consumer satisfaction.[230]

Some public agencies actually have as their remit helping individuals pursue grievances: the new Commission for Equality and Human Rights will continue the work in that regard of the Equal Opportunities Commission, the Commission for Racial Equality, and the Disability Rights Commission. It will advise individuals of their rights under discrimination and human rights law and how to secure them, including how to bring proceedings. As with its predecessor

---

[223] 116 below.   [224] C. Hodges, *Multi-Party Actions* (Oxford, 2001).

[225] Department for Constitutional Affairs, *Representative Claims. Proposed New Procedures*, Consultation Paper, February 2001; Consultation Response, April 2002.

[226] C. Scott & J. Black, *Cranston's Consumers and the Law* (London, 2000), 120–33; Lord Woolf, *Access to Justice. Final Report* (London, 1996), ch. 17. And see the excellent R. Mulheron, *The Class Action* (Oxford, 2004).   [227] See www.dti.gov.uk/coalhealth

[228] K. Hawkins, *Law as a Last Resort* (Oxford, 2003).

[229] A. McHarg, 'Separation of Functions and Regulatory Agencies: Dispute Resolution in the Privatised Utilities', in M. Harris & M. Partington, *Administrative Justice in the 21st Century* (Oxford, 1999), 235, 244.   [230] See R. Cranston, *Regulating Business* (London, 1979), ch. 4.

bodies, it will also support litigation or litigate itself if that has a potential strategic impact.[231] Non-government organizations (NGOs) such as Justice, Friends of the Earth, and Greenpeace also litigate strategically on behalf of individuals or groups of individuals.[232] Public interest litigation of this character can involve the agency or NGO acting in its own name, but in particular cases to the advantage of individuals with grievances.

Procedurally, the major issue about public interest litigation has been that of standing. Standing seems no longer to be a problem with judicial review. Outside judicial review there must be a specific statutory authority for the agency or NGO to litigate as a surrogate for individuals. In Britain there is only a limited conferral of such power, and this is mainly as a result of European directives. For example, the Director General of Fair Trading, certain utility regulators, trading standards departments, and the Consumers' Association (an NGO), can take up complaints about unfair consumer terms, ultimately seeking an injunction against their use.[233] By contrast legislation in some civil law systems empowers a range of agencies and NGOs—environmental, consumer, and trade groups—to take various types of legal action in the name of the public interest generally. The late Professor Cappelletti wrote of such devices:

The advantages of this solution vis-à-vis the isolated litigator are clear: on the one hand, they are 'specialised' in the area they represent. However, unlike the 'specialised governmental agencies', they are better suited to preserve the 'seal' of the private persons involved, while at the same time representing the *entire* interest and not merely a fragment of it. They can also multiply the resources of isolated individuals.[234]

Cost is, as ever, a problem, especially if NGOs are to initiate this type of collective action. A coalition of environmental interests has recommended that the cost-shifting rule be abandoned in public interest litigation; this would have obvious benefits where, say, an environment group wanted an order against government or an industry and knew that, if unsuccessful, it would not be ordered to pay the other side's costs.[235] Ontario's Intervenor Funding Project Act 1988 provided for finance for interest groups appearing before certain administrative agencies in the province. The Act was not a unique feature in Canadian public life: there have been other sources of public moneys for those wishing to intervene in the administrative process, especially in the environmental area. The Act set out criteria that intervenors had to fulfil to be eligible for funding, primarily that the

---

[231] *Fairness for All*, Cm 6185 (London, 2004), 60, 62–3.   [232] 120–1 below.
[233] Unfair Terms in Consumer Contracts Regulations 1999, SI 1999/2083, reg. 12. cf. Enterprise Act 2002 (Bodies Designated to Make Super-complaints) Order 2004, SI 2004/1517.
[234] M. Cappelletti, 'Alternative Dispute Resolution Processes within the Framework of the World-wide Access-to-justice Movement' (1993) 56 *MLR* 282, 286.
[235] Environmental Justice Project (Environmental Law Foundation, Leigh Day & Co., World Wide Fund for Nature), *Environmental Justice* (London, 2003), 39–45.

issues affected a significant segment of the public and the public interest, and that the intervenor was representative, relevant, and potentially helpful.[236]

A further possibility for collective justice would be an office of public advocate. At one level this would be an Office of Fair Trading or Commission for Equality and Human Rights writ large. It would be an independent agency with power to represent the public interest before courts, administrative agencies, and other bodies. The idea is along the lines of Lord Woolf's director of civil proceedings, who could initiate civil proceedings whenever required in the public interest and could act as *amicus* in all relevant proceedings.[237] The remedy usually sought by agencies or NGOs is non-compensatory in nature, primarily that someone act or be prevented from acting in a certain way. One of the functions of the public advocate could also be to seek a compensatory remedy on behalf of a group of the public. There are a few examples in Britain along those lines such as the action of the Parliamentary Ombudsman in obtaining around £150 million compensation for the Barlow Clowes investors.[238] The Financial Ombudsman Service has also obtained millions of pounds worth of compensation, from which many thousands of customers have benefited, after rulings in 'lead cases' that particular practices are unfair.[239]

Conclusion

In the working of the civil justice system our concern must be not only with access to justice, but with equal access to justice. At present, equality before the law is contradicted by the way the civil justice system works. Those not at the top get a bad deal in vindicating their rights and having their grievances resolved through judicial processes. Legal aid still has an important role, and there are strong arguments for financial support enhancing its operation. That may be made conditional on the adoption of new models of legal aid practice. It is unrealistic to think, however, that in the foreseeable future any government will increase the funding for legal aid at the rate experienced in the past. What, then, can be done? First, steps can be taken to facilitate the private provision of legal services such as encouraging legal expenses insurance to be taken out by individuals but also by groups such as trade unions and professional associations. Secondly, we can build

---

[236] M. Valiante & W. Bogart, 'Helping "Concerned Volunteers Working Out of Their Kitchens": Funding Citizen Participation in Administrative Decision Making' (1993) 31 *Osgoode Hall LJ* 687, 716–7. See M. Jeffery, 'Intervenor Funding as the Key to Effective Citizen Participation in Environmental Decision-making' (2002) 19 *Arizona J Int'l & Comp.L.* 643; W. Bogart, *Access and Impact. An Evaluation of the Intervenor Funding Project Act, 1988* (Toronto, 1992). The Act expired in 1996.

[237] Sir Harry Woolf, *Protection of the Public—A New Challenge* (London, 1990), 110–11.

[238] Parliamentary Commissioner for Administration, *The Barlow Clowes Affair*, HC 76, 1989–90 session (London, 1989); HC Deb, 19 December 1989, c.203.

[239] e.g. Financial Ombudsman Service, *Annual Review 1 April 2002 to 31 March 2003* (London, 2003).

on existing successful mechanisms such as law centres, advice agencies, and ombudsmen. With law centres, as well as a sideways expansion, there needs to be a deepening. National back-up or second-tier centres are one possibility—taking account of the work already done by specialist bodies such as Shelter—to conduct research, disseminate information and to act as a base for coordinating national campaigns. Advice agencies also need strengthening: more law-related training for generalists is one aspect, so that legal problems are spotted; more specialist law-related back-up is another. The concept of ombudsmen has much to commend it, while not depriving consumers of access to the courts. It is not necessarily transferable to sectors which are not tightly regulated. An additional advantage which some forms of alternative dispute resolution have is that they can penetrate behind the problem presented to its true cause, and also identify non-legal solutions. The tenant with rent arrears may have lost employment through unfair dismissal, which intervention may be able to restore.

We also need new ways of doing things which facilitate access to justice. Empowering individuals through education, training, and the provision of information will enable some to navigate the shoals of the system, although only a small number will benefit without fundamental adjustments, in particular procedural simplification. Collective mechanisms can also advance the interests of those traditionally unrepresented before decision-makers (including courts) and allow intervention in the process where this has not regularly occurred. One approach is to generalize the work of bodies such as the Commission for Equality and Human Rights and its predecessor bodies by establishing an office of the public advocate. Finally, it is as well to recall that procedural and institutional reform cannot be divorced from reform of public and private bureaucracies and of the substantive law. Better decision making by government agencies, for example, would reduce the number of reviewable decisions. Better quality housing in both the public and private sector would reduce the need for legal action by tenants or potential tenants. We need also to review the legal rights to which the civil justice system gives effect. Subtracting from and adding to these, recasting existing rights so they are self-enforcing, anticipating the additional legal costs of policy changes—such measures are a necessary step if equal access to justice is to become a reality.

3

Access to Justice: II

Access to justice measures, such as those outlined in Chapter 2, have been characterized as falling into distinct waves.[1] The first wave involved the extension of legal aid for individuals; this meant that lawyers received public funding from the state to provide legal assistance. The second wave—structural legal aid—focused upon the representation of diffuse or collective interests such as consumers and the environment, and involved liberalized standing rules, public interest litigation, multiparty actions and the like. The first and second waves are incorporated in the third, but the third is said to go beyond them to expand legal representation and change adjudicative procedures to accommodate different types of litigants, issues, and remedies. To an extent we touch on this type of procedural change in Chapter 5. A fourth wave is said to be using deregulation and privatization— 'competition policy'—to encourage alternative forms and providers of legal services.[2] In Chapter 2 we saw how this has taken form in developments like conditional fees. Each of these waves in the access to justice movement is concerned with what can be called 'social access': individuals and in some cases groups of individuals have legal rights and are then mobilized to obtain legal services to invoke these rights.

While the development of access to justice in South and South-east Asia contains elements of these 'waves', social access to justice is only part of the picture. A notable development in access to justice in the region over the last decade has been the concern with 'economic access', providing economic institutions, especially banks and other financial institutions, with a mechanism for easier access to judicial remedies. There has been no recent counterpart in Europe or North America to the notion of furthering economic access to justice, although it is fair to say that economic institutions in these places are already well served by existing arrangements.

In general terms the justifications for facilitating social access in South and South-east Asia are similar to those already canvassed in Chapter 2, although the problems to be addressed are especially acute in societies where many in the

[1] M. Cappelletti and B. Garth, 'Access to Justice: The Worldwide Movement to Make Rights Effective', in M. Cappelletti & B. Garth (eds), *Access to Justice* (Milan, 1978), vol. 1; M. Cappelletti, 'Alternative Dispute Resolution Processes within the Framework of the World-Wide Access-to-Justice Movement' (1993) 56 *MLR* 282.

[2] C. Parker, *Just Lawyers. Regulation and Access to Justice* (Oxford, 1999), 38–41.

population have limited resources and education and a lack of knowledge of law's potential.[3] There is an unacceptable incongruence between the rights recognized by the legal order and the experiences of individuals. Justice Krishna Iyer of the Indian Supreme Court has written:

> Regrettably, access jurisprudence is the Cinderella of the Indian Justice System. Ubi jus, ibi remedium is basic to the credibility of the law. But when a person goes to court in search of relief and has a case to substantiate the wrong done to him, prompt remedy must issue. Unfortunately, our Procedural Codes, Civil and Criminal, are beset with baffling steps that it is more accurate to describe our system as a government of lawyers and not a government of laws.[4]

Access to justice meets legal need and makes rights effective. In broad terms this furthers the rule of law. As the Supreme Court of India put it in a leading decision on public interest litigation, if no one can maintain an action for redress of a public wrong, 'it would be disastrous for the rule of law, for it would be open to the state or public authority to act with impunity . . .'.[5] Misuse of power by state bureaucracies or by agencies of the state such as the police underline the importance of social access.[6] Similarly with private wrongs, especially if the landlord, employer, or moneylender has legal help. In some societies women are especially disadvantaged: access to justice may enable them to address particular legal needs, not least in family disputes.[7] Furthermore, access to justice underpins the legitimacy of the state. Not only does it demonstrate a state's concern for the individual's plight but it can act as a channel for frustration and serve to dampen conflict. There may be an element of truth in the argument that concerns for stability, legitimacy, and economic justice in developing countries leads some courts to favour those who have less.[8] Finally, there is the important point that economic development might actually reduce access to justice to the less well-off, since the price of legal services is bid up substantially as a result of the increased demand by government and upper income groups. The legal profession 'tends to

---

[3] *Legal Empowerment: Advancing Good Governance and Poverty Reduction* (Law and Policy Reform at the Asian Development Bank 2001, Manila, 2001), 30–41.

[4] Justice V.R. Krishna Iyer, *Justice and Beyond* (New Delhi, 1980) 68–9.

[5] *S.P. Gupta v Union of India*, AIR 1982 SC 149, 190.

[6] World Bank, *World Development Report 2000/2001* (Washington, DC, 2001), 100, 103; Department for International Development, *Making Government Work for Poor People* (London, 2001), 22; M. Anderson, 'Getting Rights Right', *INSIGHTS*, No. 43, 2002, 1.

[7] e.g. S. Ali, 'Using Law for Women in Pakistan', in A. Stewart (ed.), *Gender, Law and Justice* (London, 2002); R. Mukherjee, *Women, Law and Free Legal Aid in India* (New Delhi, 1998); M. Dasgupta, 'Social Action for Women? Public Interest Litigation in India's Supreme Court', *Law, Social Justice & Global Development Journal* (LGD) 2002 (1), http://elj.warwick.ac.uk/global/02-1/dasgupta.html. A pilot study in Karachi found that use by women of justice institutions was uncommon: of over 1,800 respondents 3 per cent had used the services of the police or the courts, 4 per cent had consulted a lawyer and 1 per cent had used legal aid: S. Mhatre, N. Anderson, N.M. Ansari, & K. Omer, *Access to Justice for Women of Karachi. A Pilot Assessment* (CIET [Community Information and Epidemiological Technologies], Canada, 2002), vii.

[8] S. Haynie, 'Resource Inequalities and Litigation Outcomes in the Philippine Supreme Court' (1994) 56 *J.Pol.* 752, 753–4, 765, 770.

gravitate toward the most lucrative work—in a developing society, the rapidly growing commercial work—with a resultant decrease in legal services available for purchase at the lower margin.'[9] That points in the direction of more legal services, not less.

Economic access to justice has a quite different basis. In broad terms it is founded on the notion of 'improving the efficacy or competence of judicial systems to reduce the costs of economic transactions'.[10] It is part of a favourable investment environment and is thus premised on the assumption that economic development has an important legal component. While this is problematic as a universal truth, we can see particular cases where a causal link between legal innovation and development can be identified.[11] At its most basic a political system must ensure effective property rights and the enforcement of contractual obligations. That means a comprehensive legal framework policed by an impartial, competent, and accessible judicial system.[12] Western-style courts transplanted to the region in the colonial period and post-Independence have played an important role in settling commercial disputes as economies have become more complex. In some countries they have continued to do that in a very effective fashion.[13] In the south and south-east Asian region the Singaporean courts are an exemplar in dealing with business and other disputes in an efficient manner.

Elsewhere in the region factors such as delays encountered in litigation create one of the barriers to economic access. In 1987 the Supreme Court of India noted that even if no new cases were subsequently filed it would take 15 years to dispose of all pending cases.[14] Reporting in early 2002, a standing committee of the Indian Parliament expressed grave concern over the mounting arrears in the country's courts: as of 31 October 2001, it estimated that some 24 million cases awaited hearing in different courts throughout India. Of these nearly 20 million were pending in the district and subordinate courts, and the bulk of the remainder in the high courts.[15] This results in an inefficiency in the business environment. One study examined 1849 companies in the process of liquidation before the Indian high courts: in 59 per cent of these cases the procedure took more than 10 years, and in 32 per cent of cases more than 20 years.[16] The upshot is that in the meantime value has been stripped out by controllers and middle-men, leaving little for the creditors and employees. As we see in Chapter 9, weak mechanisms for debt recovery have been a constant factor in the high level of non-performing

---

[9] B. Metzger, 'Legal Services to the Poor and National Development Objectives', in *Committee on Legal Services to the Poor in Developing Countries, Legal Aid and World Poverty* (New York, 1974), 9.

[10] World Bank, *Governance and Development* (Washington, DC, 1991), 32. See also H. de Soto, *The Mystery of Capital* (New York, 2000), 158–88.   [11] 26–7 above.

[12] 25 above.   [13] 284 below.

[14] *P.N. Kumar v Municipal Corporation of Delhi* [1987] 4 SCC 609, 610.

[15] Parliament of India, Rajya Sabha, Home Affairs Standing Committee, *Law's Delays: Arrears in Courts*, 85th Report, Delhi, 2002.

[16] World Bank, *India. Policies to Reduce Poverty and Accelerate Sustainable Development* (Poverty Reduction and Economic Management Unit, South Asia Region, 2000), 45.

bank assets. No country has matched India in the size of the problem, although it would be wrong to think that it has been unique.

The reasons for the crisis in access to justice in the region are not central to present concerns. Instead the chapter concentrates on the measures taken to foster access to justice. It focuses largely on the Indian sub-continent, with references to Malaysia, Indonesia, Singapore, and the Philippines. Given the enormity and diversity of the region, the paucity of information about some jurisdictions and my lack of familiarity with them, the chapter can only provide a sketch of the issues involved. The discussion in this chapter is by no means exhaustive of the measures which can address access to justice problems. For example, other institutions such as ombudsmen can further access to justice: they can provide a relatively inexpensive remedy to individuals and groups not only in relation to public administration but also to bodies such as financial institutions.[17]

Social Access

Mirroring the waves of access to justice in Europe, north America and Australasia are the comparable measures in South and South-east Asia such as legal aid, public interest litigation, and innovative court structures. Because law and legal institutions are moulded by their economic and social context, facilitating social access to justice in these ways often has a different character in different jurisdictions. As in countries outside the region, there has also been a move to encourage the extra-judicial settlement of disputes, although informal justice and alternative dispute resolution (ADR) take a particular turn when drawing on traditional institutions.

Yet these measures are far from being the complete story of social access to justice. The nature and operation of the legal profession can block access to justice. This occurs if lawyers do not have a *pro bono* ethos or if they are not available in the village and rural areas, being geographically concentrated in the major cities, have commercial (rather than individual) clients, or require a down payment on fees before taking action.[18] The Indian Law Commission has said that the profession itself has an ethical obligation to ensure equal access to justice for all.[19] Greater thought is being given to how lawyers in South and

[17] The concept is known in Asia: an Asian Ombudsman Association was formed in 1996. See also M. Cooray, 'Ombudsman in Asia' and R. Jha, 'The Ombudsman Scene in India,' in R. Gregory and P. Giddings (eds), *Righting Wrongs: The Ombudsman in Six Continents* (Amsterdam, 2000); L. Reif, *The Ombudsman, Good Governance and the International Human Rights System* (Leiden, 2004), 242–6.

[18] See K.G. Machado and Rahim Said, 'The Malaysian Legal Profession in Transition', in C.F. Dias *et al.*, *Lawyers in the Third World: Comparative and Developmental Perspectives* (Uppsala, 1981), 256, 260, 262; *Legal Empowerment: Advancing Good Governance and Poverty Reduction, op.cit.*, 33–4.

[19] Law Commission of India, *One Hundred and Thirty-First Report on Role of the Legal Profession in the Administration of Justice* (Delhi, 1988), 13, 20. See 205–6 below.

South-east Asia can be attuned in their education to the problems of social access.[20] There are a number of lawyers undertaking public interest work.[21] Paralegals might in some respects compensate for the impediments on access to lawyers: India has its pleaders, Malaysia its petition writers and Indonesia its 'pokrol bambu'. All make the law more comprehensible and accessible to the less well-off, although the trade-off is that they may not have comparable access to the formal institutions of the law or the degree of competence expected of lawyers.[22]

A different type of paralegal in the region is that trained by some of the non-government organizations (NGOs) to provide a cost-effective source of legal advice and assistance to the disadvantaged. There are examples as well of volunteer paralegals, belonging to local associations who operate in partnership with NGO lawyers to protect legal rights in their communities. An example is provided by the Philippines legal services NGO, Saligan, which works on land reform and development issues. How it assisted a 1,200 household association of coconut farmers to achieve more secure and potentially profitable land tenure arrangements, through training some of its members as paralegals, has been described as follows:

The fifteen paralegals gathered data, interviewed farmers, prepared affidavits, processed land reform applications, and taught their communities about the law. They also countered landlord resistance in various ways. Where the landlords sought to evade the law by hiding ownership or revenue information, the paralegals tracked it down. Where the landlords brought in lawyers to fight agrarian reform at the quasi-judicial hearings of the relevant government agency, the paralegals represented the farmer applicants. And where landlords filed suit against farmers (alleging, for example, that the farmers had stolen crops) to frustrate the process, the paralegals helped Saligan attorneys prepare for trial in defense of the farmers. In the absence of the paralegals, most of the land reform applications would have withered due to bureaucratic delays or landlord resistance.[23]

In the Philippines, legal services NGOs such as Saligan have used the information obtained at grass-root level to work with national federations of community-based organizations to press for changes in the law.[24]

---

[20] e.g. K. Gallant, 'Learning from Communities: Lessons from India on Clinical Method and Liberal Education'; M. Pruekpongsawalee, 'Thommasat Clinical Education and the Delivery of Legal Services: A Historical and Personal Perspective', both in L. Trubek & J. Cooper (eds), *Educating for Justice Around the World* (Abingdon, Oxon, 1999); M. Gopal, *New Vision for Legal Education in the Emerging Global Scenario* (Bangalore, 2001).

[21] A. Sarat & S. Sheingold (eds), *Cause Lawyering and the State in a Global Era* (Oxford, 2001).

[22] See C. Morrison, 'Clerks and Clients: Paraprofessional Roles and Cultural Identities in Indian Litigation' (1974) 9 *Law & Soc.R.* 1; K.G. Machado & Rahim Said, *op.cit.*, 262–3; D. Lev, 'Bushlawyers in Indonesia,' in Y. Ghai *et al.*, *The Political Economy of Law* (Delhi, 1987); D. Lev, 'Between State and Society: Professional Lawyers and Reform in Indonesia', in T. Lindsey (ed.), *Indonesia. Law and Society* (Sydney, 1999), 228.

[23] S. Golub, 'Nonlawyers as Legal Resources for their Communities', in M. McClymont & S. Golub (eds), *Many Roads to Justice* (Ford Foundation, 2000), 304.

[24] S. Golub, 'Participatory Justice in the Philippines', in *ibid.*, 200, 209–10.

Legal aid: individual and structural

Typically legal aid has a dual character: it can be individual oriented, but it can also be structural.[25] The former tends to be the norm: civil legal aid is given to individuals by way of advice, assistance, or representation for family matters, disputes over property, accident compensation claims and the like. The focus is on assisting poorer individuals to cope with routine legal problems through lawyers acting in the ordinary way as advisers and advocates. While essential, individual-oriented legal aid relies on lawyer expertise rather than client empowerment. Moreover, it also has the feature that usually the work ends when the client's rights are successfully asserted 'following which neither lawyer nor the court takes any steps to prevent the same wrong from being committed against other members of the community'.[26] By comparison structural legal aid works using legal services to assist groups and communities as well as individuals in the pursuit of legal rights and social change. A solution is sought with regard to a structure or practice which causes individual injustice. Human rights issues are high on the agenda. Particular cases are conceived of as test cases; law is seen as a resource for applying pressure, especially when political institutions are unresponsive. Even if cases are unsuccessful in a legal sense they might work as part of a total strategy of publicizing an abuse and educating the populace. Structural work also encompasses lobbying and campaigning and the education and mobilization of those who are the victims of a particular injustice.

Individual-oriented legal aid schemes operate throughout the region, run both by the state but also on a voluntary basis by bar councils, law faculties and social and religious groups. Everywhere, state legal aid schemes are under fiscal pressure; this is also the case in the region. Even in a wealthy country such as Singapore the focus on national economic growth has not surprisingly been at the expense of civil legal aid. The civil legal aid scheme has been underfunded and has lacked publicity, and scant attention has been given to innovations in other comparable jurisdictions in matters such as the range of provision and the mode of delivery.[27]

Take India as another example. An obligation to provide legal aid is one of the Directive Principles of the Indian Constitution (Article 39A). These are not enforceable in a court of law but the Supreme Court has interpreted them as being

---

[25] The distinction is widely recognized, if not exactly in these terms. See, e.g., M. Cappelletti, J. Gordley & E. Johnson, *Towards Equal Justice: A Comparative Study of Legal Aid in Modern Societies* (Milan, 1975), 85, 109; M. Galanter, *Law and Society in Modern India* (New Delhi, 1989), 287. See 48–9 above.

[26] A. Valera *et al.*, 'An Integrated Approach in Providing Legal Services to the Rural Poor and other Disadvantaged Groups', in International Commission of Jurists, *Report of Seminars on Legal Services for the Rural Poor and other Disadvantaged Groups* (Geneva, 1988), 47.

[27] H.Y. Yeo, 'Assessing the State of Civil Legal Aid in Singapore,' (1992) 41 *ICLQ* 875; Y.H. Ying, 'Provision of Legal Aid in Singapore,' in K. Tan (ed.), *The Singapore Legal System*, 2nd edn (Singapore, 1999). On gaps in legal aid in Malaysia: A. Harding & A. Sharom, *Access to Environmental Justice in Kuala Lumpur* (unpublished report on Access to Environmental Justice Project, SOAS, n.d.).

addressed primarily to the legislature and executive.[28] The legal aid movement in India can be traced back to the Bombay Legal Aid Society, which began in 1925. As in many countries, however, there is a gap in India between aspiration and reality. That is not through any absence of thought about the matter: in 1949 committees in both Bombay and West Bengal were appointed to report on legal aid; in 1957 a law ministers' conference concluded that each state should formulate a scheme for legal aid; the fourteenth report of the Law Commission recommended the immediate provision of legal aid to the poor; an expert committee on legal aid under Justice Krishna Iyer reported in 1973; the constitution was amended in 1976 by the insertion of Article 39A; and the Bhagwati Committee's Report on *National Judicare; Equal Justice—Social Justice* was published in 1978.[29] Indeed the Committee for the Implementation of Legal Aid Scheme, constituted in 1980 by the central government, has achieved much, for example, a model legal aid scheme adopted by almost all jurisdictions, paralegal training, grants in aid to particular legal aid programmes, and legal aid teaching materials. Yet overall the funds allocated for legal aid have been inadequate, and when allocated have been under-utilized.[30] The Legal Services Authorities Act 1987 provides for a comprehensive, nationwide scheme of publicly funded legal services, but it was not brought into force until 1995.[31]

Structural legal aid in the region has had some noticeable, if isolated, successes. Proponents include the Indonesian Legal Aid Foundation, the Free Legal Assistance Group in the Philippines, the Union of Civil Liberties in Thailand, and the legal resources centre of the Consumers' Association of Penang (Malaysia).[32] In India, the Supreme Court has recognized structural legal aid by holding that Article 39A of the Constitution obliges a state to encourage and support social action groups in their legal aid programmes.[33] Structural legal aid is also recognized in the Legal Services Authorities Act 1987: the National Legal Services Authority must, among other things, support public interest litigation with regard to consumer protection, environmental protection, or other matters of special concern to the weaker sections of society. A number of social action groups have been responsible

[28] *Ranjan Dwivedi v UOI*, AIR 1983 SC 624.

[29] See also S. Sharma, *Legal Aid to the Poor* (New Delhi, 1993); L. Singhvi & D. Friedman, 'Free Legal Services in Delhi and Bombay, India,' in *Legal Aid and World Poverty* (New York, 1974).

[30] See the report on Himachal Pradesh in M. Chitkara & P. Mehta, *Law and the Poor* (New Delhi, 1991), 106–22.

[31] I. Jaising, 'India's Legal Services Authorities Act 1987,' in Legal Action Group, *Shaping the Future. New Directions for Legal Services*, Seminar 1 (unpublished, 1994); Rajeev Dhavan, 'Law as Struggle: Notes on Public Interest Law in India' (Madison, Wisconsin: Institute for Legal Studies, Working Paper, 1993), 37–9; Rajeev Dhavan, 'The Unbearable Lightness of India's Legal Aid Programme', in S. Hossain, S. Malik, & B. Musa (eds), *Public Interest Law in South Asia* (Dhaka, 1997).

[32] e.g. D. Lev, 'Lawyers' Causes in Indonesia and Malaysia,' in A. Sarat & S. Scheingold (eds), *Cause Lawyering. Political Commitments and Professional Responsibility* (New York, 1998); A. Harding, 'Practical Human Rights, NGOs and the Environment in Malaysia', in A. Boyle & M. Anderson (eds), *Human Rights Approaches to Environmental Protection* (Oxford, 1998).

[33] *Centre of Legal Research v State of Kerala*, AIR 1986 SC 2195.

for the pubic interest litigation instituted before Indian courts.[34] In Bangladesh the Bangladesh National Women Lawyers Association and others have used high-profile cases, with media work, to educate the public about problems such as the police treatment of women and to generate pressure for a government response to crimes such as the trafficking of females for prostitution.[35]

Some of the legal aid organizations in Indonesia have been notable for their structural approach. To an extent they are moulded by their history. Concrete steps to establish legal aid organizations began in 1967–8 as a reaction to a wave of preventive detentions and arrests; thus the movement for structural legal aid in Indonesia grew out of a struggle for constitutionalism and the rule of law.[36] Later on the process of implementing the national plan of development brought about the forcible eviction of people from their homes with large construction works and this led to a legal reaction which was attuned to the political and economic context. A national legal aid workshop agreed in 1980 that 'conscientiasation'— making people aware of their rights—should be the aim of structural legal aid which, accompanied by organizational efforts, would gradually change the unjust social structure. The Legal Aid Institute of Jakarta, which has a dozen active branches around the country, became a model for NGO socio-legal and politico-legal reform activity.[37] Daniel Lev has described the approach in his excellent account of the legal aid movement in Indonesia:

If the disabilities of the majority poor were understood to result from social and economic inequality, protected by an authoritarian and repressive state, legal aid narrowly conceived was obviously inadequate. Even in legal terms it was limited by bureaucratic and judicial corruption, inefficiency, and lack of independence—and, further, by the reality that neither state nor society took law and legal process all that seriously. In these circumstances, offering nothing more than legal counsel to the needy was hopelessly beside the point. It might even lend legitimacy to the political order that sustained the conditions of the poor.[38]

Not surprisingly, the Soeharto government criticized structural legal aid as 'politicisation' and sought alternatively to confine it to individual service provision, to co-opt it and in part to prohibit it. At one point the government denied legal aid workers permission to engage in relevant research, and district heads around Jakarta refused to allow legal aid posts to be established.[39]

[34] 92–3 below.
[35] S. Golub, 'From the Village to the University: Legal Activism in Bangladesh', in M. McClymount & S. Golub (eds), *op.cit.*, 135.
[36] B. Nasution, 'The Legal Aid Movement in Indonesia: Towards the Implementation of the Structural Legal Aid Concept,' in H. Scoble & L. Wiseberg (eds), *Access to Justice* (London, 1985), 34.
[37] D. Lev, 'Between State and Society: Professional Lawyers and Reform in Indonesia', in T. Lindsey (ed.), *op.cit.*, 230, 241, 245.
[38] D. Lev, *Legal Aid in Indonesia* (Melbourne, 1987), 20.
[39] T. Mulya Lubis, 'Legal Aid: Some Reflections' in H. Scoble & L. Wiseberg (eds), *op.cit.*, 44. See also D. Lev, *Lawyers as Outsiders: Advocacy versus the State in Indonesia* (London, 1992), 31–2.

There are many obstacles to an adequate system of legal aid. Countries, especially developing countries, have many calls on national resources and in the main legal aid (indeed, the law generally) ranks low in the list of priorities. Even when resources are available these might not be effectively employed because of ignorance of law's potential within the community or poor infrastructure for the delivery of services. Government-organized legal aid has been perceived, at certain times and in certain places, as a 'gimmick of the Government'.[40] Legal aid channelled through voluntary groups, bar associations, and law schools does not have the same complexion. If legal aid goes beyond its traditional confines of being orientated to the individual, to challenge social values or public policy, government opposition is likely. Writing in 1988, one commentator saw a variety of laws springing up all over Asia to threaten or impede the activities of the rural-based and social action groups.[41] As a Filipino legal aid lawyer put it: 'To talk of human rights, or structural change, will already raise eyebrows, and might be construed as subversive or seditious.'[42] The experience of the Indonesian Legal Aid Foundation in this regard has already been referred to. In Malaysia, lawyers with the Consumers' Association of Penang were fined for contempt of court when they criticized a Supreme Court decision made in the course of a campaign for enhancing tenant farmers' rights.[43]

Public interest litigation

One of the most dramatic examples of the courts themselves furthering social access is through their facilitating public interest litigation. Public interest litigation provides collective access to justice: although it can protect individual interests, the focus is on a remedy which can apply to all such cases of that wrong-doing, so furthering social justice or vindicating the rights of groups or communit-ies of people. Complementing public interest litigation might be a media strategy or political mobilization to build up pressure for a change in the practices of government, government agencies such as the police, or corporations.[44] For example, while Malaysian NGOs have tended to prefer political action over litigation, not least because the judiciary have taken a restrictive view of standing,

[40] S. Sharma, *op.cit.*, 80.

[41] C. Dias, 'Obstacles to Using Law as a Resource for the Poor, the Recapturing of Law by the Poor', in International Commission of Jurists, *Report of Seminars on Legal Services for the Rural Poor and other Disadvantaged Groups* (Genera, 1988), 40. See also C. Dias, 'Problems and Challenges Faced by Legal Resource Groups in South Asian Region' (1988) 30 *Journal of Indian Law Institute* 63.

[42] H. Soliman, 'A Critical Analysis of Legal Services for the Rural Poor and other Disadvantaged Groups,' in International Commission of Jurists, *Report of Seminars on Legal Services for the Rural Poor and Other Disadvantaged Groups* (Geneva, 1988), 47.

[43] A. Harding, 'Public Interest Groups, Public Interest Law and Development in Malaysia' [1992] *Third World Legal Studies*, 231, 232–3.

[44] H. Hershkoff & A. McCutcheon, 'Public Interest Litigation: An International Perspective', in M. McClymont & S. Golub (eds), *op.cit.*

several test cases have been instituted before the courts so as to attract publicity, boost the morale of community groups, or as a delaying tactic.[45] There are elements of collective access to justice in many countries in the region, in some instances statute based.[46] By common consent, public interest litigation in India has been the most dramatic example; its procedural aspects are the focus of the following discussion.[47]

Procedurally, Indian public interest litigation represents a dramatic break with the traditional common law model, although in broad terms it can be thought of as the functional equivalent of the multiparty or class action.[48] In terms of access to justice a public interest suit can be initiated by a simple letter addressed to the court, rather than by filing a written claim; hence the term the 'epistolary jurisdiction'.[49] Public interest litigation has swept away the doctrine of standing, which demands that a litigant have a direct interest in the proceedings being instituted. Any member of the public who is not a 'busybody' is able to assert diffuse, collective and meta-individual rights such as that to a healthy environment.[50] Petitioners are permitted to represent those who are not free to approach the court directly by reason of poverty, helplessness or disability or socially or economically disadvantaged position.[51] Public interest groups, lawyers, academics, journalists, and individuals have been among the petitioners recognized by the court.[52] A further procedural

---

[45] A. Harding & A. Sharom, *op.cit.*, 10–11, 12, 14, 25.

[46] As well as references cited elsewhere in this chapter see D. Harland, 'Collective Access to Justice—Some Perspectives from Asia and the Pacific' (1989–90) 6 *Chulalongkorn Law Review* 126.

[47] For elsewhere see Mansoor Khan, *Public Interest Litigation: Growth of the Concept and its Meaning in Pakistan* (Karachi, 1993); M. Amir-ul Islam, 'A Review of Public Interest Litigation Experiences in South Asia', and A. Mahmudur Rahman, 'Existing Avenues for Public Interest Litigation in Bangladesh', both in S. Hossain, S. Malik, & B. Musa (eds), *op.cit.*; N. Ahmed, *Litigating in the Name of the People: Stresses and Strains of the Development of Public Interest Litigation in Bangladesh* (University of London, PhD thesis, 1998); World Bank, *Taming Leviathan. Reforming Governance in Bangla Desh* (Washington DC, 2002), 26–8; S. Rachagan & M. Jain (eds), *Public Interest Law* (Louvain, 1998); S. Millie, 'The Tempo Case', in T. Lindsey (ed.), *Indonesia, Law and Society* (Sydney, 1999).   [48] 79 above.

[49] Substantively there must be a violation of a fundamental right, since public interest litigation (PIL) is founded on the constitution. There is a great deal of writing about Indian PIL, e.g. G. Peiris, 'Public Interest Litigation in the Indian Subcontinent: Current Dimensions' (1991) 40 *ICLQ* 66; Rajeev Dhavan, *op.cit.*, 14–22; S. Sorabjee, 'Obliging Government to Control Itself: Recent Developments in Indian Administrative Law' [1994] *PL* 39; K. Bhatia, *Judicial Activism and Social Change* (New Delhi, 1990); C.D. Cunningham, 'Public Interest Litigation in Indian Supreme Court: A Study in the Light of American Experience' (1987) 29 *Journal of Indian Law Institute* 494; S. Rizvi, *Public Interest Litigation. Liberty and Justice for All* (Delhi, 1991); S. Tripathi, *The Human Face of the Supreme Court of India* (Varanasi, 1993); S. Susman, 'Distant Voices in the Courts of India: Transformation of Standing in Public Interest Litigation' (1994) 13 *Wisc.Int'l.L.J.* 57; S. Ahuja, *People, Law and Justice* (New Delhi, 1997), vol.1 and 2; M. Jain, 'The Supreme Court and Fundamental Rights', in S. Verma (ed.), *Fifty Years of the Supreme Court of India* (New Delhi, 2000), 76–86; S. Sathe, *Judicial Activism in India* (Oxford, 2002).

[50] *S.P. Gupta v Union of India*, AIR 1982 SC 149, 192.

[51] *ibid.*; *Forward Construction Company v Prabhat Mandal*, AIR 1986 SC 391, 393.

[52] For example, *Upendra Baxi v State of UP* (1983) 2 SCC 308; *Sheela Barse v State of Maharashtra*, AIR 1983 SC 378. See Mool Chand Sharma, 'Court as an Institution for the Delivery of Socio-Economic Justice in India' in Ram Avtar Sharma (ed.), *Justice and Social Order in India* (New Delhi,

innovation has been in the conduct and outcome of litigation. The Supreme Court has emphasized the need to depart from an adversarial procedure 'which will make it possible for the poor and weak to bring the necessary material before the Court for the purpose of securing enforcement of their fundamental rights'.[53] The inquisitorial procedure which has replaced it has taken various forms. Special commissions have been appointed by the court to collect and determine facts and to propose and monitor remedies.[54] Interim remedies have been granted pending a decision on the factual and legal issues. Final remedies have been in the nature of legislative instruments with detailed proscriptions and penalties.[55]

Public interest litigation in India has not been without its critics. While the Supreme Court has acknowledged the need for judicial deference to executive, government, and parliament, its orders have sometimes demanded a reallocation of budgetary priorities.[56] Critics have contended that the Supreme Court lacks jurisdiction to frame such orders, indeed that in doing so the court impermissibly trenches on the role of government.[57] Another line of attack is that the Supreme Court has not met the high expectations created by this new jurisdiction, which has in turn engendered disillusionment and cynicism.[58] Public interest lawyers have also criticized the delay in getting cases on and the dismissive way that some judges have handled matters when they have reached the top of the queue. Even when successful, public interest lawyers point to the barriers placed in the way of implementing the resulting orders.[59] One recent assessment is that public interest litigation before the Supreme Court has achieved little, and practices condemned by the court continue unabated.[60] From the outsider's perspective, however, whatever its practical limitations in particular cases, public interest litigation seems to have raised the profile of access to justice within the general population and achieved at least symbolic outcomes over a range of public policy issues from the operation of the police, the jails, and other public authorities, through the location and environmental impact of industry, to the treatment of child labourers.

1984), 37–8; A. Perry, 'Lawyers in Urban Development: Providing a Means to an End?', *Law, Social Justice & Global Development (LGD)* 2001 (2). http://elj.warwick.ac.uk/global/issue/2001-2/perry.html.

53 *Bandhua Mukti Morcha v Union of India*, AIR 1984 SC 802, 815.

54 e.g., *M.C. Mehta v Union of India*, AIR 1987 SC 965 (the Sri Ram Fertilizers Gas Leak case); *Olga Tellis v Bombay Municipal Corp.*, AIR 1986 SC 180 (the Bombay Pavement Dwellers case); *Vishal Jeet v Union of India*, AIR 1990 SC 1412.

55 See also *Lakshmi Kant Pandey v Union of India*, AIR 1984 SC 469; *Vishaka v State of Rajasthan*, [1997] INSC 701. See U. Baxi, 'The Avatars of Indian Judicial Activism: Explorations in the Geographies of [In]Justice', in S. Verma & K. Kumar (eds.), *op.cit.*

56 e.g., *State of Himachal Pradesh v V.R. Sharma*, AIR 1986 SC 847.

57 See, e.g., Bakhshish Singh, 'Law in India and Weaker Sections—A Judicial Perspective,' in Ram Autar Sharma (ed.), *op.cit.*

58 U. Baxi, 'The Avatars of Indian Judicial Activism', in S. Verma & K. Kumar (eds), *Fifty Years of the Supreme Court of India* (Delhi, 2002).

59 Madu Kishmar, 'Public Interest Litigation', *Manushi*, No 81, March–April 1994, 11.

60 A. Shourie, *Courts and their Judgments* (Delhi, 2001).

Alternative dispute resolution

If by ADR is meant dispute resolution 'alternative' to the mainstream courts, then it takes various forms. Unlike Britain, where small claims courts are part of the ordinary court machinery,[61] elsewhere they are physically separate, with their own rules and different procedures. Malaysia and Singapore have legislated for separate small claims courts for matters such as defective goods, repayment of money lent and small debts. Legal representation is forbidden.[62] The Singapore small claims court permits electronic filing and conducts evening hearings. When ADR is discussed these days, however, informal proceedings or mediation, rather than tribunals or new courts are taken as its archetypal form. Conciliation procedures have long been established, even in colonial times, to handle industrial and labour matters.[63] Mediation procedures have been adopted in a number of countries. One strand is ADR encouraged by courts, along the lines adopted in Britain and North America.[64] Another strand is community-based mediation, which brings us to informal justice.

Informal justice, that is justice removed from the panoply of mainstream courts and similar dispute-resolving mechanisms, exists in all societies. In broad terms it can be either unofficial or state-sponsored law. Unofficial law ranges from the folk law of, say, an Indonesian village;[65] through the caste ('jati') panchayats of India, which might have considerable territorial scope;[66] to the rules and sanctions operated by trade associations or chambers of commerce. In many societies unofficial law is more important than formal justice; in that sense the term informal justice is a misnomer in suggesting something subsidiary. Unofficial law facilitates access to justice. Depending on the power configurations, unofficial law might be much more user-friendly and accessible than the official machinery of justice, which is light years away from the experiences of ordinary people.[67] However, there is the evident danger to be guarded against that unofficial law may reinforce the power of a local elite and existing patterns of informal influence, to the detriment of the disadvantaged.

State-sponsored informal justice has obvious attractions to policymakers: relative cheapness, wide geographic dispersal, and a lack of technicality in its procedures and orders. However, access to justice pursued through more informal

---

[61] 168–73 below.

[62] e.g. Ho Peng Kee, 'Small Claims Process: The Singapore Experience' (1988) 7 *CJQ* 329. See www.smallclaims.gov.sg

[63] e.g. P.G. Lim, 'Malaysia', in M. Pryles (ed.), *Dispute Resolution in Asia* (The Hague, 1997), 160. See 71 above.

[64] C. Abraham, 'Alternative Dispute Resolution in Malaysia' (1998) 1 *Int.Arb.LR* 235. See 173 below.

[65] K. von Benda-Beckmann, *The Broken Stairways to Consensus* (Dordrecht, 1984).

[66] U. Baxi, 'People's Law in India—The Hindu Society', in Masaji Chiba (ed.), *Asian Indigenous Law* (London, 1986) 235 ff.

[67] R. Green, 'Bureaucracy and Law and Order Have Something to Be Said about and for Them', in J. Faundez (ed.), *Law and Good Government* (London, 1996).

settings than the mainstream courts throws up immediate problems. What is the relationship with the formal system, and to what extent is it a mask for an unacceptable extension of state or other power? How informal is the informal system and is the informality a trap for the citizen who finds that more assistance is required than anticipated? Does informal justice compromise the individual's rights either because it is inferior in quality or because the nature of its decision making overrides legal rights to an unacceptable degree?[68]

There are many examples of state-sponsored informal justice in the region.[69] Let us briefly examine the experience in the Indian sub-continent, starting with India. There the British used the pre-colonial panchayats as units of local government and as simple judicial tribunals. Developments varied between provinces and overall did not fulfil expectations. However, in some places the panchayats handled considerable volumes of civil disputes.[70] For this reason some writers have said that they were based on the traditional dispute-resolving mechanisms of village elders. Since Independence Article 40 of the Indian Constitution has obliged the states to organize village panchayats and in the immediate post-Independence period there was a great burst of activity. However, factionalism and corruption led to a significant loss of faith in the panchayats as organs of local government, but the Seventy-Third Amendment to the constitution in 1992 has led to a revival in their fortunes.

In the post-Independence period nyaya panchayats were constituted as distinct bodies on the judicial side as a consequence of the separation of powers demanded by Article 50 of the constitution. Nyaya panchayats were established for a group of villages, were staffed by lay elected members, adopted an informal procedure and forbade legal representation (although in civil matters representation by an agent was sometimes permitted). Like the courts, fees were imposed (albeit minor), statutory rather than indigenous norms were imposed, and execution could be levied. The volume of cases was considerable and there were delays. Poor resourcing was at the root of many of the nyaya panchayats' problems. Despite support for them in the Bhagwati Committee's Report on *National Judicare: Equal Justice—Social Justice* (1977), the states in which they were established gradually wound them up.[71]

Yet the pressure on the formal court system in India demanded a functional equivalent of the nyaya panchayats. One informal mechanism has been the *lok*

[68] e.g. R. Abel, 'The Contradictions of Informal Justice', in R. Abel (ed.), *The Politics of Informal Justice* (New York, 1982); H. Genn, 'Tribunals and Informal Justice' (1993) 56 *MLR* 393.

[69] On state-sponsored informal justice at local level in Vietnam and the Philippines: *Legal Empowerment: Advancing Good Governance and Poverty Reduction*, (Law and policy Reform at the Asian Development Bank 2001, Manila, 2001), 47.

[70] H. Tinker, *Foundations of Local Self-Government in India, Pakistan and Burma* (London, 1954), 197 ff.

[71] P.C. Mathur, 'Re-modelling Panchayati Raj Institutions in India', in R.B. Jain (ed.), *Panchayati Raj* (New Delhi, 1981), 178. See generally, U. Baxi, 'Nyaya Panchayats: Experimentation in Legal Access for Village Population', in U. Baxi (ed.), *The Crisis of the Indian Legal System* (New Delhi, 1982). (This paper, written with Marc Galanter, has appeared in various other collections.) cf. Bangladesh's Village Courts Ordinance, Ord.LXI of 1976.

adalat (people's court). *Lok adalats* have been operating in some areas over a long period.[72] In his fascinating accounts of the Rangpur *lok adalat*, Professor Upendra Baxi describes its considerable caseload and the wide, popular support it enjoyed. He also outlines its multifunctional character: in addition to conflict management it acted as an ombudsman, performed invigilatory functions with regard to the behaviour of public officials, provided a focal point for mobilization against injustice, assisted people to prepare representations to, and obtain benefits from, the authorities, guided people with regard to their rights in relation to land and tax and performed a record-keeping role.

More recently the establishment of *lok adalats* has been fostered by bodies such as the Committee for Implementing Legal Aid Schemes (which is chaired by a sitting judge of the Supreme Court). The *lok adalats*, ordinarily comprising a retired judge, a lawyer and maybe also a social worker, mediate disputes in a non-technical manner. If there is no settlement, cases can revert to the formal system. The *lok adalats* have generally been organized by state or district legal aid or advice authorities. Justice A.M. Ahmadi describes their role as follows:

The date and place of holding a *lok adalat* are fixed about a month or so in advance. The date so fixed is, generally, a Saturday or a Sunday or some other holiday so that normal court work is not disrupted. Information about the holding of a *lok adalat* is given wide publicity through press, posters and, where possible, through radio, TV and cinema slides. Before a *lok adalat* is held, its organizers request the presiding officers of the various local courts to scrutinize cases pending in their courts which, in their opinion, are eminently fit for a negotiated settlement. Once the cases are identified, parties to the dispute are motivated by law students, para-legals and social workers to settle their disputes through *lok adalats*. By way of encouragement, the motivators are given transportation and other out of pocket expenses, food packets on the day of the *lok adalat* and also letters of appreciation but no remuneration, since the emphasis is on the system being service-oriented.[73]

Lok adalats have been most successful with motor accident claims, revenue matters and minor criminal matters, but less so with family disputes. *Lok adalats* have also handled disputes consequential on economic change, for example land claims:

In one Lok Adalat at Visakhapatnam, claims for additional compensation of about 25,000 villagers whose lands were acquired for a steel plant, were settled. Similarly, about 40,000 land acquisition cases arising out of three irrigation projects were settled in Andhra Pradesh recently. Claims of 9046 small cane growers and 1186 workmen of sick sugar factories taken over by the State Government were settled at a single Lok Adalat and payment to the tune of Rs. 12.33 million was made.[74]

---

[72] U. Baxi, 'From Takrar to Karar: The Lok Adalat at Rangpur—A Preliminary Study' (1976) 10 *J.Const'l. & Parl. Studies* 52; U. Baxi, 'Popular Justice, Participatory Development and Power Politics: The Lok Adalat in Turmoil', in A. Allott & G. Woodman (eds), *People's Law and State Law* (Dordrecht, 1985), 184.

[73] Justice A.M. Ahmadi, 'Arbitration and Alternative Forms of Justice', *Indo-British Legal Forum* (unpublished papers, London, 1992), vol. 2, 84.   [74] *ibid.*, 86.

While great store has been placed in *lok adalats* by those from the Chief Justice of India down, they have not taken root in all states, nor have they always had a significant impact on overall delay in the courts. Critics have also said that cases which would otherwise have been settled have been held over for a *lok adalat*, to give a false impression of achievement, and that the community representatives on *lok adalats* tend to remain passive.[75]

Permanent *lok adalats* are now formally constituted under the Legal Services Authorities Act 1987 (as amended in 2002). Under the Act, each state must organize permanent *lok adalats*, which have jurisdiction to decide (failing a compromise) on civil, minor criminal, or public utility disputes. After an application is made to a permanent *lok adalat* no party can invoke the jurisdiction of the court. The permanent *lok adalat* is not bound by the ordinary rules of civil procedure or evidence but decides in accordance with natural justice, objectivity, and other principles of justice, and an award operates as an enforceable decision of the court.[76] The central government and the Reserve Bank of India have advised banks to use the *lok adalats* for compromise settlements of their outstanding loans; the Bank issued guidelines in May 2001 for making use of *lok adalats* to settle disputes involving outstanding amounts to Rs. 5 lakhs.[77] In one assessment, *lok adalats* are a form of 'debased informalism', which provide an official process for claimants to secure a part of their entitlements, without the aggravation, extortionate expense, inordinate delay or tormenting uncertainty of court processes.[78]

Concerted efforts in respect of community-based mediation have been made in Sri Lanka, where it has been a prerequisite to litigation. The Conciliation Boards Act No. 10 of 1958 was intended for the amicable settlement of village disputes.[79] The aim of its main proponent has been summarized as follows:

The willingness of the rural disputants to rush into the courts for even the most frivolous causes, and the corresponding inability of the court system to cope with the flood of litigation, bred public contempt for the judicial process. One way of protecting the courts from such pressures was to establish a screening mechanism which would shut out those controversies amenable to amicable resolution. What was uppermost in [his] mind was the need for an efficient conflict-resolving mechanism to subdue the spirit of litigiousness which seemed to haunt the rural populace.[80]

[75] e.g. Sujan Singh & P. Diwan, *Legal Aid. Human Right to Equality* (New Delhi, 1996), 283 ff; Rajeev Dhavan, 'The Unbearable Lightness of India's Legal Aid Programme', in S. Hossain, S. Malik.& B. Musa (eds), Public Interest Litigation in South Asia (Dhaka, 1997), 158–9.

[76] e.g. M. Rao, *Public Interest Litigation in India. Legal Aid and Lok Adalats*, 2nd edn (Lucknow, 2004).

[77] Government of India, Ministry of Law and Justice, 'President Promulgates Ordinance for Recovery of Debts', Press Release, 22 August 2002.

[78] M. Galanter & J. Krishnan, 'Debased Informalism: Lok Adalats and Legal Rights in Modern India', in E. Jensen & T. Heller (eds), *Beyond Common Knowledge. Empirical Approaches to the Rule of Law* (Stanford, 2003), 115. See also in this volume R. Moog, 'Democratization of Justice: The Indian Experiment with Consumer Forums'.

[79] cf. Bangladesh's Conciliation of Disputes (Municipal Areas) Ordinance No. V of 1969.

[80] N. Tiruchelvam, 'Competing Ideologies of Conflict Resolution in Sri Lanka, a Multi-Religious Society', in Masaji Chiba (ed.), *op.cit.*, 179.

The success of the Conciliation Boards Act in the rural context meant it was extended five years later to the island as a whole. Unless a certificate was obtained from the chair of the local conciliation board to say that there was no possibility of a settlement, a court had no jurisdiction to entertain a matter. But membership of the boards became political, the legal profession resented its exclusion from them, and delays in the issue of certificates and the inappropriateness of some disputes for conciliation led to the discrediting of the system.[81] Its eventual abandonment came with a change of government. Soon after, however, a prominent committee of judges and lawyers in Sri Lanka called for the reintroduction of conciliation in a specified list of matters 'to considerably curtail the law's delays'.[82] The Mediation Boards Act No. 72 of 1988 answered that call: under it community-based mediators consider certain criminal offences and civil disputes (with some exceptions, for example if one of the parties is the state). Over 200 local mediation boards have been appointed throughout Sri Lanka, which mediate some 250,000–300,000 cases a year at village level. Sri Lankan mediation is considered effective, complementary to the formal justice system, with high rates of compliance and resulting in reduced court delay.[83]

Mediation in the specific area of debt recovery operated in Sri Lanka since the 1930s. Widespread distress caused to agriculturalists at that time led to the establishment of the Debt Conciliation Board.[84] A substantial increase in its work in the 1980s was due to a propaganda campaign carried out with the help of the Agrarian Services Department to popularize the activities of the Board at the rural level; most applicants were farmers and agriculturalists. Debtors in difficulty applied to the Board to effect a settlement of debts owed. The position was then frozen until the final hearing when the Board proposed a settlement, for example, repayment by instalments, extension of the repayment period, or reduction of interest. In three quarters of cases the parties accepted the Board's settlement proposal. If a creditor refused to accept the Board's proposal, the Board issued a certificate to the debtor. If the creditor then took legal proceedings, the debtor produced the certificate. The court could then grant a period of up to ten years for the debtor to pay, reduce the interest, or refuse the creditor costs. The courts applied the Board's proposals in the great majority of cases. However, there were serious limitations on the Board's jurisdiction. It did not have any jurisdiction over government-sponsored banks or institutions operating as lending or financing agencies. The justification was that the law was enacted to protect debtors from unconscionable moneylenders and state institutions were not in this category.[85] Moreover, there was the important limitation that there be a mortgage

---

[81] J. Canaga Retna, 'The Legal System of Sri Lanka', in K. Redden (ed.), *Modern Legal Systems* (Buffalo, 1985), 9, 770–1.   [82] *Seminar on the Administration of Justice* (Colombo, 1984), 21.

[83] S. Brown, C. Cervenak, & D. Fairman, *Alternative Dispute Resolution Practitioners' Guide* (Washington, DC, USAID Centre for Democracy and Governance, 1998), Appendix B (Sri Lanka Case Study).

[84] Debt Conciliation Ordinance, Chapter 91, as amended by Act No. 20 of 1983.

[85] *Report of the Bank of Ceylon Commission*, Session Paper No. xxvii, 1968, 36.

or conditional transfer of immovables. The jurisdiction of the Board was set at a time when the problem of small debtors was confined largely to agriculturalists. Since then many debtors incurred financial difficulties in relation to movables such as household goods and vehicles.

There has been a particular success in Bangladesh in adopting traditional mediation techniques (shalish) to advance women's rights and to resolve their disputes. Traditional shalish tended to be male dominated, was marked by legal ignorance and influenced by patronage ties or even corruption.[86] However, the Madaripur Legal Aid Association, which operates in that part of Bangladesh, began using shalish in the early 1980s, partly out of a frustration with the expense and delay of the courts. With donor assistance it expanded its services in Madaripur and began training mediation committee members in other parts of the country. Clients approach the association through its village-based mediation workers or its branches in the towns, and a shalish is organized to which the client and opposing party are invited. Most clients are women with marriage-based problems; low-income farmers with land disputes are the next largest group. The association has recruited respected community leaders to conduct mediations, but also trained a number of women mediators.

The actual shalish is often a loud and passionate event in which disputants, relatives, [mediation committee] members, and even uninvited community members congregate to express their thoughts and feelings. Additional observers—adults and children alike— gather in the room's doorway and outside. More than one exchange of opinion may occur simultaneously. Calm discussions explode into bursts of shouting and even laughter or tears. All of this typically takes place in a crowded schoolroom or other public space, sweltering most of the year, often with the noise of other community activities filtering in from outside. The number of participants and observers may range from a few dozen to well over one hundred. The shalish for a given dispute may stretch over several months and a number of sessions. These may be supplemented by discussions and negotiations between the sessions.[87]

The Association reports that 80 percent of disputes are successfully resolved with mediation, although this may be because expectations are low: a woman resorting to mediation rarely expects equal treatment and if her husband stops beating her, takes her back, or pays minimal maintenance that is enough. The Association backs up mediation settlements with selective litigation in the courts to enforce them.

An important argument in favour of ADR is that it avoids the costs and delays of court-based litigation.[88] ADR works more quickly and more cheaply, and if significant numbers of cases are diverted to ADR the courts ought to be able to process those remaining more quickly. Certainly in India, Sri Lanka, and

---

[86] E. Jansen, *Rural Bangladesh. Competition for Scarce Resources*, reprinted edn. (Dhaka, 1999).

[87] S. Golub, 'From the Village to the University: Legal Activism in Bangladesh', in M. McClymont & S. Golub (eds), *op.cit.*, 138. See also S. Brown, C. Cervenak & D. Fairman, *op.cit.*, Appendix B (Bangladesh Case Study).   [88] 71–8 above.

Bangladesh informal and community-based ADR appears to have had a positive effect. ADR might also widen access to justice: disadvantaged groups who would probably never approach lawyers or the courts might use ADR. The experience in India, Sri Lanka, and Bangladesh again provides an example.[89] Mediation might also have a role in meeting specialist needs, for example for a government ministry needing to settle land disputes or, as in Sri Lanka, addressing agricultural debt. Just what makes successful ADR, however, needs careful thought—the type of cases, at which point they should be mediated and whether mediation should be backed by an adjudicative capacity. It is crucial to appreciate that what on the surface seems to be a very similar mechanism for resolving disputes is in fact performing a quite different function in different societies.[90]

Economic Access

Economic access is designed to facilitate legal remedies for business. The intention is to make the legal system more responsive to the needs of a market economy. That not only demands the introduction of modern commercial codes to under-pin transactions but building institutional capacity with an efficient and transpar-ent court system and an independent and well-trained judiciary. Economic access has been promoted largely because businesses face similar barriers to access as individuals, although a concern with judicial hostility to business interests has also been articulated. Commercial arbitration offers one answer and is briefly mentioned. At its core, however, have been the problems faced by banks and other financial institutions in having credit repaid. With so many bad loans on their books a cloud has hung over the solvency of many banks in the region.[91] We will examine two aspects of how states in the region have furthered economic access. The first is relatively straightforward, the establishment of one type of special court. The second is in its infancy and involves state sanctioning of self-help by banks and other financial institutions to recover against the security (collateral) they have taken from borrowers for the credit advanced.

Commercial arbitration

Commercial arbitration has a long pedigree in Asia, although in the immediate post-Independence era it was little used in some countries, being seen as Western domination.[92] Too often when it was used it led to an appeal to the courts;

---

[89] On community-based conciliation in the Philippines: V. Lazatin, 'The Philippines', in M. Pryles (ed.), *Dispute Resolution in Asia* (The Hague, 1997), 175.

[90] D. Roebuck, 'Cultural Differences and Mediation: An Introduction' [2002] *Asian Dispute Res.* 135.

[91] Chapter 9 below.

[92] But the Indian Council of Arbitration was founded in 1965, jointly funded by the government and Federation of Indian Chambers of Commerce and Industry.

arbitration laws based on the UNCITRAL model law address this problem and have choked off appeals.[93] Arbitration has become increasingly popular because of delays in the courts and sometimes a perceived anti-business orientation in their decision making.[94] Arbitration clauses are often inserted in insurance policies, building and construction contracts, and joint venture agreements, although not as much in loan and credit agreements. Apart from the speedier resolution of disputes which arbitration might bring, the inclusion of arbitration clauses in commercial contracts has been boosted by the expertise at places such as the regional arbitration centres in Malaysia and the International Centre in Singapore.[95] The Asian Development Bank has encouraged arbitration as a fair and efficient method of reducing the risks associated with financial contracts.[96]

India modernized its arbitration law in 1996, with an Arbitration and Conciliation Act based on the UNCITRAL model law. Indonesia's Arbitration Law No. 30 of 1999 drew only partly on the model law, and many provisions of the previous legislation are still reflected in the law. Many countries in the region are parties to the New York Convention on the Recognition and Enforcement of Foreign Arbitral Awards of 1958. Unfortunately experience in Indonesia and elsewhere demonstrates that commercial arbitration can be constrained by local protectionism. Foreign investors have their reasonable expectations undermined as local courts have sometimes entertained appeals against arbitrations and also refused to enforce foreign awards despite their obligation to do so under the 1958 Convention.[97]

Special courts

India followed Pakistan and Bangladesh in constituting special debt recovery courts. The courts are designed to further economic access. Their adoption can be attributed in part to pressure from outside these countries, notably from the World Bank. These special courts enable banks and financial institutions to bypass the great delays of the ordinary courts and they offer an expedited form of relief to those seeking the recovery of credit advanced. Economic justifications for these courts are to improve the balance sheets of local banks and financial institutions and to release unproductive financial assets for reinvestment. These courts are seen as necessary to create an environment more favourable to economic growth and foreign investment.

[93] e.g. V. Taylor & M. Pryles, 'The Cultures of Dispute Resolution in Asia', in M. Pryles (ed.), *op.cit.*, 19–20.   [94] 269–70 below.

[95] e.g. G. Chandru, 'The Growth and Development of International Commercial Arbitration in Singapore' (2003) 6 Int.A.LR 95; 'Leaving Colonial Arbitration Laws Behind: Southeast Asia's Move into the International Arbitration Arena' (2000) 16 *Arbit.Int'l* 297; D. Howell, 'An Overview of Arbitration in Asia' [2002] *Asian DR* 131.

[96] *Secured Transactions Law Reform in Asia: Unleashing the Potential of Collateral* (Law and Policy Reform at the Asian Development Bank 2000, Manila, 2000), 91–2.

[97] 283 below; *Secured Transactions Law Reform in Asia: Unleashing the Potential of Collateral, op.cit.*, 94–5.

The Indian debt recovery legislation of 1993 had a long gestation. Concern stretches back several decades about the infection of the portfolios of banks and other financial institutions by so-called sick industries. The Sick Industries Industrial Companies (Special Provisions) Act 1985 constituted the Board for Industrial and Financial Rehabilitation set up with the mandate of reviving sick industries. At the same time as recommending this legislation, the Tiwari Committee spoke of the need for special courts to avoid the law's delays:

Large amounts advanced by the banks and financial institutions to defaulting industrial units and other defaulting borrowers are locked up due to the delays under the existing legal procedure and process for recovery. The Civil Courts are burdened with diverse types of cases. Recovery of dues by the banks and financial institutions is not given any priority by the Civil Courts. The progress more often gets bogged down through interlocutory petitions and stay orders from higher courts. Due to the delays involved in such elaborate process the interests of the banks and financial institutions are very often adversely affected. Attempts will, therefore, have to be made to reduce the impact of the arduous procedures presently obtaining for the recovery of dues insofar as the banks and financial institutions are concerned . . . In the light of what is stated above, it is recommended that the Central Government may set up a class of tribunals which would in a summary way but following the principles of natural justice, adjudicate finally, within a time-bound schedule, all matters in relation to recovery of dues of the banks and financial institutions. These tribunals should be manned by persons having specialized knowledge in the functioning of banks, financial institutions and industry.[98]

Draft legislation was prepared by the Vesuvalla Committee in 1986, further impetus was given by the Narasimham and Hegde Committees, and finally the legislation was adopted in 1993.

The Recovery of Debts Due to Banks and Financial Institutions Act 1993—to give it its full title—constitutes special tribunals with the sole jurisdiction over all actions to recover debts due to banks and financial institutions. Cases of this nature pending before the ordinary courts, of which there were believed to be some 10 million, were transferred to the tribunals.[99] Presided over by lawyers, the tribunals can make a determination by expedited procedure that a debt is owing. Thereupon the recovery officers appointed under the Act are empowered to appoint receivers over a debtor's property, to attach and sell any property of the debtor, and to arrest and detain debtors.[100] Appeals to a special appellate tribunal are possible. The legislation has survived constitutional challenge,[101] although it has still not met the full expectations of some of its promoters.[102] Pakistan and Bangladesh also have special debt recovery courts operating. In Sri Lanka the Presidential Banking Commission recommended a new commercial court which

---

[98] *Report of the Committee to Examine the Legal and Other Difficulties Faced by Banks and Financial Institutions in Rehabilitation of Sick Industrial Undertakings* (Bombay, 1984), 77, 79.

[99] Recovery of Debts due to Banks and Financial Institutions Act 1993, s 31; V. Shroff, 'The Indian Debt Recovery Act', *Journal of International Banking Law*, vol. 1, 1995, 29.

[100] 1993 Act, s 25.   [101] *Union of India v Delhi Bar Association* (2002) 4 SCC 275.

[102] See 288 below.

would have jurisdiction over matters of a commercial nature and over actions under the debt recovery laws.[103] This is a half-way house to a special court.

Clearly, then, special courts like these debt recovery courts facilitate access to justice. They might also have had an important shock value for borrowers, inducing the recalcitrant to repay more diligently. In considering whether they contribute to good government we must start with the proposition that there is nothing objectionable to special courts or special lists per se.[104] They have been established in many jurisdictions for many purposes. Such arrangements permit specialization by judges, promote greater consistency and expertise of decision making in particular areas, allow more authoritative decisions on certain questions of law, and allow certain types of issues to be progressed with greater speed. The decision to establish a special tribunal should turn on a detailed consideration of the benefits and costs. Special tribunals have costs, for example the extra resources needed to administer them. The major cost is that of equity—some litigants gain over others. Ought not the benefits gained, such as reduced delay for the cases handled, to accrue to other cases as well? Might not the establishment of special courts for powerful interests such as banks lessen the pressure which they would otherwise bring to bear on reform of the system as a whole? These issues would appear not always to have been properly argued in relation to the establishment of special debt recovery courts.

Self-help and security (collateral)

Professor Sally Falk Moore identifies three important qualities of self-help: it is undertaken in the name of right and is not simply for naked advantage; it is the intransigent side of conciliation, in that societies in which self-help is widely used normally have well-established conciliation procedures; and it will usually permit the mobilization of others in the individual's cause—thus she writes of the expansibility of certain disputes and the containment of others.[105]

---

[103] *Third Interim Report of the Presidential Commission on Finance and Banking and Debt Recovery Legislation* (Colombo, 1992), 24–5. This recommendation has a long history. In 1985 the Debt Recovery Committee recommended the establishment of a separate District Court in Colombo to be designated the Commercial Credit Court. It would be available to approved credit agencies, and its procedures would enable recovery of debts within six months (*Report of the Committee appointed by the Hon. The Minister of Justice Dr Nissanka Wijeyeratne*, 1985). The proposal attracted a great deal of opposition, especially from the bar. Subsequently, a special committee recommended the establishment of an additional court in Colombo to hear matters of a commercial nature: *Final Report of the Committee Appointed to Examine the Establishment of a Special Court for Commercial Matters* (Chairman: S.J. Kadirgamar QC). The District Judge of Colombo would refer to that court all 'commercial' matters. Then after several other twists and turns—including pressure from the World Bank—the Presidential Banking Commission reported.

[104] See R. Dreyfuss, 'Forums of the Future: The Role of Specialized Courts in Resolving Business Disputes' (1995) 61 *Brooklyn L.R.* 1; J. Widner, 'Are Specialized Courts the Right Approach to Effective Adjudication of Commercial Disputes in Developing Areas?' (unpublished paper, World Bank, 2000); J. Plotnikoff & R. Woolfson, *Review of the Effectiveness of Specialist Courts in Other Jurisdictions*, Department for Constitutional Affairs, Research Reports 3/05 (London, 2005).

[105] Sally Falk Moore, *Law as Process* (London, 1978), 99.

In many cases, lenders will not advance credit without security (collateral), so that in the event of default they can recoup from the debtor's assets. Typically, security will be taken over a debtor's land (including the buildings on it, and any plant and machinery) and over other business assets such as work in progress, stock in trade, receivables, and intellectual property. A crucial issue is whether on default the law permits lenders to proceed against the assets over which security has been taken without having to obtain a court order. If lenders can resort to self-help in this way it short-circuits any delay and expense involved in litigation and also curtails the opportunities for the debtor who would wrongfully dissipate assets.

In the common law, self-help for creditors and others seeking money payment has always had a place, although it has been more frowned on in civil law systems. Self-help in relation to security is the most important example. Common law courts have responded with varying degrees of enthusiasm to some of the self-help remedies and many have been diminished in scope by judicial attrition and legislative policy.[106] In South and South-east Asia this has been the case in common law jurisdictions in relation to security. It seems that this is because of a sympathy for debtors over creditors, but also because of a fear that self-help might not be socially containable. Furthering economic access to justice has led, however, to a revival of the self-help idea. As long ago as 1977 the Banking Laws Committee appointed by the Indian Government recommended that banks and financial institutions should have the power to enforce security extra-judicially. Its argument was that the general law relating to enforcing security was developed at a time when unscrupulous moneylenders were important suppliers of credit but that this had ceased to be appropriate when banks and other financial institutions were providing credit for development purposes. Moneylenders were quite rightly prohibited from exercising the right of private sale without the intervention of the court, but the continuation of this restriction with reference to banks and other financial institutions 'affects adversely the flow of credit and encourages protracted and vexatious litigation which comes in the way of expeditious recovery. . . .' The Committee concluded:

The power of sale without the intervention of the court should be allowed to all banks and certain notified financing institutions and this should be available to them with reference to all types of advances other than those made against the security of agricultural land and should be available independent of the form of the mortgage in their favour.[107]

The Committee confined its recommendations to banks and certain financial institutions on grounds of simplicity, but also because it felt that these bodies could be trusted not to abuse the power. Borrowers should be given suitable notice

---

[106] R. Pennington, 'Receiverships and Extrajudicial Remedies', in R. Cranston (ed.), *Banks and Remedies* (London, 1992) 101; Enterprise Act 2002, s 250.

[107] Indian Government Banking Laws Committee, *Report on Real Property Security Law* (New Delhi, 1977), 34.

before the secured party was entitled to sell the property without recourse to the court. The details of this aspect of self-help in India and elsewhere in the region is more conveniently told in Chapter 9.[108]

Conclusion

Access to justice is one aspect of good governance. While many disputes in modern societies are resolved extra-judicially, courts and court-like bodies exercising state power must be there as a backstop when this does not occur. To varying extents courts also have the function of determining norms so that disputes can then be settled 'in the shadow of the law'. Further, rights proclaimed by modern states must ultimately be enforceable, in some cases through judicial mechanisms, if they are not to be conceived of by the populace as illusory. So in various ways access to justice not only contributes to a peaceful society but to the rule of law and economic development.

Yet access to justice is a protean concept. This chapter has drawn an admittedly imprecise distinction between social and economic access. Both are necessary, it can be argued, to achieve the goals mentioned. In many societies the focus is quite rightly on social access, since the delays and expense of litigation are an obstacle to many individuals pursuing legal rights. Economic access has not been a pressing problem, since typically wealth and its correlates guarantee access to legal services and the courts. In the Asian sub-continent and in parts of South-east Asia, however, both social and economic access have not been achieved. The delays have been so great in India, or the courts so discouraging as in Indonesia, that even banks and financial institutions find the path to the courts barred.

The chapter has sketched some dimensions of the response to these access to justice problems. The attempted solutions for social access will be familiar; less so the measures addressing blockages to economic access. Yet it has been on the latter that bodies such as the World Bank have often focused, some would say at the expense of the total justice system and access for all.[109] Whatever the position in the past, international financial institutions such as the World Bank are now emphasizing as well the importance of social access to justice.[110] Their primary concern is promoting economic development. It is to what that entails, and in particular the role of law in facilitating it, that we return in Chapter 9.

[108] 281–82 below.

[109] P. McAuslan, 'Law, Governance and the Development of the Market: Practical Problems and Possible Solutions', in J. Faundez (ed.), *Good Government and Law* (Macmillan, 1996).

[110] e.g. Legal Vice Presidency, The World Bank, *Legal and Judicial Reform* (Washington, DC, 2002), 43–7; *Legal Empowerment: Advancing Good Governance and Poverty Reduction* (Law and Policy Reform at the Asian Development Bank 2001, Manila, 2001), esp. Parts II, V.

4

Courts

Inasmuch as writers on jurisprudence are concerned with what the civil courts do, their focus is on adjudication and law-making—matters such as the exercise of discretion in judicial decision making, resolving trouble, or hard cases, and the role of morality and policy arguments.[1] Another strand of writing, influenced in part by legal anthropology, places disputes centre stage: disputes or controversies which cannot be settled between the parties or their friends may be referred to a court. In this view the civil courts deal with disputes by the application of doctrine, a method of operation which distinguishes them from mediation and other alternative dispute resolution.[2] Influenced by the notion of politics as who gets what, when and how, a number of commentators have regarded the civil courts as part of the political process. This third approach focuses, for example, on how interest groups use the courts to attain their goals, just as they might use the legislature or the executive.[3] More radical writers see the civil courts as agencies of the state, reinforcing the position of commercial and property interests in society. One study, for instance, concludes: 'Effectively what the court is doing is continually re-stating the rules, re-stating those entitlements and obligations which constitute the legal basis of use rights ("property") in our society.'[4] Finally, lawyer-economists see the civil courts as performing allocative functions, as does the market, and examine matters such as the efficiency of the procedure used and the rules made.[5]

---

[1] The literature is vast: see, e.g., R. Dworkin, *Taking Rights Seriously* (London, 1977), esp. 81–149; N. MacCormick, *Legal Reasoning and Legal Theory* (Oxford, 1978); J. Bell, *Policy Arguments in Judicial Decisions* (Oxford, 1983); W. Lucy, *Understanding and Explaining Adjudication* (Oxford, 1999). See 133–6 below.

[2] Again, there is an academic industry: R. Abel, 'A Comparative Theory of Dispute Institutions in Society' (1973) 8 *L.&Soc.Rev.* 217; L. Nader & H. Todd (eds), *The Disputing Process* (New York, 1978); S. Roberts & M. Palmer, *Dispute Processes* (London, 1998) are examples. See 5, 71–8 above.

[3] 13 above. See also D. Woodhouse, 'The English Judges, Politics and the Balance of Power' (2003) 66 *MLR* 920.

[4] M. Cain, 'Where Are the Disputes? A Study of a First Instance Civil Court in the U.K.', in M. Cain & K. Kulcsar (eds), *Disputes and the Law* (Budapest, 1983), 130.

[5] G. Tullock, *Trials on Trial* (New York, 1980); P. Fenn & I. Vlachonikolis, 'Bargaining Behaviour by Defendant Insurers: An Economic Model' (1990) 14 *Geneva Papers on Risk and Insurance* 41; N. Rickman, *The Empirical Analysis of Litigation. A Survey of the Economics Literature*, Lord Chancellor's Department, Research Report No. 2/98 (London, 1998).

None of these approaches necessarily provides an answer, in broad terms, to the question of how civil courts work. Each may provide a persuasive account of particular aspects, and each may focus on critical or intellectually difficult parts of their operation. But none paints the whole picture—the matters going to civil courts, how they are handled, and with what result. This chapter attempts to do this. It adopts a 'systems' approach, examining the 'inputs' of the civil courts in England and Wales, then how decisions are made in relation to these inputs, before turning to the results of these decisions (the 'outputs').[6] The approach taken throws some light on the questions which the other approaches address, for example, the nature of rights in practice, how legal rules are applied, and the functions of law in society. Moreover, it identifies important areas in the operation of the civil courts of which there is presently a significant ignorance.

As institutions of the state, albeit independent of the executive and legislature, courts make authoritative decisions about certain matters presented to them. The social, political, and economic environment influences, indirectly, the nature of these matters. Granted this truism, the issues which arise for examination include how this environment produces particular 'inputs' for courts, and the nature of these and the character of those advancing them. Comparisons can then be made with the inputs of, say, the political system or the market. What happens to these inputs? First, they are converted into legal issues in accordance with procedural and substantive rules of law. Secondly, they are disposed of at different points and in different ways in the process of litigation. Whereas jurists concentrate on complex adjudication, in fact courts dispose of the majority of matters in a routine, mundane manner, or the parties settle a matter before—often well before—exhausting the legal process. The decisions of civil courts are not automatically implemented; enforcement may be necessary. In addition, there is the larger issue of the impact that decisions may have on other than those directly involved. Consideration of these aspects of court 'output' throw light on the courts' place in public policy.

Inputs

Courts operate within a particular social environment. Across societies, what are called courts do not necessarily handle the same matters. Within the one society, changes in the social environment may affect the civil courts.[7] Over the last 50 years, for example, changing social values have been at least partly responsible for

[6] cf. the systems analysis of political science, notably the seminal D. Easton, *A Framework for Political Analysis* (Chicago, 1965).

[7] S. Daniels, 'Ladders and Bushes: The Problem of Caseloads and Studying Court Activities over Time' (1984) *American Bar Foundation Research Journal* 751; L. Friedman & R. Percival, 'A Tale of Two Courts: Litigation in Alameda and San Benito Counties' (1976) 10 *L.&Soc.R.* 267; P. Vincent-Jones, 'Contract Litigation in England and Wales 1975–1991. Transformation in Business Disputing?' (1993) 12 *CJQ* 337.

the increasing number of applications involving families and children. It is well known that recession in the economy produces an upsurge in corporate restructuring and insolvency work. Even political change can produce a not inconsiderable volume of litigation, as with the increase in judicial review in recent decades with an expanding and activist state.[8] For convenience, this part eschews historical analyses to concentrate on the present-day inputs of the civil courts. The focus is on litigation, although the civil courts perform a range of administrative functions such as granting probate on wills to those properly entitled.[9] In particular, how do social and economic problems become grievances which in turn are taken to courts as legal proceedings? And who litigates what types of issues?

Sources of litigation

Ostensibly, the operation of the courts is based on the assumption that people know their rights and will take the initiative to enforce them if they expect to be successful. Success in these terms is immediate, by winning the case, or longer-term, by leading to greater pressure for change, for example through legislation, to build on or reverse a judgment. In this sense the courts parallel the 'free market', which assumes that self-interest will motivate rational activity. In fact, social and economic factors mediate legal action—for example the consciousness of rights, community and group norms, capacity, the nature of the relationship between the parties, the desire or otherwise for publicity, certainty of outcome, the type of problem (what is at stake, its complexity, its legal dimensions) and the perception of, and access to, legal assistance. To put it another way, before parties take legal action they must perceive that there is a problem, that the problem is capable of remedy, that the problem is sufficiently serious to justify doing something about it, that self-help is inappropriate, and that involving the law might offer a satisfactory solution. Because these prerequisites are not always satisfied, the result is that many problems are 'lumped', many claims abandoned, and many disputes compromised or avoided by the parties without outside assistance (let alone legal assistance).[10] For example, residents of an area affected by environmental decay might not conceptualize this as a problem but regard it as an aspect of life which must be tolerated. Consumers might not realize that a transaction has not satisfied legal requirements (for example, to be in writing) or not think it worthwhile,

---

[8] e.g. J. Jowell, 'Restraining the State: Politics, Principle and Judicial Review', in M. Freeman (ed.), *Law and Opinion at the End of the Twentieth Century* (Oxford, 1997).

[9] See Court Service, Courts and Tribunals Modernization Programme, *Review of Probate Business. A Consultation Paper* (London, 2002), 9–11, 13. The grant of probate assures those holding the assets of a deceased (e.g. banks) that the person to whom it is granted has legal authority to conduct the deceased's affairs.

[10] The classic analysis is W. Felstiner, R. Abel & A. Sarat, 'The Emergence and Transformation of Disputes' (1980–81) 15 *L.&Soc.R.* 631. See also J. FitzGerald, 'Grievances, Disputes and Outcomes' (1983) 1 *Law in Context* 25. cf. M. Baumgartner, 'Social Control in Suburbia', in D. Black (ed.), *Toward a General Theory of Social Control* (New York, 1984).

given the cost of an item or service, to do anything about it. A retailer might not want to engage in legal action against suppliers because of the risk of disturbing harmonious relations with them, and so might prefer to settle disputes by steps such as appropriate adjustments to price.

First, then, let us look at the issue of whether problems are perceived of as grievances, that is, as being the responsibility of someone else. In early 2004 the Legal Services Research Centre published its first national periodic survey of justiciable problems.[11] It drew on the methodology of the seminal *Paths to Justice* studies by Professor Hazel Genn and her colleagues.[12] Individuals were asked if they had experienced 'a problem' in the previous three and a half years which had been 'difficult to solve' in each of eighteen distinct categories: discrimination, consumer, employment, neighbours, owned housing, rented housing, homelessness, money/debt, welfare benefits, divorce, relationship breakdown, domestic violence, children, personal injury, clinical negligence, mental health, immigration, and unfair treatment by the police. For twelve of these categories respondents were presented with 'show cards' with detailed lists of problems and were then asked to indicate which of them, if any, matched their own problems. For example, listed problems relating to rented housing included difficulties in getting the landlord to make repairs, in obtaining repayment of a deposit, and eviction.[13] Of the 5,611 respondents, 36 per cent reported one or more non-trivial justiciable problems in the survey period.[14] The study then ranked the problems and found that consumer problems were reported most frequently (13 per cent of respondents), followed by those relating to noisy or anti-social neighbours (8 per cent), money and debt (8 per cent), employment (6 per cent), housing (owned or rented) (6 per cent), personal injury (4 per cent), and family breakdown (4 per cent). Rarely reported problems were those relating to unfair treatment by the police (2/3 per cent), homelessness (2/3 per cent), mental health (1/2 per cent) and immigration and nationality (1/3 per cent).[15] Naturally the figures represent the recall by individuals of certain problems and their willingness to reveal them to the interviewers. Importantly, the relative significance of problems which individuals identified had, as we will see, no necessary correlation with whether respondents pursued any legal remedies, in particular by going to court. With most problems there was an apparent lack of association with gender and ethnicity, but age, economic circumstances, and housing and tenure type had a significant influence in predicting many of the problems experienced.[16] The

[11] P. Pleasence, A. Buck, N. Balmer, A. O'Grady, H. Genn & M. Smith, *Causes of Action: Civil Law and Social Justice* (London, 2004) (hereafter *Causes of Action*).

[12] H. Genn, *Paths to Justice. What People Do and Think about Going to Law* (Oxford, 1999) (hereafter *Paths to Justice*). See also H. Genn & A. Paterson, *Paths to Justice Scotland* (Oxford, 2001); American Bar Foundation, *Legal Needs and Civil Justice* (Chicago, 1994).

[13] *Causes of Action*, 4. See also *Paths to Justice*, 21–2.

[14] *Causes of Action*, 9. (The comparable figure was 34 per cent in *Paths to Justice*.)

[15] *Causes of Action*, 13. (This broadly parallels *Paths to Justice*, 24.)

[16] *Causes of Action*, 15–29. See also *Paths to Justice*, 29–36.

proportion of respondents in vulnerable groups increased the more they reported problems.[17] This is confirmed by other research which shows that lone parents, as one vulnerable group, are more likely than other family types to experience justiciable problems and when they do those come in bigger groups (family, debt, domestic violence, welfare benefits and so on).[18]

Now some such grievances may be better forgotten or resolved informally. However, it seems fair to say that there are a substantial number of grievances, objectively significant, which although they could be are not pursued. In some cases people simply decide to 'lump it' because they do not think anything can be done, it is not sufficiently important, someone else has done something or it might damage an ongoing relationship.[19] In other cases they want to pursue a grievance, but do not know whom to blame. One study attributed the lower rate of personal injury litigation in England compared to the United States to a 'blaming gap' caused by cultural factors.[20] Of course, people's attitude to blaming is also influenced by the legal system as well as the other way round.[21] People may have ambivalent attitudes to those whom they can blame, may oscillate about whom to blame, or may discover they have to blame someone or transfer their blame to others having received legal advice. Complainants who start out wanting only an apology or explanation may end up blaming because of the lack of sympathy or the defensiveness they encounter.[22]

Analytically blaming is followed by claiming. Only a proportion of respondents make a claim against those perceived of as being responsible for their grievance, despite most people believing that if you make a fuss you get results.[23] There are many barriers to formal advice, which is often a prerequisite to a claim being properly advanced.[24] Organizational barriers impede a claim. For example, complaints may be filtered by front-line staff who, if not adequately trained, may discourage or deflect complainants. Claims in turn do not always give rise to legal action; in some cases the other party provides satisfaction. In only a number of cases do people seek legal assistance, and in even fewer do they institute legal action.[25] Conversely, fear of litigation may militate against some institutions offering the explanation or apology which could head off a claim.[26] Graphically,

---

[17] *Causes of Action*, 31–4.

[18] R. Moorhead, M. Sefton & D. Douglas, *The Advice Needs of Lone Parents* (One Parent Families, London, 2004), 28–31.   [19] *Causes of Action*, 50; *Paths to Justice*, 69–50.

[20] H. Kritzer, 'Propensity to Sue in England and the United States of America: Blaming and Claiming' (1991) 18 *JLS* 400.

[21] S. Lloyd-Bostock, 'Propensity to Sue in England and the United States of America: A Comment on Kritzer' (1991) 18 *JLS* 428.

[22] S. Lloyd-Bostock & L. Mulcany, 'The Social Psychology of Making and Responding to Hospital Complaints: An Account Model of Complaint Processes', in D. Galligan (ed.), *Administrative Law. Oxford Readings in Social-Legal Studies* (Oxford, 1995), 462.

[23] Office of Fair Trading, *Competition Act and Consumer Rights* (London, 2004), 24 (in a 2004 survey 65 per cent agreed with this).   [24] 9 above.

[25] e.g. *Causes of Action*, 56, 67, 96.

[26] C. Vincent, A. Phillips & M. Young, 'Why Do People Sue Doctors?' (1994) 343 *Lancet* 1609.

the process can be presented as a pyramid, showing the number of claims, disputes, times that lawyers are used, and legal cases instituted, per 1,000 problems. Not all litigation progresses step by step through such a pyramid. Persons who challenge official action against them on the basis of an administrative law or human rights doctrine may proceed directly from a grievance to litigation. More detailed analysis in some studies shows a variation with the type of matter; for example, family problems give rise to most legal actions, whereas consumer problems and employment problems are least likely to end up in a court or tribunal.[27]

Motives are one factor underlying such patterns. Towards one end of the spectrum of litigation are relatively mundane motives such as the collection of debt, the pursuit of compensation, inducing compliance with the terms of a contract, and preventing further dissemination of a publication (by seeking an interim injunction alleging defamation or breach of privacy). At the other end of the spectrum, an interest group may be advancing a political cause, or a business or government defeated in the political arena might turn to the courts for a remedy. A string of cases before the Administrative Court or the European Court of Justice are illustrative of the latter. A well-publicized example is provided by the putative European ban on tobacco sponsorship and advertising, where both the industry and the German government used the courts to overturn what other governments in the European Union had agreed to by way of a directive.[28] Along the spectrum are many motives, such as delaying the other party, seeking a decision in a forum unaffected by political considerations or disparities in power, threatening the other party, revenge, vindicating a principle, a sense of injustice, a desire to make sure what has happened to them or a relative or friend is prevented in the future,[29] gaining a tactical advantage in a continuing relationship, and obtaining a competitive advantage.

Various social and economic influences underlie decisions to pursue grievances through to the courts. In the initial stages of a complaint, in seeking advice as to what to do, cost is not a major inhibiting factor. Further on, however, cost looms larger—from the direct cost of legal action (for example, court fees), through the cost of legal services, to the opportunity cost of pursuing an action (salary/wages foregone, time expended, stress caused etc.).[30] Legal aid has had some effect in mitigating the direct costs of legal action, but, as we saw in Chapter 2, it and other publicly funded legal services are limited.[31] Under conditional fee agreements law

[27] *Causes of Action*, 96; *Paths to Justice*, 155.

[28] Case C–376/98, *Federal Republic of Germany v European Parliament and Council* [2000] ECR I-8419; Case C–74/99, *R v Secretary of State for Health ex p. Imperial Tobacco Ltd* [2000] ECR I-8599. The United Kingdom subsequently passed the Tobacco Advertising and Promotion Act 2002.

[29] e.g. L. Mulcahy, *Disputing Doctors. The Socio-Legal Dynamics of Complaints about Medical Care* (Maidenhead, 2003), 99.

[30] *Causes of Action*, 51, 53. See A. Duggan, 'Consumer Access to Justice in Common Law Countries', in C. Rickett & T. Telfer (eds), *International Perspectives on Consumers' Access to Justice* (Cambridge, 2003), 48–50.   [31] 49–53 above.

firms may be prepared to fund legal action in an accident claim (except, possibly, for direct disbursements) on the basis that a claimant will eventually recover something and legal fees be paid.[32] Wealth and education are generally associated with knowledge, skills, consciousness of rights, social contacts, and confidence, and all these may help to decide whether individuals exercise their legal rights. Generally speaking, the socially excluded are likely to be less 'legally competent'— less knowledgeable, less skilled, and less confident in relation to the law. Accordingly, although they are more likely to become vulnerable to a range of justiciable problems, they are less likely to use law to their advantage.[33]

Another aspect is whether some sections of society fail to take the initiative over matters capable of legal resolution because they are intimidated by what law is usually associated with (for example, the police, the courts, and prison). A detailed study of those involved in housing possession cases found that for some there was a deep-rooted fear of official processes and of the way they would be treated because of name, skin colour, or class.[34] As a result of their experience and the experience of others, people might feel—perhaps unjustifiably—that a matter will be brushed off and that nothing can be done. There might also be the fear that if people take action their employer, the landlord, the social welfare department, and so on will in some way retaliate.[35] While the law tends to assume that granting rights to weaker parties neutralizes differences in power, many people will regard acquiescence, avoidance, or tolerating a situation as a more rational response than asserting legal rights. There also seems to be an attitude, especially among older people, that certain problems are 'private' and 'personal', and that they should find the solution within the network of family, friends, or personal relationships rather than in the law.

There is little empirical evidence about the extent to which group and community norms affect individual legal action. One aspect is whether the propensity to litigate varies between jurisdictions. The conventional wisdom is that the United States is more litigious than other jurisdictions, a product, possibly, of a more individualistic culture and the more aggressive attitude of the American legal profession, in particular the plaintiff bar. In fact the differences in propensity to litigate depend on the type of issue: thus persons in the Untied States are more likely to bring personal injury claims but with other matters such as consumer or landlord and tenant problems the differences with, say, England, evaporate.[36] The

---

[32] 65–8 above.   [33] *Causes of Action*, 55, 58–9; *Paths to Justice*, 135–6.

[34] S. Blandy, C. Hunter, D. Lister & J. Nixon, *Housing Possession Cases in the County Court*, Lord Chancellor's Department Research Series 11/2002 (London, 2002), 54–62.

[35] A not always unjustified fear: A. Best, *When Consumers Complain* (New York, 1986), 40–2.

[36] H. Kritzer, 'Propensity to Sue in England and the United States of America: Blaming, and Claiming (1991) 18 *JLS* 400; B. Markesinis, 'Litigation-Mania in England, Germany and the United States: Are We So Different?' (1990) 49 *CLJ* 233; H. Kritzer, N. Vidman & W. Bogart, 'To Confront or Not to Confront: Measuring Claiming Rates in Discrimination Grievances' (1991) 25 *L&Soc.R.* 875; H. Kritzer, 'Lawyer Fees and Lawyer Behavior in Litigation: What Does the Empirical Literature Really Say?' (2002) 80 *Tex.LR* 1943, 1981; E. Blankenburg, 'Judicial Systems in Western Europe: Comparative Indicators of Legal Professionals, Courts, Litigation, and Budgets in the

tendency to take legal action also turns on organizational factors. Disputes may occur more often because lawyers are more inclined to encourage litigation as a way of resolving them. Institutional arrangements in some jurisdictions channel complaints to courts rather than other bodies. In the United States there are factors promoting personal injury litigation such as the contingency fee system and jury trial for civil cases. The greater involvement of counsel in Irish personal injury litigation, compared with England, is associated with the commencement of court proceedings in nearly three quarters of claims in Ireland, but only 16 per cent in England.[37]

Commercial and property interests may have a different propensity to litigate compared with individuals, not least because of the different transactions entered and interests to be protected. Commercial litigation may be only one tactic in a wider and more complex battle, where business uses it as a method of furthering interests, even if this is as simple as delaying payment or furthering or protecting against a hostile takeover.[38] Commercial and property interests may be reluctant to take their disputes to court because of the uncertainty of outcome. It may be that it is more advantageous to have a dispute undecided, or to negotiate a solution, than to litigate if the matter may be decided adversely. Certainty is a point the English courts take into account in commercial litigation.[39] Another institutional factor is the capacity of the courts to handle heavy commercial litigation—the better the judiciary, and the greater the resources available to specialist commercial courts, the more attractive they are if claims can be channelled elsewhere, be it other jurisdictions or arbitration.

Indeed, institutions other than courts may offer acceptable avenues for the resolution of a whole range of matters. Public sector bodies now have extensive internal review mechanisms handling complaints from citizens.[40] Arbitration occurs in commercial and building disputes and alternative dispute resolution (ADR) is popular in a number of areas.[41] The welfare state has spawned a huge

---

1990s', in E. Jensen & T. Heller (eds), *Beyond Common Knowledge. Empirical Approaches to the Rule of Law* (Stanford, 2003), 69–70; L. Nottage, 'What Do Courts Do?' [1996] *New Zealand LJ* 369.

[37] B. Greenford, 'The Handling of Personal Injury Claims by Insurers in England and Wales', in Department of Enterprise, Trade and Employment, *Second Report of the Special Working Group on Personal Injury Compensation* (Dublin, 2001), 115–17.

[38] Herbert Smith, *M & A Litigation* (London, 2002), 5 (survey of 100 corporate executives: over two thirds likely to consider using litigation in takeovers during coming years).

[39] *Homburg Houtimport BV v Agrosin Private Ltd.* [2003] UKHL 12; [2004] 1 AC 715, 738B, *per* Lord Bingham, is a recent statement.

[40] e.g. R. Sainsbury, 'Internal Reviews and the Weakening of Social Security Claimants' Rights of Appeal', in G. Richardson & H. Genn (eds), *Administrative Law and Government Action—The Courts and Alternative Mechanisms of Review* (Oxford, 1994); L. Mulcahy, R. Lickiss, J. Allsop & V. Karn, *Small Voices, Big Issues: An Annotated Bibliography of the Literature on Public Sector Complaints* (London, 1996).

[41] Y. Dezalay & B. Garth, *Dealing in Virtue. International Commercial Arbitration and the Construction of a Transnational Legal Order* (Chicago, 1996) is a sociological study of the former. On ADR in the commercial sector, see e.g. E. Ferran, 'Dispute Resolution Mechanisms in the UK Financial Sector' (2002) 21 *CJQ* 135. See 71 above.

range of tribunals in the areas such as education, employment, health, and social security.[42] Activities associated with modern society, such as the use of motor vehicles, have led to the establishment of special adjudicative procedures.[43] Ombudsmen in both the public and private sphere also resolve many complaints.[44] Many of the matters which these bodies deal with could go to the courts—although in some cases government has attempted to give these other bodies exclusive jurisdiction—but the cost of litigation acts as a deterrent, quite apart from perceptions about the quality of adjudication offered. The courts still act as a longstop for such disputes, for parties dissatisfied with these bodies might begin afresh in the courts or seek judicial or statutory review of a decision. However, the vast majority of such matters are handled without resort to the courts.

Further, there are the gatekeepers to litigation. Lawyers can identify avenues for litigation of which lay persons are ignorant. On the other hand, even if individuals seek legal assistance, lawyers may inhibit litigation by screening out particular types of claim. An American study found that lawyers did not regard litigation in relation to consumer claims as being worthwhile or in some cases worthy, had little or no knowledge of the applicable substantive law, but attempted to mediate some claims informally with the relevant retailer, manufacturer, or finance house.[45] These findings are likely to be replicated elsewhere and would probably extend to other matters such as disputes with neighbours. Then there are the courts, for what they say influences perceptions about what are grievances, claims, and disputes. Courts may discourage litigation through developments in procedural and substantive law.[46] In *Farley v Skinner* Lord Steyn said: 'I consider that awards in this area [damages for non-pecuniary loss] should be restrained and modest. It is important that logical and beneficial developments in this corner of the law should not contribute to the creation of a society bent on litigation.'[47] The converse, of the courts directly encouraging litigation, is unusual,[48] but courts can indirectly encourage litigation by doctrinal developments which make it worthwhile to pursue a claim. Finally, legislation can affect litigation. The introduction of new legislation may multiply the occasions for disputed interpretations, but it may also resolve points of legal contention and so discourage litigation.

---

[42] For a partial list: Council on Tribunals, *Annual Report 2003/2004* (London, 2004), 60–67; Sir Andrew Leggatt, *Tribunals for Users. One System, One Service* (London, 2001), Part II.

[43] e.g. J. Raine & S. Snape, '*It's Only Parking But . . .' Report . . . [on] the London Parking Appeals Service*, Lord Chancellor's Department Research Series 5/2002 (London, 2002).

[44] 4–6, 72–6 above.

[45] S. Macaulay, 'Lawyers and Consumer Protection Laws' (1979) 14 *L.&Soc.R.* 115.

[46] Explicitly recognized in the traditional 'floodgates' argument; e.g. *Winterbottom v Wright* (1842) 10 M&W 109; 152 ER 402. On procedure: 162 below.

[47] [2001] UKHL 49; [2002] 2 AC 732, para. 28.

[48] *Barclays Bank plc v Coleman* [2001] QB 20, 30–2, *per* Nourse LJ. But see *Royal Bank of Scotland v Etridge (No. 2)* [2001] UKHL 44; [2002] 2 AC 773, 798F–G.

Who uses the courts?

In the absence of detailed historical inquiry, it is not possible to say with precision how the matters handled by civil courts in Britain now are different from those dealt with in the past. It would seem safe to say that there are relatively more family matters before the courts than a century ago. Personal injury claims must comprise a larger percentage of matters than at the turn of the last century—how large will be seen in a moment—with the advent of motor vehicles. But although family matters and personal injury claims loom larger than they did, it would be too hasty to assume that the courts are now less important than they were for contract, property, and other claims. This is evident both in matters heard in the small claims jurisdiction (see Table 1 below) and which proceed by default or summary judgment.[49]

The nature of those involved in litigation has a profound influence on the issues courts address, the nature of lawyers' involvement, the development of doctrine and outcomes. For example, the increase over the years in the jurisdictional limit of the county court in England and Wales means that it handles much of the ordinary contract and tort litigation, to the detriment of doctrine, since its decisions are not generally reported and do not create precedent. To take another, more general, example: if a particular type of litigant constantly brought claims against another type of litigant, and the latter typically did not defend or did not obtain legal representation, it would not be surprising if outcomes tended to favour the first type of litigant. Without any conscious bias on their part, judges would simply be more exposed to the arguments favouring the first type of litigant so that these attained a more 'natural' quality. Beyond any impact on the courts, the nature of litigants may also have ramifications for society. For example, if claimants were typically commercial interests, utilities or public bodies claiming against individual defendants in debt, the courts would be functioning to reinforce other institutional outcomes in society rather than acting as an avenue redressing the balance.[50] A third example is a widely accepted notion in jurisdictions such as the United States and India that minority groups ought to look to the courts for redress if government is unsympathetic.[51] This means that the courts are making social policy as they decide cases.

There is limited evidence on the types of parties using the courts in the two main venues for hearing litigated cases in England and Wales. In 2003 there were 67,310 proceedings in the county courts disposed of by way of trial or small claim hearing. Proceedings disposed of by small claim hearing constituted the bulk of these (52,143), and an official estimate of the type of parties involved is as follows (Table 1).[52]

---

[49] 128 below.   [50] See 128–30 below.   [51] 15, 91 above.
[52] Department for Constitutional Affairs, *Judicial Statistics. Annual Report for 2003*, Cm 6251 (2004) hereafter *Judicial Statistics 2003*, 44.

Table 1. Small claims heard by type of claim and party, 2003

	Claimant			Defendant		
	Individual	Firm	Corporation	Individual	Firm	Corporation
Debt	16,170	8,060	10,220	20,440	6,760	7,240
Negligence—personal injury	1,820	240	140	1,440	380	380
Other negligence	6,330	290	670	4,650	1,010	1,630
Non possession housing dispute	620	0	100	430	0	290
Other	5,610	720	1,150	3,980	1,300	2,210
Nature of claim						
Total	30,560	9,310	12,280	30,940	9,450	11,750

More than half of both claimants and defendants were individuals. Of the proceedings by individual claimants, over one half were debt claims and nearly a quarter of claims involved negligence (personal injury or other negligence). For individual defendants, two thirds of claims against these were for debt. ('Housing' in the table does not include possession actions; the bulk of those would be claims against individuals). For the 1,642 actions set down for trial and disposed of in the Queen's Bench Division of the High Court in the same year, Table 2 sets out official estimates of the type of party and claim.[53] Note again the prominent role of individuals as claimants, quite apart from personal injury and medical negligence claims. (Of the 1,520 claims by individuals, 1,460 were by an individual, rather than a group of individuals. Groups of individuals, presumably, include multiparty actions as well as others.) Although individuals are the defendants in personal injury cases, no doubt in almost all cases the effective defendant will be an insurance company.

Individuals are therefore an important category of claimant before the civil courts. In considering the role of individuals as claimants, however, certain factors must be borne in mind. First is the obvious point already made in Chapter 2, and earlier in this chapter, that many individuals with legal problems do not get to court. Secondly, the relatively high number of individuals claiming is partly attributable, as we have seen, to the importance of personal injury and other negligence claims. Moreover, the individuals who do pursue claims are not necessarily representative of the population as a whole. Professor John Baldwin says of the small claims litigants he interviewed:

Most litigants . . . especially those who appeared as [claimants], were relatively well-heeled and articulate individuals. Over two-thirds of those in paid employment were in professional or managerial occupations, and the same applied to well over half of all defendants.

[53] *Judicial Statistics 2003*, 33. Note that the figures are rounded so there is an apparent discrepancy with medical negligence. The housing category does not take in possession claims.

Table 2. Queen's Bench Division actions set down for trial and disposal by type of party and claim, 2003

	Claimants		Defendants	
	Individual(s)	Business(es)	Individual(s)	Business(es)
Debt	20	20	20	20
Breach of contract	40	90	20	110
Personal injury	860	20	380	510
Medical negligence	430	—	90	340
Solicitors' negligence	40	—	—	40
Other negligence	110	—	—	110
Miscellaneous	20	—	20	—

Many litigants were of course businessmen and women. Almost three-quarters were car owners who had driven to the hearing. Very few litigants were from ethnic minority groups. The genuinely 'poor' make few appearances at small claims hearings, and, when they do, it is typically as defendants to face landlords or money-lenders.[54]

As well as socio-economic position, individual claimants may be unrepresentative in other ways as well. For example, because they experience a narrower range of legal problems than adults there is an under-representation of children amongst those litigating certain types of claim.[55]

However, it is clear that the civil courts cannot universally be characterized as a forum where commercial and property institutions advance claims against individuals. Of course there are many proceedings before the civil courts which involve businesses or utilities instituting debt or property claims against individuals. A great number of these proceedings are undefended and as we see below many are disposed of by way of default judgment, whereby a claimant can obtain judgment in the absence of any moves to defend a case. Many, indeed most, of such cases are legally unanswerable, because the defendant has failed to pay the debt or has fallen into arrears with rent or a mortgage. In other words, the courts are simply perfecting what the law permits, so that reform in this area of litigation needs attention to be given to the substantive law and procedural reform rather than blaming the courts.[56]

What of businesses claiming against other businesses? In a recent study of small claims, Professor John Baldwin found that a majority of the claims in the £3,000 to £5,000 band now involve commercial organizations suing other organizations with which they have done business.[57] However, litigation outside the small

[54] J. Baldwin, *Small Claims in the County Courts in England and Wales* (Oxford, 1997), 166.
[55] J. Masson & A. Orchard, *Children and Civil Litigation*, Lord Chancellor's Department Research Series 10/99 (London, 1999), 2.1, 2.6–2.7.   [56] 130 below.
[57] J. Baldwin, *Lay and Judicial Perspectives on the Expansion of the Small Claims Regime*, Lord Chancellor's Department Research Series 8/02 (London, 2002), 28. See 170 below.

claims jurisdiction is far from the stereotype of where 'two mighty goliaths are combating, head to head, through teams of in-house lawyers or retained counsel'; rather, it is 'more like the image of litigants in person'.[58] In the figures for Queen's Bench cases set down for trial in Table 2, breach of contract actions feature only 90 businesses (40 individuals) as claimants, and in some of these 90 cases proceedings would likely have been against individuals, not other businesses. The Commercial Court characteristically involves business v. business claims—contracts related to ships, cargo, insurance and aircraft, claims involving banking and finance and the purchase and sale of commodities and cases arising from arbitration. In 2003 there were 81 trials heard by the court. It is fair to add that hearings in the Commercial Court often involve massive claims and last months. Over half the cases in the Commercial Court emanate from foreign businesses on both sides.[59] The work of the Chancery Division also includes business disputes, for example intellectual property claims, partnership disputes, and contracts for the sale and purchase of shares and businesses. In the Chancery Division in 2003, 2,553 cases were set down in London, and 1,077 cases ultimately disposed of by way of a hearing. Many of these cases would not have been of a commercial character nor would they have involved business v. business claims.[60]

Overall, then, what is surprising is that commercial interests seem to use the courts little, comparatively speaking, for dispute settlement amongst themselves. As we have seen, one answer may be that other institutions provide a less expensive but still convenient forum for commercial parties: for example, they may go to arbitration. Perhaps more importantly, the relative infrequency of disputes between businesses may testify to sound planning, with legal help, thus avoiding their arising in the first place. Several notable studies have also demonstrated that businesses will try to avoid invoking the law because of the desire to maintain continuing good relations with those such as suppliers, commercial customers, and financiers.[61] It may be that competitive pressures and economic restructuring leads to an increase in business litigation and a breakdown of the non-contractual and harmonious nature of business relations which these earlier studies demonstrated.[62] As Professor Hugh Collins notes: 'The switch to the contractual discourse

[58] J. Shapland, 'The Need for Case Management? Profiles of Liquidated and Unliquidated Cases' (2003) 22 *CJQ* 324, 331–2.

[59] Court Service, *Commercial and Admiralty Courts, 2002–2003 Report* (London, 2003), paras 13, 15.   [60] *Judicial Statistics 2003*, 25.

[61] The seminal study was S. Macaulay, 'Non-Contractual Relations in Business: A Preliminary Study' (1963) 28 *Amer.Sociological R.* 55. British studies include H. Beale & T. Dugdale, 'Contracts Between Businessmen: Planning and the Use of Contractual Remedies' (1975) 2 *BJLS* 45; R. Lewis, 'Contracts Between Businessmen: Reform of the Law of Firm Offers and an Empirical Study of Tendering Practices in the Building Industry' (1982) 9 *JLS* 153; T. Daintith, 'The Design and Performance of Long-Term Contracts', in T. Daintith & G. Teubner (eds), *Contract and Organisation: Legal Analysis in the Light of Economic and Social Theory* (Berlin, 1986); S. Wheeler, 'Lawyer Involvement in Commercial Disputes' (1991) 18 *JLS* 241.

[62] P. Vincent-Jones, 'Contract Litigation in England and Wales 1975–1991' (1993) 12 *CJQ* 337. See also M. Galanter & J. Rogers, *A Transformation of American Business Disputing? Some Preliminary Observations*, DPRP 10-3, Institute for Legal Studies, University of Wisconsin (1991).

of rights occurs only when no long-term business relation seems to be practicable and the parties feel unable to achieve an accommodation that preserves some diminished benefits for both'.[63] Occasionally a business sues government in relation to the regulation of some aspect of its activity. Such cases are a relatively small component of the work of the Administrative Court.[64]

Government is rarely a claimant in the civil courts. One exception is with social housing, when local government as landlord seeks possession orders against tenants for rent arrears or other breaches of their tenancy conditions. Utilities also bring debt claims. Individual v. government claims can be against government on the basis of vicarious liability (as with motor vehicle accidents), as employer (as with negligence claims by civil servants or members of the armed forces), or for a breach of duty in the performance of functions (for example, the growing number of claims by pupils against the local education authority).[65] Although it was expected that the Human Rights Act 1998 would have a marked effect on litigation rates, that has not occurred and human rights arguments have typically been invoked to bolster other claims.[66] Litigation may have been lengthened as the result. The police are sued by members of the public who claim, say, to have been assaulted or falsely imprisoned.[67] The concern with medical negligence claims against national health service bodies is mentioned elsewhere.[68]

The claims against government which attract most attention are those for judicial and statutory review. In 2003 the Administrative Court received some 5,704 applications in non-criminal cases for permission to apply for judicial review, which is the first, filtering, stage of the process. Of these, only 1,354 applications were granted (just over two fifths).[69] At the next stage, determination by the court, of some 338 cases, in only 144 cases was the application allowed, the rest being dismissed or withdrawn. The figures provide some support for the general proposition that government comes out ahead in litigation. Whether this is because of superior resources, extensive screening so that dubious cases are conceded, or broader structural factors is for further inquiry in Britain.[70] The largest single category of judicial review cases was immigration (3,848 applications; 114 court determinations), although subsequent legislation means that this source has been choked off and replaced by a statutory review procedure.[71] As to statutory review,

---

[63] H. Collins, *Regulating Contracts* (Oxford, 1999), 329.   [64] 119–20 below.

[65] e.g. N Harris, 'Liability under Education Law in the UK—How Much Further Can it Go?' (2001) 4 *European Journal for Education Law and Policy* 131.

[66] J. Raine & C. Walker, *The Impact on the Courts and the Administration of Justice of the Human Rights Act 1998*, Lord Chancellor's Department, Research Report No. 9/2002 (London, 2002).

[67] R. Clayton, H. Tomlinson, E. Buckett & A. Davies, *Civil Actions Against the Police*, 3rd edn. (London, 2003).   [68] 5–6 above.

[69] *Judicial Statistics 2003*, 20.

[70] See H. Kritzer, 'The Government Gorilla: Why Does Government Come Out Ahead in Appellate Courts?', in H. Kritzer & S. Silbey (eds), *Litigation: Do the 'Haves' Still Come Out Ahead?* (Stanford, 2003).

[71] Nationality, Immigration and Asylum Act 2002, s 101. The next highest non-criminal category was homelessness: 199 applications for permission and 8 determinations by the court.

the largest identified category of cases was planning and related matters, with 197 applications and 96 determinations by the court (33 allowed, 63 dismissed).[72]

Institutions may stand behind some of the individuals who sue or are sued. It is difficult to uncover this in a systematic way. However, even with personal injury claims litigants may be supported by institutions. On the claimants' side are trade unions and, more recently, specialist law firms and claims management companies with large portfolios of claims funded by conditional fees or similar arrangements. With regard to defendants, although individuals appear as such in personal injury motor vehicle cases, in practice the third-party insurers conduct the defence, often without any continuing involvement from those against whom the action is nominally being brought. Repeat players such as defendant insurance companies have an advantage in litigation in their resources and their ability to construct long-term litigation strategies; in their insight into which cases to compromise; and in their potential influence over the legislative and administrative processes which mould the law.[73] Since its formation in 1990, the Association of Personal Injury Lawyers (APIL) has been a counterweight on the claimant side in personal injury matters to the insurance companies.

Public interest litigation attempts to build on the insights of commercial repeat players. Perhaps ironically, the lead in public interest litigation in England has been taken by quangos, notably the Equal Opportunities Commission, which over many years has funded a series of test cases before domestic courts and the European Court of Justice, designed to change policies and practices in the treatment of women at work.[74] Democracy in Britain is mature enough to have one arm of the other state suing another. Non-government organizations (NGOs) also litigate. The relative volume of cases is small, not least because issues must be cast in legal terms. Amnesty International intervened by way of counsel in the well-known case involving the application by Spain to extradite the former military leader of Chile, Senator Pinochet.[75] Liberty, founded as the National Council for Civil Liberties, and Justice, the British arm of the International Commission of Jurists, has intervened in a number of important human rights

---

[72] *Judicial Statistics 2003*, 21.

[73] The classic study of repeat players is M. Galanter, 'Why the "Haves" Come Out Ahead: Speculation on the Limits of Legal Change' (1979) 9 *Law & Soc.R.* 95. See also D. Songer, R. Sheehan & S. Brodie Haire, 'Do the "Haves" Come Out Ahead over Time? Applying Galanter's Framework to the Decisions of the U.S. Courts of Appeals, 1925–1988' (1999) 33 *Law & Soc. R.* 811; R. Smyth, 'The "Haves" and the "Have Nots": An Empirical Study of the Rational Actor and Party Capability Hypothesis in the High Court 1948–99' (2000) 35 *Australian Journal Political Science* 255; P. McCormick, 'Party Capability Theory and Appellate Success in the Supreme Court of Canada, 1949–1992' (1993) 26 *Canadian Journal of Political Science* 521. See H. Kritzer & S. Silbey (eds), *op. cit.*

[74] C. O'Cinneide, *A Single Equality Body. Lessons from Abroad* (Manchester, 2002), 18–20. The White Paper says that strategic interventions in litigation by the new Commission for Equality and Human Rights is to be provided for in statute: *Fairness for All*, Cm 6185 (London, 2004), 40.

[75] *R v Bow Street Metropolitan Stipendiary Magistrates, ex P Pinochet Ugarte (No. 2)* [1999] UKHL 1; [2000] 1 AC 119.

cases.[76] Other groups such as Child Poverty Action Group, the Rape Crisis Federation, the Pro-Life Alliance, and Public Concern at Work have also brought or intervened in litigation to further the causes they espouse.[77] Although quangos must be able to justify intervention under their constitutive document, the only legal constraint otherwise on third party intervention seems to be whether a court considers intervention helpful.[78] Rather than simply intervening, some interest groups, as mentioned, litigate directly. Friends of the Earth and Greenpeace have proceeded against government directly as the courts have stretched the rules of standing.[79] NGOs advancing a case of general public importance, which the court considers in the public interest to resolve may also benefit from a protective costs order, under which they are exposed to limited or no costs, should they lose.[80] Such involvement of NGOs in litigation can be a useful corrective to social and economic inequalities.[81] However, there is no guarantee that NGOs claiming to represent the public interest do so and there is a danger that the law's claims to neutrality and objectivity may be diluted by an excessive participation of interest groups before the courts.[82]

The Conversion Process

Procedure has long been recognized as playing a central role in how cases are handled in courts. Jeremy Bentham's concern about 'the burthens of judicial procedure' takes form in current interests such as widening access to justice and reducing delay and expense.[83] The majority of cases commenced never go

[76] e.g. *R v Khan* [1997] AC 558; *R v Lambert* [2001] UKHL 37; [2002] 2 AC 545; *R (Anderson) v Secretary of State for the Home Department* [2002] UKHL 46; [2003] 1 AC 837; *R (Saadi) v Secretary of State for the Home Department* [2002] UKHL 41; [2002] 1 WLR 3131; [2002] 4 All ER 785; *R v Special Adjudicator, ex p Ullah* [2004] UKHL 26; [2004] 2 AC 323.

[77] e.g. *R v Lord Chancellor, ex p CPAG* [1999] 1 WLR 347; [1998] 2 All ER 755; *R v A (No. 2)* [2001] UKHL 25; [2002] 1 AC 45; *Re A (Children) (Conjoined Twins: Surgical Separation)* [2000] 4 All ER 961; *Street v Derbyshire Unemployed Workers Centre* [2004] EWCA Civ 964; [2004] IRLR 687, para. 34.

[78] *Re Northern Ireland Human Rights Commission* [2002] UKHL 25; [2002] NI 236; *Heil v Rankin* [2001] QB 272, 298–9; CPR r.54.17. See generally R. Rawlings, 'Courts and Interests', in I. Loveland (ed.), *A Special Relationship? American Influences on Public Law in the UK* (Oxford, 1995).; D. Smith, L. Bridges & K. Ashton, *Third Party Interventions in Judicial Review. An Action Research Project*, Public Law Project (London, 2001); C. O'Cinneide & M. Arshi, 'Third-Party Interventions: The Public Interest Re-affirmed' [2004] *PL* 69.

[79] *R (Friends of the Earth Ltd) v Secretary of State for the Environment Food and Rural Affairs* [2001] EWCA Civ 1847; *R (Greenpeace Ltd) v Secretary of State for the Environment, Food and Rural Affairs* [2002] EWCA Civ 1036; [2002] 1 WLR 3304.

[80] *R (Cornerhouse Research) v Secretary of State for Trade and Industry* [2004] EWHC 3011 (Admin).

[81] Justice and Public Law Project, *A Matter of Public Interest* (London, 1996); Public Law Project, *10th Anniversary Report* (London, 2000); D. Songer, A. Kuersten & E. Kaheny, 'Why the Haves Don't Always Come Out Ahead: Repeat Players Meet Amici Curiae for the Disadvantaged' (2000) 53 *Political Res. Q.* 537.   [82] C. Harlow, 'Public Law and Popular Justice' (2002) 65 *MLR* 1, 16.

[83] See Chapter 2 above and Chapter 5 below.

through the full process to hearing. Mention has been made of the many debt
claims disposed of by default judgment. In addition substantial numbers of
cases which are commenced end up settling. Substantive law, too, channels civil
litigation. Of primary interest here is the extent to which the substantive law
enables social issues to be converted into legal problems so that the courts can deal
with them. To put it another way, only if there is a cause of action is it worth suing.
Related to this is that legal claims may in turn be replaced by welfare claims: thus
workers' compensation and now industrial injuries disablement benefits
substitute for many personal injury claims before the courts. In some jurisdictions
tort has been replaced by a compensation scheme for personal injury claims.[84] All
this can be termed the conversion process for cases.

Court procedures

Procedural law can have an influence on those resorting to the courts, the matters
litigated and the results obtained. Technicalities, anomalies, and complexities in
procedural rules may discourage claims, delay them unnecessarily, or distort
outcomes by preventing all meritorious points being heard. Consider, for example
if court procedures facilitate delay in cases in which the outcome is reasonably
clear-cut. Certain parties have an obvious motive to delay: activity in violation of
the law, for example, can be continued up to the hearing, unless interim relief can
be obtained. Similarly, a person may be induced to abandon a claim, or a case may
be weakened with time because witnesses are no longer available. The reform of
procedural rules initiated by Lord Woolf, and considered in the next chapter, were
designed in part to simplify and expedite litigation. Evidential rules can throw up
barriers to establishing a case. Statistical evidence, for example, is not readily admissible to show, say, that a surgeon has a much higher mortality rate than average.[85] Yet
if only one case is examined, it may be much easier for the surgeon to argue chance
and to have an inference of negligence rejected. Of course such evidence, if admitted, would need to be carefully scrutinized: a higher mortality rate might simply
mean that a surgeon was operating on older or more at-risk patients.[86]

At one time rules of standing acted as a barrier to what issues could be litigated
in public law. In recent decades, as we have noted, the English rules have been
liberalized to such a degree that most interest groups with only an ideological connection with an issue can now claim standing.[87] Although multiparty actions are
available for what Americans call mass torts, we have seen other types of class
action still has a considerable way to go to facilitate access to justice.[88] Another

---

[84] P. Cane & P. Atiyah, *Atiyah's Accidents, Compensation and the Law*, 6th edn. (London, 1999), ch. 13.
[85] M. Powers & N. Harris, *Clinical Negligence*, 3rd edn. (London, 2000), ch. 26
[86] B. Bridgewater *et al.*, 'Surgeon Specific Mortality in Adult Cardiac Surgery: Comparison
between Crude and Risk Stratified Data', *BMJ*, vol. 327, 5 July 2003, 13.
[87] Lord Woolf, J. Jowell & A. Le Sueur, *de Smith, Woolf & Jowell, Judicial Review of Administrative
Action* (London, 1995), 119–22.   [88] 79 above.

area for debate is whether there is scope in England for something comparable to the Brandeis brief. In the United States the parties to litigation can file a Brandeis brief, which may include government reports, research by social scientists, and laws in other jurisdictions. The brief broadens a court's perspective by introducing it to wider policy considerations. Argument before English appellate courts is generally confined to evidence admitted at any hearing and to competing contentions as to the relevant law. Courts might benefit in the occasional case where an important public policy issue is raised and they had systematically collected information about the potential economic or social implications of their decision. Often those implications are simply assumed, sometimes without the benefit of full argument.[89]

Transformation of issues

Categories for the subject matter of litigation, such as the description 'personal injury claims', coincide roughly with an everyday understanding of cases. If cases were to be categorized by the relief requested (damages, possession, injunction, declaration, etc.), there would be some move away from that everyday under-standing. And if cases were to be analysed according to legal categories such as tort or equity, the masking of social issues would be even greater. At one level this transformation is relatively straightforward and widely recognized, as a motor vehicle accident becomes a claim in negligence for money damages, a quarrel between two neighbours changes into a dispute over planning approval, family breakdown takes form as a child contact case, and an undefined housing difficulty becomes a claim under the homelessness legislation.[90] At least on the surface, certain standards in civil law, notably that of the 'reasonable person', draw on community notions of proper behaviour. Standards in the European Convention of Human Rights, such as the prohibition on inhuman or degrading treatment (Article 3) and the guarantee of respect for family life (Article 8) also have some resonance with community standards even when stretched to claims for social welfare and housing.[91]

The transformation may be more fundamental as regards the number of parties involved or the issues addressed. Conflicts over economic resources, moral or political principle, the exercise of government power or use of the environment become conflicts over the meaning and application of legal doctrine.[92] Take the campaign by Greenpeace against depletion of the Brazilian rain forests, which has

---

[89] e.g. *Barclays Bank plc v O'Brien* [1994], 1 AC 180, 188C–H, *per* Lord Browne-Wilkinson. See also J. Stapleton, 'Tort, Insurance and Ideology' (1995) 55 *MLR* 820.

[90] R. Atkinson, T. Buck, D. Pollard, & N. Smith, *A Regional Study of Local Authority and Court Processes in Homelessness Cases*, Lord Chancellor's Department Research Series 9/99 (London, 1999), 6.

[91] 223, 225 below.

[92] See generally B. Yngvesson & L. Mather, 'Courts, Moots, and the Disputing Process', in K. Boyum & L. Mather, *Empirical Theories About Courts* (New York, 1983), 64.

involved tracking illegal logging, for example by aircraft, mapping logging areas and taking direct action against companies within Brazil and internationally.[93] In *R (Greenpeace Ltd) v Secretary of State for the Environment, Food and Rural Affairs*[94] the campaign took the form of an argument about whether the UK relevant authorities should permit the import of a particular cargo of Brazilian mahogany. The cargo was accompanied by a valid export certificate issued under order of a Brazilian lower court, but contested by the Brazilian environmental body which was the designated management authority of the Brazilian state under the Convention on International Trade in Endangered Species of Wild Fauna and Flora.[95] Under that Convention there are strict controls on the export and import of an endangered species such as Brazilian mahogany. Article II(3) of the Convention requires the prior grant and presentation of an export permit, and that a number of conditions be met. One of these is that the management authority of the state of export has to be satisfied that the specimen had not been obtained in contravention of the laws of that state for the protection of flora and fauna. The Convention is incorporated into European Union law by a Council Regulation.[96] Article 4(3)(a) of the Regulation requires that any import has to be accompanied by an export permit that has been issued in accordance with the Convention by an authority of the issuing country and that it should state that it has been obtained in accordance with the national legislation on the conservation of the species concerned.

So in general terms the issue before the Court of Appeal was whether an importing state in the European Community should reject an importation under Article 4(3)(a) where a valid export permit had been issued by an exporting state but the state was not satisfied that the specimen had not been obtained in contravention of its laws. In legal terms it was a narrow issue of the construction of that Article: was there a proper export certificate? The majority held that until an authentic export permit was revoked by the authority which issued it, or was set aside by agreement or court order, the importing authorities were entitled to treat it as valid. The need for commercial certainty in international trade supported this conclusion, for otherwise doubts would be introduced about whether importers and others involved in trade could reasonably rely on the documents, and shipments would be liable to be held up indefinitely as enquiries were made.[97] Laws LJ dissenting held that in interpreting Article 4(3)(a) environmental concerns trumped commercial certainty:

The interpretation of statutes is hardly ever entirely value-free. It is neither surprising nor regrettable that in confronting their task of interpretation, the judges have to a greater or lesser degree been moved by the aspirations of their time. Such a process does no more than

---

[93] See 'Logging in the Amazon' at www.greenpeace.org
[94] [2002] EWCA Civ 1036; [2002] 1 WLR 3304, CA.
[95] The text with amendments and resolutions is at www.cites.org
[96] Regulation (EC) 338/97, of 9 December 1996 [1997] OJ L61/40, 3 March 1997.
[97] [2002] EWCA Civ 1036; [2002] 1 WLR 3304, paras 49, 61–62, *per* Dyson and Mummery LJJ.

bring to life the plain fact that the law—perhaps especially the common law—will reflect contemporary influences, even though it is not a creature of them; it must do so, or it would ossify. In the century before last, the sanctity of contract, with all that said for trade across the British empire and beyond, was a powerful engine of statutory construction. Now, the world is a more fragile place. Considerations of ecology and the protection of the environment are interests of high importance. The delicate balances of the natural order are continuously liable to be disturbed by human activity, which in particular threatens the survival of many flora and fauna. These concerns are today well known and well accepted. Within the proper limits of the courts' role, and in appropriate contexts, I think we should now be ready to give them special weight.[98]

Another illustration of the transformation of social issues is provided by the legal claims made against banks after several economic recessions by those purchasing property on mortgage. The economic context—the collapse in the property market—unveiled claims in law which were removed from the basic reality that people could no longer pay the mortgage. Claimants contended that there were vitiating factors in the mortgage documentation, their banks had breached a duty toward them such as adequately advising on the original transaction, there had been misrepresentation, undue influence or unconscionable conduct by a third party (for example, the spouse conducting the loan negotiations with the bank) or the mortgage transaction was somehow in breach of statutory law.[99] Each legal claim was designed to produce a result which reduced or expunged the amount to be paid. So as these two examples illustrate what may at base be an environmental or an economic dispute in a broad sense is transformed into a dispute about the application of legal doctrine when it is brought before the courts.[100]

The transformation of social into legal issues is facilitated by detailed regulatory legislation. In addition to relying on broad common law principles, a party may be able to invoke a range of statutory law relevant to a particular issue. The meaning of statutory language being oftentimes arguable, the potential for legal action is considerable in the modern state. In addition, procedural law may open further avenues to contested legal points. The result may be what has been called the 'lawsuit before the lawsuit', the second of which may never eventuate. Conversely, a case may settle but generate satellite litigation about costs. Such satellite litigation may be deprecated by the courts.

Transformation of an underlying social issue is contingent on the legal doctrines arguable, whether statutory or otherwise. This is the explanation that, in different jurisdictions, a similar social reality, such as the collapse of the property market, gives rise to legal claims formulated doctrinally in different ways. In the

---

[98] *ibid.*, para 33.
[99] e.g. W. Blair (ed), *Banks, Liability and Risk*, 3rd edn (London 2001); J. O'Donovan, *Lender Liability* (Sydney, 2000); R. Cranston, *Principles of Banking Law*, 2nd edn, (London, 2002), 183–228.
[100] C. Howard, 'Public Law and Common Law', in D. Galligan (ed.), *Essays in Legal Theory* (Melbourne, 1984), 8–13.

one jurisdiction the doctrinal arguments may be narrowed during the life of a case as the litigator finds that not all those points advanced at the outset prove plausible on testing by the other side or the court. The legal doctrine in which a social problem finds expression may also be reformulated in the course of case. On the surface *Attorney General v Blake*[101] involved a claim by the government to the profits of an autobiography of a self-confessed spy, who had escaped from prison to the Soviet Union in 1966. More fundamentally it was an assertion by the state that it should continue to pursue those who betray it to ensure they are accorded just punishment. At first instance this political principle was formulated by the government in terms of a breach of fiduciary duty by Blake; in the Court of Appeal public law was invoked;[102] while in the House of Lords the case was decided in favour of the government on restitutionary principles.

Lawyers handling a case are clearly important in this transformation process. The focus may be narrowed to one legally relevant issue or widened from a private dispute into one involving issues of public importance. A significant development in the law may result from a strategy adopted in relation to a client's case. In rare cases, it may emerge from a decision on an issue not raised by the party's lawyers but by the court itself. Is it any wonder that many clients do not understand why they succeed, or more importantly, fail in court, when the matter has been transformed beyond their recognition? Moreover, if the legal process is dealing with legal concepts, it will understandably not usually address the underlying social issue. Neither point is necessarily objectionable: many approach lawyers precisely so that the legal implications of their problems can be deployed to their advantage (or to the disadvantage of their opponents). Avoiding the underlying social issue may also be functional for society. In general terms courts resolve disputes; it is up to others to address issues of social, economic, or political contention.

Attrition of cases

At the centre of thinking about civil courts is the model of formal adjudication—parties present their cases to a court, the adversary process operates and a matter is disposed of by formal adjudication. Despite this popular picture, relatively few of the cases which are begun in court are adjudicated. Instead, the great majority are disposed of by default judgment, discontinued, or settled. Figures on this for the courts as a whole are set out in the next part of this chapter. The attrition evident in these global figures is replicated in specific areas. Of 16,500 personal injury cases a leading British insurance company closed in the twelve months to October 1999, 87 per cent settled without any legal proceedings being started, 12 per cent

---

[101] [2000] UKHL 45; [2001] 1 AC 268; [1997] EWCA Civ 3008; [1998] Ch 439, CA; [1997] Ch 84.

[102] The Court of Appeal held that the Attorney General as guardian of the public interest could invoke the civil law in aid of the criminal law (the Official Secrets Act 1989).

settled after that point, and only 1 per cent resulted in a trial.[103] A study of 762 personal injury cases drawn from solicitors' files found that in only one third of cases were proceedings issued, and of these only five went to trial.[104] In an examination of 920 requests for the issue of a summons in relation to a liquidated claim made over a four-week period in the county court in Sheffield, it was found that 878 (95 per cent) resulted in the summons being issued. In 16 per cent of cases there was no action known to the court post-issue and they were eventually struck out. In another 7 per cent the claimant withdrew the action, and in 130 cases (14 per cent) the court was notified of a settlement. Over half the cases (58 per cent) continued to either default judgment (44 per cent) or a defence being entered (19 per cent). There were successful applications to set aside default judgment in 17 cases (2 per cent). Hearings were scheduled in 144 cases (16 per cent), and held in 112 cases (12 per cent). Most of those were small claims hearings, or a hearing preparatory to that, with just four resulting in trial before a county court judge. There were no appeals from any of those cases.[105] If cases had gone to appeal, however, there might well have been a further attrition. Overall, then, the passage of cases through the courts can be characterized as a continuation of the pyramidal structure already seen with grievances. Not all cases pass through each stage of the process, with many dropping out along the way and being dealt with other than by active intervention of courts. Contact with the courts may well contribute to this attrition, however, as parties are confronted with their case and that of the other side.

Decision Making

Formal adjudication of civil law cases begun is atypical. Civil courts dispose of the bulk of cases by routine administration or by providing a forum in which cases are settled or abandoned. Characterized in this way, the civil courts parallel other organizations in society to a greater extent than if the focus were to be, as it often is, on adjudication alone. Whether the way in which courts handle cases by routine administration or by facilitating settlement is ideal is a separate issue. The concern here is primarily with the way courts actually work in practice. However, the normative question inevitably arises, just as it does in the criminal courts, where the counterpart of routine administration and settlement is the sentencing of those pleading guilty, in some cases after the prosecution has agreed to drop a more serious charge against the defendant (popularly characterized as plea bargaining).

---

[103] M. Zander, *The State of Justice* (London, 2000), 41.

[104] P. Pleasence, *Report of the Case Profiling Study. Personal Injury Litigation in Practice* (London, 1998), 51–2 (hereafter *Case Profiling Study*).

[105] J. Shapland, A. Sorsby, J. Hibbert, *A Civil Justice Audit*, Lord Chancellor's Department Research Series 2/02 (London, 2002), 55–62.

Routine administration

Much of what the courts do in disposing of cases involves routine administration—approving outcomes sought by a claimant without opposition from the defendant, those agreed elsewhere or those determined by social or economic factors. A court order may be desired to guarantee compliance with those outcomes or because it is a precondition to further action. One aspect of routine administration is the consent judgment, where parties have settled a case and simply enter judgment as a formal record.[106] Another is default judgment where the claimant gets judgment straightforwardly since the defendant has not filed an acknowledgement of service or a defence to a claim.[107] To be distinguished is the summary judgment, which may be given against a claimant or defendant on the whole of a claim or on a particular issue, but only if the court considers that the other side has no real prospect of succeeding and there is no other compelling reason for a hearing.[108] Originally summary judgment was to dispose of cases expeditiously where there was simply no defence. Later it was extended to defences where there were merits but not sufficient in the eyes of the court to justify the development of their evidential or legal basis for an ultimate hearing.

With much routine processing, court officials undertake a limited inquiry to ensure that an application fits established categories (often, this only involves checking that documents are correctly completed) and then give their imprimatur by entering judgment. There is no judicial input, not least because there are no contested issues. For example, both parties want a divorce and have agreed on care and contact in relation to the children and the division of the family property. (Divorce is an example of a court order being a legal prerequisite to persons taking further action, in the particular case, remarriage.) As with divorce, a court may order an individual's bankruptcy or the winding up of a company in a routine manner when there are no disputed matters.[109] Nonetheless, such orders have profound consequences—a change in a person's status in the case of divorce or bankruptcy, and the end of a company's existence in the case of a winding up.

Debt collection and possession actions are well recognized as areas where the civil courts frequently engage in the routine processing of cases. As noted, such claims typically result from institutions such as businesses, banks, building societies, utilities, and social and private landlords taking action against individuals. By having a

---

[106] CPR r 40.6(2), (3). See D. Foskett, *The Law and Practice of Compromise*, 5th edn. (London, 2002), 178.

[107] CPR r 12.3. See CPR r 13.3 on setting aside default judgment if there is a real prospect of success. See *ED & F Mann Liquid Products Ltd v Patel* [2003] EWCA Civ 472.

[108] CPR r 24.2. Granting summary judgment must be in accordance with the Overriding Objective in CPR r 1.2 (see 149 below) and the requirements of Article 6 of the European Convention on Human Rights.

[109] During 2003 the number of bankruptcy petitions was 36,581 and the number of company winding-up petitions was 9,829.

judgment entered, even a default judgment, the claimant is then able to invoke the court's enforcement powers, however illusory these may prove to be in practice. In fact many financial institutions see the main advantage of court action as increasing the pressure on the individual to come to an agreement about repaying the debt rather than as a direct means of recovering the money.[110] A judgment may be a legal prerequisite to further action where, for example, on mortgage default the bank or building society wishes to resell the property. While not legally necessary, a judgment may be valuable to a claimant, for example the creditor contemplating further action, such as seeking the insolvency of a debtor or writing off the debt for regulatory or tax purposes. Although individuals may possibly have a defence or counter-claim in relation to a debt or possession claim, these are not always raised because of the cost—the very fact of a debt or possession action usually indicates a lack of financial resources—or because of social factors, including a lack of access to legal advice and assistance.

Most money claims in the county court in England and Wales are entered by default—1,317,206 default actions out of 1,354,446 money claims begun in 2003—or by the claimant accepting the defendant's offer to pay all or part of the amount claimed.[111] Typically no judge is ever involved in such claims. The Claim Production Centre was established in 1990 to process bulk claims from those such as banks, credit and store card issuers, and utilities, which supply the information to the centre electronically. It issued 631,667 claims in 2003 representing almost half of total default claims. Debtors often ignore default judgments and the court's enforcement procedures may prove ineffective.[112] Over the last 15 years there has been a fall in money claims issued by the county court.[113] Some creditors now use arrears management and recovery teams in preference to the courts.[114] Litigation is the last resort, and then only for larger debts.

There were 217,530 actions for the possession of land in the county courts in 2003. The bulk of these divided as shown in Table 3:[115]

Table 3. Possession action, county court, 2003

	Private mortgagees	Social landlords	Private landlords
Actions entered	63,465	135,829	17,485
Orders made	15,999	29,285	8,352
Suspended orders	22,838	62,217	3,100

[110] M. Hope, *Household Indebtedness, Voluntary and Involuntary. A Study of Court Summonses*, Lord Chancellor's Department Research Series 8/97 (London, 1997), 29.

[111] *Judicial Statistics 2003*, 42.

[112] J. Baldwin, *Evaluating the Effectiveness of Enforcement Procedures in Undefended Claims in the Civil Courts*, Department for Constitutional Affairs Research Series 3/2003 (London, 2003).

[113] *Judicial Statistics 2003*, 41.

[114] N. Dominy & E. Kempson, *Can't Pay or Won't Pay? A Review of Creditor and Debtor Approaches to the Non-Payment of Bills*, Department for Constitutional Affairs Research Series 4/2003 (London, 2003), 39.   [115] *Judicial Statistics 2003*, 43.

Actions for possession involve a judicial hearing, although typically cases are heard in groups. An order for possession entitles the claimant to obtain a warrant for possession, to evict the mortgagor or tenant, although the parties may still negotiate a compromise to prevent that occurring. Duty solicitor schemes may help in this.[116] As indicated in the table, the court orders many possession orders to be suspended, so that as long as the defendant complies with the terms of the suspension to pay, say, current instalments and something towards the arrears, the order cannot be enforced.

Greater safeguards ought to be introduced in the routine processing of cases, especially default work. Claimants' cases may not always be unassailable.[117] More importantly, many debtors, tenants, and mortgagors would pay were it not that their ability to do so is affected by the vicissitudes of life. One approach, pursued by the government, is to encourage institutional creditors to be sensitive to the distinction between those who can't and won't pay, and to ensure that court action is only taken 'where it is genuinely necessary'.[118] This can be done, in the first instance, through self-regulation, for example industry codes of practice. Social housing landlords can provide debt advice and assistance for those potentially with rent arrears to avoid unnecessary repossessions where other ways of recovering them are possible.[119] Another approach, more a long-stop, would be to have stronger vetting of a claimant's case as a precondition to obtaining a default judgment. At present claimants who obtain a default judgment are in a strong position, because of the difficulties of having it set aside. The costs of legal action can be added to the original claim, and if judgment is entered an order for costs can be obtained. Even if there is no defence to a claim for debt or for possession, it is desirable to have procedures whereby the possibility of assisting individuals to repay by instalments but over a longer period is always properly explored.

Settlement

The conventional legal wisdom is that civil litigation is wasteful and disruptive, and that strong efforts ought to be made to settle cases out of court. The law facilitates settlement in various ways, especially through its procedural rules.[120] Clearly courts do have an influence on settlements; as some writers put it, settlements occur in the 'shadow of the law'.[121] Courts do this through their decisions, which are used in bargaining and which shape expectations as to what would

---

[116] 58 above.

[117] e.g. J. Luba, N. Madge & D. McConnell (eds), *Defending Possession Proceedings*, 5th edn. (London, 2002).

[118] Department of Trade and Industry, *Fair, Clear and Competitive. The Consumer Credit Market in the 21st Century* (London, 2003), 91.

[119] L. Phelps, M. Carter, *Possession Action—The Last Resort?* Citizens Advice, (London, 2003), 49–54.   [120] 162–8 below.

[121] R. Mnookin & L. Kornhauser, 'Bargaining in the Shadow of the Law: The Case of Divorce' (1979) 88 *Yale LJ* 950.

occur if a matter went to a hearing. An obvious example is the amounts awarded in personal injury cases, which are taken into account in settling similar, later claims.[122] In addition, the cost of litigation, in particular the rule that costs follow the event, induces settlements. Settlements occur because most cases are relatively straightforward and once the facts are clear do not involve major uncertainties about the law.

Settlement practices, and the potential for settlement, vary with a range of factors including the parties involved, the existing or future relationship between them, their relative strengths, the type of case, legal costs, the certainty of outcome,[123] and the attitude and reputation of the lawyers involved.[124] Some cases are more difficult to settle than normal because of the personal animosity of the parties, because they are test cases, or because of what is at stake. A continuing relationship between the parties, on the other hand, is conducive to settlement because a range of informal sanctions push in that direction. On the basis of reputation and experience lawyers evaluate whether their opponents genuinely want settlement. Lawyers may not rush into settlement for fear of giving the impression that their case is shaky or not worth much. Clients sometimes determine the pace of settlement negotiations; financial necessity, for example, may make them interested in a quick settlement. Lawyers sometimes delay matters deliberately in the interests of clients, for example, if they are representing a defendant debtor, a person who wishes a particular arrangement for child contact to continue, or a target company in a takeover battle. In commercial litigation, where large sums of money are at stake, it is possible by procedural manoeuvres and appeals to wear down the weaker side and possibly to force it to a settlement. The practices of institutional litigants regarding settlements is also an important factor; for instance, certain insurers now favour an early settlement of claims in personal injury litigation.[125]

There is a high incidence of settlements. Sometimes these occur after proceedings have begun but before the hearing, at the door of the court or during the hearing itself. An official estimate is that of the cases set down for trial in the Queen's Bench Division of the High Court in 2003, 1,070 were withdrawn before a

---

[122] *Heil v Rankin* [2001] QB 272, para. 6. There are a number of services providing information on awards in personal injury cases, including online: e.g. *Kemp and Kemp The Quantum of Damages* (London, looseleaf).

[123] Theoretically the decision to settle is reciprocal in character: the claimant with a high probability of success is usually matched by a defendant with a low probability.

[124] For general discussion of settlement: R. Dingwall, T. Durkin, P. Pleasence, W. Felstiner & R. Bowles, 'Firm Handling: The Litigation Strategies of Defence Lawyers in Personal Injury Work' (2000) 20 LS 1; H. Genn, *Hard Bargaining. Out of Court Settlement in Personal Injury Actions* (Oxford, 1987); S. Wheeler, *Reservation of Title Clauses* (Oxford, 1991); D. Harris *et al.*, *Compensation and Support for Illness and Injury* (Oxford, 1984). For US literature: e.g. S. Gross & K. Syverud, 'Don't Try: Civil Jury Verdicts in a System Geared to Settlement' (1996) 44 *UCLA LR* 1, 51; C. Silver, 'Does Civil Justice Cost Too Much?' (2002) 80 *Tex. LR* 2073, 2107–11.

[125] T. Goriely, R. Moorhead & P. Abrams, *More Civil Justice? The Impact of the Woolf Reforms on Pre-action Behaviour*, The Law Society and Civil Justice Council, Research Study 43 (London, 2002), 58.

hearing, struck out, or settled by consent order; 150 were settled at the door of the court or during the course of the hearing; and 370 were tried to completion.[126] Of the 363 cases disposed of by the Technology and Construction Court, 297 were struck out, settled or discontinued, 41 tried and 9 transferred.[127] Settlement occurs as well in the Administrative Court.[128] For the county court, the official estimate is that of actions set down for trial in 2003, 2,980 were settled at the commencement or during the hearing, 11,130 were tried to completion, and 1,060 were struck out.[129] In the small claims jurisdiction, however, settlements are fewer since lay people representing themselves appear not to regard it as appropriate, or even proper, to engage in out-of-court discussions once a claim is issued.[130]

Lawyers sometimes defend late settlements as being necessary if they are to perform their duty to their clients. This view is put strongly by lawyers who believe that it is only with hard bargaining that realistic offers are made.[131] However, another explanation for such settlements is that where late briefing occurs it is only on the eve of a hearing that the barristers properly and realistically appraise a case. Yet another explanation, given by practitioners, is that settlements often occur late because only then do the parties appreciate what a court hearing involves. Practitioners' perceptions of the particular judge allocated to hear a case may also affect whether or not they try to settle it. Late settlement is increasingly discouraged.[132] Traditionally, the civil courts facilitated settlement mainly indirectly, through the 'radiating' effects of their decisions and the existence of rules such as those relating to payment into court. Following the introduction of pre-action protocols and other Woolf reforms, the civil courts now play a more direct role in the settlement of cases. To that and its desirability we return in the following chapter.

Adjudication

Attrition means that in terms of cases begun it is relatively rare that the courts give authoritative rulings after a completed adjudication. Even cases which obtain a date for hearing may have settled by the hearing. In addition, cases sometimes settle after the hearing has commenced, which may occur because the weaknesses of a party's case are exposed or because the partial hearing resolves important issues, with the result that the parties are able to agree on the others. Cases where there is a completed adjudication do not always match the adversary model of the conventional wisdom. It may be that there is only an applicant, and no defendant,

---

[126] *Judicial Statistics 2003*, 33.   [127] *ibid.*, 38.
[128] L. Bridges, G. Mezaros & M. Sunkin, 'Regulating the Judicial Review Case Load' [2000] *PL* 651.
[129] *Judicial Statistics 2003*, 45.
[130] J. Baldwin, 'Litigants' Experiences of Adjudication in the County Courts' (1999) 18 *CLQ* 12, 17.
[131] H. Genn, *Hard Bargaining*, (Oxford, 1987), 46, 53, 134.
[132] e.g. *Lownds v Home Office* [2002] EWCA Civ 365; [2002] 1 WLR 2450, para 9.

as where a party obtains an *ex parte* injunction, an executor seeks an authoritative construction of a will, a company applies for its winding up, or a liquidator of a company wants a ruling on how to proceed.

Even if these qualifications are taken into account, adjudication is often still far removed from a world where evenly matched parties are able to place all relevant considerations before the court, which then decides the matter by the rational application of the law to the facts. Delays, expense, and tactics all distort the ideal model. Outcomes may reflect the nature, interests, and representation of the parties, as well as the legal merits. An obvious point is that even at appellate level there are many litigants in person facing represented parties.[133] Llewellyn described the position neatly in relation to the right to sue for damages for breach of contract:

[T]he right could rather more accurately be phrased somewhat as follows: if the other party does not perform as agreed, you can sue, and if you have a fair lawyer, and nothing goes wrong with your witnesses or the jury, *and* you give up four or five days of time and some ten to thirty percent of the proceeds, and wait two to twenty months, you will probably get a judgment for a sum considerably less than what the performance would have been worth—which, if the other party is solvent, and has not secreted his assets, you can, in further due course, collect with six percent interest for delay.[134]

At the end of the process, after the parties present their positions, courts do give authoritative rulings on matters. But if there is an underlying dispute, adjudication will not necessarily lead to its resolution. Obvious examples are provided by courts deciding family issues, whose decisions exacerbate, rather than resolve, the underlying dispute between the parties involving, say, contact with a child. As will be seen, in all areas where an adjudication has occurred the parties may do nothing, may refuse to accept the outcome, or may pursue non-legal avenues for more favourable redress of the matter.

Rules are central to adjudication, although not determinative. (For present purposes rules include legal principles, standards, and values.[135]) They are supplemented by norms, such as those falling under the rubric of legal ethics, which influence the behaviour of lawyers and judges involved in the process.[136] The basis of the rules and norms is to ensure that decisions accord with the relevant law and facts. But they also affect matters such as the participation of parties in the decision, procedural fairness, rationality, finality and public support for the courts. Adjectival rules (procedural and evidentiary) must address matters such as the definition of issues, the identity of the adjudicator and whether he or she ought to be disqualified in the particular case, the hearing of the matter (for example, requiring the adjudicator to give all parties an opportunity to present their case, determining how matters are to be proved), the method of decision making (for example, allocating responsibility for decisions between judge and jury, confining a decision to

---

[133] e.g., *Ali's case*, 1–2 above.

[134] K. Llewellyn, 'A Realistic Jurisprudence—The Next Step' (1930) 30 *Colum.LR* 431, 437–8.

[135] See R. Dworkin, *Taking Rights Seriously* (London, 1997), 14. ff; K. Sullivan, 'Foreword, The Justices of Rules and Standards' (1992) 106 *Harv.LR* 24.　　　　[136] Chapter 6 below.

evidence and arguments presented by the parties at the hearing with all present), the nature of the decision (for example, whether it is to be announced in open court, whether reasons are needed in support), and the extent of any appeals (for example, time limits, whether confined to issues of law).

Under the common law adversary system, procedural rules confine adjudication, in the main, to the issues raised by the documents which commence the proceedings (the so-called 'statements of case', previously the 'pleadings'). Courts are reluctant to force a party to pursue what they think are important issues, just as they do not interfere by calling witnesses without the consent of the parties. While courts are under some duty to assist in ensuring justice there are cases where, through ignorance or incompetence of the parties, matters are not raised on which a party might succeed or the court may come to a different conclusion. The Overriding Objective of the Civil Procedure Rules puts a greater onus on courts to ensure an equality of arms.[137] Evidentiary rules are designed to elicit relevant evidence and to minimize distortions.[138] There is still the problem that evidence might be inaccurate for reasons such as honest mistake and lapses of memory. Under the common law system courts make definitive findings of fact and use them as a basis for judgment, even though they have only been established on the preponderance of evidence.[139] Overall, the adversary system is based on the assumption that, apart from management issues, the judge should play a relatively passive role during the trial, relying largely on the parties to present their side of the matter to what they see as the best advantage. The stance is said to aid neutrality, since the judge need not make any premature decisions about a matter.[140]

Substantive rules of law have a direct application to results. A variety of issues arise. Which rules of law are relevant? What do they mandate, if anything, in the particular case? How are they to be applied consistently with what has occurred in prior similar cases? What if they do not clearly cover the issue in dispute: is reference made, or should it be, to analogous rules, to underlying principles of law, to the public interest, to morality, to justice, or to yet other factors? Do the results the rules produce accord with community notions of morality and justice? To what extent do and should courts develop new rules?

What actually determines the judicial response to these issues—the 'silent true reason for decisions'[141]—may not always coincide with what judges say are the relevant considerations. In practice, social needs, public policy, general legal

---

[137]   149 below.

[138]   Twining notes the variety of perspectives on trials:'[T]rials are referred to as forensic lotteries or degradation ceremonies or licensed battles or conveyor belts'.See 'Evidence and Legal Theory' (1984) 47 *MLR* 261, 274.

[139]   Alternative approaches, such as the use of presumptions, are discussed in M. Shapiro, *Courts* (Chicago, 1981), 11–12.

[140]   See J. Jolowicz, 'Adversarial and Inquisitorial Models of Civil Procedure' (2003) 52 *ICLQ* 281.

[141]   Lord Browne-Wilkinson, 'The Impact on Judicial Reasoning', in B. Markesinis (ed.), *The Impact of the Human Rights Bill on English Law* (Oxford, 1998), 22. See also R. Stevens, *The English Judges* (Oxford, 2002), 73–6.

values, a judge's background and values may blend with specific legal rules in a complex mix. The issue has given rise to considerable jurisprudential discussion. The point to highlight here is that there is some element of choice in judicial decision making.[142] The distinction between the literal and purposive interpretation of legislation—what the language says or what it was intended to accomplish when drafted—masks, rather than illuminates, this truth.[143] Language is open-textured, and there is always some scope for discretion in its interpretation. What is said to be a literal interpretation may be impregnated with policy choices, albeit downplayed or passed over.

In some areas common law courts have given some emphasis to policy considerations and values in decisions. Risk-spreading through insurance has featured in negligence cases; the right to be able freely to consult one's lawyer in professional privilege cases; access to justice in cases dealing with court procedures; and the importance of deferring to the executive in relation to issues of national security in immigration cases.[144] Most judges now acknowledge that they have some role in making law, although this may be within the confines of extending established principle by means of inference, deduction, and analogy. Occasionally the courts will abrogate an existing common law rule, as in *Kleinwort Benson Ltd v Lincoln CC*[145] where there was a Law Commission report recommending legislation to do this. When its principles apply the Human Rights Act 1998 entrusts the courts with a wider purchase on public policy than before.[146] Yet the activism which the principles suggest must be restrained in their application, as Professor Conor Gearty argues, because in a properly functioning representative democracy judges should simply not do certain things.[147] Gearty also argues for restraint to avoid disproportionate intrusion on the legal system and analytical incoherence.

The dominant view is the belief that if the law is settled, judges ought to apply it even if the particular results are undesirable. Change in such circumstances must come from Parliament, possibly at the initiative of law reform bodies, but not from the courts, which do not have the institutional capacity to handle issues with major social or economic ramifications. Lord Nicholls of Birkenhead put the matter this way in a case involving a claim by a transsexual person of one sex to be recognized by the law as of the other sex:

This would represent a major change in the law, having far reaching ramifications. It raises issues whose solution calls for extensive enquiry and the widest public consultation and

---

[142] e.g. T. Bingham, *The Business of Judging* (Oxford, 2000), chs 2–3; S. Sedley, *Freedom, Law and Justice* (London, 1999), 42–3, 56; J. Griffith, *The Politics of the Judiciary*, 5th edn. (London, 1997).

[143] See *R v Secretary of State for the Environment, Transport and the Regions ex p Spath Holme Ltd* [2000] UKHL 61; [2001] 2 AC 349, paras 388–396.

[144] e.g. *Smith v Eric S Bush* [1990] 1 AC 831, 858–9; *R v Derby Magistrates, Court, ex p B* [1996] 1 AC 487, 507; *R v Lord Chancellor, ex p Witham* [1998] QB 575; *Secretary of State for the Home Department v Rehman* [2001] UKHL 47; [2003] 1 AC 153, 195G–H, *per* Lord Hoffmann.

[145] [1999] 2 AC 349.

[146] e.g. *R (Kebilene) v Director of Public Prosecutions* [2000] 2 AC 326, 374–5 *per* Lord Hope.

[147] C. Gearty, *Principles of Human Rights Adjudication* (Oxford, 2004), ch. 6.

discussion. Questions of social policy and administrative feasibility arise at several points, and their interaction has to be evaluated and balanced. The issues are altogether ill-suited for determination by courts and court procedures. They are pre-eminently a matter for Parliament, the more especially when the government, in unequivocal terms, has already announced its intention to introduce comprehensive primary legislation on this difficult and sensitive subject.[148]

This approach is consistent with those who believe in the supremacy of politics in our society. However, a view with some support is that judges ought to be more active in changing settled law. A justification for this is said to be that Parliament is increasingly paralysed by an institutional inability to cope with change.[149] The evidence for this is tenuous. In any event, advocates of judicial activism fail to specify in detail the respective spheres of judicial and parliamentary action or to give sufficient attention to the issue of judicial accountability in a democratic society.[150] The conventional view is that it is the task of the executive, with Parliament, not the courts, to govern the country and to determine moral and social disputes.[151]

Outputs

That legal maxims hunt in pairs is neatly illustrated in relation to remedies: *ubi jus ibi remedium* (where there is a right, there is a remedy), as opposed to *ubi remedium ibi jus* (where there is a remedy, there is a right). Whatever the truth of the matter historically, it is certainly the case that the law relating to remedies has a profound influence on what the civil courts can do. Remedies, however, are only part of the outcome of cases. It may be that a remedy has to be enforced by a separate procedure to ensure compliance. And there is much more besides. Two issues are discussed here: first, the outcome of cases for the parties involved, and secondly, whether those outcomes have an impact on wider social behaviour.

Outcomes

Various outcomes of civil cases have already been alluded to—settlements, discontinuances, consent orders, default judgments, summary judgments, and judgments after a hearing. The remedies granted by civil courts range from declarations as to what the law is, through money awards (damages), to specific orders such as injunctions, specific performance, company and child care and contact

---

[148] *Bellinger v Bellinger* [2003] UKHL 21; [2003] 2 AC 467, para. 37. cf. *Ghaidan v Godin-Mendoza* [2004] UKHL 30; [2004] 2 AC 557, para. 33.

[149] See M. Kirby, *Judicial Activism* (London, 2004), 56–8.

[150] J. Griffith, 'The Common Law and the Political Constitution' (2001) 117 *LQR* 42, 65–6.

[151] See e.g. *R v Home Secretary, ex p Fire Brigade Union* [1995] 2 AC 513, 567, *per* Lord Mustill; *R (Pretty) v DPP* [2001] UKHL 61; [2002] 1 AC 800, 810A–B, *per* Lord Bingham.

orders. In addition to lump sum awards courts can now order structured settlements for periodic payments of damages.[152] The grant of specific orders such as injunctions is hedged with limitations, however, and overall the range of court orders is far narrower in scope than the sort of solutions possible through legislation.[153] Typically, civil courts have only a limited concern with the parties before them, unlike, say, some youth courts or the courts in theocratic or authoritarian societies, where a case provides an avenue for the examination of a person's larger personality and behaviour.

Court orders typically decide that one party is legally right and the other legally wrong. Compromise is not generally the order of the day, even though it might be in keeping with community views of doing justice, or conducive to resolving the social dispute underlying litigation. The issue arises in an acute form when two parties are adversely affected by the fraud of a third party, who disappears or is unable to pay compensation to the person suffering the loss. Both parties may be innocent or both may share some responsibility for the fraud having occurred. Yet the courts do not formally divide the loss according to the justice of the case as once suggested by Lord Devlin but decide the issue in black and white terms.[154] Exceptionally legislation has provided for an apportionment of loss in some cases, most notably with contributory negligence.[155] Prior to the relevant legislation, a claimant who was negligent was barred completely from recovering against a negligent defendant, but now the courts need only reduce the damages recoverable to the extent thought just and equitable given the claimant's share in the responsibility for the accident.

The majority of claimants before the civil courts are successful. As well as for those instituting actions which result in a default judgment or possession order, the same applies to cases which are tried. There were 760 judgments in the Queen's Bench Division of the High Court in 2003 in cases set down for trial, more than 80 per cent in favour of the claimant only.[156] Over 14,000 actions were set down for trial in the county court that year, in addition to those cases disposed of by a small claims hearing. Just less than three quarters were in favour of the claimant.[157] Table 4 gives the details and shows that more claimants in debt cases were successful than claimants in negligence cases.

The evidence from these official figures is replicated in more detailed studies. Of the 81,142 legal aid certificated personal injury cases closed in the 1996–7 financial year, 63 per cent were successful overall, although the success rate ranged from 80 per cent with motor vehicle injury cases to less than 20 per cent with medical negligence cases.[158] In the study of 762 legal aid certificated personal

---

[152] Courts Act 2003, ss 100–101.
[153] But see J. Young, 'The Constitutional Limits of Judicial Activism: Judicial Conduct of International Relations and Child Abduction' (2003) 66 *MLR* 823, 834.
[154] *Shogun Finance Ltd v Hudson* [2003] UKHL 62; [2004] 1 AC 919, 933H.
[155] Law Reform (Contributory Negligence) Act 1945, s 1(1).
[156] *Judicial Statistics* 2003, 33.   [157] *ibid.*, 45.   [158] *Case Profiling Study*, 58–9.

Table 4. Actions set down for trial in county court, by result, 2003

	For claimant	For defendant	For both	Total
Debt	1,890	230	170	2,280
Personal injury	6,010	1,410	170	7,580
Other negligence	620	120	20	770
Other	2,510	580	390	3,480
Total	11,020	2,340	750	14,110

injury cases from 1996–7, 92 per cent of the motor vehicle injury cases were successful, but only 19 per cent of medical negligence cases.[159] Cases relating to minor injuries generally enjoyed greater success rates than those relating to severe injuries, which lends some support to the notion that defendants will sometimes settle smaller claims because of the nuisance value.[160]

Perhaps all this should not be surprising. It seems a reasonable assumption that most claimants act rationally and have calculated that they are likely to succeed before they institute legal action. However, just because a claimant succeeds does not mean that the defendant has lost. For the purposes of settlement negotiations, claimants may claim for more than they know they will obtain, and defendants may deny liability whatever their real views. The final result in which the claimant ostensibly succeeds may be closer to what the defendant, rather than the claimant, really wanted all along. When damages are recovered individual parties do not necessarily win substantial amounts. In fewer than one fifth of successful cases in the *Case Profiling Study*, relating to all legal aid certificated personal injury cases closed in 1996–7, did recoveries exceed £10,000, and in only 2 per cent of such cases were damages £1,000,000 or more. Almost 70 per cent of all successful cases saw damages of less than £5,000.[161] Because claimants who litigate are successful overall in obtaining relief, courts authorize the transfer of considerable sums of money. The Court Funds Office—part of the Court Service—acts as a banker when there have been payments in relation to court awards, for example for children.[162] The sums involved are considerable.[163]

The binding quality of court decisions derives partly from the standing which courts have in society. Many parties obey the decision of a court, whether or not they agree with it, because it issues from an institution with authority and thus there is no need for enforcement action. However, the binding quality of court decisions may involve an element of coercion. In some cases parties have to have judgment executed by obtaining the appropriate order, for example, a warrant of execution, or a warrant of possession. Often, an order for execution is obtained by institutions such as social landlords *in terrorem* (as a warning). Court officials need

[159] *Case Profiling Study*, 60.   [160] *ibid.*, 61.   [161] *ibid.*, 40.
[162] CPR r 21.2; CPR r 40.6(2), (3).   [163] *Judicial Statistics 2002*, 92 (£3.1 billion in 2002).

never implement it, for subsequently the sum of money is eventually paid, the property transferred, or other appropriate action taken. Sometimes coercion is necessary because of evasion or defiance of a court order. Enforcing judgment generally requires parties to approach the court afresh and may even involve them in further litigation. The unscrupulous and knowledgeable have been too easily able to frustrate the enforcement process. The steps to reform the process are well overdue.[164]

Social impact

There are many conceptual problems in assessing the social impact of judicial decisions, as opposed to the outcomes for particular litigants. These parallel those outlined in Part II of the book about the general impact of law. What is evident is that a limited number of decisions do have a significant impact on public policy. The decisions affirming values such as access to justice, equality before the law and the rule of law are especially important. These are also decisions which touch specifically on important areas of the political process, determine major human rights issues, result in the delay or abandonment of major developments, or dispose of important economic prizes or impose burdens. For example an English court has set the parameters within which the Boundary Commission must determine constituency boundaries for elections; the House of Lords held that transsexual employees who have undergone gender reassignment are entitled to be treated equally with non-transsexual members of that gender; a leading case in judicial review declared that government funding towards a dam development project overseas was unlawful because it failed to meet the conditions for granting foreign aid; and in holding that disabled patients had a legitimate expectation to live in a new facility as long as they chose, which it would be an abuse of power to upset, the Court of Appeal was conferring on them a substantive financial benefit.[165] Examples are also available in the judgments of the European Court of Justice having a significant impact on public policy in each of these broad areas.

In areas of public law the impact of judicial decision may generally be more important than elsewhere. Judicial review of administrative action provides an example. For any individual organization the incidence of judicial review is relatively small, so it is unlikely to touch the core of its operation. Moreover, many challenges are unsuccessful, thus upholding, possibly reinforcing, government policy. Even if successful, the particular applicants may not succeed when the

[164] *Effective Enforcement*, Cm 5744 (London, 2003); Courts Act 2003, s 99; J. Baldwin & R. Cunnington, 'The Crisis in Enforcement of Civil Judgments in England and Wales' [2004] *PL* 305.

[165] *R v Boundary Commission for England, ex p Foot* [1983] QB 600; *Chief Constable of West Yorkshire Police v A* [2004] UKHL 21; [2004] 2 WLR 1209; *R v Secretary of State for Foreign and Commonwealth Affairs, ex p World Development Movement Ltd* [1995] 1 WLR 386; [1995] 1 All ER 611; *R v North and East Devon Health Authority, ex p Coughlan* [1999] EWCA Civ 1871; [2001] QB 213 respectively.

matter is administratively redetermined, and other applicants in a similar position may be thwarted by regulatory or administrative changes.[166] Nonetheless, a decision sometimes has effects on government administration beyond its particular circumstances. Thus the considerable volume of judicial review cases on homelessness, while not having a profound repercussion on street-level administration, made a significant impression on the interpretation and shaping of the legislation.[167] A study of the impact of judicial review on the Independent Review Service of the Social Fund found some influence in its early days as it sought to establish its legitimacy, but less over time as service efficiency became the watchword of the organization.[168] In the area of asylum the courts' main impact was in the area of procedure, enabling asylum seekers to put their case, but there was little influence on the functioning of administrative justice and none whatsoever on public policy.[169] As far as the consequence of judicial review on tribunals is concerned, one study found that it was patchy. While compliance was fairly readily achieved with the requirement, for example, for Mental Health Review Tribunals to give reasons, that was not the case in relation to even a core legal value such as procedural fairness, as applied to the role of the medical member of that tribunal.[170]

If we turn to private law, it is difficult overall to identify a large number of decisions which have had an impact on general social behaviour. Despite the attention lawyers lavish on private law decisions, they do not generally have the same dramatic social consequences as legislation, even legislation which is rarely, if ever, litigated. For example, the establishment of small claims courts has been of far greater social importance for consumers than the many cases on contract, consumer credit or the Trade Descriptions Act 1968, although it is the cases which tend to feature in the text books and law school teaching. Similarly, town planning legislation has been more influential for the environment than decisions on the law of nuisance, and employment legislation for workers than decisions on the contract of employment. Perhaps this limited impact of case law should not be surprising. Common law cases are decided in the context of particular disputes—the wider context is not generally of concern. A second factor in the lack of impact is that the implications of particular cases are not obvious to most members of the community.[171] While social and economic arrangements are built around new legislation, a court case only unusually provokes the same response. Finally, case law is generally

---

[166] An Australian study found that applicants ultimately succeeded in 60 per cent of cases: R. Creyke & J. McMillan, 'The Operation of Judicial Review in Australia', in M. Hertogh & S. Halliday (eds), *Judicial Review and Bureaucratic Impact* (Cambridge, 2004).

[167] S. Halliday, 'The Influence of Judicial Review on Bureaucratic Decision-Making' [2000] *PL* 110, 121.

[168] M. Sunkin & K. Pick, 'The Changing Impact of Judicial Review: The Independent Review Service of the Social Fund' [2001] *PL* 736.

[169] R. Thomas, 'The Impact of Judicial Review on Asylum' [2003] *PL* 479.

[170] G. Richardson & D. Machin, 'Judicial Review and Tribunal Decision-Making' [2000] *PL* 494, 514.

[171] M. Galanter, 'Justice in Many Rooms: Courts, Private Ordering, and Indigenous Law' (1981) 19 *J. Leg. Pluralism* 1, 11–15.

not a powerful factor in constituting economic and social relations when compared with legislation. The latter has a better chance of moulding community mores or the drive for profits because it can create administrative structures and establish a sophisticated scheme of sanctions.

This is not to deny that some private law cases can have an effect beyond the immediate parties to the litigation. Three examples suffice. First, a judgment of the House of Lords in July 2000 precipitated a crisis in Equitable Life, the oldest mutual life assurance company in the United Kingdom, by exposing deep-seated financial management problems.[172] What followed was loss to individual policyholders and possibly also a further loss of public faith in the financial services industry.[173] Secondly, the decision of the House of Lords in the *Fairchild* case meant those contracting mesothelioma when negligently exposed to asbestos by more than one employer could recover compensation, even though they could not prove which employer had exposed them to the fatal asbestos fibre.[174] An inkling of the ramifications of this decision for asbestos alone comes from a report of the Trade Union Congress, that over the four years to 2001 some 18,000 people died as a result of working with the material.[175] The third example concerns the guidelines laid down by the courts in a number of important banking cases, concerning the steps which a lender should take to satisfy itself that the consent of wives (and others in a similar close relationship with a borrower) to act as surety was properly obtained.[176] A study of the impact of these guidelines on banks and building societies found that they did have a positive effect on institutional practices in explaining matters to customers.[177]

A cluster of cases, or repeated litigation, in an area of private law is usually going to have greater social significance than the isolated case. It is a truism that the whole complex of contract law, say, has had an effect on the way commercial contracts are negotiated and implemented. A series of tort cases 'opened the floodgates' to persons injured in motor vehicle and industrial accidents, allowing them to obtain compensation through litigation. As a result, the courts perform what is effectively a social welfare function, rather than a government agency. The doctrinal developments favouring this must be seen against the background of the growth of liability insurance.[178] However, it is doubtful whether liability rules

---

[172] *Equitable Life Assurance Society v Hyman* [2002] 1 AC 408; *Report of the Equitable Life Enquiry*, HC 290, 2004, 39–40 (the Penrose Report).

[173] Parliamentary Commissioner for Administration, *The Prudential Regulation of Equitable Life*, 4th Report, Session 2002–2003, HC 809, 2003.

[174] *Fairchild v Glenhaven Funeral Services Ltd* [2002] UKHL 22; [2003] 1 AC 32, reversing the Court of Appeal.

[175] *Mapping the Misery of Asbestos* (London, 2001). The figure of £6 billion for victims has been mentioned. See also the Rand Corporation study, S. Carroll *et al.*, *Asbestos Litigation Costs and Compensation* (Santa Monica, CA, 2002).

[176] R. Cranston, *Principles of Banking Law*, 2nd edn. (Oxford, 2002), 213–20.

[177] M. Pawlowski & S. Greer, 'Constructive Notice and Independent Legal Advice: A Study of Lending Institution Practice' (2001) 65 *Conveyancer* 229.

[178] See J. Morgan, 'Tort, Insurance and Incoherence' (2004) 67 *MLR* 384.

have had any deterrent effect on the way people drive or work, compared with the influences of road traffic penalties and health and safety at work legislation. This is notwithstanding that the way damages are assessed in such cases—generously or otherwise—affects the level of premiums payable by motorists and employers to insure against liability. Still in the area of tort law, it is said that defamation law in Britain greatly inhibits investigative journalism.[179] Although there may be an element of truth in this it is difficult to accept the proposition wholesale when many areas ripe for investigative journalism, but in which defamation is irrelevant, go unexplored. And there are whole areas of economic and social life—education, transport, the arts, and so on—where private law litigation is largely irrelevant. As well as social factors, the courts' own institutional limitations cause their decisions to have little impact. Most common law courts rely on the executive to enforce judgments and on others to initiate punishment of those in contempt of its orders. Public interest litigation such as that in the United States, where the courts transferred themselves into administrative agencies developing, overseeing, and implementing structural reform of prisons, is exceptional in Britain.[180]

Naturally, courts also have a limited impact if their decisions are reversed, either directly or indirectly, by administrative or legislative action. Admittedly, courts may be able to limit legislative amendment of their decisions by their interpretation of the relevant legislation or the application of other common law doctrines. The upshot may therefore be that judicial decisions and legislation are part of a continuing process, adjusted by the judges or by government in a dialectic with each other.

Where there are financial consequences of a court's decision for the public revenue, Parliament may act relatively quickly to overturn it.[181] So, too, where public policy is firmly set, as with asylum.[182] An adverse decision under the European Convention on Human Rights may also provoke a prompt legislative response.[183] Without such incentives spurring them to action, however, governments are usually more dilatory about introducing legislation to amend or reverse a judicial decision. For example, in 1947 the House of Lords confirmed that farmers could not be liable in negligence if their animals strayed onto a road and caused an accident.[184] Considerable criticism of the decision followed on the basis that it was inappropriate in societies with heavy, fast-moving traffic on the roads. Yet it was not until 1971 that the rule was abrogated and this subsidy to farmers at the

---

[179] G. Robertson & A. Nicol, *Media Law*, 4th edn. (London, 2002), x, ch. 1 *passim*. See I. Hargreaves, *Journalism. Truth or Dare?* (Oxford, 2003), 179–204.

[180] M. Feeley, 'Implementing Court Orders in the United States: Judges as Executives', in M. Hertogh & S. Halliday (eds), *Judicial Review and Bureaucratic Impact* (Cambridge, 2004). See 315 below.

[181] e.g. Finance Act 2004, ss 30–37, Sch 5; Case C–324/00 *Lankhorst-Hohorst GmbH v Finanzampt Steinfurt*, [2003] STC 607.

[182] See the examples in R. Thomas, *op.cit.*, 500, 502–3.

[183] e.g. Prevention of Terrorism Act 2005; *A v Secretary of State for the Home Department* [2004] UKHL 56; [2005] 2 WLR 87.   [184] *Searle v Wallbank* [1947] AC 341.

expense of road-users greatly reduced.[185] The time which elapses before the effect of a decision, or body of decisions, is amended or reversed may be compounded if a matter is referred to a law reform body for comment and recommendation. It may be that some governments have taken this course with a view to delaying controversial legislation.

With legislative amendment or reversal of court decisions, much also depends on whether a government is motivated enough about an issue to act swiftly. The motivation may be ideological because of pressure from outside interests. Under the Trade Union and Labour Relations (Consolidation) Act 1992, discrimination against employees on the ground of trade union membership is prohibited.[186] When the Court of Appeal in *Wilson and Palmer*[187] held that restricting pay rises to people who transferred from collective bargaining to personal contracts discriminated against trade union members, the Conservative government introduced the so-called 'Ullswater amendment' to the 1992 Act. It permitted action short of dismissal against trade union members if the employer's purpose in taking such action was 'to further a change in his relationship with all or any class of his employees'.[188] Subsequently on appeal, the House of Lords held that the discrimination in *Wilson and Palmer* was permissible, since it was discrimination by omission, not action.[189] In 1999, the Labour government amended the Act to outlaw discrimination by omission.[190] (In 2004 the Ullswater amendment was repealed, following a ruling of the European Court of Human Rights in the *Wilson and Palmer* cases.[191]) Compare the reaction to the *Shimizu* case,[192] which gave rise to a concern that minor features on buildings in a conservation area could be demolished without the need for planning consent. Although, in response to the judgment, the government announced in 2001 an intention to strengthen planning controls, nothing had been done by October 2004.[193] The ideological imperative is absent and the pressure from outside interests not of sufficient salience to have government pull out the stops.

Separate from, although analogous to, legislative reversal of a court decision is where a court judgment is used as an occasion to facilitate legislation. In *Quintavalle* the High Court held that the system of licensing for the use of embryos in treatment and research under the Human Fertilization and Embryology Act 1990 was confined to those the product of fertilization, not those

---

[185] Animals Act 1971, s 8(1).   [186] Section 137. See also ss 146, 152.

[187] *Associated Newspapers Ltd v Wilson; Associated British Ports v Palmer* [1994] ICR 97 CA.

[188] Trade Union and Labour Relations (Consolidation) Act 1992, s 148(3).

[189] [1995] 2 AC 454.   [190] Employment Relations Act 1999, s 2, Sch 2, para. 2.

[191] See Employment Relations Act 2004, ss 29–32; *Wilson and the National Union of Journalists, Palmer, Wyeth and the National Union of Rail, Maritime & Transport Workers, Doolan & others v United Kingdom* [2002] IRLR 568.

[192] *Shimizu (UK) Ltd v Westminster CC* [1997] UKHL 3; [1997] 1 WLR 168.

[193] See Office of the Deputy Prime Minister, *Review of Permitted Development Rights* (London, 2003), paras 35.24–35.29.

created by cell nuclear replacement.[194] While that decision was being appealed, the government took the opportunity of rushing through legislation, previously promised, to ban human reproductive cloning.[195] Despite a perception that the legislation was intended to reverse the High Court decision,[196] in fact it did not extend to the problem which the case raised, although the government indicated that it would introduce further legislation, when parliamentary time allowed, should its appeal be unsuccessful. Shortly after the 2001 Act became law, the Court of Appeal reversed the High Court decision—and the Court of Appeal decision was upheld by the House of Lords[197]—so it became unnecessary to legislate further. However, the original High Court decision was a convenient peg on which to hang legislation that was planned anyway.

Conclusion

Concentrating on trouble or hard cases misses much of the process of the civil courts as institutions. In many respects, the courts are functioning as administrative agencies or as facilitators of compromises rather than directly resolving contested issues of law and fact. Even if the concern is hard or trouble cases, it would seem crucial to understand how these cases percolate up to the relevant court for decision. Exclusive use of disputes as an organizing category for understanding courts overlooks other aspects such as their role in law-making, the assertion of values, and social policy. In addition, there are the occasions when parties approach courts to obtain the imprimatur of the state in relation to a matter, without any suggestion that there is a dispute, or even a potential dispute, involved. A corporate rearrangement is an example. So in theory courts are institutions of the state through which power can be asserted or confirmed. Most litigation, however, is oriented to the claims of individuals and organizations, removed from what is ordinarily obtainable, under existing arrangements, through the political process. And so long as individuals continue to advance so many claims through the courts, in particular with accident litigation, it is difficult to sustain an argument that the courts are simply ratifying the legal claims of dominant groups in society. Moreover, given the limited impact of liability rules on behaviour, it seems beside the point to concentrate attention, as lawyer-economists might be tempted to do, on the efficiency of those rules.

By contrast, the approach to courts adopted in this chapter provides a framework for understanding their internal operation, as well as their relationship with

---

[194] *R (Quintavalle) v Secretary of State for Health* [2001] EWHC 918. See S. Pattinson, 'Reproductive Cloning: Can Cloning Harm the Clone?' (2002) 10 *Medical LR* 295.

[195] Human Reproductive Cloning Act 2001.

[196] e.g. G. Hurst & N. Hawkes, 'Ministers Rush to Close Cloning Loophole', *The Times*, 23 November 2001, 16.

[197] [2003] UKHL 13; [2003] 2 AC 687; [2002] EWCA Civ 29; [2002] QB 628, CA.

their society. It lays a tentative basis for formulating theories about matters such as how courts operate and the functions of law. Take just a few of the issues touched on here. First, there is the uneven use of courts in terms of who brings cases and over what issues. How else are grievances dealt with in society, how is conflict otherwise channelled, and how are challenges to basic political and economic structures filtered so that the courts rarely deal with them directly? Secondly, there are the many cases before the civil courts where commercial and property interests obtain judgment in default against individuals. How is it possible to talk about the latter having legal rights if those rights are not properly explored in what actually happens? Thirdly, the transformation of issues, and the identification of the legally relevant, raise questions about power, in particular about how the understanding and interpretation of events takes place in a legal context. Finally, there is the role of courts in public policy. Compared with government which can work through the executive arm of the state, it seems that courts overall are not central in this regard. If the outcomes in particular cases have unacceptable ramifications, these can generally be reversed by legislation. Nonetheless, courts have an important function in reminding society, especially speaking to those with power, of the importance of values such as equality before the law, the need to respect civil, political, human, and social rights and that acting in accordance with law is a cardinal feature of liberal democratic society.

5

Procedure

In an ideal world of making public policy, problems and objectives would be clearly defined, options rigorously canvassed and calculated choices made. In the real world this is a counsel of perfection; rationality must be pursued under severe constraints. Not only does one never start with a blank sheet but resources are limited (time being one of the most important); the problem as opposed to its symptoms may not be immediately identifiable; there are opposing interests which close off certain lines of inquiry and outcome; and values might be contested and a trade-off necessary. For these reasons it has been popular to conceptualize public policy making as 'the science of muddling through' rather than as a completely rational process. In this interpretation large policy changes ('big bang') are not typical; rather there is a public policy cycle in which incremental changes are adopted, these giving rise to further demands, this in turn producing more adjustments.[1]

The Woolf Report, and the changes it has brought about to civil procedure in England and Wales, fit more a big bang than an incremental model of public policy making.[2] Case management in particular constitutes a radical break with the adversary nature of English civil procedure. In its implementation, Lord Woolf had argued for an early and wholesale, rather than a more staged, introduction of the changes. The latter was the approach ultimately adopted.[3] Nevertheless, big bang it remained. Aspects of the reform such as the emphasis on speed and reduced cost accorded with the sense of crisis and the need for significant change felt by leading judges, practitioners, and court administrators.[4] Lord Woolf was

---

[1] C. Lindblom, 'The Science of "Muddling Through"' (1959) 19 *Public Admin. R* 79. See also C. Lindblom, *The Policy-Making Process*, 2nd edn (Englewood Cliffs, NJ, 1980); *The Intelligence of Democracy* (New York, 1965); H. Redner (ed.), *An Heretical Heir of the Enlightenment. Politics and Science in the Work of Charles E. Lindblom* (Boulder, 1993); M. Bayes, *Incrementalism and Public Policy* (New York, 1992).

[2] Lord Woolf, *Access to Justice. Interim Report* (London, 1995) (hereafter *Interim Report*); *Access to Justice. Final Report* (London, 1996) (hereafter *Final Report*).

[3] e.g. *Final Report*, 31; *Report to the Lord Chancellor by Sir Peter Middleton* (London, 1997), 53–7. For recent examples of a staged implementation of civil procedure reform: *Report of the Civil Procedure Review Committee: A New Judicial Culture* (Quebec, 2001); Australian Law Reform Commission, *Review of the Adversarial System of Litigation: Rethinking the Federal Civil Litigation System*, Discussion Paper No. 62 (Sydney, 1999).

[4] For one of the most elegant: Sir Thomas Bingham, 'The Price of Justice' (1993–94) 16 *Holdsworth L.R.* 4; T. Bingham, *The Business of Judging* (Oxford, 2000), 386. See also G. Lightman, 'The Civil Justice System and Legal Profession—The Challenges Ahead' (2003) 22 *CJQ* 235.

able to build a coalition favouring fundamental change to address these issues. His critics were routed since they had no ready solutions to the problems and were reduced either to defending the status quo or to contending that radical change was impossible.[5] Overall the adoption of the bulk of the Woolf proposals has seen a fundamental change in legal practice and culture in a remarkably short space of time.

One dimension to the formulation and implementation of public policy is the role of social research. However one might conceptualize the process to what extent do the findings of social research feed into policy making? If so do they broaden or limit the range of choices? Is social research taken seriously by policy makers and are their recommendations consistent with it? Are policy changes monitored by social researchers for unintended consequences so that adjustments to redress these can be made? Is social research less necessary with incremental change since by definition knowledge is acquired in doing and large-scale change never made?

Over 100 years ago Holmes took the view that social research is necessary for the rational study of law.[6] Efforts were made by legal realists in the 1920s to redirect Yale Law School to 'fact research'. Yet there is still an uneasy relationship between law and social research. Judicial decision making in England is mainly untouched by social research although the Law Commission makes occasional use of it. While the former is perhaps excusable given its focus, the style of reasoning and how information enters the process, the latter is at first glance more difficult to fathom.[7] Perhaps one explanation is that the law schools have proved remarkably resistant to using social research and this affects law reform generally. Most forms of legal scholarship are non-sociological or anti-sociological.[8] The tone is set by the fashions in contemporary legal theory, which largely eschew social research as a source of understanding and as a guide to law.

Unfortunately civil justice has been a Cinderella subject and not a great deal of social research has been done. In 1994 four directors of leading research institutions into civil justice in the United States called for a systematic collection of data

---

[5] See e.g. M. Zander, 'Why Lord Woolf's Proposed Reforms of Civil Litigation Should be Rejected' in A. Zuckerman & R. Cranston (eds.), *Reform of Civil Procedure* (Oxford, 1995); C. Dehn, 'The Woolf Report: Against the Public Interest', *ibid.*; M. Zander, 'The Woolf Report: Forwards or Backwards for the New Lord Chancellor?' (1997) 16 *CJQ* 208.

[6] Oliver Wendell Holmes, 'The Path of the Law' (1897) 10 *Harv.LR* 457, 469.

[7] One valuable inquiry, sponsored by the Law Commission, is H. Genn, *Personal Injury Compensation: How Much is Enough?*, Law Com. No 225 (London, 1994). See J. Tanford, 'Law Reform by Courts, Legislatures, and Commissions following Empirical Research on Jury Instructions' (1991) 25 *Law & Soc.Rev.* 155. The need for empirical research upon which to propose law reform has been increasingly acknowledged by law commissions. See, e.g., Australian Law Reform Commission, *Review of the Adversarial System of Litigation: Rethinking the Federal Civil Litigation System*, Discussion Paper 62 (Sydney, 1999), para. 1.25, and the various empirical studies referred to there (e.g. T. Matruglio & G. McAllister, *Part One: Empirical Information about the Federal Court of Australia* (Sydney, 1999)).

[8] W. Twining, *Blackstone's Tower: The English Law School* (London, 1994), 144–5. See also L. Friedman, 'The Law and Society Movement' (1986) 38 *Stan. L.R.* 763.

so that reasoned and effective policy could be made.[9] There has been a notable response by social scientists.[10] How much worse the position has been in England, although the Civil Justice Review did commission some important studies,[11] and the Woolf Inquiry drew on existing social research and conducted some itself, in particular in relation to legal costs.[12] The recommendations of the Inquiry were broadly consistent with the existing social research. In line with Lord Woolf's own advice that his recommendations be carefully monitored, government has funded a limited amount of social research. There has been some other relevant social research as we shall see, some under the auspices of the Department for Constitutional Affairs (previously the Lord Chancellor's Department). This chapter draws on the social research, such as it is, to examine civil procedure in England and Wales, mainly the big bang brought about by the Woolf reforms.[13] In addition to what has been described as managerial judging or court control, the chapter discusses some other broad themes of the procedural change such as facilitating settlement, dealing with cases proportionately and encouraging alternative dispute resolution. Let us begin first with a sketch of the procedural changes themselves.

Procedural Change

Procedural rules loom large in discussion by lawyers about the cost and efficiency of litigation. Changes in the rules of court are regularly proposed as solutions to these problems. Procedural proposals are sometimes radical, as with Adrian Zuckerman's argument for a more truncated form of procedure along the lines of

---

[9] M. Galanter, B. Garth, D. Hansler & F. Zemans, 'How to Improve Civil Justice Policy' (1994) 77 *Judicature* 185.

[10] In addition to the sources below see S. Djankov, R. La Porta, F. Lopez-de-Silanes & A. Shleifer, 'Courts' (2003) 118 *Q J Econ* 453.

[11] Civil Justice Review, *Report of the Review Body on Civil Justice*, Cm 394, 1988, para. 349 (hereafter, 'Civil Justice Review').   [12] *Final Report*, Annex III (by Professor Hazel Genn).

[13] Apart from the Woolf Inquiry, there have been several reform proposals in other Commonwealth jurisdictions to achieve a more accessible and efficient civil procedure. See, e.g., in New Zealand: New Zealand Law Commission, *Striking a Balance: Your Opportunity to Have Your Say on the New Zealand Court System* (Preliminary Paper, 2002); in Canada: (*Canadian Bar Association, Report of the Canadian Bar Association Task Force on Systems of Civil Justice* Ottawa, 1996); Canadian Bar Association, *A National Agenda for Civil Justice Reform* (Consultation Document, 1996); *Civil Justice Review: Supplemental and Final Report* (Ministry of the Attorney General, Toronto, 1996); *Report of the Civil Procedure Review Committee: A New Judicial Culture* (Quebec, 2001); Ontario Law Reform Commission, *Study Paper on Prospects for Civil Justice* (Executive Summary, 1995); Ontario Law Reform Commission, *Rethinking Civil Justice: Research Studies for the Civil Justice Review* (Toronto, 1996); Law Reform Commission of Nova Scotia, *Reform of the Administrative Justice System in Nova Scotia* (1997); Manitoba Civil Justice Litigation Committee, *Civil Justice Review Task Force Report* (1996); Australia: Australian Law Reform Commission, *Managing Justice: A Review of the Federal Civil Justice System* (2000); Law Reform Commission of Western Australia, *Review of the Criminal and Civil Justice System* (2002).

summary judgment.[14] While it cannot be denied that procedural rules have an effect on cost and efficiency, they are only part of the equation, a point almost universally acknowledged. As already mentioned we have been hampered by the relative lack of empirical data. For example, there was no systematic evidence that the enhancement to the central philosophy of 'cards on the table' in the early 1990s improved the rate of settlement.[15] Responding to a chorus of criticism about the rule, the Woolf Report contained recommendations for its modification.[16] The impact of major changes introduced following that report have been more closely monitored and we return to some of the evidence below.

Procedural reform was central to the Woolf Inquiry. The Report laid the groundwork for a new procedural code, as well as making recommendations on specific matters such as the handling of disputes before action. The Report sets out Lord Woolf's philosophy for a new procedural code. It is incorporated in the Overriding Objective of the Civil Procedure Rules. Dealing with cases justly is the lodestar, but that is defined as a matter of reaching the right result in terms of the facts and the law, but mindful that resources are not unlimited and that decisions must be reached within a reasonable time.

1.1. (1) These Rules are a new procedural code with the overriding objective of enabling the court to deal with cases justly.

(2) Dealing with a case justly includes, so far as is practicable—

    (a) ensuring that the parties are on an equal footing;

    (b) saving expense;

    (c) dealing with the case in ways which are proportionate—

        (i) to the amount of money involved;

        (ii) to the importance of the case;

        (iii) to the complexity of the issues; and

        (iv) to the financial position of each party;

    (d) ensuring that it is dealt with expeditiously and fairly; and

    (e) allotting to it an appropriate share of the court's resources, while taking into account the need to allot resources to other cases.

Ensuring cases are on an equal footing as an aim of the civil justice system has been touched on in Chapter 2 and is developed further in Chapter 7.[17] Procedurally it takes shape in matters such as court fees, the treatment of litigants in person and in the responsibility on the court to ensure that one side does not use procedural devices such as excessive disclosure (discovery) to browbeat the other.[18] Crucially, the Overriding Objective, indeed the Civil Procedure Rules as a whole, is based on the important assumption that cases do not all need the same preparation or same

---

[14] A. Zuckerman, 'A Reform of Civil Procedure—Rationing Procedure Rather Than Access To Justice' (1995) 22 *JL&Soc* 155.

[15] Sir Leonard Hoffmann, 'Changing Perspectives on Civil Litigation' (1993) 56 *MLR* 297, 306.

[16] See now CPR rr 32.2, 32.4. On the statement of truth to accompany witness statements: CPR r 22.1(1)(c).   [17] 36 above, 218 below.

[18] e.g. CPR r 31.3(2).

lengthy trial. Procedures must be proportionate to the type of case hence, for example, the three tracks—the small claims track, fast track and multi-track.[19] The greater control over the resources allocated to individual disputes has rightly been categorized as a new philosophy of distributive justice in procedure, ensuring resources are allocated fairly to litigants and would be litigants and that the allocation of resources is proportionate to the importance of each dispute.[20]

The Civil Procedure Rules (CPR) are a new procedural code and represent without doubt the greatest change in English civil procedure since the Judicature Acts 1873–5.[21] Simplification is one theme running through the Woolf reforms. It was a reaction to the complexity which Lord Woolf saw in the existing procedures and substantive law. Complexity in Lord Woolf's view facilitates the aggressive tactics of lawyers which he deprecates, and indeed 'is considered by many to require it'.[22] Simplification is the goal for the new rules. By statute the rules must be simple and simply expressed.[23] A primary aim of the new rules is understandability. Not only is there now a single set of rules applying to the High Court and county courts, but there is simplification of specific procedures. For example the number of ways of commencing an action and the plethora of initiating documents (writ, default summons, fixed date summons, originating summons, originating application) have been abolished, to be replaced by the issue of a claim form.[24] As Lord Woolf put it, reducing the size of the rules and the number of propositions contained in them, using simpler and clearer language and adopting a simpler drafting structure are all aimed 'at enabling the rules to perform their proper function once more'.[25]

Perhaps the most radical innovation in procedure has been the emphasis on party cooperation, a distinct break from the adversary culture. In particular this has been furthered by the introduction of pre-action protocols. As a result, court procedure now reaches back to mould behaviour before the parties have even invoked court processes. Their aim is to encourage settlement and promote a culture where litigation is a last resort.[26] Overall the protocols require the early exchange of information about a claim. Thus claimants must send a detailed letter about a prospective claim, which defendants must respond to in full within a specified period. Claimants must generally hold back from litigating in the meantime. Under the protocols parties must cooperate to varying degrees on matters such as experts, and under them there is an obligation on the parties to demonstrate a willingness to settle. There are pre-action protocols for specific areas such as personal injury, clinical negligence, housing disrepair, defamation,

---

[19] 158, 168 below.

[20] A. Zuckerman, 'Justice in Crisis: Comparative Dimensions', in A. Zuckerman, *Civil Justice in Crisis* (Oxford, 1999), 51. See also *Jones v University of Warwick* [2003] EWCA Civ 151, para. 25 [2003] 1 WLR 954, 962; [2003] 3 All ER 760, 767.

[21] See generally N. Andrews, *English Civil Procedure* (Oxford, 2003); A. Zuckerman, *Civil Procedure* (London, 2003). [22] *Interim Report*, 7.

[23] Civil Procedure Act 1997, s 2(7). [24] CPR r 7.2.

[25] *Final Report*, 281. See also 272. [26] CPR Protocols PD, 1.4(1)–(3).

disease and illness, and judicial review. A general pre-action protocol was proposed, but not proceeded with on the basis that it was too ambitious and likely to lead to confusion.[27] Absent a pre-action protocol in an area parties still are expected to act reasonably in exchanging information and documents at an early stage and must generally seek to settle their dispute without recourse to litigation. The protocols are guides to good practice, although the courts take breach into account in giving case management directions and making orders for costs.[28] Overall, the practitioners' view of pre-action protocols is positive.[29] Their success has been greatest when accompanied by other changes such as the greater specialization in solicitors' practices brought about by factors such as the changed funding of legal aid.[30]

One aspect of the new procedure is the greater control on cost. Lord Woolf had seen the problem of cost as the most serious besetting the litigation system. One aspect is that costs can be used as an instrument of war, to drain, or deter an opponent.[31] Under the Overriding Objective of the CPR, the court must consider whether the likely benefits of taking a particular step justify the cost of doing so.[32] There is also a wide power for the court to take any step or make any order for the purpose of managing a case and furthering the Overriding Objective.[33] The Costs Practice Direction sets out steps which lawyers must take to keep clients informed about their potential liability in respect of costs and in order to assist the court in case management. Thus the court can require the parties to file cost estimates to show the likely effect on costs of making specific case management decisions. The implication is that the court can limit costs at the outset by a protective costs order so that they are proportionate to the amount involved or where a public interest is involved.[34] This can be done through a case management decision that the costs of a party are to be limited to a certain figure, proportionate to the amount involved and reflecting whether they are a claimant or defendant. In heavier litigation a costs cap may be administered by the court and be altered to reflect changed circumstances.[35]

Costs are normally awarded on a standard, rather than an indemnity, basis. Under the CPR standard basis costs are confined to items proportionately and reasonably incurred and which are proportionate and reasonable in amount.

---

[27] Lord Chancellor's Department, *General Pre-action Protocol*, Consultation Paper, December 2001.   [28] *Carlson v Townsend* [2001] 1 WLR 2415, CA.

[29] Lord Chancellor's Department, *Civil Justice Reform Evaluation. Further Findings* (London, 2002), paras 3.13–3.26.

[30] T. Goriely, R. Moorhead & P. Abrams, *More Civil Justice? The Impact of the Woolf Reforms on Pre-action Behaviour*, The Law Society and Civil Justice Council, Research Study 43 (London, 2002), 45, 296–8 (hereafter *More Civil Justice?*) See 48 above.

[31] *Merck & Co. Inc. v Generics (UK) Ltd* [2003] EWHC 2842, para. 83; [2004] RPC 31.

[32] CPR r 1.2(h).   [33] CPR r 3.1(2)(m). See also CPR r 3.1(5).

[34] *Solutia (UK) Ltd v Griffiths* [2000] EWCA Civ 736, paras 28, 29, 33; *King v Telegraph Group Ltd* [2004] EWCA Civ 613; *R (Corner House Research) v Secretary of State for Trade and Industry* [2005] EWCA Civ 192.

[35] C. Lethem, 'Costs as a Case Management Function' (2001) 151 *NLJ* 1276, 1276.

Whether the costs incurred by claimants are proportionate is to be judged in part having regard to what it is reasonable to believe they might recover at the time of the claim; with defendants regard is to be had to the sum it was reasonable for them to believe the claimant might recover should the claim succeed.[36] If the costs as a whole are proportionate, all that is normally required is that each item should have been reasonably incurred and the cost of that particular item is reasonable. If the costs as a whole are disproportionate, the court will have to be satisfied that the work in relation to each item was necessary, and if so that the cost of that particular item is reasonable.[37] Initially, empirical work suggested that the goal of making costs proportionate was being missed. For example, average costs in a sample of fast track personal injury cases were nearly 70 per cent of damages, both prior to and immediately after introduction of the CPR in 1999.[38] Courts are now adopting a robust approach and disallowing disproportionate costs.[39]

Fixed costs in the fast track are another method of addressing the problem of disproportionate costs. The original intention was that costs in the fast track should be fixed.[40] Here Lord Woolf was influenced by the German experience, where control on litigation costs has meant that litigation is less expensive than in England.[41] There are few examples of fixed litigation costs in the common law world. Following Lord Woolf's recommendation, research was conducted into costs in the proposed fast track. The Institute of Advanced Legal Studies used hypothetical personal injury and contract case studies to determine the amount of work for conducting a case through the fast track. Invited groups of solicitors, district judges, and claims managers were asked to talk through their likely approach to the case studies under the new procedures and to provide detailed estimates of the time each stage would take. The research concluded that a consensus was possible over the processing of personal injury cases, so that a cost matrix for claimants and defendants could be devised.[42] With contract cases participants gave widely differing estimates, both of the work required and the time it would take. The researchers therefore concluded that it was not possible, at that stage, to estimate cost levels based on the amount of work demanded of a client's lawyer. Instead, they suggested that the amount payable by the loser to the winner should be proportionate to the value in dispute.[43]

As a result of subsequent work by the Civil Justice Council, established as a result of the Woolf reforms,[44] fixed costs now exist for road traffic accident cases.

---

[36] CPR rr 44.4(1), (2), 44.5(3).

[37] *Lownds v Home Office* [2002] EWCA Civ 365; [2002] 1 WLR 2450; [2002] 4 All ER 775, CA.

[38] *More Civil Justice?*, 177.   [39] *Habib Bank Ltd v Ahmed* [2004] EWCA Civ 805.

[40] *Final Report*, ch. 7.

[41] e.g. M. Roth, 'Towards Procedural Economy: Reduction of Duration and Costs of Civil Litigation in Germany' (2001) 20 *CJQ* 102; D. Leipold, 'Limiting Costs for Better Access to Justice—The German Experience' in A. Zuckerman & R. Cranston (eds), *Reform of Civil Procedure* (Oxford, 1995).

[42] T. Goriely, F. Butt & A. Sherr, *Costing Fast Track Procedures Through Hypothetical Studies*, Lord Chancellor's Department, Research Series 4/98, London 1998), 119–20.

[43] *ibid.*, vi, 148–9, 155, 160.   [44] Civil Procedure Act 1997, s 6.

This is a model to be extended to other litigation.[45] Costs are fixed according to a scale based on damages recovered, rather than hours spent on advancing the claim.[46] The scheme does not cover disbursements (e.g. a medical or other report), liabilities such as insurance premiums or success fees, neither does it affect any contractual right of solicitors to recover costs from their client. Fixed costs are predictable costs and should therefore facilitate access to justice. In Lord Hoffmann's view, they are also 'a more rational approach than to leave the matter to individual costs judges'.[47]

Traditionally disclosure (discovery) was justified in the UK system—civil law jurisdictions which do not permit it to any like the same extent—on the ground that it enables parties to make a more accurate evaluation of the strengths and weaknesses of a case, with the result that issues are narrowed or cases settled, thereby saving time and costs. Surprise at trial is also supposed to be reduced in that disclosure exposes false or misleading evidence. But the arguments about the deleterious effect of disclosure are well known: it became increasingly common for there to be a lack of cooperation, with parties adopting an adversarial and obstructive manner. In major cases the documentation was said to be enormous, with much of it unnecessary and irrelevant. The adverse consequences were said to be complicated pleadings, more witnesses and experts, obfuscation of issues, proceedings becoming more labour intensive, and if a settlement were achieved it tended to be after the costs have mounted up.[48] But if these have been common arguments, it has also been said that the problem is not so much disclosure as the complexity of modern commercial litigation, modern technology (for example the photocopier, electronic data) and the adversarial system which is not always conducive to a spirit of cooperation.

There has been virtually no empirical evidence about disclosure in England. Has intensive disclosure been common, or a feature of only a small number of cases? How costly has it been—not neglecting, of course, indirect costs such as the disruption to a party's business when documents relating to the matter are being rooted out? In making his recommendations, Lord Woolf was obliged to resort to a number of United States studies of the cost of disclosure and its effects on delay. For example, an influential study funded by the American Bar Foundation conducted with a sample of Chicago lawyers argued that the world of disclosure was not monolithic.[49] In smaller cases disclosure was not a consumer of time, but

---

[45] Department of Work and Pensions, *Review of Employer's Liability Compulsory Insurance. Second Stage Report* (London, 2003), 13–14.

[46] CPR Part 45, II. See J. Peysner, 'Finding Predictable Costs' (2003) 22 *CJQ* 349; J. Peysner, 'Predictability and Budgeting' (2004) 23 *CJQ* 15. K. Underwood, *Fixed Costs* (London, 2004).

[47] *Callery v Gray* [2002] UKHL 28; [2002] 1 WLR 2000, para. 36.

[48] e.g. Report by the Independent Working Party set up jointly by the General Council of the Bar and the Law Society, *Civil Justice on Trial—The Case for Change*, June 1993, paras 5.1–5.3 (the Heilbron–Hodge Report).

[49] W.D. Brazil, 'Views from the Front Lines: Observations by Chicago Lawyers about the System of Civil Discovery' [1980] *ABF Res.J.* 218; *ibid.*, 'Civil Discovery: Lawyers' Views of its Effectiveness, its Principal Problems and Abuses' [1980] *ABF Res.J.* 787; *ibid.*, 'Improving Judicial Controls Over

was straightforward and not greatly encumbered by friction or evasion. With larger cases, however, there were problems in the view of the lawyers interviewed. Delay was used as a tactic and there was over-disclosure and over-production. Many lawyers believed that the expense was often disproportionate to the benefits. Indeed in 50 per cent of the large cases at least one party believed at the end of the day that it still knew something of significance which the other party did not. Accusations were also made of abuse. Importantly the problem with disclosure in larger cases was attributed to lawyers failing to think through a case before entering discovery and because judges were inhospitable or superficial in handling disclosure disputes.

As evidenced by submissions to the Woolf Inquiry, there has been a widespread view in the profession in England that disclosure was over-used, costly, and lead to delay. While the United States research lends some support to these views, it is only in particular cases: disclosure is not a problem in the great majority of small and average cases. Too often in England the issue is looked at through the lens of the larger, commercial case. The recommendations of numerous reports in the United States—not all backed by empirical study—are based on the premise that disclosure needs control. These recommendations include beginning disclosure early, imposing judicial controls on the amount of disclosure, establishing separate disclosure 'tracks' for cases of different complexity, and imposing judicial sanctions to enforce orders and to control disclosure abuses. 'Disclosure events' have been limited in several federal judicial districts in the United States.

With all this as background Lord Woolf decided that reform was in order, although not to certain classes of cases where disclosure was not perceived of as a problem (for example running down cases).[50] To encourage settlements pre-action disclosure, which previously only applied to personal injury cases, can be ordered, and in any event is encouraged by the pre-action protocols.[51] For fast track cases, disclosure is standard disclosure; indeed the court can order that it be even more limited than that.[52] This is consistent with the objective of proportionality and with the evidence that in these cases disclosure was limited and in the main not a

the Pretrial Development of Civil Actions' [1981] *ABF Res.J.* 875. For an Australian study replicating this research: B. Cairns, *The Use of Discovery and Interrogatories in Civil Litigation* (Australian Institute of Judicial Administration, 1990). See also Australian Law Reform Commission, *Managing Justice: A Review of the Federal Civil Justice System* (Report No. 89 2000), 511 for the particular and newly emerging problems associated with disclosing electronic documents. The very large Wisconsin Civil Litigation Project, funded by the US Department of Justice, found that there was no discovery at all in 37 per cent of the cases it sampled. In the majority of cases where there was discovery it took less than 20 per cent of the time spent on the case: D. Trubek *et al.*, *Civil Litigation Research Project Final Report*, University of Wisconsin Madison Law School, Part B (1983), III, 358–60, Part C (1987), 119, 132–134, 321–322. See also J. McKenna & E. Wiggins, 'Empirical Research on Civil Discovery' (1998) 39 *BC.L.R.* 785; J. Kakalik *et al.*, 'Discovery Management: Further Analysis of the Civil Justice Reform Act Evaluation Data' (1998) 39 *BC.L.R.* 613.

[50] CPR r 31.16.

[51] *Interim Report*, ch. 21; *Final Report*, 37–52. See B. Cairns, 'Lord Woolf's Report on Access to Justice: An Australian Perspective' (1997) 16 *CJQ* 98.   [52] CPR, PD 28, para. 3.6(1)(c), (4).

problem. As regards the fast track the reforms do seem to have had a beneficial impact. With larger cases disclosure is under the control of the court, which consistently with the Overriding Objective can conduct a cost-benefit analysis of the value of going beyond the limited, standard disclosure required by the rules to more detailed disclosure.[53] This is consistent with the rather sceptical light which some of the American research throws on the value of disclosure, while recognizing that because of the cultural belief that disclosure contributes to just outcomes it cannot be curtailed too much.[54] It is also consistent with surveys of English commercial lawyers which found a majority opinion that disclosure had become too burdensome.[55] The experience so far seems to be that while at county court level disclosure has been reigned in, the higher courts are not acting consistently in keeping it within bounds, not a easy task.

Managerial Judging

In his Report, Lord Woolf developed his ideas for greater court control of litigation. The courts through new mechanisms and the work of the procedural judges would decide what procedure was suitable for each case, set realistic timetables and ensure compliance. The objective would be to define the issues and to encourage the settlement of cases at the earliest stage. A less combative approach would be required of the parties and those who did not behave reasonably would be penalized. If settlement were not achieved, court control would ensure that a case was tried as quickly and economically as could be.[56]

This aspect of Lord Woolf's Report conforms in its broad thrust to the modern trend in judicial administration, towards greater court control as the way to reduce delay and possibly costs. There is also the assumption, as in the title of Lord Woolf's report, that court control relates to greater access to justice.[57] The key element is said to be early and continuous judicial control of cases by contrast with the traditional laissez-faire approach of the adversarial system.[58] The belief is that

[53] CPR rr 31.3–31.6, 31.12.

[54] A US study suggests that in medical negligence cases disclosure is conducive to just results: H. Farber & M. White, 'Medical Malpractice: An Empirical Examination of the Litigation Process' (1991) 22 *RAND J.Econ.* 199.

[55] Herbert Smith, *Reform of the Civil Justice System. The Views of UK Corporations* (London, 1995) (41 industrial companies and 20 financial organizations interviewed, sampled from top 400 companies in Times Top 100); Simmons & Simmons, *A Paper on Lord Woolf's Proposals for the Reform of the Civil Justice System* (London, 1995) (40 clients and contacts, typically in-house lawyers with large organizations).

[56] These are of course the bare bones of the case management approach: see *Interim Report*, Section II, and *Final Report*, Section II.

[57] See also Access to Justice Advisory Committee, Commonwealth of Australia, *Access to Justice* (Canberra, 1994), para. 17.6.

[58] I. Scott, 'Case-flow Management in the Trial Court', in A. Zuckerman & R. Cranston (eds), *Reform of Civil Procedure: Essays on Access to Justice* (Oxford, 1995); R. Turner (Senior Master, Queen's Bench Division), 'The Overriding Objective and the Proactive Judge', *JSB Journal*, Issue 13, 2001, 14.

although a court should be prepared to reach a reasonable accommodation with lawyers, it should be wary about allowing lawyers to breach orders made. In other words, the court should create among lawyers the expectation that events will occur as ordered and when scheduled. Essential for greater court control is the routine collection of statistics and the constant monitoring of case progress.

Court control as envisaged in the modern judicial administration literature already existed in a form in North America and Australia and in England in the Commercial Court and the Technology and Construction Court, and with multi-party actions.[59] Outside these three areas attempts at court control in England seemed to have floundered. The Evershed Committee advocated court intervention by means of a 'robust' summons for directions whereby the Master would consider the state of the pleadings, any outstanding orders that were required, and then give directions to enable the case to be set down for trial.[60] The scheme was a failure without a serious commitment to provide the sub-judicial time required to make it effective, and lacking the sanctions needed to persuade parties to complete their preparations at an earlier stage.[61]

Despite past failures there was a strong head of wind in favour of greater court control by the time Lord Woolf reported. In one study about 140, mainly barristers, responded to questionnaires about their experience with the Commercial and Technology and Construction Courts and multiparty actions. Ninety-eight per cent of respondents agreed that timetables reduced delay with the use of fixed dates for trial being particularly useful. Over 98 per cent thought that timetables should be formulated as early as possible, and the need for strict enforcement of timetables was mentioned by many. However, a majority thought that the best method of devising a timetable was by party agreement, followed by court scrutiny. Importantly, respondents were divided as to whether 'contact time' with the court would be reduced by the use of timetabling. Almost three quarters of respondents thought that the court could play a useful role in defining the issues.[62] Similarly, surveys of the clients of two large commercial law firms found widespread support for court control.[63] Giving control of the timetable to specially appointed procedural judges and taking it away from parties and their lawyers was an especially popular reform in one of the surveys. Many respondents in the other study supported greater control, although some cautioned that the reformed system should not operate to the detriment of justice in the larger or more complex cases.

---

[59] See Australian Law Reform Commission, *Managing Justice. A Review of the Federal Civil Justice System*, Report No. 89 (Sydney, 1999), chs 6–8; N. Armstrong, A Question of Priorities: Court Management of Civil Litigation in England and Wales, PhD thesis, Nottingham Trent University, 1995, ch. I.

[60] *Final Report of the Committee on Supreme Court Practice and Procedure*, Cmd. 8878 (1953), 70–83.

[61] C. Glasser, 'Civil Procedure and the Lawyers—The Adversary System and the Decline of the Orality Principle' (1993) 56 *MLR* 307, 313.

[62] N. Armstrong, 'Perspectives on Court Management' (1994) 144 *NLJ* 131.

[63] See n. 55 above.

Various strands of court control can be identified. The first, case management, involves in broad terms a judge taking charge of a case early on and establishing a programme for its resolution.[64] Case management under the CPR occurs at various points. One is the point at which cases are allocated to one of the three tracks, the small claims track, fast track, and multi-track. Allocation occurs once the parties have responded to the allocation (trial information) questionnaire, which is generally served on the parties by the court after a defence is filed.[65] In the small claims and fast tracks, court control generally follows automatically, under the relevant rules and practice directions, without much in the way of specific court intervention.[66] In the multi-track, which is for the larger or more complex claims, the court may give directions and set a timetable, if the parties agree suitable proposals.[67] Otherwise the court may fix a case management conference or pre-trial review. If a party has a lawyer, a representative familiar with the case and with sufficient authority to deal with issues likely to arise must attend the case management conference or pre-trial review.[68] Case management of multi-track cases is generally handled in civil trial centres rather than feeder courts.[69] At the case management conference the court reviews the steps the parties have taken, gives directions as to the progress of the case, and ensures that as far as possible the parties have agreed on the matters in issue and conduct of the claim.[70] There are now standard directions needed to prepare most multi-track cases for trial and these have enabled parties to agree acceptable directions in a majority of cases.[71] A pre-trial review may be held after the parties have returned the requisite pre-trial check list (or listing questionnaire).[72]

Differential case management is a second strand of court control. It was given a definite boost in the United States by the Brookings Institute study which recommended that it be adopted in all courts. Cases of different complexity are to be placed on different time tracks of procedure and trial.[73] The Brookings study suggested three tracks: track one to apply to 'simple' or expedited cases, which require little or no judicial intervention prior to trial and can be resolved in fairness to all parties relatively quickly; track two, to apply to complex cases[74] which are

---

[64] See CPR r 1.4(2), which lists some twelve aspects to active case management.

[65] CPR r 26.3; PD 26, para. 2.   [66] CPR, PD 26, paras 8.2, 9.2.

[67] CPR rr 29. 2(1), 29.4.   [68] CPR r 29. 3(2).

[69] CPR, PD 26, para. 10(2), PD 29.

[70] CPR, PD 29, para. 5.1. See also para. 5.3 on topics to be covered.

[71] In specialist disciplines, such as clinical negligence, the specialist Masters have devised suitable draft directions with aid of the lawyers practising in these areas.

[72] CPR rr 29.6–29.7.

[73] R. Litan *et al.*, *Justice for All: Reducing Costs and Delays in Civil Litigation* (Washington, DC, 1989). See also H. Bakke & M. Solomon, 'Case Differentiation: An Approach to Individualized Case Management' (1989) 73 *Judicature* 18.

[74] At the IXth World Conference on Procedure Law the following were identified as complex cases: major disasters (e.g. train/plane crashes) or the distribution of defective products resulting in injury to large numbers of people; environmental law disputes regarding major projected or existing projects; insolvency cases involving large numbers of litigants, which are potentially complex; possibly expropriation proceedings; large corporate and commercial disputes in particular instances—e.g.

characterized by the need for early and intense judicial involvement; and track three, to apply to standard cases, which do not fall into the other two categories. This early categorization of cases was designed to facilitate individual case management so that a case could be moved to disposition with appropriate efficiency. The National Center for State Courts in one of its studies examined differential case management in six demonstration sites for the Department of Justice (only two were civil courts).[75] Unfortunately it was not possible to evaluate on the civil side whether it produced cost savings or benefits which exceeded its costs. Certainly in one of the sites differential case management reduced delay by early disposition of easily disposable cases. At no site was it possible to develop quantitative data on whether it improved use of judge and lawyer time. Regarding participant satisfaction the study found little outright opposition.

Lord Woolf recommended adoption of differential case management, and as a result there are the three tracks under the CPR already mentioned. The first is the existing small claims system, although it now encompasses claims up to £5,000 (with personal injury and housing repair claims, this limit is £1,000).[76] Then there is the fast track for claims not exceeding £15,000. The financial level is a fairly rough dividing line but avoids the problems of applying other criteria for identifying less complex cases. Fast track cases are subject to fairly standard directions: there is a typical timetable for preparation of a case and the trial should be in hours (and certainly not exceed a day), with disclosure and oral expert evidence being restricted.[77] The third tier is the multi-track, which deals with all other cases. These include claims exceeding £15,000, but also those for less than that amount, but which are in the multi-track because they raise an issue of public importance or involve extensive oral evidence or a hearing longer than a day.[78]

A third strand of court control is the use of time standards for case processing. Well known are those of the American Bar Association: for general civil cases 90 per cent should be disposed of within a year of filing and the remainder within two years (unless there are exceptional circumstances).[79] California, for example, adopted case processing time standards modelled on the ABA standards pursuant to its Trial Court Delay Reduction Act of 1986. The ABA has also promulgated *Trial Management Standards* for trials; one aspect is the setting of reasonable time limits (after consultation with counsel) and maintaining momentum once the

---

major corporate crashes, corporate takeovers, shareholder suits: H. Lindblom & G. Watson, 'Complex Litigation—A Comparative Perspective' (1993) 12 *CJQ* 33.

[75] T. Henderson *et al.*, *Differentiated Case Management. Final Report*, National Center for State Courts (Williamsburg, 1990). Differential case management has emigrated from the United State; e.g. it was introduced in the New South Wales Supreme Court, the largest of the state jurisdictions in Australia: Practice Note 81 (1994) 32 NSWLR 243.   [76] 170 below.

[77] CPR r 26.6(4)–(5); CPR 28, PD 28. See *Maguire v Molin* [2002] EWCA Civ 1083; [2003], WLR 644.

[78] CPR rr 26.6(6), 26.8(1).

[79] American Bar Association, Standards Relating to Trial Courts, 1992 edn. See also H. Schwartz & L. Ratliff, 'Delay in State Courts: Are Time Standards An Answer?' (1986) 70 Judicature 124.

trial has begun. It is a combination of these approaches which is adopted in the CPR. For example, the trial of fast track cases should typically occur within 30 weeks of directions being given and there is a timetable of steps during this period for preparation of the case for trial. With multi-track cases, however, the court sets a timetable of steps necessary to be taken and fixes the trial date or period as soon as it can. The periods can be tailored to each case and there is no norm in the rules for multi-track cases.[80] In practice the protocols provide clear time periods for all cases during the pre-action phase, and for standard multi-track cases informal norms have evolved.

The philosophy of greater court control through involvement in the interlocutory stages of civil cases is not an uncontroversial matter. The proponents argue that civil litigation can no longer be regarded as a private matter between parties who conduct it at their own pace. Since the courts are blamed for overall delay in the system, it is said, they must take action to reduce it. Thus the philosophy of court control is said to represent the public interest by improving efficiency. In its most developed form it involves having for each case someone in the court who has responsibility for moving it expeditiously to completion. There must always be a scheduled next date by which certain specified tasks are to be completed, and that next date must always be quite short in relation to what the lawyers think is desirable or possible. Efficient court management is an integral part of attacking court delay involving measures such as classifying cases for handling in ways depending on their particular type, and using information to monitor the progress of cases through the pre-trial process. There are other justifications apart from delay reduction which can also be advanced: thus some proponents of court control see an improved quality of justice through a fairer allocation of court resources.

One of the most powerful critiques of court control is by Professor Judith Resnik.[81] Apart from questioning the empirical basis and arguing that issues of quality are neglected—we return to both these matters below—she argues that court control results in judges having a broad and uncontrolled discretion since pre-trial conferences are not recorded and the institutional constraints which ordinarily operate, such as appeal, are reduced. Parties might capitulate and comply with judicial pressure to settle. Moreover, Professor Resnik contends that no explicit norms guide judges in their decisions about what to demand of litigants; there is consequently a threat to judicial impartiality, especially where judges later try cases which they have attempted to settle.

In the debate over appropriate responses to the increasingly heavy workload of the federal courts, I am concerned about preserving the uniqueness of the judicial function . . . Among all of our official decisionmakers, judges—and judges alone—are required to provide

---

[80] CPR rr 29.2, 29.8(c), PD 29, para. 5.4.
[81] J. Resnik, 'Managerial Judges' (1982) 96 *Harv.LR* 374; 'Trial as Error, Jurisdiction as Injury' (2000) 113 *Harv.LR* 924.

reasoned explanations for their decisions. Judges alone are supposed to rule without concern for the interests of particular constituencies. Judges alone are required to act with deliberation—a steady, slow, unhurried task.[82]

These views have not passed unchallenged. Apart from the arguments in favour of court control which have been mentioned, some proponents argue that judges are representatives of litigants and the public and need to act as a check on the practice of lawyers. Court control can actually enhance accountability, not least because it can generate more management information in the courts.

What of the empirical point raised by Professor Resnik, that research on its impact means the case for greater court control is unsupported? In summarizing the quite considerable body of US research it can be said that there is *some* evidence that court control expedites cases; its impact on the private cost of litigation is, however, less sure. An early study by the Federal Judicial Center of federal district courts suggested that the success or otherwise of strong case management turned on its appropriateness. While most of the courts it investigated were characterized by strong case management, the differences lay in the relative effectiveness of alternative forms. Moreover, the courts which enforced a comprehensive pre-trial order were not necessarily the speediest or the most efficient.[83] The National Center for State Courts has conducted a number of major research projects into the impact of court management on efficiency. The National Centre for State Courts is, as a body, dedicated to the concept. In the classic study, *Justice Delayed*, the authors found that structural, caseload and procedural factors were not associated with the pace of litigation and they advanced their well-known theory that the pace of litigation is most strongly associated with the 'local legal culture'.[84] A subsequent study, *Changing Time in Trial Courts*, examined the case processing times in eighteen general jurisdiction trial courts located in urban areas. The study found that based only on qualitative observation courts with relatively fast case processing times tended to exhibit some common characteristics, including leadership, commitment to achieving time goals, and effective communication with the local Bar. In relation to case-flow management procedures, the authors write that managing cases 'is clearly much more an art than a science at the present time.'[85]

---

[82] J. Resnik, 'Managerial Judges', *op. cit.*, at 445.

[83] S. Flanders, *Case Management and Court Management in United States District Courts* (Washington, DC, 1977).

[84] T. Church *et al.*, *Justice Delayed*, National Center for State Courts (Williamsburg, 1978).

[85] B. Mahoney *et al.*, *Changing Times in Trial Courts*, National Center for State Courts, (Williamsburg, 1988), 120. See also W. Hewitt *et al.*, *Courts that Succeed*, National Center for State Courts (Williamsburg, 1991). Not all ascribe to it as leading a role. See J. Grossman *et al.*, 'Measuring the Pace of Civil Litigation in Federal and State Trial Courts' (1981) 65 *Judicature* 86, 102–3. See also T. Sullivan *et al.*, 'The Persistence of Local Legal Culture: Twenty Years of Evidence from the Federal Bankruptcy Courts' (1994) 17 *Harv.J.L.* & *Pub.Pol'y* 80; M. Heise, 'Justice Delayed? An Empirical Analysis of Civil Case Disposition Time' (2000) 50 *Case Western Reserve LR* 813.

Examining Court Delay,[86] and its follow-up,[87] analysed data from 39 urban trial courts. The former concluded that two case management characteristics, strict time disposition goals and early court control, were generally associated with courts that featured a faster pace of litigation. The latter also found that case management, especially early court intervention in scheduling case events, was correlated with a faster case processing time. In the latter, more extensive, study, however, stricter time goals displayed only a moderate correlation with a speedier pace of litigation for cases reaching the trial calendar. Yet even the finding about early case control was heavily qualified by the authors, since further analysis found that in relation to the 'typical' civil case, case management had no effect, although it did have an impact on the oldest cases. Moreover, the number of pending cases per judge displayed a stronger association with the pace of contested cases than did the point of court control. The authors conceded that it may have been because early court control was implemented in courts with smaller pending case loads per judge which produced the correlation between early court control and the quicker pace of litigation.[88]

The most influential study of the impact of court management in the United States was conducted by the Rand Corporation and published in 1996. It resulted from a Congressional decision to require ten courts to adopt specific rules and programmes involving managerial judging and compared these with another ten courts doing nothing (the intended control group). Over six years information on some 12,000 cases was collected from court files and from the judges, lawyers, and parties involved in the cases.[89] In summary it is said that Rand found the impact of managerial judging less than expected. While early judicial management signi-ficantly reduced time to disposition, it also increased the cost to litigants, although in some cases the latter was offset by the decrease in costs associated with control of discovery.[90] Yet a more careful evaluation of the Rand research does not support any adverse conclusion about the impact of court management. In this argument the context of the Rand research—the Congressional experiment—is crucial. It cannot be assumed that simply ordering the ten courts to adopt new practices would have much effect. On the whole judges and officials could continue with the same approach to handling litigation as they already had. Importantly, many courts were already using the managerial techniques required by the new

[86] J. Goerdt *et al.*, *Examining Court Delay*, National Center for State Courts (Williamsburg, 1989).

[87] J. Goerdt *et al.*, *Reexamining the Pace of Litigation in 39 Urban Trial Courts*, National Center for State Courts (Williamsburg, 1991).

[88] *ibid.*, 59, 68. These studies focused mainly on overall disposition times, but a separate study of 1500 trials in nine courts found that court control reduced actual hearing times: D. Sipes, 'The Lengths Courts Go to Try a Case—And Possible Remedies' (1988) 12 *State Court Journal* 4.

[89] J. Kakalik *et al.*, *Just, Speedy, and Inexpensive? An Evaluation of Judicial Case Management under the Civil Justice Reform Act*, Rand Corporation (Santa Monica, 1996).

[90] J. Kakalik, 'Just, Speedy and Inexpensive' (1997) 80 *Judicature* 184, 187. Critics of the Woolf reforms have argued it has increased costs, e.g. M. Zander, *The State of Justice* (London, 2000), 42. Empirical evidence on this is lacking at the time of writing.

programmes—managerial judging has been a procedural norm in the United States over several decades. Thus it was not surprising that the impact of the programmes in these courts was less than might have been expected.[91]

The adoption of the Woolf reforms in England and Wales was different: the baseline of managerial judging was much lower than in the United States. It has been introduced wholesale into the court system. The legal culture has been transformed and is generally supportive.[92] Evidence in the early years is that court control reduced delay—the average length of time for a case from issue to trial went down from 639 days in 1997 to 498 days in 2000–1[93]—although this may also have been because of the fall-off in litigation. Costs have been the Achilles heel of case management, as evident in the United States research. What seems to have happened is a front-end loading of costs to meet the demands of the early production of information especially under the pre-action protocols. Whether this means higher costs, as costs are incurred even for cases which would have settled, must await detailed evaluation.[94]

Facilitating Settlement

The movement for greater court control runs in parallel with that to facilitate more settlements. The first of the ten basic principles of reform set out in the Heilbron–Hodge Report was that the philosophy of litigation should be primarily to encourage early settlement of disputes.[95] Lord Woolf conceived of litigation as a last resort and saw his proposals for case management as encouraging settlements at the earliest possible stage.[96] And settlement is of course pivotal to the smooth functioning of the legal process. The courts could not cope if there was not a substantial attrition of cases as they passed through the different stages of litigation.[97] But it would be wrong to draw too strict a line between settlement on the one hand and adjudication on the other. Although a case might not be tried to completion, court resources might have been involved. Decisions at interim points may lead the parties to settle and cases may also settle during trial. Settlements also occur, as the literature puts it, in the shadow of the law. A decision in a particular case may lead to the settlement of a tranche of similar cases.

---

[91] S. Flanders, 'Case Management: Failure in America? Success in England and Wales?' (1998) 17 *CLQ* 308. Flanders points out that the finding of increased costs to litigants came mainly from estimated attorney hours worked, recalled well after the event and gathered through mail surveys (at 317), and thus of questionable reliability.

[92] Surveys of solicitors show overwhelming support for the Woolf reforms, including managerial judging, and 'there is a widely held view that there has been a change of culture . . .': Lord Chancellor's Department, *Civil Justice Reform Evaluation. Further Findings* (London, 2002), paras 2.5, 2.7.   [93] *ibid.*, para. 6.4.

[94] *More Civil Justice?*, 174.   [95] Heilbron–Hodge Report, para. 1.8.
[96] *Interim Report*, 30; *Final Report*, 4, 16–17.   [97] 126 above.

Recognizing its importance, the law facilitates settlement in various ways, such as the protection given to 'without prejudice' communications.[98] The way interest rates are calculated on judgment may also provide an incentive to settle, although other things being equal much depends on the comparison between that and market rates of interest. Then there are the rules about formal offers to settle, which are designed to facilitate settlement by providing for a costs penalty if a rejecting party obtains less by judgment than the amount the other side offers.[99] That costs follow the event in our system is also said to facilitate settlement, possibly unfairly to one of the parties, compared with the American rule that in general each party bears his or her own costs.[100] In fact if a litigant were confident of winning the rule may encourage the pursuit of smaller cases which otherwise it would not be economical to litigate.[101]

Settlement practices vary with a range of factors including the parties involved, the type of case and the attitudes and reputation of the legal representatives. Some cases are more difficult to settle than normal, for example if they are test cases. Solicitors might not rush into settlement negotiations for fear of giving the impression that their case is shaky. Clients might sometimes determine the pace of settlement. In some areas solicitors may delay matters deliberately in the interests of clients, for example if they are representing a defendant debtor or a person who wishes a particular contact arrangement with children to continue. The practices of institutional litigants regarding settlement are clearly important. It is said that now insurance companies generally follow a policy of settling cases earlier, one reason being the economic advantages of doing so.[102] One complaint is that settlements occur too late in the process. The criticism is that there are unnecessary delays and that costs are unnecessarily incurred. If settlement has occurred on the eve of the trial 'the litigant has to make within minutes a decision which may affect his or her whole life'.[103] The contrary view of late settlements is that if lawyers are to perform their duties to their clients then they must wait until realistic offers are made. Settlements at the door of the court are fewer after the Woolf reforms and the number occurring before the hearing day have increased.[104]

---

[98] e.g. *Rush & Tompkins v Greater London Council* [1989] AC 1280, 1299; *Unilever plc v Procter and Gamble Co.* [2000] 1 WLR 2436; *Berry Trade Ltd v Moussavi* (No. 3) [2003] EWCA Civ 715; *The Times*, 3 June 2003.

[99] CPR rr 36.20, 36.21. Part 36 is an advance on the previous rules: claimants as well as defendants can make offers and offers can be made before a claim is issued or during proceedings.

[100] C. Glasser, 'Civil Procedure and the Lawyers—The Adversary System and the Decline of the Orality Principle' (1993) 56 MLR 307, 309.

[101] H. Kritzer, 'Lawyer Fees and Lawyer Behavior in Litigation: What Does the Empirical Literature Really Say?' (2002) 80 *Tex LR* 1943. See also N. Rickman, 'The Economics of Cost Shifting Rules', in A. Zuckerman & R. Cranston (eds), *Reform of Civil Procedure—Essays on 'Access to Justice'* (Oxford, 1995).

[102] KPMG Peat Marwick, *Study on Causes of Delay in the High Court and County Courts. Final Report* (London, 1994), 26; *More Civil Justice?*, 58.

[103] *Royal Commission on Legal Services*, Cmnd 7648 (1979), 300.

[104] Lord Chancellor's Department, *Civil Justice Reform Evaluation. Further Findings* (London, 2002), paras 4.1–4.4.

The issue that arises is whether courts should intervene more to promote earlier settlements, and also to facilitate more settlements. There is quite a powerful literature which gives an emphatic no to this question. Its argument is that courts should have nothing to do with settlement because settlement is a negation of the judicial process. This view can be traced back at least 150 years to Bentham. He abhorred compromise as a denial of justice. However equal the parties, he argued, compromise involves a sacrifice of results. In discussing Bentham's views, Professor William Twining says that it seems likely that he 'would have looked with deep suspicion on modern efforts to promote mediation, negotiation or arbitration (especially in private) . . .'.[105] The most notable modern critic is a leading Yale professor, Owen Fiss. In his 'Against Settlement'[106] Fiss attacks what he calls the dispute perspective. Equating this with adjudication is based on a fundamental misunderstanding of the nature of law as well as of judicial institutions. Fiss argues that advocates of the dispute perspective 'act as though courts arose to resolve quarrels between neighbours who had reached an impasse and turned to a stranger for help'.[107] This 'trivialises' adjudication by which courts possess 'power that has been defined and conferred by public law not by private agreement'.[108] Fiss' argument is that the job of courts is not to maximize the ends of private parties but to give force to the public values embodied in law. In the judicial administration perspective, he would argue, the opportunity to articulate legal values gives way to an over-emphasis on efficiency and technique, which diminishes the value of law.

The implications of Fiss' argument cannot go unchallenged. Quite apart from anything else there are the practicalities that without settlement the courts would not be able to handle their caseload. Moreover, Fiss' arguments turn partly on the more prominent role which US courts take in enunciating and applying general public policy and to that extent do not have the same relevance in this country. Professor Menkel-Meadow attempts a balance between Fiss and his critics. After finding wanting the efficiency arguments for settlement, she observes that:

What settlement offers is a substantive justice that may be more responsive to the parties' needs than adjudication. Settlement can be particularised to the needs of the parties, they can avoid win/lose, binary results, provide richer remedies than the commodification or monetarization of all claims and achieve legitimacy through consent. In addition, settlement offers a different substantive process by allowing participation by the parties as well as the lawyers. Settlement fosters a communication process that can be more direct and less stylised than litigation, and affords greater flexibility of procedure and remedy.[109]

To an extent the issue resolves into an empirical question about the quality of settlements and whether they are oppressive and one-sided.[110] Are parties pressured

---

[105] W. Twining, 'Alternative to What? Theories of Litigation, Procedure and Dispute Settlement in Anglo-American Jurisprudence: Some Neglected Classics' (1993) 56 *MLR* 380, 385.
    [106] (1984) 93 *Yale LJ* 1073. See also *The Law As It Could Be* (New York, 2003), ch. 5.
    [107] O. Fiss, 'Against Settlement' (1984) 93 *Yale LJ* 1073, 1082.   [108] ibid., 1085.
    [109] 'For and Against Settlement: Uses and Abuses of the Mandatory Settlement Conference' (1985) 33 *UCLA LR* 485, 504–5.   [110] H. Collins, *Regulating Contracts* (Oxford, 1999), 351.

into accepting redress considerably less than their full entitlement? In particular, do the delays associated with formal litigation compel parties to settle and to abandon valid claims and defences? Professor Hazel Genn's *Hard Bargaining* found that hard bargaining did achieve better results. In many cases, however, she found that solicitors were not achieving the best they could for their clients. She attributes this partly to inequalities in power, for example that claimants' solicitors felt that they had to cooperate when they were in a disadvantageous position with insurance company representatives. But partly also it was because of solicitors inexperienced in personal injury work and their approach to negotiations and the preparation of the particular case they were presenting.[111] Since the time of that research, there has been a much greater concentration of personal injury work in specialist lawyers, and 'dabblers' have been discouraged by market pressures.[112] The authors of some research, which thoroughly analysed eighty financial relief cases, concluded that the system was characterized by settlement but not necessarily by purposeful settlement-seeking, one reason being inactivity on the part of solicitors.[113] The authors were especially critical of the 'settlement culture' among practitioners, necessary they conceded because of the huge caseload the lawyers carry. Settlements in the authors' view were too often the product of fatigue and domination rather than the triumph of a strategic and effective approach.[114] Again specialization over the last decade is likely to be producing more effective settlement techniques among family lawyers than this research found.

The Winn Committee considered the idea of formal settlement conferences conducted by the courts ('court-annexed', in US terms). It rejected it on empirical grounds, that the American evidence did not show clearly that it led to a higher level of settlements, but also because it would delay and increase the cost of litigation as well as putting undesirable pressure on the parties to settle.[115] Likewise the Civil Justice Review, which concluded that its proposals for early exchange of witness statements would increase opportunities for settlement and that pre-trial intervention by judges should be reserved to a pre-trial hearing in the more substantial cases.[116] Yet the idea of court-annexed settlement conferences has swept important parts of the common law world and they are now an accepted feature in the United States and in some Canadian and Australian jurisdictions.[117] In the United States, settlement conferences are part of a whole managerial philosophy, that judges should be actively involved in promoting settlement. The

---

[111] H. Genn, *Hard Bargaining* (Oxford, 1987).   [112] *More Civil Justice?*, 54–6.

[113] G. Davis, S. Cretney & J. Collins, *Simple Quarrels* (Oxford, 1994), 257.

[114] Echoing Fiss they also say that the courts too have developed methods which ensure that very few trials are held: *ibid.*, 167.

[115] *Report of the Committee on Personal Injuries Litigation*, Cmnd 3691 (1968), para. 355.

[116] Civil Justice Review, para. 259.

[117] For a somewhat dated account of settlement conferences in New South Wales: R. Cranston, P. Hayes, J. Pullen & I. Scott, *Delays and Efficiency in Civil Litigation*, Australian Institute of Judicial Administration (1985), ch. 19.

assumption is that more settlements result and in some quarters that settlements produce superior results to trial. Even if cases do not settle, settlement conferences may shorten any hearing by narrowing the issues, eliciting admissions and eliminating non-contested matters. The settlement efforts of judges in the United States are sustained and various, although it would be wrong to think it is intensive in all, or even a majority of cases.[118] Opponents of court-annexed settlement conferences see any advantages more than counterbalanced by the way in which they might coerce parties into unwanted settlements and generally undermine the adversary system. It is also said by opponents that parties do not receive the same fair hearing which they would otherwise and that cases are resolved away from public view. Settlement conferences are said by the opponents to take time and to involve costs, and if judges are involved their impartiality and dignity might be undermined.

Which side of the argument does the empirical evidence about court-annexed settlement conferences support? Comparing the quality of settlement with adjudication is fraught with difficulties and it should not be surprising that there do not seem to be any studies attempting it. As far as efficiency is concerned, an early study over a six-month period of personal injury motor vehicle claims in New Jersey concluded that in all likelihood settlement conferences did not lead to fewer cases reaching trial. More definitely it concluded that mandatory settlement conferences achieved neither a higher settlement rate nor shorter trials than where the parties had a choice about the matter. However, it did find a gain in the fairly definite improvement in the quality of trials in an appreciable fraction of cases which had been to a settlement conference but not settled.[119] The classic study of delay for the National Center for State Courts found that those courts exerting more effort in settling cases did not necessarily dispose of more cases per judge than those where less was expended.[120] Similarly, the important study by the Federal Judicial Center reported that the courts with the strongest settlement activity had the fewest civil terminations per judge, while the court with the least settlement involvement had the second most civil terminations.[121] So none of this is very encouraging. One consistent finding of a variety of studies is that the use of settlement conferences does not increase disposition times; indeed it might actually increase delays.[122] The puzzle is then why many US judges are enamoured of the

---

[118] See the current handbook, D.M. Provine, *Settlement Strategies for Federal District Judges* (Federal Judicial Center, Washington, DC, 1986).

[119] M. Rosenberg, *The Pretrial Conference and Effective Justice* (New York, 1964), 29–41, 45–53. As a result of the study, New Jersey promptly made settlement conferences in personal injury vehicle claims optional rather than mandatory.

[120] T. Church *et al.*, *Justice Delayed*, National Center for State Courts (Williamsburg, 1978), 33.

[121] S. Flanders, 'Case Management in Federal Courts' (1978) 4 *Justice System J* 147, 161. See also S. Flanders, *Case Management and Court Management in United States District Courts* (Federal Judicial Center, Washington, DC, 1977), 37–9.

[122] But there may be greater predictability and hence more efficient listing: C. Baar, *The Reduction and Control of Civil Case Backlog in Ontario* (Advocates' Society, Toronto, 1994), 4.

settlement role, in particular in settlement conferences.[123] In the light of this evidence it was not surprising that, while Lord Woolf assumed that case management would facilitate settlement, he eschewed the idea that courts should formally conduct settlement conferences.[124]

Settlement has clearly been facilitated by the Woolf reforms. This is partly evident in the fall in the overall number of claims initiated in the courts since their introduction, although other factors such as the decision on public funding for civil litigation must be taken into account in explaining some of the figures. Between May 1999 and April 2001 the average number of contract and tort claims issued in the county court fell by 20 per cent, whereas the average number of possession of land and recovery of goods claims (which only benefited from the new procedures in October 2001) dropped less than 1 per cent. The comparison between the two sets of figures seems good evidence of the impact of the reforms.[125] Especially important to settlement before claims are issued are the pre-action protocols. Researchers commissioned by the Law Society and the Civil Justice Council interviewed lawyers, insurers, and claims managers specialising in personal injury, clinical negligence, and housing disrepair, and reviewed the solicitors' files of 158 personal injury claims finalized pre-CPR and those of 152 personal injury claims finalized post-CPR.[126] Overall they concluded that the Woolf reforms provided a clearer structure and greater openness and meant a cultural change in favour of settlement.[127] The pre-action protocols were said to encourage negotiation at an early stage, meant the parties had information to make more realistic appraisals of a case, and consequently made settlements easier to achieve.[128] Claimant solicitors involved in personal injury litigation welcomed the changes to the final offer rules in Part 36 of the CPR, as providing 'a way to

---

[123] Professor Marc Galanter offers a number of reasons, which are certainly suggestive:

1. Resource savings: imposed decisions require the decision maker to employ elaborate procedures and to supply elaborate justifications.
2. Avoidance of supervisions: settlements are largely unreviewable and their occurrence increases the autonomy of the forum from its hierarchic superiors.
3. Minimisation of enforcement problems: imposed decisions are less likely to be complied with than decisions that are consented to.
4. Vertical credibility: imposition endangers credibility since at least one party is agreed with the forum. Settlement enables avoidance of untoward results which would attract attacks on the forum.
5. Sense of accomplishment: participation in settlements induces a feeling of accomplishment and control.
6. Fun: finally, participation in settlements may strike a judge an engaging activity that enables him to employ beneficially his talents as a negotiator.'

M. Galanter, 'A Settlement Judge, Not a Trial Judge: Judicial Mediation in the United States', in S. Shetreet (ed.), *The Role of Courts in Society* (Dordrecht, 1988), 310–11 (footnotes omitted).

[124] In May 2004 a pilot scheme began in Manchester for joint settlement meetings in personal injury actions for more than £100,000. It is not court-annexed settlement, but the court will consider at case management conferences whether to order one.

[125] Lord Chancellor's Department, *Civil Justice Reform Evaluation. Further Findings* (London, 2002), paras 3.9–3.12.   [126] *More Civil Justice?*, 403–8.

[127] *ibid.*, 158–60, 163, 165.   [128] *ibid.*, 45, 83, 168–70, 296.

make things happen' without issuing proceedings, and helped speed up the settlement process.[129]

Proportionality and Small Claims

The Overriding Objective requires dealing with cases proportionately. Proportionality constantly enters case management decisions and has driven structural changes such as the introduction of fixed costs in the fast track. For some thirty years the small claims procedure has offered a proportionate method of resolving disputes. It thus offers a sound basis for appraising other experiments in proportionality, such as the fast track. Apart from an expansion of monetary jurisdiction, however, it was largely untouched by the Woolf reforms. That does not mean that the small claims jurisdiction has achieved perfection in facilitating access to justice. Experience elsewhere provides an agenda of possible reforms.

In *Afzal v Ford Motor Co. Ltd*[130] the Court of Appeal drew attention to the main aims of the small claims procedure of furthering access to justice, dealing with matters in an inexpensive, informal manner and getting directly to the real issues in dispute.[131] The small claims procedure now disposes of the majority of cases which go to a hearing in the county court—in 2003, 15,167 cases were disposed of by trial, while the number of small claims hearings was 52,143.[132] Of these 52,143 cases, most (34,440) involved debt claims, with the next highest categories being personal injury (2,210) and other negligence claims (7,290). As Lord Woolf said: 'I see the small claims scheme as the primary way of increasing access to justice for ordinary people.'[133] Particularly important in this regard is the 'no costs' rule, whereby in small claims unsuccessful parties cannot in general be ordered to pay the other side's cost.[134] Thus claimants should not be deterred from taking legal action because of the risk of penury if they fail. The problem, however, is that small claims in England and Wales is largely a middle-class preserve.

In other jurisdictions small claims courts are separate from the ordinary courts. In the past the issue has been raised whether this should happen in England and Wales so as to symbolize and foster a completely new, and simpler, approach. In some fairly extensive but dated research into small claims, the National Consumer Council recommended against an entirely separate system of small claims courts.[135] However, it did suggest that each county court should have a separate 'Small Claims Division' clearly labelled and recognized as such, intended to promote the creation of a distinctive new identity for small claims. It also recommended a separate, simplified procedural code. In the early 1990s the Scottish Office commissioned detailed

---

[129] *More Civil Justice?*, 143, 367–9.   [130] [1994] 4 All ER 720, 747.
[131] See also Civil Justice Review, paras 505, 510, Recommendation 68.
[132] *Judicial Statistics 2003*, Cm 6251 (2004), 44.   [133] *Interim Report*, 100.
[134] CPR r 27.14.   [135] National Consumer Council, *Simple Justice* (London, 1979).

research into the small claims procedure there. Significantly no one claimed to have used the rules as a source of information 'and most advisers considered they were too complex for the average member of the public to comprehend'.[136] The Touche Ross research for the Civil Justice Review found—rather disturbingly given that the procedure is supposedly straightforward—that the most frequently used source of help with small claims was solicitors.[137] In his survey of higher value small claims litigants in 2000, Professor John Baldwin found that despite the apparent simplicity of the procedures, well over a third of the sample said that they had to complete a great deal of paperwork before the hearing. Over 70 per cent of the sample who were not themselves lawyers or others accustomed to appearing at those hearings had taken legal advice beforehand, almost all from solicitors.[138]

The current rules for small claims are part of the Civil Procedure Rules. Part 27 and the accompanying practice direction set out the special procedure for the small claims track. CPR r 27. 2 disapplies other Parts of the CPR for those claims such as those relating to disclosure, evidence, experts, and offers to settle. Otherwise other Parts of the CPR apply to small claims. There are provisions for standard directions—these are set out in the practice direction for a typical claims, for example road accidents, building disputes, return of tenants' deposits—and for preliminary hearings. Accompanying the rules are explanatory leaflets which have the crystal mark for clarity in plain English. There is nothing comparable to the explanatory video which jurors view before entering court to hear a criminal trial. A completely separate and simplified 'code' would contribute to sweeping away the residual view that anything less than the traditional court system is somehow inadequate. Coupled with a separation of 'small claims' matters within the county court this would serve to provide an irreversible psychological break from the traditional procedures in the ordinary courts and further access to justice.

For a time the cause of proportionality was not assisted by the Court of Appeal view that the small claims procedure ought not to be fundamentally different from the ordinary adversary process. In *Chilton v Saga Holidays plc*[139] the district judge had quite sensibly ruled that where one side was unrepresented he did not allow cross-examination and questions had to be put through him. Yet the Court of Appeal upheld an appeal—it was fundamental that each party should be able to probe the accuracy and completeness of the evidence of the other side. The decision was unfortunate to say the least. Many unrepresented individual litigants are generally not capable of framing questions so there is an immediate advantage

---

[136] H. Jones *et al.*, *Small Claims in the Sheriff Court in Scotland*, Scottish Office Central Research Unit (Edinburgh, 1991), 105–6.

[137] Touche Ross, *Civil Justice Review: Study of the Small Claims Procedure* (London, 1986), Table 18.

[138] J. Baldwin, *Lay and Judicial Perspectives on the Expansion of the Small Claims Regime*, Lord Chancellor's Department Research Series No. 8/02 (London, 2002), 28, 38 (hereafter 'Small Claims I'). [139] [1986] 1 All ER 841.

given to the represented or sophisticated. In 1989 the National Consumer Council recommended that all questions to witnesses should be put through the judge, whether or not the parties were represented, and the Civil Justice Review endorsed this.[140] Again unfortunately in the *Afzal* case the Court of Appeal has opined that 'the process [is] adversarial . . .'.[141] In his Inquiry Lord Woolf made it quite clear that he sees the process as interventionist.[142] The rules now enable the judge to adopt any method of proceeding that it considers to be fair and provides specifically that hearings are to be informal, the strict rules of evidence do not apply, evidence need not be taken on oath, and the court may limit cross-examination.[143] In particular the practice direction provides that the judge may ask questions of any witness before allowing others to do so, refuse to allow cross-examination until all the witnesses have given evidence in chief, and limit cross-examination to a fixed time or to a particular subject or issue.

A key recommendation of Lord Woolf's Report was that the small claims jurisdiction be increased from £1,000 to £3,000, with consideration being given to a possible further increase to £5,000.[144] The general limit is now £5,000, which is probably the highest in the world for small claims courts.[145] Many consumer representatives favoured an expansion—albeit with the qualification that more assistance be available for individual litigants—as a way of furthering access to justice. Yet powerful voices were raised against expanding the small claims jurisdiction for all cases, especially for personal injuries. The latter have been accommodated by locating personal injuries and housing disrepair claims above £1,000 in the fast track.[146] When British Columbia increased its small claims jurisdiction an evaluation concluded that this increase provided access for disputes which did not previously exist. New cases came 'out of the woodwork'—previously they were neither litigated in the small claims court or the superior courts. However, the evaluation observed that whereas some 70 per cent of cases involved lay claimants *and* lay defendants (both before and after the change), for claims over the old limit this dropped to 55 per cent.[147] So far this has not occurred in England and Wales. The annual increases in small claims has not been significant and the changes of jurisdiction have been easily absorbed by the system.[148]

A minority of North American and Australasian jurisdictions bar lawyers from small claims jurisdictions. The rationale is that lawyers mean longer, more costly and complex hearings and that they perpetuate inequalities if employed by one party only. Access to justice for individuals might be compromised since those

[140] National Consumer Council, *Ordinary Justice* (London, 1989), 303; Civil Justice Review, R68.
[141] [1994] 4 All 720, 733.   [142] *Interim Report*, 100, 108.
[143] CPR r 27.8. See also PD 27, para. 4.3.   [144] *Final Report*, recommendation 274.
[145] CPR rr 26.6, 27.1(2).
[146] The Better Regulation Task Force has recommended that the limit for personal injury claims in the small claims court be increased from £1,000 to £5,000 in order to reduce legal costs: *Better Routes to Redress* (London, 2004). See 11 above.
[147] Semmens & Adams, *Evaluation of the Small Claims Program*, Ministry of Attorney General, 1991, 21.   [148] J. Baldwin, Small Claims II, 9–10.

who cannot afford lawyers will be deterred from suing. The National Consumer Council at one time wanted a ban on legal representation in the great majority of cases, although subsequently it has relented, on the philosophical basis of freedom of choice, and for the practical reason that there has been an expansion in lay representation (a doubtful proposition). In his 1994 survey of small claims cases, Professor John Baldwin found that legal representatives appeared in just under a quarter of them, three times as often for the claimant as the defendant. In only one case were both sides represented. Baldwin noted that in the majority of cases the district judges either sidelined legal representatives or preserved their interventionist role (with an accommodation to the lawyers present).[149] He concluded that the benefits of legal representation in the small claims arena are unlikely to be great. That does not accord with anecdotal accounts of small claim litigants in person, who felt hampered when confronting legal representation on the other side. Moreover, it does not go to the important issue of preparation before the hearing. Baldwin's research in 2000 found that solicitors acted in only a minority of hearings in higher value claims (£3,000–£5,000). Only 30.9 per cent of the litigants who turned up for court had a legal representative. The proportion of litigants who were represented was higher when the litigant was a private individual (36.4 per cent) than in the case of commercial organizations (27.90 per cent), indicating that there is 'a cadre of business personnel with considerable expertise and experience in presenting cases in the small claims arena'.[150]

Research suggests, albeit not unequivocally, that a ban on legal representation might be unnecessary so long as other steps are taken to assist the unrepresented litigant beforehand. Thus the leading American research found, surprisingly, that a sizeable number of litigants sought legal advice for small claims, even if they were not represented at the hearing. It also found that the presence of a lawyer tended to increase significantly the time necessary for a hearing. As well as the obvious conclusion that more had to be done to assist the unrepresented before a hearing, the study argued for careful control of legal representatives—'their participation should be limited to presenting additional legal or evidentiary points at the end of a case, and that questioning of witnesses should be conducted by the judge'.[151] The follow-up study by the National Centre for State Courts found that representation at trial by a lawyer was not a statistically significant correlate of success after controlling for other independent variables. It suggested that one explanation might be that, if permitted, lawyers were usually not given the opportunity to dominate the unrepresented party.[152] Baldwin's earlier small claims

---

[149] J. Baldwin, *Small Claims in the County Courts in England and Wales* (Oxford, 1997), 82–4, 87 (hereafter 'Small Claims I').

[150] J. Baldwin, Small Claims II, 30. See also C. Whelan, 'Small Claims in England and Wales: Redefining Justice', in C. Whelan (ed.), *Small Claims Courts* (Oxford, 1990), 119.

[151] J. Ruhnka & S. Weller, *Small Claims Courts*, National Center for State Court (Williamsburg, 1978).

[152] J. Goerdt, *Small Claims and Traffic Courts*, National Centre for State Court (Williamsburg, 1992), 69.

research found that most district judges thought self-represented litigants did well, even when the other side was represented. Over half of individual claimants thought the procedure was easy enough to use without a solicitor, although as long as the matter was straightforward.[153] In his 2000 research Baldwin found only 14.7 per cent of the 75 litigants who represented themselves at full hearings experienced difficulty in coping without a lawyer.[154]

For many years a more interventionist approach has been used by those conducting small claims cases (in practice, district judges). We have seen that Lord Woolf gave his official blessing to this. It is essential for various reasons, including the simplicity of the proceedings. Earlier research threw up some disturbing findings about the district judges conducting small claims hearings—a dislike for the work, undue formality, and an adherence to adversary modes.[155] While some of this might still occasionally exist the overwhelming judicial approach now is positive although Baldwin cautions against complacency: '[A] judicial concern with ensuring that litigants understand what is happening at hearings and feel able to participate effectively in them needs to be recognised both in training and in practice'.[156] From his observations Baldwin found that there were differences in judges' interpretation of what it means to be interventionist. However, in his studies, he has found that there is now widespread acceptance of the desirability of the interventionalist role, that hearings be conducted in a pragmatic, down-to-earth manner, and that unrepresented litigants must be assisted in presenting their case.[157]

The small claims procedure is designed, of course, to be informal. Critics have argued that informality leads to overlooking rights and subverting the goal of preserving public rules and standards of conduct. From the point of view of litigants the reality is different. Empirical evidence tends to identify as the critical factor whether the procedure is perceived as fair and dignified.[158] United States evidence has confirmed an overwhelmingly high degree of satisfaction among small claims litigants, even those who lost. The more highly educated were more satisfied, perhaps because they were better able to understand the procedures. Treatment by the judge was the strongest correlate of litigant satisfaction along with both outcome and procedures.[159] Litigant satisfaction in the Scottish research could not be explained entirely by whether they had won or not. The overwhelming majority of litigants praised the sheriffs for their fairness, irrespective of the outcome of cases.[160] In the Touche Ross research for the Civil Justice Review reactions varied

[153] J. Baldwin, Small Claims I, 38–9, 87, 104–5, 113.

[154] J. Baldwin, Small Claims II, 26, 60.

[155] G. Applebey, 'Small Claims in England and Wales', in M. Cappelletti and J. Weisner (eds), *Access to Justice Vol. 2: Promising Institutions* (Alphen aan den Rijn, 1979).

[156] Small Claims I, 29. He identified four main judicial approaches: going for the jugular; hearing the parties; passive; mediatory.   [157] e.g. J. Baldwin, Small Claims II, 61–2, 64–5.

[158] E. Clark, 'Recent Research on Small Claims Courts and Tribunals: Implications for Evaluators' (1992) 2 *J.Judicial Admin.* 103, 117.   [159] J. Goerdt, *op.cit.*, 64, 68.

[160] H. Jones *et al., op.cit.*, 100.

with whether a party was successful, although nearly half of those who lost their cases thought the proceedings were fair.[161] Baldwin's latest research found that litigant satisfaction remained high, regardless of outcome.[162] (As noted earlier, Baldwin found the higher socio-economic groups were disproportionately litigating in small claims.)[163] All these results accord with the conventional wisdom that the opportunity to give their grievance a good airing is perceived by litigants as important, if not more important for some, than outcome.[164]

Court-annexed Alternative Dispute Resolution

Alternative dispute resolution (ADR) is the flavour of the decade. Lord Woolf's Interim and Final Reports are not immune to fashion.[165] One way the new system of case management encourages settlement is by suggesting the use of ADR when this is likely to be beneficial. Judges are to be able to take into account a litigant's unreasonable refusal to attempt ADR in awarding costs.[166] Certain forms of ADR are positively encouraged.[167] Agreements to refer disputes to ADR have been held to be contractually binding.[168] Yet it would be wrong to think that ADR has the wholly uncritical imprimatur of the Woolf Report. The Report identifies the enormous variety of initiatives—from informal mediation through conciliation to arbitration—and cautions that claims of success are sometimes exaggerated. It points to the need for monitoring and evaluation with support for the most promising and successful schemes.[169] The issue discussed here is the narrow use of court annexed ADR.[170]

So far there has been only limited social research to monitor and evaluate court annexed ADR in Britain. Professor Genn examined an experimental scheme to promote ADR at Central London County Court, whereby those involved in larger civil disputes were offered ADR for nominal cost. Very few took advantage

---

[161] Touche Ross, *Civil Justice Review: Study of the Small Claims Procedure* (London, 1986), 24.

[162] J. Baldwin, Small Claims II, 26, 34, 58. See also Small Claims I, 102, 113, 126.

[163] 116 above. See also I. Ramsay, 'Small Claims Courts: A Review', Ontario Law Reform Commission, *Rethinking Civil Justice: Research Studies for the Civil Justice Review* (1996), vol. II, 505–6.

[164] T. Tyler, 'What Is Procedural Justice? Criteria Used by Citizens to Assess the Fairness of Legal Procedures' (1988) 22 *Law & Soc.Rev.* 104; W. O'Barr *et al.*, 'Lay Expectations of the Civil Justice System' (1988) 22 *Law & Soc.Rev.* 137.

[165] *Interim Report*, 22, 136 ff. See also recommendations 296–303 of the *Final Report* 'alternative approaches to dispensing justice'. Subsequent discussion and descriptions of ADR processes are contained in: Lord Chancellor's Department, *Alternative Dispute Resolution—A Discussion Paper* (London, 1999); M. Palmer and S. Roberts, *Dispute Processes: ADR and the Primary Forms of Decision Making* (London, 1998); M. Partington, 'Alternative Dispute Resolution: Recent Developments, Future Challenges' (2004) 23 *CJQ* 99.

[166] *Dunnett v Railtrack plc* [2002] EWCA Civ 303; [2002] 1 WLR 2434; [2002] 2 All ER 850; *Halsey v Milton Keynes General NHS Trust* [2004] EWCA Civ 576; [2004] 1 WLR 3002; [2004] 4 All ER 920. [167] CPR rr 1.4(2)(e), 26.4.

[168] *Cable & Wireless plc v IBM United Kingdom Ltd* [2002] EWHC 2059.

[169] *Final Report*, 146. For similar comments, see Australian Law Reform Commission, *Review of the Adversarial System of Litigation: ADR—Its Role in Federal Dispute Resolution* (Issues Paper 25, 1998), 35–7. [170] For ADR more generally: 71–8 above.

of it, in part because their solicitors saw it as an admission of weakness. However, over three fifths of those who went to ADR settled their case expeditiously. Where cases failed to settle, ADR pushed up overall costs, not surprisingly since ADR is an additional step in the process.[171] The general satisfaction of those undertaking ADR in the Genn study has been replicated in research by Brooker and Lavers with ADR in commercial and construction litigation in the High Court. In those areas ADR is driven by lawyers' support for the concept, ADR clauses in contracts and the satisfactory settlement rate which occurs.[172] Professor Genn has also examined 233 ADR non-mandatory orders of the Commercial Court between 1996 and 2000. She found that where ADR was attempted, 52 per cent of cases settled as a result, and 20 per cent settled some time after the conclusion of ADR. Of those cases in which ADR was not attempted following an ADR order, about 63 per cent eventually settled. This was attributed to the order in about a fifth of cases. The rate of trials among those cases was much higher (15 per cent) than in cases where ADR was unsuccessfully attempted (5 per cent). Experience of successful ADR was overwhelmingly positive and even when unsuccessful some solicitors though the process was constructive.[173] Research for the Civil Justice Council of small claims mediation at Exeter County Court found it saved judicial time and facilitated settlement. Parties undertaking mediation generally felt that it was useful and appreciated that it was informal, saved time, and achieved a result. Mediations which involved a heavy emotional or complex relationship were less successful.[174]

Social research has been extensive in relation to court-annexed arbitration in the United States. Sometimes called court-administered arbitration, compulsory arbitration or mandatory arbitration, such programmes channel the less important civil litigation for a speedy hearing before a judicial officer (not a judge) or lawyer or panel of lawyers, whose order can then become an order of the court. If either party wishes to challenge the decision an appeal can be taken to the court and the matter heard *de novo*. Cases can be heard more quickly than before the courts, it is said, and the courts should be able to expedite the matters which remain because there are fewer of them. Although in broad terms similar to traditional arbitration, court annexed arbitration differs in its coverage and if it has a compulsory character. Typically in the United States smaller civil cases are assigned to arbitration, automatically in some jurisdictions, after screening in others. Lawyers act as arbitrators for a small or nominal fee in most jurisdictions. Lawyers, the parties, and any witnesses appear before the arbitrator for a private

[171] H. Genn, *The Central London County Court Pilot Mediation Scheme*, Lord Chancellor's Department Research Series 5/98 (London, 1998).

[172] P. Brooker & A. Lavers, 'Commercial and Construction ADR: Lawyers' Attitudes and Experience' (2001) 20 *CJQ* 327.

[173] H. Genn, *Court-Based ADR Initiatives for Non-Family Civil Disputes: The Commercial Court and the Court of Appeal*, Lord Chancellor's Department Research Series 1/2002 (London, 2002).

[174] S. Prince, *Court-based Mediation: A Preliminary Analysis of the Small Claims Mediation Scheme at Exeter County Court* (London, 2004).

hearing where the rules of evidence are relaxed and matters expedited. The parties have a specified period in which to reject the award and request a trial *de novo*. As a disincentive to reject awards, most programmes include a monetary disincentive in the form of a penalty or costs if the party's position is not improved at trial. With some of the programmes fees must be paid before the *de novo* hearing so as to discourage frivolous requests.

An early evaluation by the Federal Judicial Center of court-annexed arbitration in three federal district courts had produced strong evidence that it decreased time from filing to disposition in two of the three districts, attributable almost exclusively to settlement of cases prior to the arbitration hearing. In the third court no such effect was found, probably because of the court's procedures for the scheduling of arbitration hearings. However, in about 60 per cent of arbitrated cases the arbitration award was voided by a demand for a trial *de novo*.[175] An evaluation of compulsory court-annexed arbitration in Rochester, New York, found that the total disposition time for arbitration did not vary from the total time taken previously.[176] Another study of a court-annexed arbitration programme in California found that the hearing time spent per personal injury case arbitrated averaged 2.5 hours, compared to 3.3 days for the average trial.[177] Research into civil claims in a county of Pennsylvania suggested that court-annexed arbitration had made progress in limiting the length and number of protracted cases. Whether this had happened by chance or by a concerted effort to monitor cases to identify those most likely to be complex was not clear.[178] An evaluation of ten mandatory federal court schemes in 1990 found that from 5 per cent to just over one quarter of the civil caseload in the ten districts went to arbitration. Depending on the district, cases resolved by arbitration were disposed of from two to eighteen months sooner than cases resolved by trial. However, less than one half of arbitration awards were accepted in eight of the ten districts, with parties exercising their right to a *de novo* hearing in the ordinary way. One of the most important findings was that a majority of lawyers reported a saving in costs. As would be expected, no such savings were reported in cases going to a *de novo* hearing. Moreover, over two thirds of those participating in arbitration cases were corporations or business parties.[179]

Perhaps the most impressive study to date of court-annexed arbitration is one by the Institute for Civil Justice of the Rand Corporation and the Duke School of Law Private Adjudication Center. It is distinguished in two ways from earlier

[175] E. Lind & J. Shepard, *Evaluation of Court Annexed Arbitration in Three Federal District Courts* (Federal Judicial Center, Washington, DC, 1981).

[176] S. Weller *et al.*, 'American Experiments for Reducing Civil Judicial Trial Costs and Delays' (1982) 1 *CJQ* 151, 161–4.

[177] E. Johnson *et al.*, *Outside the Courts* (National Center for State Courts, Denver, 1977), 46. However, this was at a time when the Californian programme was voluntary so there is no certainty that the cases going to arbitration were comparable with those going to trial.

[178] D. Steelman *et al.*, *Case Processing in the York County Court of Common Pleas* (National Center for State Courts, Denver, 1979).

[179] B. Meierhoefer, *Court-Annexed Arbitration in Ten District Courts* (Washington, DC, 1990).

research: first, it covered high-value claims, whereas research previously had focused on smaller claims; secondly, and more importantly, it used a control group which was randomly removed from arbitration and dealt with by ordinary pre-trial processes. There were a number of important findings. One was that arbitration increased the likelihood that a case would receive some form of adjudication since one third of the arbitration cases, but only 15 per cent of the control group, went to a hearing. Next, there was no significant difference in delay between the two groups of cases. Unfortunately the data on costs was not as good as that on other matters. But a cost difference was found for parties, although the lower cost of arbitration for parties was for defendants, not plaintiffs. Importantly, there was no difference in the public costs, i.e. to the courts. In interviews with litigants it was found that those whose cases went to a hearing were more frequently disposed of, and since a greater proportion of the arbitration group went to a hearing than those dealt with ordinarily, overall litigants in the arbitration group were more favourable in their ratings. The study concluded that court-annexed arbitration increased access to justice: there was no evidence of increased filings of claims but in substituting arbitration hearings for bilateral settlement, it gave litigants something they wanted—an opportunity to have their cases adjudicated.[180]

There would therefore seem to be no savings of public expenditure with court-annexed arbitration, although there is some (but not strong) evidence of cost advantages to litigants. Arbitrated cases are not necessarily processed quicker.[181] One reason might be that lawyers carry the same workload whether their case is going to arbitration or the courts, so that inasmuch as delay can be attributed to lawyers' practices arbitration might not have a great impact. There is some evidence in the US studies that parties welcome court-annexed arbitration as an opportunity to have an official decision on their cases, but in a high number of cases the parties are dissatisfied with the result since they request a *de novo* hearing. With this as background Lord Woolf concluded that it was not the appropriate time to introduce court-annexed alternative dispute resolution, although he referred expressly to other reasons—the burden for the courts of adopting his other recommendations and the plethora of private ADR schemes.[182]

---

[180] E. Lind, *Arbitrating High-Stake Cases* (Santa Monica, 1990). For a later study of mediation and neutral evaluation programmes, see J. Kalalik *et al.*, *An Evaluation of Mediation and Early Neutral Evaluation under the Civil Justice Reform Act* (Santa Monica, 1996), in which the research evaluated six federal district courts that had mediation or early neutral evaluation programmes. See also: D. Hensler, 'A Glass Half Full, A Glass Half Empty: The Use of Alternative Dispute Resolution in Mass Personal Injury Litigation' (1995) 73 *Tex.LR* 1587; CPR Judicial Project Advisory Council of the CPR Institute for Dispute Resolution and Other ADR Experts, *Statement of Concerns regarding the Rand ADR Study* (New York, 1997).

[181] cf. a Canadian study, which found cost and time advantages to court-annexed mediation: R. Hann & C. Baar, *Evaluation of the Ontario Mandatory Mediation Program* (Toronto, 2001).

[182] *Interim Report*, ch. 18.

Conclusion

Making public policy is not an exact science. Quite apart from the difficulty in some instances of identifying how to reach a particular goal, there is the problem in foreseeing all the ramifications of reform. One such consequence is that individuals and organizations can adjust their behaviour to change and by doing so undermine its very purpose.[183] Part of the folklore in American judicial administration concerns the introduction of a speedy trial list in Baltimore. That list soon became so clogged that if lawyers wanted to delay matters they would ask for a speedy trial. This is not an argument for petty tinkering and against comprehensive change.[184] The Woolf reforms were a big bang change and, on the whole, have been successful. But in achieving comprehensive change incrementalism can have the advantage that corrections can be more easily made as any undesirable consequences of a change in policy become manifest. In any event incrementalism is all that is possible in some instances because of resource constraints, a clash of interests, and a lack of consensus on values.

In advance of policy changes it is desirable to bring to bear relevant social research. What really is the problem? How has it been dealt with successfully in the past, or in similar settings? What unintended side effects must be guarded against? These are some obvious questions which social research may have addressed. Systematically monitoring change once it is introduced is also essential. Unfortunately social research and monitoring have not been prominent features of the civil justice system. By comparison with what has been achieved in criminology, research into civil justice is minimal. Significant changes in civil justice are constantly made without monitoring. This does not mean that social research is non-problematic. Research findings clearly turn on the questions asked. In order to reduce life's complexity researchers must structure their observations and highlight the characteristics which they regard as important. Findings can hardly be said to be definitive or to reveal universal truths. Sometimes research misleads us into thinking that it has uncovered more than is actually known and evidence which is not persuasive is put forward as supporting the author's own particular dispositions. But the dearth of research is clearly not helpful to the policymaker who is already under pressure to make decisions and take action quickly but on the basis of inadequate analysis. We must know more of the operation of the civil justice system in England and Wales if we are to pursue avenues for its future operation which accord with existing principle and achieve values such as equality before the law and more effective access to justice.

---

[183] e.g. G. Priest, 'Private Litigants and the Court Congestion Problem' (1989) 69 *Boston ULR 527*.

[184] See J. Jolowicz, 'Comparative Law and the Reform of Civil Procedure' (1988) 8 *LS* 1, 13.

6

Lawyers' Conduct; the Professional Standards

Prominent in the obituaries for Gregory Peck were references to his Oscar-winning role as the lawyer Atticus Finch in the film version of Harper Lee's novel *To Kill a Mocking Bird*.[1] The obituaries remind us of the parallels in the characters of Peck and the fictional Finch—graciousness, integrity, and courage: courage in Peck's case in resisting the blandishments of the Hollywood moguls and standing up for causes he believed in, a greater courage in Finch's case in defending an innocent black man, Tom Robinson, accused of raping a white woman in a segregated, Alabama town of the 1930s. The film was one of a number of American criminal trial dramas from the mid 1950s through the 1960s, where lawyers were portrayed as labouring heroically for justice.[2] Its qualities at many levels—its faithfulness to the text, the cinematography and the acting—mean that it will outlive many of that genre. The novel itself is well known. It has frequently been a set-text for secondary school students in various parts of the English-speaking world. It is none the worse for that. For lawyers it throws up a range of issues. One concerns access to justice: the court had assigned Finch to defend Robinson, who as a poor black could not afford legal representation. Another involves the administration of justice: the innocent Robinson is convicted by the all-white jury despite Finch showing that the accusation is a tissue of lies.

For present purposes the interest is in Finch's conduct as a lawyer. He defends Robinson, at a cost to himself and his family. He and his family are shunned for siding with black people, he could have been lynched when he defends Robinson against the fury of the mob, and his children only just manage to escape violence from the vengeful father of the lower-class woman alleging rape. He is a Brahmin and a lawyer in a small town, setting an example to his children. No doubt one way of understanding all this and Finch's behaviour is sociologically.[3] As several legal scholars have pointed out, Finch's actions can also be understood against the

---

[1] *The Times*, 13 June 2003; *New York Times*, 13 June 2003, Section A,1. Harper Lee, *To Kill a Mocking Bird* (New York, 1960).

[2] N. Rafter, 'American Criminal Trial Films: An Overview of their Development, 1930–2000' (2001) 28 *JL&Soc* 9, 15.

[3] Professor John Dollard's approach to understanding a comparable Southern town in his classic study from the 1930s: *Class and Caste in a Southern Town*, 3rd edn (New York, 1949).

backdrop of the standards of legal professional responsibility.[4] These standards of professional responsibility—legal ethics—are more elaborate than in Finch's day and now need address the whole complexity of modern lawyering. They may need creative interpretation in their application to particular circumstances; lawyers may fall short of what is demanded; and in everyday situations they may only inform behaviour in an indirect way. Nonetheless, they throw significant light on lawyers' conduct. By examining their contours we further our understanding of how law works.

The profession's ethical rules have sometimes had the appearance of protectionism and as being not at all concerned with the public interest or the proper administration of justice.[5] Important ethical rules have not been ethical truisms: they have often been concerned with the gathering and retention of clients or been directed more at professional conformity rather than right behaviour.[6] This lends support to one interpretation of professionalism.[7] Yet any association with the profession dispels the suggestion that the profession's ethical codes for conduct are self-interest writ large. There is a genuine concern with high ethical standards, not least so as to maintain the profession's public standing and confidence. Nor would it be correct to suggest that professional standards are completely divorced from ordinary morality. There is old authority, for example, that despite fidelity to the client being a paramount consideration, lawyers must not, in the words of Lord Esher MR, 'degrade' themselves personally for the purpose of winning their client's case.[8] This example raises important issues to which we return. The first is the need to reconsider the boundaries between, on the one hand, a lawyer's obligation to a client and, on the other, the public interest. And the second is the danger that focusing simply on the profession's ethical rules can lead to moral blindness: legal ethics and professional responsibility are more than a set of rules, they are also a commitment to honesty, integrity, and service in the working of the law.

The Regulatory Regime

The general law has a great deal to say about professional behaviour. The law of agency, contracts, torts, fiduciary obligations and evidence, and in its blunt way, criminal law, all have a bearing on lawyers' behaviour in their professional lives. Sometimes the general law speaks in surprising, and not completely unwelcome, ways. In one case a firm of solicitors was held to be potentially liable for

---

[4] T. Dare, 'The Secret Courts of Men's Hearts: Legal Ethics and Harper Lee's *To Kill a Mockingbird*' in K. Economides (ed.), *Ethical Challenges to Legal Education and Conduct* (Oxford, 1998); T. Shaffer, 'The Moral Theology of Atticus Finch' (1981) 42 *U.Pitts.LR* 181; cf. S. Lubet, 'Reconstructing Atticus Finch' (1999) 97 *Mich.LR* 1339.

[5] *R v Visitors to the Inns of Court, ex p Calder* [1994] QB 1, 63. See M. Zander, *Lawyers and the Public Interest* (London, 1968).

[6] e.g. B. Abel-Smith & R. Stevens, *Lawyers and the Courts* (London, 1967), 138–9, 160–1, 196.

[7] 18–19 above.   [8] *Re G. Mayor Cooke* (1889) 5 TLR 407, 408.

restitutionary orders under the Financial Services Act 1986 for loss to an investor. Liability was held to be possible if the solicitors were knowingly concerned in the contravention of the Act, notwithstanding that they received nothing under the impugned transactions.[9] Nowadays solicitors are on guard against being the vehicles of fraud, given the reinvigorated application of claims for the proceeds and the more likely personal claims for having 'assisted' the fraud.[10] Getting to grips with money laundering and terrorist financing has meant legislative incursions onto the lawyer's duty of confidence.[11] It is not before time since there is clear evidence from other jurisdictions that legal professional privilege and the duty of confidence have been used to cloak the identities of the beneficial owners of laundered bank accounts.[12]

In addition to the general law there are, secondly, the specific standards of good professional conduct which the courts have elaborated both through their direct control of lawyers and through their review of the decisions of professional disciplinary bodies.[13] Direct control has often been based on the commonplace observations that lawyers are officers of the court and therefore can be disciplined for misconduct.[14] There is now a statutory duty for advocates to act with independence in the interests of justice.[15] The most basic misconduct is to mislead the court, although there is considerable refinement in how this can be constituted. Passively standing by and seeing the court misled is not such misconduct—for example, when the prosecution does not present a complete list of the defendant's previous convictions—unless the error is a material part of the case, where the lawyer must withdraw if the client does not consent to the disclosure being made.[16] Other duties to the court include not abusing the court processes, corrupting the administration of justice, or handling litigation in a dilatory or inefficient manner.[17] In recent times the courts' reach has extended beyond court behaviour to sharp practice in legal negotiation.[18] On occasions professional misconduct can extend to personal misbehaviour, sufficiently close to the administration of justice for it to be labelled as such (for example, the lawyer who fails to

---

[9] *Securities and Investments Board v Pantell SA (No 2)* [1993] Ch 256.

[10] C. Mitchell, 'Assistance'; B. Birks, 'Receipt', both in P. Birks & A. Pretto (eds), *Breach of Trust* (Oxford, 2002).   [11] Proceeds of Crime Act 2002, s 330; Terrorism Act 2000, s 19(2), (5), (6).

[12] e.g. *Republic of Haiti v Duvalier* [1990] 1 QB 202, 207 (continental lawyers expert in concealment of funds). See R. Bosworth-Davies, 'Money Laundering and Lawyers' (1994) 138 *SJ* 626; W. Park, 'Anonymous Bank Accounts, Narco-Dollars, Fiscal Fraud, and Lawyers' (1991–2) 15 *Fordham Int.L.J.* 652.

[13] On the inherent jurisdiction of the court: e.g. *Re the Justices of Antigua* (1830) 12 ER 321; *Re S (a barrister)* [1970] 1 QB 160; *John Fox v Bannister King & Rigbeys* [1988] QB 925.

[14] Solicitors Act 1974, s 50(1). Barristers are not officers of the court but are bound by the same standards.   [15] Access to Justice Act 1999, s 42.

[16] *Vernon v Bosley (No 2)* [1999] QB 18, CA.

[17] D. Ipp, 'Lawyers' Duties to the Court' (1998) 114 *LQR* 63.

[18] *Commission for the New Towns v Cooper (Great Britain) Ltd* [1995] Ch 259, CA; *The Stolt Loyalty* [1995] 1 Lloyd's Rep 598, CA. See A. Boon, 'Ethics and Strategy in Personal Injury Litigation' (1995) 22 *JLS* 353, 355.

pay tax over nearly four decades).[19] Coupled with the inherent jurisdiction of the court to control lawyers are specific statutory controls, for example the wasted costs jurisdiction which enables a court to sheet home to solicitors and barristers the loss and expense to litigants caused by the unjustified conduct of litigation, misconduct, default, or serious negligence.[20]

Examples of the behavioural standards which the courts have evolved for the profession arise throughout the discussion. Suffice to say here that the courts reiterate that in matters of professional discipline the touchstones are public confidence in the profession and public protection from the unscrupulous or incompetent. Notwithstanding that its exercise may cause deprivation to the lawyer involved, the power of discipline is protective in purpose, rather than punitive. As Lord Mansfield said in 1778 the question is: 'Whether, after the conduct of this [person], it is proper that he should continue a member of a profession which should stand free from all suspicion . . . It is not by way of punishment . . .'.[21] For this reason the considerations which ordinarily weight in mitigation of penalty for a particular individual have less effect in cases of professional discipline.[22] Whether the possibility of disciplinary action has any general deterrent effect is a matter for inquiry; it may enter the consciousness of most lawyers too sporadically to influence behaviour.

The third set of rules governing professional behaviour are the codes of practice issued by the Bar and the Law Society.[23] In important respects they go beyond the requirements of the general law; conversely, breach of them is not conclusive of breach of the general law. Historically the codes have evolved from the practical workings of the discipline which the profession itself has exercised. The inns of court have a long history of controlling both the admission and conduct of barristers subject, however, to the jurisdiction of the visitors and then review by the courts.[24] Under s 42 of the Access to Justice Act 1999 advocates are now under a duty to comply with the codes. A disciplinary committee for solicitors was established under the Solicitors Act 1888, although it was not until 1919 that legislation empowered the committee to exercise actual disciplinary powers.[25] The courts have generally deferred to a positive finding of misconduct by the profession's disciplinary bodies, and have also been reluctant to mitigate penalty,

---

[19] *New South Wales Bar Association v Cummins* (2001) 52 NSWLR 279, CA.

[20] e.g *Ridehalgh v Horsefield* [1994] Ch. 205, CA; *Harley v McDonald* [2001] 2 AC 678, PC; *Medcalf v Mardell* [2002] UKHL 27; [2003] 1 AC 120.

[21] *Ex p Brounsall* (1778) 98 ER 1385, 1385.

[22] *Bolton v Law Society* [1994] 1 WLR 512, 519, CA; *Law Society of New South Wales v Foreman* (1994) 34 NSWLR 408, 441–51, 471–3, CA.

[23] Bar Council, *Code of Conduct* (London, 2004) (hereafter BC); The Law Society, *The Guide to the Professional Conduct of Solicitors*, 8th edn, 1999 (hereafter LSG).

[24] *Lincoln v Daniels* [1962] 1 QB 237. See also *R v General Council of the Bar ex p Percival* [1991] 1 QB 212; B. Lee, 'The Constitutional Power of the Courts over Admission to the Bar' (1899) 13 *Harv.LR* 233; J.H. Baker, 'Judicial Review of the Judges as Visitors to the Inns of Court' [1992] *PL* 411.

[25] See B. Abel-Smith & R. Stevens, *Lawyers and the Courts* (London, 1967), 188–90; R. Abel, *The Legal Profession in England and Wales* (Oxford, 1988), 133–6, 248–60, 285–7.

on the basis that the representatives of the profession itself are the best judges of misconduct and its seriousness.[26]

Public pressure has meant that the professional machinery for regulating behaviour has become increasingly elaborate. There has been a disciplinary tribunal for solicitors for many years.[27] In 1986 the Law Society established the Solicitors Complaints Bureau as a quasi-independent body to handle, as the name suggests, complaints about solicitors. Following criticism of its performance, the Bureau was reconstituted as the Office for the Supervision of Solicitors.[28] The majority of complaints are resolved by agreement between the client and the solicitor concerned although a number of cases undergo formal investigation, and an order may be made that the solicitor rectify an error or pay compensation. Insurance cover under the Solicitors' Indemnity Fund has since 1987 extended to any legal liability, including dishonesty. A compensation fund was inaugurated in 1941 to cover situations where there is no one against whom a claim for misappropriated money can be made. The drain on the fund has led to increased scrutiny by the Law Society of solicitors' practices. Under the Courts and Legal Services Act 1990 the government appointed a legal services ombudsman to review how both branches of the profession handle complaints. The ombudsman may recommend that a complaint be reconsidered and compensation paid. In 2004 the government invoked a reserve power in the Access to Justice Act 1999 and appointed a non-lawyer as legal services complaints commissioner with statutory power to regulate the way complaints are handled. The ombudsman presently performs this function. The new arrangements followed the ombudsman's finding that the existing regulatory labyrinth was not delivering an acceptable level of success in complaints-handling.[29] At the time of writing the regulatory framework for legal services is undergoing change.[30]

The codes are not like some ethical codes, which are aspirational in character. As indicated they can lead to legally enforceable consequences, such as intervention in a lawyer's practice, and ultimately disbarment of a lawyer from practice. In many respects the codes are simply restating and expanding the general law; they are not exhaustive of all the ethical problems which lawyers face. While the codes surface in judicial decisions, they have a far more important, daily application in decisions by the profession, rulings by the Bar and the Law Society about their application, and advice given to members of the profession by the professional bodies and others on the basis of the code provisions.

---

[26] See *Bolton v Law Society* [1994] 1 WLR 512, CA.

[27] e.g. *Camacho v Law Society* [2004] EWHC 1675 (Admin); [2004] 1 WLR 3037; [2004] 4 All ER 126.

[28] e.g. V. Lewis, *Complaints Against Solicitors: The Complainant's View*, Law Society RPPU Research Study No. 19, 1996.

[29] *In Whose Interest*, Legal Services Ombudsman, Annual Report 2003/4 (London, 2004).

[30] *Review of the Regulatory Framework for Legal Services in England and Wales* (London, 2004) (the Clementi Review), See www. legal-services-review.org.uk/content/report/index.htm

Nor are the codes ordinary law and they are not applied as if they were. In their application the professional bodies adopt a creative role in interpretation. Many situations do not fall within the four corners of the codes, but it is not uncommon for the professional bodies to reason by analogy from other provisions and to invoke principle. The justification for this liberal, purposive approach is that lawyers should know that certain conduct is wrongful, even if not expressly proscribed by the codes. But any uncertainty in application may expose lawyers to disciplinary action when their behaviour is only questionably unethical or represents the unconventional or politically unpopular. This last point is certainly not an argument against a purposive approach to the codes but simply a caution about their application. Even if the codes only repeated the standards contained in the general law they would be more accessible and provide a more practical basis for professional discipline. In fact the codes do more: they identify the main lines of the profession's thinking on professional responsibility and have both educative and moulding effects. New members of the profession can be more easily instructed into acceptable standards of behaviour, and members of the profession generally may be dissuaded from unacceptable behaviour and may have any disposition to act correctly reinforced.

An important policy issue is the extent to which the codes ought to be infused by wider ethical notions. There are two aspects to this. One is encapsulated in the question: 'Can a good lawyer be a bad person?'[31] In other words, are the standards in the codes too lax when laid alongside common morality? The second aspect is that if there is a discrepancy between the codes and common morality, what is special about lawyers that exempts them from the precepts of the latter? To put it another way, how is it that lawyers can decide ethically on a course of action for a client which is different from that they would adopt for themselves in everyday life? While there is a certain force in these questions, it seems that those who argue for the primacy of moral considerations do not give enough attention to their contingency in real life. One response to this might be to try to give moral values a greater objectivity in the legal context. For example, the Overriding Objective of the Civil Procedure Rules is to ensure cases are dealt with justly. Thus seeking justice should be the lodestar for lawyers engaged in litigation. This may be helpful but still does not give sufficient guidance to the lawyer wanting to know how to act ethically in particular situations. Ethical issues arise in specific contexts and we need detailed guidelines for resolving the practical problems which arise.

None of this is to advocate moral relativism. In many cases the rightness or wrongness of conduct can be identified and reflection on what ethical thought might demand should inform any discussion of professional responsibility. Lawyers cannot remain free from moral responsibility simply by pointing to a provision in the codes. Nor are lawyers simple technicians; they must not submerge

---

[31] D. Luban, *Lawyers and Justice: An Ethical Study* (Princeton, 1988); D. Luban (ed.), *The Good Lawyer: Lawyer's Roles and Lawyers' Ethics* (Totowa, NJ, 1983).

their own moral standards to the pursuit of a client's interest irrespective of what that might be. In any event, there is high authority that they must also serve other interests such as those of third parties and, more generally, justice. There are problems, then, in putting ethical thought to the fore, not least lawyers' own unfamiliarity with this field. That does not mean that it has no role to play, just that it cannot be determining.

There is also another problem. In important respects the present professional codes are too vague. In some especially difficult areas lawyers are given no guidance as to how they should act—the level of charging is an important one—although in a few they are told that they have a discretion to withdraw from providing further services to a particular client. We return to some of these below. While it is impossible for the codes to be more specific in many areas, there seems to be more scope in them for standards, such as the public interest—familiar to lawyers in other contexts—which would force lawyers to confront more directly the creative aspect of professional judgment and require them to justify a particular course of action.[32] The final point to make is that many of the issues are also about values. This is apparent in matters such as *pro bono* work and furthering access to justice.

With the codes themselves there is the obvious point that control over their content rests largely in the profession itself, the very group whose ethical behaviour is in issue. In this area self-regulation has many advantages, not least in identifying wrongdoing and fissures in the codes. As I have said, it is wrong to characterize the codes as wholly, or mainly, self-serving. Yet there are dangers in self-regulation here as elsewhere. One is cartelization. Another is that the codes might not adopt the strict line suggested by public interest legal values if economic pressures push in the opposite direction. The obvious conclusion is that lawyers should not have a completely free hand in writing the codes; there must be some mechanism for ensuring that what is contained in them is subject to public scrutiny and really is the best for justice and for society as a whole.

Confidentiality, Competence, Loyalty

In an address to the new serjeants at law in 1648 Law Commissioner Whitelock said that the duties of advocates to their clients were general and particular. The general consist in three things, secrecy, diligence, and fidelity.[33] These three duties, identified 350 years ago, provide the pegs for a relatively brief exposition of the central rules of professional responsibility.

---

[32] W. Simon, 'Ethical Discretion in Lawyering' (1988) 101 *Harv.LR* 1083.
[33] Sir Bulstrode Whitelock, *Memorials of the English Affairs*, 1853, vol. 2, 454. Whitelock was one of the commissioners of the great seal in the period of the Commonwealth.

Confidentiality

So first, secrecy or, more familiarly, the duty of confidentiality. In general terms the law implies a term into the contract which a lawyer has with a client 'to keep [the] client's affairs secret and not to disclose them to anyone without just cause'.[34] Consent of a client to disclosure lifts the duty of confidentiality. A client might well condone disclosure, when the lawyer thinks the circumstances demand it, even though the law does not require it. But the purposes behind and contours of the duty of confidence are sometimes as difficult for lawyers as they are for other professionals. Privacy, and protecting the client's expectations and other interests, are clearly important rationales of the duty, although as we will see there are larger public interests as well, such as encouraging the utilization of legal services and enhancing the system of civil justice. The duty applies to 'secrets which are confidentially reposed' in the lawyer,[35] and that goes some way to embracing other than what is directly communicated by the client (for example information generated by professional skill). The duty is not absolute in character, and is trumped if the public interest favours disclosure.[36] Statute expressly dissolves the duty of confidentiality in a variety of situations: for example, a solicitor is protected in disclosing to the police a suspicion or belief that a person is involved in terrorist offences or that money or property is associated with terrorism.[37] However, there is no obligation to disclose terrorist offences if this would be in breach of legal professional privilege.[38]

There are general injunctions about preserving the confidentiality of a client's affairs in the professional codes.[39] The duty for solicitors extends to making sure that their staff as well maintain confidentiality. In accordance with the general law, the duty of confidentiality stated in the codes continues after the lawyer/client relationship has ended. Apart from these general provisions there are a limited number of specific rules in the codes relating to confidentiality. For example, barristers must not act if there is a risk that information confidential to another client or former client might be communicated to or used for the benefit of anyone else without their consent.[40] Another example is that solicitors must not disclose the content of a will they have drawn before probate, except with the consent of the executors.[41]

Under the general law disclosure in breach of confidence is permissible on grounds of public interest.[42] The Bar Code does not expressly acknowledge this public interest exception. It posits withdrawal from a case where, for example, the barrister has a duty of disclosure to the court and the client refuses to sanction it.[43] The Law Society Code is more in line with the general law. It says that a duty to keep a client's confidences can be overridden if there is powerful

---

[34] *Parry-Jones v Law Society* [1969] 1 Ch 1, 7, *per* Lord Denning.

[35] *Re a Firm of Solicitors* [1992] QB 959, 966.

[36] See F. Gurry, *Breach of Confidence* (Oxford, 1984), esp. 149 ff.; P. Finn, 'Professionals and Confidentiality' (1992) 14 *Syd.LR* 317.   [37] Terrorism Act 2000, ss 19, 20.

[38] *ibid.*, s 19(5).   [39] BC §603(f); LSG §16.01.   [40] BC §603(f).

[41] LSG §16.01(3); §24.02(3)–(4).

[42] *Attorney-General v Guardian Newspapers (No. 2)* [1990] 1 AC 109.   [43] BC §608(d).

justification.[44] Apart from statutory provisions and rules of court which permit or oblige disclosure, the Law Society Code gives only limited exceptions: first, where the solicitor has been used by the client to commit crime or perpetrate fraud; secondly, if the solicitor believes disclosure is necessary to prevent the client or a third party committing a crime, which the solicitor believes on reasonable grounds is likely to result in serious bodily harm; thirdly, if abuse of children is involved; and fourthly, where disclosure is reasonably necessary to establish a defence to a criminal charge or civil claim by the client against the solicitor.[45] It is important to appreciate how narrow these exceptions are. First, and obviously, disclosure in such instances is not obligatory, however serious the wrongdoing. Secondly, the exceptions are limited to crime and fraud, and do not extend generally to deliberate wrongdoing or breaches of a court order. The solicitor who learns of a client's intention to murder has a right to disclose, but not all crimes are covered even if they cause serious damage to property, nor are regulatory offences involving damage to the environment or financial interests. Critics have noted the self-interested hierarchy of exceptions: least protected are third-party interests, then come the interests of those paying the lawyer's fees, i.e. clients, but most protected are the interests of lawyers, where there is a claim against them by a client.[46]

Running along parallel lines with the duty of confidence, but narrower in scope, is lawyer/client privilege. Legal professional privilege is an evidential rule which precludes other parties by way of pre-trial discovery, or in the course of judicial or quasi-judicial proceedings, from obtaining access to (1) communications between a lawyer and client with the dominant purpose of obtaining advice and assistance in relation to legal rights and obligations, and (2) communications between a lawyer or client and third party involving potential litigation.[47] The privilege is absolute in its effect—unless waived by the client[48]—and public interest cannot enter the balance as in the general duty of confidentiality.[49] If it is to trump legal professional privilege, legislation must be in the clearest possible terms.[50] The main rationale of the privilege is that it encourages clients to reveal all to their lawyers, thereby facilitating effective legal advice and assistance and facilitating settlement of hopeless claims. In this regard Lord Brougham's justification is still used.[51] At times, lawyer/client

---

[44] LSG §16, Introductory note.			[45] LSG §16.02.

[46] R. O'Dair, *Legal Ethics. Text and Materials* (London, 2001), 249.

[47] *Re L (a minor)* [1997] AC 16; *Three Rivers DC v Bank of England* [2004] UKHL 48; [2004] 3 WLR 1274.

[48] There can be considerable scope for argument about whether, and to what extent, the client has waived: *Goldberg v Ng* (1995) 60 ALJR 19, HC of A.

[49] *R v Derby Magistrates' Court, ex P B* [1996] AC 487.

[50] *R (Morgan Grenfell & Co. Ltd) v Special Commissioner of Income Tax* [2002] UKHL 21; [2003] 1 AC 563.

[51] *Greenough v Gaskell* (1833) 39 ER 618, 620–1. See *English & American Insurance Co. v Herbert Smith* [1988] FSR 232; *Balabel v Air India* [1988] Ch 317, 329–30; *R v Derby Magistrates' Court, ex P B* [1996] AC 487, 507; *B v Auckland District Law Society* [2003] UKPC 38; [2003] 2 AC 736.

privilege is even represented as a right fundamental to liberty and liberal democratic society.[52]

All this must be treated with some scepticism.[53] It seems doubtful whether empirical evidence would lend much support to the rationale of encouraging the use of lawyers and maximum client disclosure. Whether legal advice is sought depends in most cases on factors other than legal professional privilege. There is a plain necessity on the part of commercial interests to use lawyers, and it would be surprising if in marginal situations they did not sometimes finely calculate whether and what they needed to disclose for the purposes of obtaining legal advice. It is highly likely anyway that many people are ignorant of the privilege so it is not going to influence their behaviour. Among the arguments Jeremy Bentham advanced against the privilege was that the innocent had no need of it and that it protected only the guilty. In his view the privilege should not exist and lawyers should have to warn their clients that their revelations could be disclosed.[54] Certainly on first impression the privilege would seem to be as likely to lead to more effective avoidance of the law as to more effective utilization of legal services. In theory a client can shop around to discover from one lawyer what will ground a claim, then tailor what is told to a second lawyer retained to bring the claim. Subject to the possible application of the fraud/crime exception, of which more below, the communication with the first lawyer would be privileged.

Although the privilege is of ancient lineage too much should not be made of this since over time its content has moved in unpredictable and surprising ways, and its present shape has been importantly determined by redundant evidentiary rules, false assumptions and high falutin rhetoric about its centrality to liberty.[55] The fact that the courts have refused to extend the privilege to other professions, especially those doing similar work, such as auditors, accountants, and tax advisers, must also give pause to the notion that it is somehow a fundamental right.[56] This is not to deny the value of legal professional privilege. As with the duty of confidence, it protects interests such as privacy, important to the dignity of the individual. But as with the duty of confidence, countervailing public interest

---

[52] *Australian Mining & Smelting Europe Ltd v EC Commission* [1982] ECR 1575, 1610–14; [1982] 2 CMLR 264, 320–1; *General Mediterranean Holdings SA v Patel* [1999] 3 All ER 673, 688; *R (Morgan Grenfell & Co. Ltd) v Special Commissioner of Income Tax*, [2002] UKHL 21; [2003] 1 AC 563.

[53] See e.g. G. Dehn & M. Brindle, 'Confidentiality and the Public Interest', in R. Cranston (ed), *Legal Ethics and Professional Responsibility* (Oxford, 1994); G. Watson & F. Au, 'Solicitor–Client Privilege and Litigation Privilege in Civil Litigation' (1998) 77 *Can.Bar R.* 315; F. Zacharias, 'Rethinking Confidentiality' (1989) 74 *Iowa LR* 351.

[54] J. Bowring (ed)., *The Works of Jeremy Bentham* (Edinburgh, 1843), vol. 7, 474–5.

[55] M. Radin, 'The Privilege of Confidential Communication between Lawyer and Client,' (1928) 16 *Calif.LR* 487; G. Hazard, 'An Historical Perspective on the Attorney–Client Privilege' (1978) 66 *Calif.LR* 1061.

[56] e.g. *Price Waterhouse (a firm) v BCCI Holdings (Luxembourg) SA* [1992] BCLC 583. Consideration has been given to the position of lawyers and others providing services in the one practice: Sir David Clementi, *Report on the Review of the Regulatory Framework for Legal Services in England and Wales* (London, 2004), 135–7.

arguments should be capable of being weighed in the balance, or otherwise the privilege could become a mask for abuse. In the context of litigation, for example, justice may be better served by truncating the privilege in the quest for justice.

The privilege does not countenance communications which are not relevant to the client's legal business. This is the effect of the seminal decision *Annesley v Anglesea*,[57] where the court ordered disclosure by the Earl's solicitor of the Earl's statement that 'I would give £10,000 to have him hanged', the 'he' being a rival for his estate. More importantly, for reasons of public policy, the privilege has never been held to apply to communications by a client for the purpose of being guided or helped in the commission of a crime or the perpetration of fraud (the crime/fraud exception).[58] The House of Lords has held that this exception to the general rule applies even if the client is the innocent tool of a third party who has the unlawful purpose.[59] A simple example would be solicitors giving advice to a borrower making a deliberate misrepresentation to a building society, for the purpose of procuring a loan, whether or not the solicitors are aware that their involvement is furthering the fraudulent purpose.[60] The exception also extends to steps taken to conceal the unlawfulness or to spirit away the resulting profits.[61] The crime/fraud exception does not extend to lawyer/client communications about matters of which legality is only in doubt; the requisite purpose is said to be absent. In any event confidentiality fits here with the rationale of encouraging persons to seek legal assistance regarding compliance with the law. In practice, there can be a fine line between the innocent desire to comply with lawful requirements and the dishonest quest for knowledge as to how to avoid the law. In a valuable decision the Court of Appeal has held that lawyers realizing or suspecting that they have been unwittingly used as a conduit for fraud may apply to the court for an order that they be at liberty to disclose the fact to the victims.[62]

Competence

Lawyer misbehaviour can cover the range from bad manners and poor attitude through to dishonesty.[63] Competence falls along the spectrum. It is something about which clients can have a fairly accurate picture when compared with the judgments of peer reviewers.[64] As a matter of law lawyers must be skilful and must

---

[57] (1743) 17 State Trials 1140, 1223–6, 1241.

[58] See J. Auburn, *Legal Professional Privilege* (Oxford, 2000), ch. 9; A. Newbold, 'The Crime/Fraud Exception to Legal Professional Privilege' (1990) 53 *MLR* 472.

[59] *R v Central Criminal Court, ex p Francis & Francis* [1989] AC 346.

[60] *Nationwide Building Society v Various Solicitors, The Times*, March 1 1999.

[61] *Derby & Co. Ltd v Weldon (No. 7)* [1990] 1 WLR 1156; [1990] 3 All ER 161.

[62] *Finers (a firm) v Miro* [1991] 1 WLR 35; [1991] 1 All ER 182.

[63] For examples: A. Baron, 'A Law Unto Themselves', *Which?*, July 2004, 109; P. Pleasence, *Report of the Case Profiling Study*, Legal Aid Board Research Unit (London, 1998), 96; Legal Service Ombudsman, Annual Reports.

[64] R. Moorhead, A. Sherr & A. Paterson, 'What Clients Know: Client Perspectives and Legal Competence' (2003) 10 *Int'l J.L. Prof.* 5

exercise the skill they have.[65] The law reports contain examples of lawyers being liable to clients for a lack of competence, and there are also cases where they have been held to be liable to third parties where a client's instructions have been negligently effected.[66] Indeed, lack of competence might be raised collaterally as in the very exceptional cases where a conviction will be quashed because of the failure of the lawyer adequately to advise or act.[67] Competence can include a failure to advise about obvious risks, even if that is not within the strict ambit of matters on which advice has been sought.[68] This is in addition to the duty of solicitors to advise, which arises in special circumstances, such as when a wife gives security over her share in the domestic home for her husband's business debts.[69]

It goes without saying that lawyers must have a sound knowledge of the law. Thus they may be liable for wrongful advice, albeit that the questions are obscure and difficult. Clients must be advised of the legal consequences of any step which they propose to take, about the alternative avenues, and that any particular step ought to be taken without delay.[70] But lawyers will not be treated as responsible where the law is unsettled or capable of being changed on appeal, where the matter is characterized by obscurity in language or expression or where the circumstances demand quick and clear advice rather than reasoned and comprehensive precision.[71] Moreover, lawyers are not business advisers and although solicitors might offer business-related advice and try to protect clients against themselves, they are not under a legal duty to do so.[72] And a lawyer is under no duty to cross-examine clients, in addition to reading relevant materials, in order to discover inaccuracies in their account.[73] As with others providing services, lawyers must act with reasonable competence and skill. Liability might arise simultaneously under contract and tort.[74] The courts have now overturned the immunity of barristers and solicitor-advocates from suits in negligence in respect of the carriage of a case in court and the pre-trial work connected with it.[75] The strongest argument for the immunity was ensuring finality in litigation, although this assumed that losing

---

[65] *Norton v Lord Ashburton* [1914] AC 932, 956.

[66] *Ross v Caunters* [1980] Ch. 297; *White v Jones* [1995] 2 AC 207. Recent cases include *Moy v Pettman Smith (a firm)* [2002] EWCA Civ 875 (on the solicitors' liability).

[67] *Boodram v The State of Trinidad and Tobago* [2001] UKPC 20; [2002] 1 Cr App R 12.

[68] *Credit Lyonnais SA v Russell Jones & Walker* [2002] EWHC 1310; [2002] EGLR 65, Ch. cf. *Clark Boyce v Mouat* [1994] 1 AC 428, 437D, PC; *Heydon v NRMA Ltd* (2000) 51 NSWLR 1, 118, *per* McPherson A-JA.

[69] *Royal Bank of Scotland v Etridge (No. 2)* [2002] 2 AC 773. See R. Cranston, *Principles of Banking Law*, 2nd edn (Oxford, 2002), 216–20 and the references there.

[70] *Re a Solicitor ex p Incorporated Law Society* (1895) 39 SJ 219, 219; *Otter v Church Adams, Tatham & Co.* [1953] Ch. 280; cf. *Griffiths v Evans* [1953] 1 WLR 1424; [1953] 2 All ER 1364.

[71] *Richards v Cod* [1943] KB 139; *Sykes v Midland Bank Executor & Trustee Co. Ltd* [1971] 1 QB 113; *County Personnel (Employment Agency) Ltd v Alan R. Pulver & Co.* [1987] 1 WLR 916; [1987] 1 All ER 289; *Heydon v NRMA Ltd* (2000) 51 NSWLR 1; *Moy v Pettman Smith (a firm)* [2005] UKHL 7; [2005] 1 WLR 581.   [72] *Haigh v Wright Hassall & Co.* [1994] EGCS 54.

[73] *Dawson Cornwell & Co. (a firm) v C.J. Nicholl & Associates Ltd.* (2002) 152 NLJ 1434.

[74] *Midland Bank Trust Co. Ltd v Hett, Stubbs & Kemp* [1979] Ch 384.

[75] *Arthur J.S. Hall & Co. (a firm) v Simons* [2002] 1 AC 615.

clients had the stamina for relitigation. Competence also arises in the general law in other ways. Lawyers must not misrepresent their competence. When handling moneys they must account and not make improper investments.[76] Lawyers must not stray beyond the task their client has authorized: if a lawyer acts without authority he or she may not only be liable to the client but to third parties for breach of warranty of authority.[77]

In the past there was a reluctance to treat a failure in care and skill as professional misconduct.[78] This was reinforced in practice because the professional bodies often gave precedence to the client's interest in obtaining compensation over disciplining the lawyer. The law now recognizes that serious negligence can amount to professional misconduct.[79] Both codes clearly equate lack of care and skill with professional misconduct. Not only that, but they add some meat to the duty to act with care and skill. Thus both codes say that lawyers must not act if they lack the experience or competence, or if in the circumstances (for example, pressure of time) they cannot adequately represent a client.[80] These provisions are directed at any temptation, especially in today's competitive environment, for lawyers to take on any work which comes their way although, for example, it falls outside the area in which they practice. The Bar Code obliges barristers to take steps to ensure that their practices are run efficiently and are properly administered, and that proper records are kept.[81] Heads of chambers have specific obligations to ensure an efficient operation.[82] The Law Society Guide states explicitly that solicitors are under a duty to act with care and skill, diligence and, promptness, and to keep their clients properly informed.[83] Solicitors must not act or continue to act in circumstances where the client cannot be represented with competence or diligence. This applies if they have insufficient time to devote to a matter, or insufficient experience or skill to deal with it competently.[84] There is also an express principle in the code obliging solicitors to deal promptly with correspondence.[85]

Care and skill under the Law Society Guide covers behaviour which falls short of negligence. Unlike negligence, however, breach of the code does not lead to an award of damages although the Office for the Supervision of Solicitors can intervene and direct a solicitor to afford redress to the client. Frequent reasons for the Office to order redress are delay and a failure to communicate.[86] Delay can lead to the Law Society taking a matter from a solicitor and ultimately to serious disciplinary action. Most importantly nowadays it is a breach of the care and skill obligation to provide services which are not of the quality which is reasonable to expect.[87] So-called inadequate professional service covers a wider field than

---

[76] *e.g. Lee v Sankey* (1873) LR 15 Eq 204; *Blyth v Fladgate* [1891] 1 Ch 337.
[77] *Yonge v Toynbee* [1910] 1 KB 215.   [78] *Re a Solicitor* (1974) 118 *SJ* 737.
[79] *McCandless v General Medical Council* [1996] 1 WLR 167, PC.
[80] BC §§603(a), (b); 701(b)(e).   [81] BC §403.2(a).   [82] BC §§404.1–404.2
[83] LSG §§12.08; 13.01.   [84] LSG §12.03.   [85] LSG § 12.10.
[86] *e.g.* Law Society, *Annual Report for year ending 30 April 2003* (London, 2003), 11.
[87] LSG §12.08(5)–(7).

professional incompetence and include organizational incompetence.[88] Prejudice to a client does not have to be shown before a solicitor can be found to have failed to provide adequate professional service.[89]

Loyalty

Thirdly, then, to loyalty. As a matter of law the duty of loyalty has derived primarily from the position of lawyers as fiduciaries. As a matter of public policy loyalty is probably grounded on the nature of the lawyer as a professional who places skills and knowledge at the disposal of the client. As with any professional, clients are entitled to place a certain trust in their lawyer that he or she will act loyally and competently. The strain comes when loyalty is, or ought to be, trumped by public interest.

(a) Devotion to the client's interests

Loyalty's first face is devotion to the client's interests. That demands competence, commitment, and zeal. Not being frank with a client, and dissembling, would be a breach of the duty.[90] The Bar Code says that barristers must promote and protect fearlessly their lay clients' best interests without regard to their own interests or the consequences.[91] If there is a conflict, loyalty to the client comes before loyalty to the instructing solicitor. Thus the Bar Code says that barristers owe their primary duty to their lay client and must not permit any intermediary (for example, a solicitor) to limit that.[92] The Law Society Guide requires solicitors to act in the best interest of their client, although this may need to be tempered by the requirement that cases be pursued only in a way proportionate to the benefit.[93] More detailed consequences of loyalty include the principle that solicitors must not take advantage of the age, inexperience, want of education, business experience, ill health, and so on of a client.[94] Moreover, the code says specifically that solicitors must not take unfair advantage of a client by overcharging.[95]

The Bar has always put its claim to loyalty boldly in espousing the fearless promotion of a lay client's best interests, without regard to the barrister's own interest. Atticus Finch provides an American example. Lord Brougham's defence of Queen Caroline has been portrayed as an exemplary example of such zeal. Brougham's alluded in his defence of the Queen to evidence which might harm the King, but argued that no matter what the consequences his duty as an advocate demanded that he take every step necessary to defend his client.[96] Advocates are constantly

---

[88] Solicitors Act 1974, s 37A; LSG §30.02. See A. Paterson, 'Professional Competence' (1983) 28 *J.Law Soc.Scot.* 385.

[89] *R v The Law Society, ex p Singh & Choudry (a firm)*, The Times, 1 April 1994.

[90] *Somatra Ltd v Sinclair Roche and Temperley* [2003] EWCA Civ 509, CA.

[91] BC §303(a).   [92] BC §303(b).   [93] LSG §2.02(c); §1.02(8). See 149 above.

[94] LSG §12.09.   [95] LSG § 14.12.

[96] *Hansard*, New Ser., iii, 3 October 1820, 114. See W. Forsyth, *Hortensius, or the Advocate*, 3rd edn (London, 1879), 389; D. Rhode, 'An Adversarial Exchange on Adversarial Tactics' (1991) 41

reminded that they must not act as judges. Rights, it is said, are determined by the courts and not by advocates. 'It is for want of remembering this that foolish people object to lawyers that they will advocate a case against their own opinions.'[97] It is also said advocates sometimes find that arguments which they do not think to be especially good are accepted by the courts. Notwithstanding all this lay people do not share the same confidence as do advocates that the adversarial system always works.

What are the public interest limits on loyalty? There are few common law boundaries to advocate zeal. One is honesty; advocates must present their client's case to the best of their ability, without making themselves a judge of its correctness, but they must not be dishonest.[98] Lord Denning MR, in his own inimitable way, summed up the boundaries for advocates as follows: 'It is a mistake to suppose that [an advocate] is the mouthpiece of his client... to say what he wants: or his tool to do what he directs. He is none of these things. He owes allegiance to a higher cause. It is the cause of truth and justice.'[99] So advocates must not assert what they know to be a lie, nor must they connive at, much less attempt to substantiate, a fraud, but they are entitled to require the other side to prove its case. In theory the adversary system produces just results based on laws fairly applied to accurate facts.

The professional codes contain injunctions similar to the common law against acting dishonestly, unlawfully, or in any way likely to diminish public confidence in the profession.[100] The codes also say that although there is a duty to advance a client's interests, this must not be so as to compromise professional standards.[101] As the Law Society Guide puts it, a solicitor 'must not allow clients to override the solicitor's professional judgment, for example, by insisting on the solicitor acting in a way which is contrary to law or to a rule or principle of professional conduct'.[102]

Specific guidance on these limits is harder to come by. There is a well-known limit, restated in both codes, that lawyers must not deceive or mislead a court.[103] *Meek v Fleming*[104] is an example. A press photographer brought an action against

---

J. Leg. Ed. 29. On Lushington's involvement in the defence: S.M. Waddams, *Law, Politics and the Church of England* (Cambridge, 1992), 144–50.

[97] *Johnson v Emerson* (1871) LR 6 Ex 329, 367.

[98] W. Boulton, *A Guide to Conduct and Etiquette at the Bar*, (London, 1975), 69. In *Abraham v Jutsun* [1963] 2 All ER 402, 404, Lord Denning said: '[It is an advocate's] duty to take any point which he believed to be fairly arguable on behalf of his client. An advocate is not to usurp the province of the judge. He is not to determine what shall be the effect of legal argument. He is not guilty of misconduct simply because he takes a point which the tribunal holds to be bad. He only becomes guilty of misconduct if he is dishonest. That is, if he knowingly takes a bad point and thereby deceives the court.'

[99] *Rondel v Worsley* [1966] 3 WLR 950, 962. Compare a similar statement by Crampton J in *R v O'Connell* (1844) 7 Irish LR 261, 313.   [100] BC §301(a); LSG §§1.01; 12.02.

[101] BC §307(c); LSG §§1.01; 12.02.   [102] LSG §11.01(2).

[103] BC §302; LSG §21.01.

[104] [1961] 2 QB 366. Advising a client to wear conventional clothing, never otherwise worn except to marriages or funerals, has not been thought to be misleading, presumably because the judge/jury realizes the truth.

'Chief Inspector Fleming' for, *inter alia*, assault. Between the issue of the writ and the trial the defendant was demoted to station sergeant for being a party to an arrangement to practice deception on a court. He was asked in cross-examination: 'You are a chief inspector and you have been in the force, you told us, since 1938'. His answer was yes. During the summing-up the judge referred to the defendant as 'inspector' or 'chief inspector' many times. The fact of the demotion was known to the defendant's legal advisers but they decided not to reveal it to the court. A new trial was ordered, since to allow the defendant to retain the 'judgment unfairly obtained would be a miscarriage of justice'. By contrast, *R v Visitors to the Inns of Court, ex p Calder*[105] involved a barrister who had made a mock-up of a receipt purportedly signed by her client, the plaintiff. Believing it to be forged she put it to the defendant in cross-examination—'Have you ever seen anything like this before?'—in an attempt to undermine the defendant's credibility. At that stage the original of the receipt could not be found, nor a photocopy. Subsequently it was found and the mock-up played no further part in the trial. The barrister was nonetheless charged with misleading the court by failing to explain fully the provenance of the mock-up. The Court of Appeal quashed the conviction by the Visitors; the original not being disclosed, the barrister was entitled to assume it might well have been destroyed, and therefore it was a legitimate tactic to cross-examine on the basis of the mock-up. The court was not misled and there was no evidence that the barrister had attempted to mislead it.

Derived from the obligation not to deceive or mislead the court are the more specific duties not to coach witnesses, not to devise facts to assist a client, and to ensure that the court is informed of all relevant decisions and legislation, however unfavourable.[106] A client's admission of perjury or of misleading a court, prior to or in the course of proceedings, obliges both a barrister and solicitor to decline to act further, unless the client agrees fully to disclose the matter. Presenting perjured evidence would, of course, constitute misleading the court. These various aspects of the duty of honesty derive partly from the adversary system: courts must be able to rely on the honesty of opposing parties since there is generally no inquisitorial machinery whereby they can investigate facts, and the pressure of business and absence of law clerks at first instance mean that judges are reliant on the advocates to research the law fully. While placing obligations on lawyers in this way compensates for certain features of the adversary system, it does not address other matters such as any inequality of legal representation.

(b) Conflicts of interest

The other face of loyalty is avoiding conflicts of interest, although this principle is also underpinned by the duty of confidentiality. Echoing the general law, the

---

[105] [1994] QB 1. Generally speaking, in presenting a document to a court an advocate is in effect warranting that it is what it purports to be and that it is accurate.

[106] BC §§705(a), (b); 708(c), (e); LSG §21.01.

professional codes contain a variety of provisions addressing conflict of duty and interest (between lawyer and client) and conflict of duties (duty to different clients or duty to a new client and a former client). Illustrative in the Bar Code are the rules relating to barristers likely to be a witness in a case, barristers having a connection with a client or court, and barristers with two or more clients whose interests conflict.[107] The general thrust of these rules is replicated for solicitors in the Law Society Guide, although the scope is wider, disqualifying a solicitor's partners as well as the individual solicitor with the conflict.[108]

As with general fiduciary law, to avoid a conflict of interest lawyers might have to decline to act altogether. Their duty is to inform their client of that and, if relevant, that he or she should seek legal advice from other lawyers, starting afresh and not relying on any advice already given.[109] Thus the Law Society Guide provides that solicitors who have acted for both lender and borrower must not subsequently act for the lender against the borrower to enforce repayment if in doing so he or she has obtained confidential relevant information, for example about the borrower's financial position.[110] Nor may a solicitor who has acted for a company in a particular matter, and has also acted separately for directors or shareholders in a personal capacity in the same matter, now act for either the company or the other parties if litigation ensues between them in respect of it.[111] Mundane examples of conflicts of duty and interest, where solicitors must generally decline to act, involve transactions with clients, gifts, and legacies.[112]

Conflicts of interest are pervasive; the problem is that they may be so common that lawyers do not recognize them as such. In a survey of 100 leading companies in 2004, more than a third reported at least one conflict of interest involving their legal advisers in the past year, and almost as many had been forced to appoint a different lawyer as a result of a conflict during the past two years.[113] For this reason it is often better to attack an undesirable practice directly instead of imposing on the lawyer the obligation to take action if that practice gives rise to a 'conflict'. Take the basic potential conflict between a client and a lawyer—the lawyer is being paid which, especially if at an hourly rate, creates a potential incentive for the lawyer to contrive work. Matters which are better closed might be unnecessarily prolonged. In fact the empirical evidence does not lend support to differences in work content related to the type of fee arrangement.[114] Inasmuch as there could

---

[107] BC §307(b), (d), (f).
[108] LSG §§15.01–15.03. See, e.g., *Lewis v Hillman* (1852) 10 ER 239; *Brown v Inland Revenue* 1964 SC (HL) 180; *R v Ataou* [1988] QB 798; *Perry v Edwin Coe (a firm), Independent*, 1 April 1994.
[109] *Hilton v Barker Booth & Eastwood (a firm)* [2005] UKHL 8; [2005] 1 WLR 567, para.32.
[110] LSG §15.02(4).   [111] LSG §15.02(6).
[112] LSG §15.04. See *Stewart v MacLaren* 1920 SC (HL) 148; *Re a Solicitor* [1975] QB 475; *Longstaff v Birtles* [2001] EWCA Civ 1219; [2002] 1 WLR 470, CA.
[113] D. Bedlow, 'Conflicts in Crisis', *Legal Week*, 25 June 2004. Apparently the Law Society's ethics guidance team receive about 6000 inquiries a year on conflicts of interest: E. Fennell, 'Rules Not Made to be Broken', *The Times*, 12 October 2004.
[114] H. Kritzer, 'Lawyer Fees and Lawyer Behaviour in Litigation' (2002) 80 *Tex.LR* 1943, 1967–71.

be a problem the basic conflict is dealt with in the professional codes by general rules such as those relating to lawyers acting with reasonable skill, care, and diligence. It might also be helpful to tackle the problem directly with specific code provisions against undertaking unnecessary work. Such a rule would reflect for litigation the obligation on lawyers in the CPR.[115]

The restructuring of law firms has given rise to conflict problems where different parts of the amalgamated firm have represented opposing clients. The Law Society has issued guidance on the matter. The amalgamated firm must cease to act for both clients, although in 'exceptional' circumstances outside litigation the amalgamated firm may continue to act for one client, or just possibly both clients, if it is in the best interests of the clients. An effective Chinese wall must be erected, and both clients must give their consent after having had the risks fully explained. The guidance adds that there is a heavy onus on the amalgamated firm to show the wall is effective.[116] One study found that circumstances would drive some firms away from adherence to the letter of the guidance. Indeed some large City firms would pay little or no attention to the guidance and were prepared to act in most conflicts other than where clients were directly opposed. Where they considered there was little or no risk of complaint, they were prepared to act without explicitly getting consent.[117]

The guidance does not cover an increasingly regular occurrence of younger solicitors, and increasingly partners, moving firms, so that a client finds that a solicitor has moved to a firm on the other side of a matter. Here the circumstances should be determinative: there should be no objection if the transferring solicitor can show that there is no risk of possessing relevant confidential information, or gives a plausible undertaking not to have anything to do with the matters dealt with at the previous firm.[118] The courts have not approached the problem consistently. In *Rakusen v Ellis, Munday and Clark*,[119] the Court of Appeal took a relaxed position and allowed one of two partners to represent a company defending a wrongful dismissal action when the plaintiff had consulted the other partner earlier in the proceedings, in the course of which he had disclosed much confidential information. There was an undertaking that the latter would not act in any way in the proceedings and would not say anything about his consultations with the plaintiff. Indeed the facts were peculiar in that the two partners effectively conducted separate practices without any knowledge of each other's clients. However, the decision dates from a different age of smaller firms and, it might be added, lower standards. When the House of Lords had to consider the issue in 1998 it rejected an objective test, whether a reasonable person would anticipate

---

[115] 149 above.   [116] LSG, Annex 15A.

[117] J. Griffiths-Baker, *Serving Two Masters. Conflicts of Interest in the Modern Law Firm* (Oxford, 2002), 120–40. For the United States: S. Shapiro, *Tangled Loyalties. Conflict of Interest in Legal Practice* (Ann Arbor, 2002).

[118] *Koch Shipping Inc. v Richards Butler (a firm)* [2002] EWCA Civ 1280; [2002] 2 All ER (Comm) 957; *Re a Firm of Solicitors* [1997] Ch. 1.   [119] [1912] Ch. 831.

that there was a danger that information gained from acting for a former client would be used against that client in representing the new client. Instead it held that the onus was on a law firm to show that there was no risk of disclosure. The risk of disclosure had to be real, not fanciful or theoretical. However, only in exceptional cases would a Chinese wall be considered a suitable arrangement to prevent the leakage of information since, however conscientious members of the firm might be, confidential information could inadvertently seep.[120]

In this area desirable public policy is not clear-cut. The argument for a liberal standard is that there is a countervailing, public interest in not unduly restricting a client's choice of lawyer, and that depriving persons of their chosen lawyer may cause inconvenience, expense, and disruption. The problem is especially acute when representation is well under way so the change in lawyer will have a very considerable impact on the client who has to find a new one. Disqualification suits can be a forensic tactic, generating satellite litigation and, of course, cost and delay. What seems necessary is not automatic disqualification but a close empirical inquiry as to whether there is or will be a conflict, and how that might be mitigated by realistic arrangements within the firm.

Lawyer Control and Lawyer Zeal

A distinction—albeit glib—can be drawn between at one end of the spectrum lawyers taking advantage of clients, and at the other lawyers taking advantage on behalf of clients. The first conceives the lawyer/client relationship as one of control with lawyers imposing their agenda on clients. The second conceives of the client as autonomous, with the lawyer zealously pursuing the client's interests, as the North American literature puts it, as hired gun. In fact the reality of domination or autonomy falls along a spectrum and varies with the circumstances. Certainly the socially excluded are likely to be ignorant of and mystified by the law. However unconsciously, the lawyer might drift into imposing his or her agenda on the relationship.[121] On the other hand, the commercial client might

---

[120] *Bolkiah (Price Jefri) v KPMG (a firm)* [1999] 2 AC 222. See also *Marks & Spencer Group plc v Freshfields Bruckhaus Deringer* [2004] EWCA Civ 741; [2005] PNLR 4. Elsewhere see *McDonald Estate v Martin* [1991] 1 WWR 705, SCC; *National Mutual Holdings Pty Ltd v Sentry Corp.* (1989) 87 ALR 539. The seminal US decision is *T.C. Theatre Corp. v Warner Brothers Pictures*, 113 F.Supp. 265 (SDNY 1953). On Chinese walls see, e.g. *Analytica Inc. v NPD Research Inc.*, 708 F.2d 1263 (7th Cir.1983). See F.M.B. Reynolds, 'Solicitors and Conflict of Duties' (1991) 107 LQR 536; R. Tomasic, 'Chinese Walls, Legal Principles and Commercial Reality in Multi-Service Professional Firms' (1991) 14 *U.NSW. LJ* 46; Note, 'The Chinese Wall Defense to Law-Firm Disqualification' (1980) 128 *U.Penn. LR* 677; R. Mulheron, 'Solicitor's Conflicts of Duty and Interest. Three Different Scenarios' (1999) 1 *U.Notre Dame Aust. LR* 83; Law Commission, *Fiduciary Duties and Regulatory Rules*, Consultation Paper No. 124 (1992), 144–51.

[121] The classic study is D. Rosenthal, *Attorney and Client: Who's in Charge?* (New Brunswick, NJ, 1974). See also M. Cain, 'The General Practice Lawyer and the Client: Towards a Radical Conception', in R. Dingwall & P. Lewis (eds), *The Sociology of the Professions* (London, 1983); A. Sarat &

know exactly what it wants to achieve, with lawyers and others being employed as tools to facilitate this. The problem then might be not the autonomy of the client but that of the lawyer. In one sense lawyer control is a corollary of the law's mystery: the lawyer has a superior learning and knowledge of legal processes which clients cannot hope to acquire (without a substantial investment), even if they had the inclination. Lawyer control can have a functional justification in suppressing anti-social behaviour. To use a sociological term, lawyers are gatekeepers. They advise clients about how to behave lawfully, they screen out unjustified claims, they encourage the settlement of disputes, and they damp down abuse of the legal process. In this regard, the lawyer's role as gatekeeper should be enhanced.

The profession's codes exhibit a concern with both tendencies. Concern that the lawyer might take advantage of the client is evident in the Bar's standards applicable to criminal cases. Barristers should advise defendants about their plea ('he may, if necessary, express his advice in strong terms') but must make clear that the client has complete freedom of choice.[122] They should advise clients about whether or not to give evidence in their own defence, but the decision should be taken by clients themselves.[123] Similarly, the Law Society code says that solicitors must act in the best interests of clients.[124] There are various warnings that solicitors must keep clients properly informed. The aim in relation to communications with clients is to ensure that those unfamiliar with the law receive the information needed to understand what is happening. No doubt more could be done both through the codes about the way lawyers treat clients. Legal education has a role in lawyers learning how to be more responsive, for example to the human as well as to the legal dimensions of clients' problems. What of the other tendency, lawyer zeal?

Lawyer zeal and its limits

In considering lawyer zeal it is useful to begin with the role of a leading City of London law firm in the well-publicised acquisition of House of Fraser by the Fayeds. House of Fraser was then the largest group of department stores in Europe and included the prestigious Harrods store. The firm represented the Fayeds at crucial points in the acquisition process. Inspectors were appointed to inquire into the circumstances surrounding the takeover, notably the impression conveyed to the government that the Fayeds were a family with widespread, international business interests who had sufficient funds to finance the takeover without assistance from any third party. In the course of their report, the inspectors (Henry Brooke

---

W. Felstiner, 'Law and Strategy in the Divorce Lawyer's Office' (1986) 20 *Law & Soc.Rev.* 93; G. Lerman, 'Lying to Clients' (1990) 138 *U.Penn.LR* 659; M. McConville, J. Hodgson, L. Bridges & A. Pavolvic, *Standing Accused. The Organisation and Practices of Criminal Defence Lawyers in Britain* (Oxford, 1994); R. Moorhead, A. Sherr & A. Paterson, *op.cit.*, 7–13.

[122] BC, Written Standards for the Conduct of Professional Work, §11.3.   [123] *ibid.*, §11.4.
[124] LSG §2.02.

QC, as he then was, and Hugh Aldous, an accountant) concluded that in deciding not to refer the acquisition to the Monopolies and Mergers Commission the government had taken comfort from the assurances which were given to the Office of Fair Trading (OFT) and the Department of Trade and Industry (DTI) by the Fayeds and, more importantly, from an impression which had been created that the Fayeds' merchant banker, the board of House of Fraser (which recommended acceptance of the bid), and the law firm had all aligned their reputations with those of the Fayeds. In response to this the law firm contended that in acting, speaking, and making submissions for their clients, solicitors do not generally give an imprimatur of any sort. If regard was had to what it had said and written it would be concluded that the firm had declined to give any assurance or endorsement. The inspectors rejected this.

We have little difficulty in accepting that these submissions were correct as a matter of theory. A High Court judge or an experienced lawyer would have little difficulty in detecting when a solicitor was ceasing to act as a mere advocate and becoming more and would also probably try and stop him from changing his role because he would know the problems this causes. In their relationships with the OFT, however, solicitors are not dealing with High Court judges or experienced lawyers. They are dealing with intelligent lay people. [The OFT officer] and, at one remove, [the DTI officer] told us the impression which [the firm] created on their minds and were not surprised that the firm created that impression. The firm has said that they should have read the words which [it] used and that they were wrong to receive that impression. We do not agree. Anyone reading [the] letter would have obtained the impression that the firm was in a certain sense vouching for the accuracy of what their clients had said.[125]

In the result the inspectors did not blame the firm for failing to take further steps to ensure that the assertions by their clients were based on fact. They thought that the problem arose from a confusion of roles, in particular that solicitors when they act as advocates do not appreciate the dangers of identifying with their clients, ready to vouch for their cause. Barristers, of course, however passionately they may argue their client's case, do not as a practice assert a personal opinion as to the facts or the law.[126]

The House of Fraser takeover raises in stark form the dangers of lawyer zeal. Identifying (or being perceived, to identify) too closely with a client's case as in that instance misled others as to the strength of the clients' arguments. Of course zeal *per se* is admirable. The problem in some areas is an under-representation of interests, not excessive zealousness. The tragedy as we have seen earlier in the book is that constraints on access to justice mean that many ordinary people with a need for legal services are not well served, let alone zealously. Coupled with the problem

---

[125] Department of Trade and Industry, *House of Fraser Holdings plc* (London, 1988), 491. On the Law Society's response to this report: HC, Trade & Industry Committee, *Company Investigations*, HC 36, 1990, 285–6 (with limited exceptions 'a solicitor is under no obligation to check the accuracy of any statement he makes on behalf of a client...'). See also R. Rice, 'Salutary Lessons from the Fayed Affair', *Financial Times*, 26 March 1990, 8.   [126] BC §708(b).

of under-representation is the unenthusiastic representation of clients. For a variety of financial and other reasons lawyers may not show the devotion, which would ordinarily be expected, in pursuing certain claims.[127]

Zeal, however, must have its boundaries. The client's own interests will delineate the first. It may be that the client's interests are best served by compromise and accommodation with opponents, rather than the zealous insistence on pursuing legal rights to the hilt. Moreover, a lawyer may not give sufficient attention to the object of zealousness; in other words, the problem may not be excessive zealousness, but excessive zealousness on behalf of the wrong person. Instructed by a company, for example, zealousness on behalf of the company as a whole, rather than the directors with whom the lawyer actually deals, could lead to greater corporate social responsibility. A second boundary to zeal is that demanded by the interests of others directly involved in the matter. Even in the arena of criminal defence zeal needs to be mitigated in the interests of victims. An example is the shield against defence attacks which the victims in rape cases now have.[128] The final boundary to zealousness is that imposed by the public interest. This is the hardest to define. It is clear that a Darwinian struggle between adversaries will not necessarily produce a result which is in the public interest. We now know enough about the adversary process to realize that, quite apart from anything else, the different sides may be unequally matched. Moreover, many aspects of a lawyer's work do not involve another side, for example the lawyer giving advice to a client as to how to structure a transaction to comply with company law and to minimize taxation.

Before proceeding further to delineate this third boundary, it is as well to recall the origins of lawyer zeal. They lie in criminal defence, and there the justification is obvious. Zealousness guarantees a thorough preparation of the case, not simply by the defence lawyers. Without it, the police and prosecution authorities would not have the same incentive to investigate a matter thoroughly, for example by investigating any corroboration for the defendant's account. Recent miscarriages of justice underlie how much worse the situation would be in the absence of zealous defence. Putting that to one side, however, the crucial issue is that the approach with criminal defence cannot automatically be extended to other cases, in particular the lawyer giving advice to, negotiating on behalf of, or representing a client where no litigation is in contemplation. Here we are not concerned with the state operating against the individual or with the possibility that the client might be deprived of his or her liberty. For good reasons the zeal which we expect of a lawyer in criminal defence is not necessarily appropriate in these other, more common, situations.

Generally speaking, of course, the client will have no truck with illegality and will want to stay well within the four corners of the law. But sometimes clients will want to push the law to its limit and will expect their lawyer to facilitate this. They

---

[127] 114 above.
[128] Youth Justice and Criminal Evidence Act 1999, s 41. See J. Temkin, *Rape and the Legal Process*, 2nd edn (Oxford, 2002), 9–10, 196–225.

will want their bid for a target company to succeed, financing to be obtained for their enterprise, or tax to be avoided. These days in commercial law the lawyer becomes closely involved in business decision making. Competitive pressures may impel lawyers to tread on very thin ice. It was probably only a matter of time before prosecuting authorities should bring proceedings against a City solicitor. Although when this occurred the judge directed a not guilty verdict against the partner of the large law firm who was involved in the Blue Arrow affair, the prosecution was a salutary warning, as the *Financial Times* put it, 'of the dangers inherent in the proactive role commercial lawyers are required to play these days'.[129] As one expert in commercial fraud from another prominent large law firm said: 'The apparently aggressive attitude of the prosecution towards professionals is moulded by a belief that many sophisticated frauds... cannot be carried out without the active and knowing participation of a solicitor or other advisor.'[130] It is in these areas of potential wrongdoing by clients, or suspected wrongdoing, that the problems for lawyers are acute.

Client wrongdoing

Over the years the Bar has been able to refine its approach to a client's confession of wrongdoing. In 1915 the English Bar Council drew a sharp distinction between confessions which were made to counsel before the proceedings commenced and those which were made subsequently. If the former it was said to be most undesirable for an advocate to whom the confession had been made to undertake the defence, since he would most certainly be seriously embarrassed in the conduct of the case. In any event no harm could be done by requesting the accused to retain another advocate. Other considerations applied in cases in which the confession was made during the proceedings, or in circumstances where the advocate could not withdraw without seriously compromising the position of the accused. In addressing this the Bar Council said it was essential to bear in mind that the issue in a criminal trial was always whether the accused was guilty of the offence charged, not whether the accused was innocent, and secondly that the burden rested on the prosecution to prove the case. Thus the advocate's duty was to protect a client as far as possible from being convicted, except by a competent tribunal and upon legal evidence sufficient to support a conviction, although in the event of a confession there were very strict limitations on how the defence was to be conducted since no advocate should assert what he or she knew to be a lie, nor connive at, much less attempt to

---

[129] R. Rice, 'Blue Arrow and the Role of the Solicitor', *Financial Times*, 20 November 1989, 15. See also Department of Trade and Industry, *County NatWest Limited. County NatWest Services Limited* (London, 1989).

[130] D. Kirk, 'Blue Arrow: A Legacy of Suspicion', *Lawyer*, vol. 5, n. 43, 5 November 1991, 4. See P. Stewart, 'Lawyers in the Firing Line', *Int'l. Financial LR*, April 1991, 12.

substantiate, a fraud.[131] This approach is, in substance, contained in the current code.[132]

Illustrative of the principle is the Australian decision, used in some of the American texts, *Tuckiar v The King*.[133] The accused, a nomadic aboriginal, was charged with the murder of a police constable in the Northern Territory. During the trial counsel for the accused interviewed his client at the suggestion of the trial judge to ascertain whether he agreed with evidence given by a witness for the Crown of a confession alleged to have been made by the accused to the witness. After interviewing the accused his counsel said in open court that he was in a worse predicament than he had encountered in all his career. The implication was obvious, and the accused was found guilty of murder. In a joint judgment the High Court of Australia (Gavan Duffy CJ, Dixon J, Evatt J, McTiernan J) said of counsel:

Why he should have conceived himself to have been in so great a predicament, it is not easy for those experienced in advocacy to understand. He had a plain duty, both to his client and to the Court, to press such rational considerations as the evidence fairly gave rise to in favour of complete acquittal or conviction of manslaughter only.[134]

Outside the law this approach has never been universally accepted. Jeremy Bentham regarded the lawyer assisting a guilty client to an acquittal to be an accessory after the fact of the offence.[135] Contemporary commentators query whether advocates for criminal defendants can be completely oblivious to the harm done to victims when there are outcomes contrary to the merits.[136] However, the approach addresses cases of unequivocal guilt, not those of doubtful guilt. In practice the former will be rare and the reality is of a 'confession' (if any) in relation to which the lawyer will rarely, if ever, be able to conclude certain guilt. No doubt there are

[131] See also M. Hilbery, *Duty and Art in Advocacy* (London, 1959), 9.

[132] BC, Written Standards for the Conduct of Professional Work, reads:

12.2 . . . the mere fact that a person charged with a crime has confessed to his counsel that he did commit the offence charged is no bar to that barrister appearing or continuing to appear in his defence, nor indeed does such a confession release the barrister from his imperative duty to do all that he honourably can for his client.

12.3 Such a confession, however, imposes very strict limitations on the conduct of the defence. A barrister must not assert as true that which he knows to be false. He must not connive at, much less attempt to substantiate, a fraud.

12.4 While, therefore, it would be right to take any objections to the competency of the Court, to the form of the indictment, to the admissibility of any evidence or to the evidence admitted . . . a barrister must not . . . set up an affirmative case inconsistent with the confession made to him.

12.5 . . . he is entitled to test the evidence given by each individual witness and to argue that the evidence taken as a whole is insufficient to amount to proof that the defendant is guilty of the offence charged. Further than this he ought not to go.

[133] (1934) 52 CLR 335. See also 258 below.

[134] ibid., 346. After the defendant was convicted his counsel made a public statement in court to the effect that the accused admitted the evidence called by the Crown of a confession was correct. The High Court said that this was wholly indefensible; in the event it rendered a retrial impossible because that would have been known throughout the Territory.

[135] J. Bowring (ed.), *The Works of Jeremy Bentham* (Edinburgh, 1843), vol. 7, 474–5.

[136] R. O'Dair, *Legal Ethics Text and Materials* (London, 2001), 199–215, 222.

other cases, falling outside the strict words of the code, which lawyers themselves would almost universally condemn as professional misconduct. A striking example is *R v Dean*.[137] Dean was tried for attempted murder of his wife and defended by Meagher. He was convicted and after the trial Dean confessed to Meagher that he was in fact guilty. (Clearly this does not fall within the words of the code since it was not a confession before or during the trial.) Knowing this, Meagher still agitated for a Royal Commission to reopen the case, and when one was ultimately appointed Dean received a pardon as a result of its recommendations. Afterwards Meagher had to concede Dean's confession and was struck off for professional misconduct.

What of those instances which do not fall squarely within the words of the code, or clear cases such as *R v Dean*, where a lawyer knows, or more probably suspects, that he is assisting a client in wrongful conduct, wrongful in the sense that it will be a breach of the criminal or regulatory law, fraudulent or (possibly also) an intentional or bad faith breach of contract?[138] Consider these hypothetical examples.

- A solicitor appears for a landlord against an unrepresented tenant. The tenant puts arguments which are irrelevant to the issue. However, the solicitor knows that if the tenant were to put other arguments his client would not obtain the order for possession.

- An assistant solicitor in a large law firm is advising a company on the application of environmental protection legislation to some of its intended activities. It is fairly clear to her that the activities are in clear breach of the legislation, but, at the conference, her supervising partner indicates to the client that the area is doubtful legally, and that in any event it is unlikely that the enforcement authorities will discover the breach. At the end of the conference she is told by him to draft a letter of advice to the client along those lines.

- A lawyer in a law centre is advising on welfare benefit. He has doubts whether the client is telling the truth about not having worked in the relevant period, but on being assured that no work was done proceeds with the claim and as a result has been successful. A short time later he discovers for certain that the client was not telling the truth and had full-time employment for the period for which benefit was, wrongfully, obtained.[139]

One approach in addressing these hypotheticals is to ask to what extent non-lawyers would be in breach of the criminal or civil law—whether as aider or

---

[137] C.K. Allen, '*R v Dean*' (1941) 57 *LQR* 85.

[138] Counselling breach of contract would not otherwise seem to be professionally objectionable, although it might be a tort.

[139] These hypotheticals are derived from P. Heymann & L. Liebman, *The Social Responsibility of Lawyers* (New York, 1988); G. Kittleson, 'From Ethics to Politics: Confronting Ethics and Scarcity in Public Interest Practice' (1978) *Boston U.LR* 337, 363–72.

abettor, conspirator, constructive trustee, and so on—were they to advise or assist the client. On this approach if a non-lawyer were to be liable, exceptional reasons would have to be adduced to exculpate a lawyer. However, we saw at the outset that in the realm of legal ethics and professional responsibility we are not simply concerned with breaches of the criminal or civil law but with those broader standards which among other things ensure justice and maintain the public standing of the profession. Thus this approach, while fruitful, will be too narrow in a number of cases. At the other end of the spectrum is to posit the role of the lawyer not as one who maximizes a client's freedom, but as one who assists them to bring their affairs into line with the public interest and the law's values. It is said that this might involve directing a client's attention to the morally just, as well as the legally permissible course, if the latter might cause unjustified harm to others.[140] While this approach can be fruitful in exploring the issues, it lacks sufficient acceptance or bite to provide a template for action.

A third approach is to reason from the codes and from other sources about professional misconduct. In relation to the first hypothetical, a party asking for an injunction *ex parte* must bring all material facts to the notice of the court; this principle could be extended to other cases. With the second and third hypotheticals we can draw on various principles.[141] First, lawyers, as we know, are under no duty to assist a crime or fraud, or to become party to an abuse of process.[142] The duty of confidence is dissolved under the crime/fraud exception. Indeed there is even some older professional authority that in the case of a serious crime a solicitor has an *obligation* to convey the information to the relevant authorities—thus going beyond the crime/fraud exception—notwithstanding the duty of confidence.[143] Moreover, there is the central duty of lawyers to uphold the law and not by their actions to subvert or subtract from its legitimacy. Thus lawyers believing that a client will in all probability use advice or assistance to disregard the law should be loath to act. In terms of our hypotheticals, these existing principles are only a baseline to providing definite guidance on what are patently troubling cases.

Whatever approach is adopted, much depends on the knowledge of the lawyer with respect to the wrong the client will effect and on what the lawyer actually

---

[140] See D. Nicolson & J. Webb, *Professional Legal Ethics* (Oxford, 1999), 219–24; R. O'Dair, *op. cit.*, 334, 338–60; C. Samford & S. Parker, 'Legal Regulation, Ethical Standard Setting and Institutional Design', in S. Parker & C. Samford (eds), *Legal Ethics and Legal Practice* (Oxford, 1995), 20–4; J. Webb, 'Being a Lawyer/Being a Human Being' (2002) 5 *Leg. Ethics* 130, 132–3.

[141] *Dalglish v Jarvie* (1850) 42 ER 89. See also *Garrard v Email Furniture Pty Ltd* (1993) 32 NSWLR 662, 677.

[142] 188 above; *Batchelor v Pattison* 1876 3 R 914, 918 (lawyers cannot be asked to follow the client's instructions beyond what is lawful and proper); *Clark v United States* 289 US 1, 15 (1933), *per* Cardozo J for the court: 'A client who consults an attorney for advice that will serve him in the commission of a fraud will have no help from the law.' Solicitors who have strong evidence of suspected fraud on the part of a client are entitled to apply to the court for directions as to how to deal with the fruits of the fraud. *Finers (a firm) v Miro* [1991] 1 All ER 182.

[143] T. Lund, *A Guide to the Professional Conduct and Etiquette of Solicitors* (London, 1960), 103. In less serious cases the lawyer might only be obliged to withdraw: *ibid.*, 105, 107.

does to achieve it. As to the first, does culpable knowledge extend beyond actual knowledge to encompass wilfully shutting one's eyes to the obvious, or wilfully and recklessly failing to make the inquiries an honest and reasonable lawyer would make? Perhaps *R v Delaval*[144] is as relevant as it was when Lord Mansfield decided it over 200 years ago. There a young woman was removed from Bates, to whom she was apprenticed, and placed in the hands of Sir Francis Delaval, ostensibly for musical training but in fact for the purposes of prostitution. Not only was the information for conspiracy of Bates and Delaval upheld, but also that of the lawyer who drafted the documents of assignment. The attempt to portray the lawyer simply as an amanuensis was unsuccessful. He could not imagine that she really bound herself to Delaval to be taught music, said Lord Mansfield; he could not have been ignorant of the true purpose of the transaction.[145] In practice it should not be forgotten that lawyers by training should be able to make astute judgments as to their clients' purposes. If, as Hazard notes, a lawyer can assess how the purposes of others may affect his or her client, a lawyer can have the same knowledge of how a client's purposes can affect others.[146]

Measuring the second factor, the extent of the lawyer's activity in effecting the wrongdoing, is similarly difficult. Much will turn on the circumstances. Performing an act which substantially furthers the client's wrongdoing should give rise to culpability. In *Johnson v Youden*[147] a solicitor did the conveyancing of a house, knowing the price to be in breach of the price control regulations. The court held that since he did know how the price was calculated he was guilty of aiding and abetting the offence. The attempt to portray him as a mere scrivener failed. The conveyancing effected the wrongdoing. If the principles applying to accessory liability are relevant, there seems no reason why in some circumstances, if the lawyer knows what is going on, giving advice should not make the lawyer guilty of professional misconduct if it enables the client to pursue the unlawful conduct. In practice the lawyer should never be in this position. Knowledge should result in the lawyer declining to act. Indeed in the United States there has been much discussion about whether the lawyer discovering corporate wrongdoing might have to report it to the regulatory agencies or stage a 'noisy withdrawal', which is tantamount to reporting it.

The Profession's Wider Responsibilities

So far the focus has been on the profession's responsibilities in relation to clients. Although only partly articulated and patchy lawyers have acknowledged wider responsibilities. One aspect is within the profession itself, for example the obligation

---

[144] (1763) 97 ER 913.   [145] *ibid.*, 916.
[146] G. Hazard, 'How Far May a Lawyer Go in Assisting a Client in Legally Wrongful Conduct?' (1981) 35 *U.Miami LR* 669, 672.   [147] [1950] 1 KB 544.

not only to end racial and sexual discrimination in the profession, but positively to advance the position of minorities and women.[148] Lawyers are under a legal duty to assist the court in furthering the Overriding Objective of the CPR, which includes as far a practicable, ensuring that parties are on an equal footing.[149] Another wider aspect is the responsibility to the law itself, ensuring simplification if possible, legal reform and renewal in the light of changing social and economic circumstances and more generally the maintenance of the rule of law and its institutional manifestations such as the independence of the judiciary. Then there is what could in broad terms be described as the duty to facilitate access to justice. This has obvious links with the rule of law and equality before the law.[150] In this regard high legal fees are a very significant issue. Moreover, the limits on publicly funded legal services highlight the importance of new initiatives. These wider responsibilities deserve attention; let us briefly examine a few.

The profession engages in law reform activity, primarily through official committees of both the Bar Council and Law Society which comment on proposed legislation and in some cases promote statutory change. But there is nothing comparable in the English codes to the obligations stated in the Model Rules of the American Bar Association, that lawyers 'should cultivate knowledge of law beyond its use for clients, employ that knowledge in reform of the law and work to strengthen legal education'.[151] The underlying rationale of this provision, as set out in 1952 in a seminal report from the Joint Conference of the American Bar Association and the Association of American Law Schools, is partly to enhance the standing of the legal profession itself.[152] Partly also it was felt that lawyers who saw an injustice in practice, or who brought about an injustice by their advocacy, should seek legal reform. As the statement put it, a lawyer has both the best chance to know when the law is working badly and the special competence to put it in order. Detached from the immediate representation of client interest, lawyers involved in law reform activity can and should adopt a more detached view.[153]

Access to justice has a number of strands. One is ensuring that persons are not handicapped from establishing the rightness of their position because they are, or their cause is, unpopular. Representation of unpopular causes is an essential component of public confidence in the legitimacy of the legal system. The cab-rank rule for the Bar demands that barristers accept any instructions or brief to

---

[148] See Courts and Legal Services Act 1990, s 64; BC, §§305.1–305.2, 403.2, 404.1–404.2 (Equality and Diversity Code for the Bar); LSG §7.01–7.02, Annex 7A.

[149] CPR rr 1.1(2)(a), 1.3.   [150] R. O'Dair, *op. cit.*, 365.

[151] American Bar Association, *Model Rules of Professional Conduct*, Preamble, para. 6, §6.1.

[152] L. Fuller & J. Randall, 'Professional Responsibility' (1958) 44 *Amer. Bar Assoc. J.* 1159.

[153] Compare Justice Brandeis' oft quoted remarks: '[T]he leaders of the bar with few exceptions have not only failed to take part in constructive legislation designed to solve in the interest of our people our great social, economic and industrial problems, they have failed likewise to oppose legislation prompted by selfish interests. They have often gone further in disregard of the public interest. They have, at times, advocated as lawyers, legislative measures which as citizens they could not approve . . .'. L. Brandeis, 'The Opportunity in the Law' (1905) 39 *American Law Review* 555, 560–1.

represent any client at a proper professional fee in the fields in which they profess to practice, irrespective of the nature of the case or any belief or opinion which the barrister might have formed as to the character, reputation, cause, conduct, guilt, or innocence of that person.[154] Extravagant claims have sometimes been made for the cab-rank rule,[155] and in some cases unpopular clients have found that barristers of their first or even second choice have been unavailable because of 'prior commitments'.[156] On the whole, however, the rule has worked remarkably well and unpopular clients have been better served in England than in the United States, where there is no equivalent obligation.[157] Not only has the rule ensured representation for unpopular clients, but it has gone a considerable way to removing the stigma from those barristers who have stuck their neck out to represent unpopular causes.

Unlike the Bar solicitors are free to decline instructions, although any refusal must not be based on racial, sexual, or religious grounds. Solicitors can therefore refuse assistance to those to whom they have moral or political objections. By the same token if they accept a retainer they are bound to the duties of confidence, diligence, and loyalty already examined, however morally or politically obnoxious they find their client's cause. (There is nothing equivalent for the profession here to the American ethical rule whereby a lawyer might explicitly base advice to a client on his or her personal views of morality and similar non-legal values[158].) Representation of a client by a solicitor does not constitute endorsement of that client's morals or politics. But since solicitors are free to choose their clients on such grounds, it follows that their decisions to do so may be criticized. A solicitor's choice of client or cause is a moral decision and the solicitor must be prepared to justify it along with other decisions.[159]

Another strand of access to justice concerns the maldistribution of legal services. Corporations and the very wealthy pay for and receive excellent legal advice and assistance. Criminal legal aid ensures that most defendants are represented. This is clearly necessary when the exercise of state power might result in a custodial sentence. Elsewhere, as we have seen earlier in the book, there are problems with access to justice. *Pro bono* work has a long history: in the first part of the twentieth century there was the 'dock brief' system[160] and lawyers also offered advice sessions in settlement houses in inner city areas. Now with the squeeze on coverage

---

[154] BC §601.

[155] Erskine's is well known in his defence of Tom Paine: 'From the moment that any advocate can be permitted to say, that he will or will not stand between the Crown and the subject...from that moment the liberties of England are at an end': (1792) 22 State Trials 358, 412.

[156] S. Sedley, 'The Future of Advocacy', in P. Thomas (ed), *Discriminating Lawyers* (London, 2000).

[157] It has been said that in the United States ethical rules have been used against lawyers associated with unpopular causes: J. Auerbach, *Unequal Justice* (New York, 1976), 289.

[158] American Bar Association, *Model Rules of Professional Conduct*, §2.1, Comment.

[159] M. Freedman, 'Ethical Ends and Ethical Means' (1991) 41 *J. Leg. Educ.* 55, 56.

[160] 46 above.

of legal aid, the profession has taken some steps in response.[161] To see this as simply self-interest or economic advantage—for recruitment and retention purposes, or to counter lawyers' poor public image—is to misconceive its motivation.[162] Whether *pro bono* work should be compulsory, however, has been fiercely contested. The *pro bono* working party of the Law Society rejected the idea as wrong in principle and counterproductive—wrong in principle, since it would be no more appropriate than to require a minimum level of charitable giving, and counterproductive, since solicitors' existing involvement in voluntary legal services depends on goodwill and enthusiasm.[163] Instead, it recommended a variety of initiatives to encourage voluntary legal services. Other measures need to be considered; for example a well developed technique in Australia and some parts of the United States is to use interest on general client accounts to fund subsidized legal services and legal education. The position in England and Wales has direct ethical connotations because legislation promoted by the Law Society reversed the common law duty of solicitors not to profit from the use of clients' moneys.[164] For the United States Professor Marc Galanter has suggested that the many partners from large law firms who retire early could be mobilized to meet unmet legal need—an idea with application elsewhere, which would utilize a valuable resource of human capital.[165]

Finally, those who are primarily law teachers need to turn the spotlight on legal education. Partly this concerns the role as teacher. There are many problems which are by no means unique to law teachers. How should they relate to students, professionally and socially; what steps should be taken to further equal access to educational opportunities; how extensively should they engage in consultancy or practice to the detriment of academic duties—these are a few examples. Partly also it concerns the responsibility to teach legal ethics. For too long law schools washed their hands of this on the grounds that legal ethics were for vocational training. Traditional courses on legal ethics focused on specific points of professional practice and behaviour. Unfortunately they strayed heavily into areas which, while useful to the young practitioner, had nothing to do with ethics but were really issues of etiquette. This has changed as traditional courses have been revamped and refined. In the last decade there has been a very welcome development in academic interest in legal ethics.[166]

---

[161] e.g. the Bar supports a Pro Bono Unit (court representation) and the Free Representation Unit (tribunal representation): see Bar Pro Bono Unit, *Annual Review 2003–2004* (London, 2004). The Solicitors Pro Bono Group coordinates a not inconsiderable volume of legal help (e.g. Solicitors Pro Bono Group, *A Guide to Law Firm Pro Bono Programmes in England and Wales* (London, 2004), not confined to large law firms. See 57 above.

[162] A Boon & R. Abbey, 'Moral Agendas? *Pro Bono Publico* in Large Law Firms in the United Kingdom' (1997) 60 *MLR* 630; M. Galanter & T. Palay, 'Large Law Firms and Professional Responsibility', in R. Cranston (ed.), *Legal Ethics and Professional Responsibility* (Oxford, 1994); R. Katzmann (ed.), *The Law Firm and the Public Good*, Brookings Institution (Washington, DC, 1995).

[163] *Solicitors Serving Society* (London, 1994), 8.   [164] Solicitors Act 1974, s 33(3).

[165] M. Galanter, 'Old and in the Way' [1999] *Wisc LR* 1081.

[166] Legal ethics was the focus of my presidential year of the Society of Legal Scholars and led to R. Cranston (ed.), *Legal Ethics and Professional Responsibility* (Oxford, 1995). There followed some

As Menkel-Meadow has rightly noted: '[Law teachers] cannot avoid teaching ethics. By the very act of teaching, law teachers embody lawyering and the conduct of legal professionals. We create images of law and lawyering when we teach doctrine through cases and hypotheticals.'[167] That does not mean that law schools need convey the technical detail of professional responsibility, which might still be left to vocational training. Nor should law schools delude themselves that they can effectively socialize their students to behave ethically when, in practice, groups and institutional pressures will produce in them certain types of behaviour. Yet all law teachers have a responsibility to give some attention to the ethical underpinnings of legal practice, a responsibility to sensitize students to the ethical problems they will face as practitioners, to provide them with some assistance in the task of resolving these problems, and to expose them to wider issues such as access to justice.[168]

Conclusion

On the whole there is a high level of satisfaction with lawyers' services.[169] But there is still a worrying level of complaints among clients—delays, mistakes, lost documents, and unprofessional behaviour.[170] Defalcations by solicitors, and the substantial amounts involved, have put the spotlight on professional standards. In recognition of such developments, lawyers and law firms are becoming more vigilant in preventing the possible conflicts and temptations which can arise in the course of servicing clients. For example, some large law firms operate a two partner rule on large transactions, to ensure collective decision making on difficult advice. (The cost to the client, of course, escalates.) Similarly, a number of regulatory initiatives have been taken at the level of the profession as a whole with respect to professional standards. Just one example is the establishment of the Legal Services Ombudsman.

While the ethical rules themselves have not attracted the same public attention, there has been a quiet transformation in recent decades. From some rather general standards which it was thought all lawyers would know there has evolved a more legalized system based on codes of conduct. One interpretation of this development is that it reflects both movements in the market for legal services and

excellent books: S. Parker & C. Sampford (eds), *Legal Ethics and Legal Practice* (Oxford, 1995); K. Economides (ed.), *Ethical Challenges to Legal Education and Conduct* (Oxford, 1998); A. Boon & J. Levin, *The Ethics and Conduct of Lawyers in England and Wales* (Oxford, 1999); D. Nicholson & J. Webb, *Professional Legal Ethics* (Oxford, 1999); R. O'Dair, *Legal Ethics. Text and Materials* (London, 2001). The subject now has its own journal, *Legal Ethics*, published by Hart.

[167] C. Menkel-Meadow, 'Can a Law Teacher Avoid Teaching Legal Ethics' (1991) 41 *J.Leg.Ed.* 3, 3.
[168] D. Rhode, *In the Interests of Justice* (New York, 2000), 200–3.
[169] R. Moorhead, A. Sherr, A. Paterson, 'What Clients Know: Client Perspectives and Legal Competence' (2003) 10 *Int'l J.L. Prof.* 5, 13–14.
[170] e.g. J. Farrar, 'Investigation. Solicitors', *Which Magazine*, 8 August 2001, 8.

the transformation of the profession. A socially homogeneous, relatively cohesive profession, with shared understandings, has become a much larger and variegated one, with members playing a variety of new roles. There has been a consequent need for rules and a bureaucratic machinery to assimilate and discipline the profession's disparate parts. Moreover, greater attention has had to be given within the profession to ethical standards because in many ways they are symbolic of how the profession sees itself. Disputes about the rules are to an extent surrogates for disputes about the future of the profession.[171]

An underlying theme of the chapter has been that the move to more definite rules is not only inevitable but also desirable. Intuition or appeals to secular or other morality are no substitute for a framework of rules. Not only may there be no consensus over the former, but in some important respects the correct ethical position is not immediately apparent. Issues of legal ethics do not come identified as such but arise in particular contexts of legal practice. Without definite rules it is not only difficult to see how professional behaviour will be constrained but the problems of teaching legal ethics would be considerably compounded. By the same token a second underlying theme of the discussion has been that the existing codes of professional practice cannot simply be treated as a system of specific rules. The correct ethical stance will very infrequently come ready labelled. If that were to be the case they would become like any other body of rules which lawyers would manipulate, and if needs be seek to avoid. The ends lawyers are pursuing, the ethics of their clients, the standing of the profession, and the wider interests of justice and legal values—these are just some of the matters which must also be considered in channelling and justifying professional behaviour. Moreover, the present professional codes do not give specific guidance in important respects. To return to one of the hypotheticals above: if breach of a regulatory law is tolerated by officials, should lawyers counsel a client to disregard it? Arguably desuetude is distinguishable from under-enforcement of a regulatory law because of lack of resources. Without a reasoned elaboration of the ethical position, however, lawyers will be at a loss as to which course to pursue in the absence of a definite rule.

A further underlying theme has been that in important respects the current set of ethical rules is contestable. I have focused on the duties of confidentiality and loyalty which lawyers are mandated to give to a client's interests. The lynchpin of the present rules is that lawyers need not be convinced of a client's case; that is for the courts. In single-mindedly serving a client's interest, the assumption is that a lawyer is serving justice. As a lawyer one need not be primarily concerned with any wider interest. This argument and its conclusion is still largely valid. But there are

---

171 Thus the debate about advertising: on the one hand advertising is correctly said to inform the public about legal services and to further competition; on the other hand there is some truth in the claim that advertising transforms the profession into a body of business hucksters. See Editorial, 'Trading Standards' (1993) 143 *NLJ* 1249.

a number of difficulties. First, there is the widespread public perception these days that the self-interest of the lawyer is masquerading as public service. The unequal access to legal services and the unequal matching of lawyers in particular cases undermine the validity of the model. Secondly, we have seen that however unformulated or inadequate they might be, there are limits to the lawyer acting as hired gun. For advocates, Lord Reid sums up the position this way:

> Every counsel has a duty to his client fearlessly to, raise every issue, advance every argument, and ask every question, however distasteful, which he thinks will help his client's case. But, as an officer of the court concerned in the administration of justice, he has an overriding duty to the court, to the standards of his profession, and to the public, which may and often does lead to a conflict with his client's wishes or with what the client thinks are his personal wishes.[172]

The corollary is that in some circumstances the law and the profession's ethical rules recognize that unquestioning zeal in a client's interest may cause social harm.

What is necessary in this area is a further refinement of the provisions in the codes. When do the interests of others and the public interest trump devotion to the client's interest? When should a lawyer question his or her client's intentions and activities and be justified by code provisions in doing so? When should a lawyer cease to act for a particular client or indeed disclose suspected wrongdoing to the relevant regulatory agency? Such questions demand careful analysis. One difficulty is that the current rules were forged in the context of the criminal law where the notion of the fearless advocate, zealously defending the client, come what may, is more understandable. But extension of the arguments in the criminal context to other areas, in particular advice to clients, does not always make sense. The enormous legal resources which powerful interests can marshall—whatever the cause—might well be politically contentious, socially harmful, and possibly morally objectionable. Ultimately this phenomenon might also undermine the standing of the legal profession and the legitimacy of the law.

A final underlying theme of this chapter has been that legal ethics have to be conceived of within the more general area of professional responsibility. The wider ethical issues of the operation of the legal profession as a whole are now firmly on the agenda. The obvious example is the unequal utilization of legal services and of access to justice. As indicated, this wider conception links with the rules in the professional codes, since many of these are based on the notion that clients will be competently and adequately represented. Another aspect of this wider topic is inequality of access to the profession itself. The professional bodies have taken this on board in the realization that the profession is failing to tap vital resources and denying opportunities to, for example, a significant minority of young people with black and minority ethnic backgrounds. Law schools too must provide

---

[172] *Rondel v Worsley* [1969] 1 AC 191, 227. See also S. Rogers, 'The Ethics of Advocacy' (1899) 15 *LQR* 259.

students with guidance on the ethical issues which they will face when they enter the profession. Successful lawyers these days reap great rewards, but in the process will face many temptations to barter their integrity. We must remember they are members of a noble profession. The public rightly expects of them a high standard in how they go about their calling.

PART II
LAW'S IMPACT

7

Rights in Practice

What a society labels as a right might be illusory in a substantive sense or, the main focus of this discussion, might not be implemented in practice. To explore this theme this chapter examines rights which have a strong legal connotation. It is in this regard that the dichotomy between the values of society and everyday reality can be most pronounced. Although embodied in law or the legal system some civil, political, or social rights are not exercised, or are exercised to only a limited extent. Indeed, it may come to pass that they cannot really be regarded as rights at all. Professor Sam Stoljar put it this way:

You cannot have a right unless it can be claimed or demanded or insisted upon, indeed claimed effectively or enforceably...Rights thus are performative-dependent, their operative reality being their claimability; a right one could not claim, demand, ask to enjoy or exercise would not merely be 'imperfect'—it would be a vacuous attribute.[1]

Among the explanations for rights being imperfect are practical impediments, limited resources, desuetude, and perhaps most importantly, social and economic inequality. One of the law's greatest challenges is making rights work in practice in the face of those social realities. First we examine civil and political rights, primarily those which relate to equality before the law, before turning to the social rights of the modern welfare state.

Civil and Political Rights

Liberal democratic societies have typically asserted that their citizens enjoy certain civil and political rights—for example: freedom of speech, freedom of assembly, the right to a fair trial, and the right to property. In his *Commentaries on the Laws of England* (1765), Blackstone reduced the absolute rights of individuals to three categories: the right of liberty, the right of personal security, and the right of property.[2] England remained unusual before the Human Rights Act 1998 in leaving civil and political rights to be recognized largely by the common law.[3]

---

[1] S. Stoljar, *An Analysis of Rights* (New York, 1984), 3–4.
[2] (London, 1783), vol. 1, 121–45.
[3] e.g. D. Feldman, *Civil Liberties and Human Rights in England and Wales*, 2nd edn (Oxford, 2002), 58–70; S. Finer, V. Bogdanor & B. Rudden, *Comparing Constitutions* (Oxford, 1995), 36–9, 95–101.

Elsewhere it became usual for such rights to be formally incorporated in a statement or bill of rights.

Although possibly unfashionable to say so at the present time, the US Constitution has been the important progenitor of modern statements or bills of civil and political rights.[4] The First Amendment to that constitution provides in pellucid terms that Congress shall make no law prohibiting the free exercise of religion, abridging freedom of speech or of the press, or the right of the people peaceably to assemble and to petition the government for the redress of grievances. Under the Sixth Amendment, in all criminal prosecutions, an accused enjoys the right to a speedy and public trial, by an impartial jury, to be informed of the nature and cause of the accusation, to be confronted with the witnesses against him, to have compulsory process for obtaining witnesses in his favour and to have the assistance of counsel for his defence. Similarly, the European Convention on Human Rights provides rights to life, liberty, privacy and family life, and expression. Reflecting the US Sixth Amendment, Article 6 of the European Convention contains fair trial rights in the determination of criminal charges and civil rights and obligations.

Not only have liberal democratic societies asserted that there are certain civil and political rights but also that these rights are recognized by, and enforceable at, law. Some draw on *Magna Carta*, which provides that no person's freedom could be passed upon or condemned, but by lawful judgment of his peers or by the law of the land (cap.xxxix).[5] Among the ancillary rights of individuals to secure the protection of the primary rights he outlined, Blackstone identified the right of access to the courts. Judicial review is sometimes a feature of bills of rights, either expressly or by implication as a matter of law. Article 13 of the European Convention on Human Rights imposes an obligation to ensure appropriate rules and institutions to give people an effective remedy for violations of Convention rights. There is a strong, practical argument that some form of legal process will always be necessary to identify bearers of rights, resolve conflicts over rights and protect against the violation of rights. While some form of legal process is necessary to make legal rights work, it is far from being sufficient and both political commitment and cultural change are also essential.[6]

Equality before the law

At least three issues arise in relation to the issue of making civil and political rights work: first, to what extent does the detailed substantive law reflect the rights espoused; secondly, are the rights enforced in practice; and thirdly, do they govern

---

[4] On borrowings: e.g. V. Jackson & M. Tushnet, *Comparative Constitutional Law* (New York, 1999), 168–73; cf. M. Glendon, *Rights Talk. The Impoverishment of Political Talk* (New York, 1991), ch. 6.

[5] S. Finer, *The History of Government* (Oxford, 1997), vol. 2, 905.

[6] e.g. F. Krug, *Values for a Godless Age*, (Harmondsworth, 2000); P. Alston, 'A Framework for the Comparative Analysis of Bills of Rights', in P. Alston (ed.), *Promoting Human Rights through Bills of Rights* (Oxford, 1999), 12–13.

what actually happens. To a degree the second and third issues are related, although they do not overlap completely. To throw light on these issues, this part examines a fundamental value in liberal democratic states, equality before the law. The value predates the modern liberal democratic state. Insistence on the equal application of laws was common to Rousseau, John Stuart Mill, and Dicey. For Dicey, writing at the turn of the century, equality before the law was one element of the rule of law, the basis of the constitution.[7] In the modern age, equality before the law is widely accepted as 'probably the most generally respected of all egalitarian ideals'.[8] It is enshrined in various written constitutions, notably in the Fourteenth Amendment of the US Constitution, in European constitutions such as Article 3(1) of the German Basic Law, in Article 14 of the Indian Constitution, and in Article 15(1) of the Canadian Charter of Rights and Freedoms.[9] It is regarded as fundamental in modern liberal democratic societies, although this does not mean that it is always justiciable.[10]

One interpretation of equality before the law is formal in character; it requires impartiality (not permitting bias to influence decisions) and treating like cases alike (ensuring that people's rights are equally protected and their duties equally enforced). In this sense it is part of the rule of law. In this interpretation, equality before the law does not touch the substance of the law. Certainly this standard of equality before the law is not to be lightly dismissed. It imposes checks on power and wealth, inasmuch as these subvert impartiality and prevent like cases being treated alike in the administration and enforcement of the law. For instance, the rules of legal order are applied in the same way to all persons independently of matters such as their power, status, race, or wealth.[11] Equality before the law also establishes a safeguard against the misuse of power and discretion by the state for it is on the same footing before the law as the individual.[12] The interpretation of equality before the law is the minimal position espoused by all liberal democratic societies.

A second interpretation of equality before the law goes one step further and demands that in practice rights be equally the subject of protection and the duty of enforcement. As Professor Bernard Williams pointed out, equality before the

---

[7] A.V. Dicey, *An Introduction to the Study of the Law of the Constitution*, 10th edn (London, 1965), 193–4, 202–3.

[8] S. Benn & R. Peters, *Social Principles and the Democratic State* (London, 1959), 122. See also J. Jowell, 'In Equality a Constitutional Principle?' (1994) 47 *CLP* 1; 309 below.

[9] It will be enshrined in the Treaty Establishing a Constitution for Europe, Article II-80. See also European Convention on Human Rights, Protocol 12, not ratified by the United Kingdom. At an international level there is Article 14(1) of the International Covenant on Civil and Political Rights: D. McGoldrick, *The Human Rights Committee* (Oxford, 1994), 396–7.

[10] *Matadeen v Pointu* [1999] 1 AC 98, 109F, PC.

[11] J.-E. Lane, *Constitutions and Political Theory* (Manchester, 1996), 224.

[12] E.P. Thompson, *The Poverty of Theory* (London, 1978), 288–9; *Whigs and Hunters* (Harmondsworth, 1977), 168; J. Waldron, 'Rights and Needs. The Myth of Disjunction', in A. Sarat & T. Kearns (eds), *Legal Rights* (Ann Arbor, 1997). cf. M. Horwitz, 'The Rule of Law: An Unqualified Human Good?' (1977) 86 *Yale LJ* 561; B. Fine, *Democracy and the Rule of Law* (London, 1984), 169–88; 310–11 below.

law means not the abstract existence of rights, but the extent to which they govern what actually happens. 'If a fair trial or redress from the law can be secured in that society only by moneyed and educated persons, to insist that everyone *has* this right, though only these particular persons can *secure* it, rings hollow to the point of cynicism.'[13] This procedural standard of equality before the law demands that steps be taken to ensure that rights are equally the subject of protection and the duty of enforcement. Under the Overriding Objective of the CPR courts must ensure that parties are on an equal footing, as one aspect of dealing with cases justly.[14] Publicly funded legal services, in the form for example of legal aid, are well accepted as another such step.[15] As we see later in this chapter, and elsewhere in the book, other steps are demanded as well.

There is a third, and not universally accepted, interpretation of equality before the law, which requires that the substance of the law treat people equally—not to disadvantage or to prefer—except where a departure from this can be justified. On one view of this interpretation equality before the law demands that people be accorded equal respect and not be discriminated against.[16] In modern society there are frequent departures from equal treatment; there is widespread classification and unequal treatment. The task is to determine whether particular instances of differentiated treatment are acceptable. Various attempts have been made to formulate tests to do this.[17] One formulation is that those with similar backgrounds or in similar circumstances must generally be equally or similarly treated. A related approach is that law-makers must treat people equally if under prevailing community standards they are considered to be equal. The 'immutable characteristics' formulation is that people must be accorded equal rights irrespective of original endowments over which they have no control, such as birth, race, and gender. Finally, it is said that distinctions in treatment are justified only if they are relevant, intelligible and reasonable.[18]

None of these tests is necessarily clear in its application. There are boundary problems with the first approach, in agreeing on the criteria to identify those with similar backgrounds or in similar circumstances. What stands in the way, say, of the assumption of the nineteenth-century poor law, that the poor justify separate, punitive, treatment? In relation to the second approach there may be considerable disagreement over prevailing community standards, and even if these can be identified their implications for minorities may be adverse. Limits may be placed

[13] B. Williams, 'The Idea of Equality', in H.A. Bedau (ed.), *Justice and Equality* (Englewood Cliffs, NJ, 1971), 128–9.   [14] CPR r1.1(2)(a).
[15] 36 above.
[16] See C. McCrudden, 'Introduction', in C. McCrudden (ed.), *Anti-Discrimination Law* (Aldershot, 1991), xi ff.
[17] See S. Fredman, *Women and the Law* (Oxford, 1997), 381–5; S. Poulter, *Ethnicity, Law and Human Rights* (Oxford, 1998), 13–29, 72–4; R. Wintemute, *Sexual Orientation and Human Rights* (Oxford, 1995), 232–8, 245–54.
[18] See T. Allan, *Constitutional Justice* (Oxford, 2001), 21, 38–40, 310–11; W. Sadurski, 'The Concept of Legal Equality and an Underlying Theory of Discrimination' (1998) *Saint Louis-Warsaw Transatlantic Law Journal* 63; P. Polyviou, *The Equal Protection of the Laws* (London, 1980).

on the application of the third approach: if race, sex, and gender are included, what of poverty which, because of the structural features of society, is involuntary for many and, indeed, for whole nations? In the application of the fourth test there are obvious difficulties in identifying intelligible, relevant, and reasonable distinctions. It should be noted that this third, substantive, interpretation of equality before the law moves beyond legal to moral values, and may well be indifferent to the formal and procedural interpretation of the idea. It is not uncontroversial and drifts into notions of equality in rather than before the law.[19]

For our purposes equality before the law means treating like cases alike in the administration of the law and, in a wider sense, ensuring that different treatment in the substantive law does not violate notions of the equal respect to which persons are entitled and can be objectively justified. (It is perhaps helpful to note in passing that objective justification of a difference in treatment is increasingly demanded by English courts as a result of Article 14 of the European Convention on Human Rights.)[20] If we take this or any of these different interpretations of equality before the law, a key issue is: to what extent are they realized in practice? If we have regard to the administration and the substance of the law, we must conclude that even the minimal, formal interpretation of equality can be far from completely realized in practice.

Law's administration

Broadly speaking, inequalities in the administration of the law are produced, if only indirectly, by economic and social inequalities. As Max Weber noted:

Formal justice guarantees the maximum freedom for the interested parties to represent their formal legal interests. But because of the unequal distribution of economic power, which the system of formal justice legalises, this very freedom must time and again produce consequences which are contrary to the substantive postulates of religious, ethnic or of political expediency.[21]

Inequalities in the administration of the law take basically two forms. First, the way state officials administer the law sometimes disadvantages certain sections of the community. Distortion can occur because of moral attitudes on the one hand, and organizational and social pressures on the other.[22] The result is that the formal standard of equality before the law—fundamental in all liberal democratic societies—is violated. Secondly, individuals do not have equal wealth and power and thus do not have equal capacity to exercise the rights which the law confers

---

[19] See e.g. R. Dworkin, *Sovereign Virtue. The Theory and Practice of Equality* (Cambridge, MA, 2000); R. Posner, *The Problems of Jurisprudence* (Cambridge, MA, 1993), 302–4, 332–4.

[20] e.g. Lord Phillips MR's judgment in *R (G) v Immigration Appeal Tribunal* [2004] EWCA Civ 1731; [2005] 1 WLR 1445; [2005] 2 All ER 165, paras 28–35. See also *R (Carson) v Secretary of State for Work and Pensions* [2005] UKHL 37; [2005] 2 WLR 1369, discussed below at 223.

[21] *Max Weber on Law in Economy and Society* (trans. E. Shils & M. Rheinstein) (Cambridge, MA, 1954), 228. [22] D. Galligan, *Discretionary Powers* (Oxford, 1986), 128–40.

on them. The unequal capacity to exercise legal rights derives not simply from an inability to pay, but also from related factors such as social confidence, knowledge, and contacts.[23] The differential capacity to exercise legal rights and liberties applies to both the civil and criminal law. The second, procedural, standard of equality before the law is relevant in this regard.

Examples from criminal law can be used to illustrate the first type of inequality in the administration of the law. Commenting generally on the operation of the criminal law, Aubert contended that it is almost as if it 'has succeeded in condemning poverty, homelessness, the lack of family and of stable work, without ever naming these characteristics as of any concern to the law'.[24] Certainly, to take just one group, white working class and ethnic minority younger men are over-represented in the official crime statistics compared with their numbers in the population as a whole.[25] There are three possible explanations. The first and simplest is that they commit more offences. There is statistical support for this, in relation to the type of offences handled by the police, even allowing for the exaggeration in police and court records because of the second and third explanations.[26] The second possible explanation is that there is distortion in the administration of criminal law. Again studies have provided some evidence of this. Certain factors suggest themselves as reasons. For example, those enforcing the law, such as the police, have considerable discretion and must often make do with limited resources or take speedy decisions without full knowledge of the facts. In making decisions, there is scope for their introducing knowledge or perceptions, for example that those from particular groups are more prone to wrongdoing.[27] The distortions which can consequently occur are well known, and training and organizational checks are in place to varying extents to counter them. Courts, too, do much these days in the way of training and through other devices attempting to eliminate similar distortions.[28]

A third, and related, explanation for the over-representation of certain sections of society in the criminal records is that they are more likely to be subjected to law-enforcement activity. Partly this is a response to public complaints but also it is a result of proactive patrolling, which becomes self-justifying. The other side

[23] 39–40, 111–2 above.

[24] V. Aubert, 'Justice as a Problem of Social Psychology' (1970) 56 *Archiv für Rechts und Sozialphilosophie* 465, 478.

[25] M. Maguire, R. Morgan & R. Reiner (eds), *Oxford Handbook of Criminology*, 3rd edn (Oxford, 2002), 362–3 (M. Maguire), 609 (C. Phillips & B. Bowling). See also *Stephen Lawrence Inquiry*, Cm 4262 (London, 1999), 321–2.

[26] M. Maguire, R. Morgan & R. Reiner (eds), *op.cit.* 365 citing J. Braithwaite, *Inequality, Crime and Public Policy* (London, 1979), 62.

[27] *ibid.*, 1011–13 (B. Bowling & J. Foster).

[28] See Dr Roger Hood's disturbing study of bias in sentencing black defendants: *Race and Sentencing* (Oxford, 1992). But there was no evidence of discrimination in a later study of possession cases in three county courts: S. Blandy *et al.*, *Housing Possession Cases in the County Court: Perceptions and Experiences of Black and Minority Ethnic Defendants*, Department for Constitutional Affairs Research Reports 11/2002 (London, 2002), 58–63, 80–5.

of the coin is that relatively little attention is directed to offences such as financial fraud and breach of environmental and health-and-safety-at-work laws. These offences tend to be hidden from the public so that they do not complain as much to enforcement agencies or demand that action be taken as with, say, anti-social behaviour by young people. There is also an ambivalence among the public about the criminality of such offences, an ambivalence which influences the approach of enforcement agencies. Even where proceedings are taken, convictions are often difficult to obtain and might simply attract a fine.[29]

The second type of inequality in the administration of the law results from the unequal capacity of individuals to exercise their legal rights. Ability to pay affects whether a person can take advantage of what the law permits. Most private law, as well as large parts of the criminal law, function to facilitate private arrangements by individuals.[30] If individuals desire, they can conclude contracts, acquire property, marry, enter civil partnerships, form companies and business partnerships, and so on, and the law imposes duties designed to make performance of these matters effective. Usually some expenditure is required for individuals to make these choices, even if there is no need to obtain legal assistance. There may be registration fees, administrative charges, or simply the opportunity costs in making the arrangement. In many of these cases cost is not an inhibiting factor, although there is the separate, but related issue, that because of the pressure of circumstances, or sometimes because of a lack of knowledge or skills, the less well-off take the more expensive path, as with entering credit contracts with higher interest rates and more onerous terms.[31] However, those able to pay for legal services may be at an advantage in terms of speed, the ease of a transaction or the ability to short circuit a queue. More importantly, those with resources can use the law to protect and fructify them: contracts can be drawn, trusts and companies established, and tax breaks exploited.

How law is administered and procedures work may also turn directly on the individual's ability to pay. A clear case is that of the person who remains in custody because they cannot provide the surety imposed as a condition of bail.[32] Fines weight more heavily on the poor than on the affluent.[33] In some cases those fined are imprisoned in default because they cannot pay. In civil proceedings people may be at a disadvantage because of inability to pay. As we saw in the discussion of *Ali's* case in Chapter 1, it is generally no longer the case under the CPR that impecunious claimants are required to provide security for costs.[34] However, there

---

[29] e.g. House of Commons, Environmental Audit Committee, *Corporate Environmental Crime*, HC 136 (London, 2005), paras 37–45.

[30] H.L.A. Hart, *The Concept of Law* (Oxford, 1961), 27.

[31] e.g. Department of Trade and Industry, *Fair, Clear and Competitive*, Cm 6040 (London, 2003), 17, 41, 53.

[32] See Law Commission, *Bail and the Human Rights Act 1998*, Law Com. No. 269 (London, 2001), 77–9.

[33] This must now be taken into account: Criminal Justice Act 2003, s 164(3), (4).

[34] 2 above.

is the cost of litigation, which includes the expense of preparing the necessary documents, court fees, and wages foregone to attend the hearing, quite apart form the expense of employing a lawyer. In 1834 James Stephen, then colonial under-secretary, remarked: 'These Irishmen are not the first, nor will they be the last, to make the discovery that a man may starve and yet have the best right of action a special pleader could wish for.'[35] A lack of means may affect the settlement process, as in motor-car and industrial accidents, if the less well-off settle a legal claim to their disadvantage because of the pressing need for compensation money.

As noted in chapter 4 wealth and education are usually associated with knowl-edge, skill, education, contacts, and confidence, and all these influence whether individuals exercise their legal rights. Evidence that some groups lack such legal competence has been uncovered in various surveys. For example, a valuable study of black and minority ethnic persons about facing housing possession proceedings in county courts in London, Birmingham and Leicester found that they were wary of seeking advice from solicitors for fear of the costs. Many participants, especially from London, were ambivalent about using local advice centres because of previous experiences, involving limited opening hours and long queues to see advisors. In terms of seeking advice, information and reassurance from friends, defendants were divided. A number felt too ashamed, embarrassed, upset or proud to do so. Older respondents in particular expressed reluctance because of the stigma they would feel if they received a possession summons. The majority of respondents had had no or only very limited experience of any type of legal pro-ceedings. Most commonly prior experience arose either in connection with crimi-nal proceedings or civil matters such as family proceedings. For some their previous experiences with the legal system had been very negative. Respondents were unsure exactly what a civil court would be like. For many the media and tele-vision drama played a strong influence in shaping their image of the courts.[36]

Substance of the law

Professor Ronald Dworkin's concern in *Sovereign Virtue* is with the unequal distribution of a nation's wealth. He argues that

a citizen's wealth massively depends on which laws his community has enacted—not only its laws governing ownership, theft, contract, and tort, but its welfare law, tax law, labor law, civil rights law, environmental regulation law, and laws of practically everything else.[37]

He goes on to contend that by enacting one set of laws rather than another, a society is to a considerable degree predicting which of its citizens will be worse off as a result. This is no doubt true and the issue of equality is still, as Professor Dworkin correctly asserts, crucial if we are to demonstrate an equal concern for

---

[35] Quoted in O. MacDonagh, ' "Pre-transformations": Victorian Britain', in E. Kamenka & A. Tay (eds), *Law and Social Control* (London, 1980), 122.

[36] S. Blandy *et al.*, *Housing Possession Cases in the County Court: Perceptions and Experiences of Black and Minority Ethnic Defendants*, Department for Constitutional Affairs, Research Paper 11/2002 (London, 2002), 45–53.   [37] R. Dworkin, *op.cit.*, 1.

all, not just in our own society, but more generally. However, the issue here is not the more general one of social and economic inequalities to which a society may give force through law. In a sense this conflates law and society, for law is simply giving expression to social facts. Rather the present concern is with the inequalities existing in the substance of the law itself which advantage or disadvantage certain sections of society. If the wider standard of equality before the law outlined earlier in the chapter is adopted, then these areas of law are inconsistent with it because the advantage or disadvantage created by them cannot be justified in the context of a liberal democratic society.

Inequality operates in at least three distinct ways in the substance of the law. First are the provisions which on their face advantage or disadvantage certain sections of society. Secondly, the law may favour certain categories over other categories, and typically identifiable sections of society occupy the less-favoured categories. Historically for example, the law has tended to favour landlords over tenants, employers over employees, and producers over consumers. Thirdly, substantive and procedural law set the parameters within which the law is administered. To the extent, for example, that the substantive law entrusts state agencies with wide discretion, they have the scope to apply the law in violation of the formal standard of equality before the law. Nothing more need be said of this third aspect here.[38]

The bulk of provisions which on their face overtly discriminate and cannot be justified have been repealed or overturned. For example, the discrimination against women in participating fully in electoral politics was finally removed in Britain in 1928.[39] Throughout most of its history, vagrancy law disadvantaged the poor in an overt manner. For example, at one time the offences of sleeping rough and not being able to give a good account only applied to those who did 'not have any visible means of subsistence'.[40] The requirement was repealed in 1935 because on its face it clearly discriminated against the poor. These days challenges to the substantive law might marshall the anti-discrimination provision (Article 14) of the European Convention on Human Rights. *R (Carson) v Secretary of State for Work and Pensions*[41] suggests an uphill battle. That case involved two issues: the exclusion of pensioners resident abroad from the annual uprating of the state retirement pension, and the payment of income support and jobseeker's allowance at a lower rate to under 25s. The House of Lords had no difficulty in finding that the different treatment in both cases was not a denial of equal respect and Parliament was entitled to draw it. By taking oneself out of the jurisdiction and therefore outside the primary scope and purpose of the social security system, a pensioner could not claim equality of treatment. As for those under 25, their situation as a whole was relevantly different in terms of their living arrangements, what they could expect to earn and their necessary expenses.

---

[38] See 232, 310 below.
[39] e.g. *Nairn v University of St Andrews* [1909] AC 147; *De Souza v Cobden* [1891] 1 QB 687. See S. Fredman, *op.cit.*, 58–66.   [40] Vagrancy Act 1824, s 14.
[41] [2005] UKHL 37; [2005] 2 WLR 1369.

There are various sources of the second type of substantive inequality: first, freedom of contract has determined important common aspects of relationships; secondly, the law, which operates in the absence of statutory regulation, has tended to favour certain categories over others; and thirdly, certain categories of persons do not take advantage of the rights which statutory law confers on them. The first source of inequality is relatively straightforward. The familiar problem of freedom of contract is that the interests of stronger parties generally prevail over those of the weaker. As a classic study put it, it enables the former to legislate in an authoritarian manner without using the appearance of authoritarian forms.[42] On the whole, landlords, employers, and producers have been in the stronger position and tenants, employees and consumers in the weaker.[43] Historically the latter have tended not to have the same bargaining power because of factors such as a shortage of rental accommodation and unemployment in certain sectors of the economy, and because lawyers and other professionals have acted more for the former than the latter.[44] The second source of inequality in the landlord–tenant, employer–employee and the producer–consumer relationships has been with what the law has allowed. The simplest example is that the common law and sometimes statutory law have generally permitted the exclusion of beneficial terms implied into the contracts between these different parties.[45] With their superior bargaining power landlords, employers, and producers have typically taken advantage of this. Regulatory legislation has progressively limited the degree to which beneficial terms can be excluded.[46]

A third source of inequality in these relationships—which relates to the discussion in earlier chapters—is that many tenants, employees, and consumers have not asserted their legal rights, no matter how favourable these might have been. Either they have not known about their rights, or if they have, they have faced social, financial, and legal obstacles to vindicating them. Nothing more need be said of this here.

Social Rights

In practical terms, social rights have still to be achieved in liberal democratic societies if, as Professor T.H. Marshall contended, these comprise not only the right to a basic standard of welfare and security but also the 'right to share to the

[42] F. Kessler, 'Contracts of Adhesion. Some Thoughts about Freedom of Contract' (1943) 43 *Colum.LR* 629.

[43] See S. Bright, & G. Gilbert, *Landlord and Tenant Law* (Oxford, 1995), 161–70, 226, 233–8; M. Freedland, *The Personal Employment Contract* (Oxford, 2003), 124–9, 178 ff; C. Scott & J. Black, *Cranston's Consumers and the Law*, 3rd edn. (London, 2000), 74–8 (hereafter *Consumers*).

[44] e.g. D. Hay, 'Master and Servant in England: Using the Law in the Eighteenth and Nineteenth Centuries'; D. Englander, 'Urban House Tenure and Litigation in Nineteenth-Century Britain', in W. Steinmetz (ed.), *Private Law and Social Inequality in the Industrial Age* (Oxford, 2000).

[45] e.g. Sale of Goods Act 1893, s 55.

[46] Unfair Contract Terms Act 1977; Landlord and Tenant Act 1985, s 12.

full in the social heritage and to live the life of a civilised being according to the standards prevailing in the society'.[47] What, however, do we mean by social rights? At the international level the United Nations Declaration of Human Rights in 1948 contains an article that everyone has a right to an adequate standard of living, including food, clothing, housing, medical care, and necessary social services, and the right to security in the event of unemployment, sickness, disability, widowhood, old age, or other lack of livelihood in circumstances beyond his control.[48] These social rights are set out in greater detail in the International Covenant on Economic, Social and Cultural Rights.[49] For Europe, the European Social Charter of the Council of Europe, which came into force in 1965, imposes obligations on states to give effect to the social rights it recognizes, including employment rights; rights to education, health care, and social welfare benefits and services; and rights to the protection of the family and its members.[50] Building on the Social Chapter in the Maastricht Treaty, which after 1997 became effective for Britain along with other European Union member states,[51] and the EU Charter of Fundamental Rights, the Treaty Establishing a Constitution for Europe will contain a number of social rights under the heading 'Solidarity'. These include employment rights, rights for family protection, and rights to social security, social assistance, housing and health care, albeit in accordance with rules laid down by European Union and national law.[52] The social rights contained in instruments such as these have never had the force of their counterpart civil and political rights in either their expression or enforcement. Even if they were to be justiciable there is an argument that social rights are not strictly rights, because full satisfaction is not possible within existing resources.[53]

Social legislation

The approach here is to eschew these broad statements of social rights to focus on what is provided for in specific social legislation, in particular to examine its realization in the substance and administration of the law. Initially, it is necessary to distinguish two broad categories of social legislation. What the first category, regulatory legislation, does is to detail the duties of the private individuals and

[47] T.H. Marshall, *Sociology at the Crossroads and Other Essays* (London, 1963), 74.

[48] Article 25.

[49] House of Lords, House of Commons, Joint Committee on Human Rights, *The International Covenant on Economic, Social and Cultural Rights*, HC 183; HC 1188 (London, 2004).

[50] The right to education is recognized in the Council of Europe's European Convention on Human Rights, First Protocol, Article 2. Article 8 of the Convention, coupled with Article 3, might oblige a state to provide welfare in some situations: e.g. *Anufrijeva v Southwark LBC* [2003] EWCA Civ 1406; [2004] QB 1124.

[51] P. Craig & G. de Burca, *EU Law*, 2nd edn (Oxford, 1998), 37.

[52] See *Treaty Establishing a Constitution for Europe. Commentary*, Cm 6459 (London, 2005), 68–71.

[53] W. Sadurski, 'Economic Rights and Basic Needs', in C. Samford & D. Galligan (eds), *Law, Rights and the Welfare State* (London, 1986).

institutions within its ambit. These might be landlords, employers, producers, or service providers. The other side of the coin is that the beneficiaries of such regulation may have a right. So landlords must not unlawfully evict tenants; tenants are now given a legal right to sue for damages, measured by the landlord's profit on obtaining vacant possession.[54] Similarly, employees can be said to have a right to be paid the minimum wage set by law since the legislation gives them a contractual entitlement to sue for any shortfall between what they should have received under it.[55] Although contracts are not usually voided if regulatory legislation is breached, consumers might be able to recover the loss following its breach, in addition to any separate civil action for damages.[56]

A second category of social legislation sets out the conditions for individuals to qualify for welfare benefits and services or, to put it more accurately for many such benefits and services, the circumstances when state and local agencies must provide them. Although sometimes described as 'rights', the term is rarely used in the legislation which covers the wide variety of welfare benefits and services such as social housing, personal care, and social services more generally. However, satisfaction of the prerequisites for some welfare benefits and services gives individuals a claim to receive them.[57] An ancillary role for both types of social legislation is to constitute machinery for its implementation. The machinery may involve regulatory agencies or those for the delivery of welfare benefits and services (called here social welfare agencies). The legal system acts to an extent to settle the disputes which arise over the ambit and operation of the regulatory and distributive rules and the operation of the machinery.

Realization of the promise of social legislation turns on various factors, in particular its emergence, its juridical form and substantive provisions, the way it is administered and its effects. As with the consideration of social and political rights, the discussion here largely ignores emergence and effect to concentrate on the juridical form of social legislation, its substantive provisions and the way it is administered. As regards the emergence of social legislation, it may be remarked briefly that this can sometimes explain why its provisions are ambiguous, over-inclusive, conflicting or otherwise not commensurate with any ostensible goal of creating particular social rights. For example, the defects may reflect conflicts between different interests at the time of enactment, because those drafting the law did not foresee particular problems, or simply because not enough attention was given to the policy issues behind it and the problems which needed surmounting in relating it to other institutions. The establishment of the Child Support Agency in the 1990s, and the ensuing chaos, is a good example of the latter.[58] As for the effects of social legislation, there are the independent and unintended,

---

[54] Housing Act 1988, s 27.

[55] National Minimum Wage Act 1998, ss 1(1), 10, 12, 17. See also s 20 (enforcement officers able to sue on behalf of workers).

[56] *Consumers*, 152, 336; R. Cranston, *Principles of Banking Law*, 2nd edn (Oxford, 2002), 203.

[57] N. Wikeley & A. Ogus, *The Law of Social Security*, 5th edn (London, 2002), 274–5, 278, 387.

[58] e.g. G. Davis, N. Wikeley, R. Young, J. Barron & J. Bedward, *Child Support in Action* (Oxford, 1998).

as well as the direct and intended, effects. Related policies can also have a bearing. Both may well undermine the direct and intended effects of establishing a particular regime of social rights. A well-known example is that failures in housing benefit administration have caused rent arrears and homelessness, which is contrary to the policy behind this benefit.[59]

Let us return to the juridical nature of social legislation. That depends on at least three factors: first, the duty set out in the relevant legislation; secondly, the provisions for accountability through internal and external review; and thirdly, the basis of any entitlement persons have. The first factor is relatively straightforward and refers to whether the relevant state or local agency has a wide discretion, or alternatively whether the legislation and rules set out relatively objective standards for individual provision. Review of the decisions of the agencies—the second factor—may be underdeveloped at one end of the spectrum, while at the other end there may be a relatively sophisticated system, for example internal review, external redress through tribunals and an appeal to the courts. Any entitlement persons have is statutory and its strength at law turns on the first two factors—the duty the relevant legislation gives its administrators and the extent to which their decisions are subject to organized review. However, it is useful to consider the basis of entitlement as a separate head because, by contrast with the statutory entitlement of welfare claimants, the beneficiaries of occupational welfare may have a contractual or equitable right to benefit which is enforceable in the courts in the ordinary way.[60] These three aspects of legal structure—statutory duty, review, and the basis of entitlement—are addressed here.

The duty imposed on state and local agencies may be clear from the legislative language. Different types of discretion can be identified falling along a continuum. In the first type an agency is entrusted with broad discretion to meet particular goals. Thus the legal duty might be to all those in need in a particular area, but not to each person in need individually. The legislation in this respect sets out the broad aims which the agency must bear in mind in performing the specific duties set out in it elsewhere.[61] Even where the legislation does impose duties to specific persons in need it might still confer a wide discretion on the agency. In practice these days the agency will have rules in such circumstances.[62] The replacement of

59 J. Neuburger, *House Keeping. Preventing Homelessness Through Tackling Rent Arrears in Social Housing*, Shelter (London, 2003), 7–9; House of Commons, Select Committee on Office of the Deputy Prime Minister, *Homelessness*, HC 61 (London, 2005), para. 98; *North British Housing Association Ltd v Matthews* [2004] EWCA Civ 1736; [2005] 2 All ER 667, para. 32.

60 R. Ellison, *Pensions Law and Practice* (London, looseleaf).

61 Children Act 1989, s 17(1); *R (G) v Barnet LBC* [2003] UKHL 57; [2004] 2 AC 208.

62 e.g. community care grants and crisis loans from the Social Fund are discretionary; moreover, there is no right of appeal to a tribunal: Society Security Contributions and Benefits Act 1992, Part VIII. But there are detailed rules. See G. Craig, 'Lump Sum and Emergency Payments: A Brief History', in T. Buck & R. Smith (eds), *Poor Relief or Poor Deal? The Social Fund, Safety Nets and Social Security* (2003); A. Barton, *Unfair and Underfunded: CAB Evidence on What's Wrong with the Social Fund*, NACAB (London, 2002); M. Howard, *Lump Sums. Roles for the Social Fund in Ending Child Poverty*, National Council for One Parent Families, Family Welfare Association, Child Poverty Action Group (London, 2003), 12–14.

discretion by definite and public rules, even if in internal codes and manuals, can be regarded as bringing social legislation more into line with the rule of law. Another type of discretion is where there are legislative rules, but the agency is empowered to depart from them in certain defined circumstances, described in such terms as 'exceptional', or 'urgent'.[63] This is increasingly unusual in social legislation.

Finally, there is the type of discretion which arises in most branches of the law because rules must be interpreted: this may be obvious on the face of legislation because the standards referred to are relatively open-textured (such as 'reasonably practicable' or 'capable of work'), but this type of discretion can also arise where officials are under a 'duty' to, or 'shall', exercise their discretion in the light of specified, relatively objective, criteria. Open-textured standards may be embodied in legislation for a number of reasons, one being because the nature of the subject matter is such that law-makers cannot decide on every situation likely to arise or cannot agree on the details of how social policy will work in practice. Objectivity may be assisted by invoking the judgment of experts.[64] Even where there are specified, relatively objective criteria, there can be disagreement on what these mean or how certain facts are to be interpreted. For instance, the statutory consequence of the provisions relating to fiscal welfare (i.e. through tax concessions on matters like pensions) tends to be in effect that taxpayers who satisfy relatively objective requirements are entitled to the concessions.[65] But avoidance of the discretionary language of benefits legislation does not mean that there is no room for disagreement over the interpretation of fiscal legislation.

The second factor in the juridical nature of social legislation is the character of the machinery available for review of primary decision making. In theory it may make no difference whether there is machinery for review, since officials are obliged to give effect to the law.[66] In practice, however, the strength of social rights depends in part on review of their implementation for that feeds back directly into the routine business of decision making and adjudication.[67] Inspectorates have a central place in the British state in reviewing the overall performance of government agencies, whether they be regulators or social welfare agencies. Although the inspectors may not review individual decisions, better decision making in this regard may result from the overall inspection of an agency.[68] As far as courts are concerned, their involvement usually arises for regulators in the context of a criminal prosecution: the responsible agency acts on behalf of the public to bring the regulated to book. Occasionally this may lead to judicial comments on the behaviour of the agency. In relation to social welfare agencies the House of Lords

---

[63] e.g., Ministry of Social Security Act 1966, ss 7, 13. See N. Wikeley & A. Ogus, *op.cit.*, 274–5, 313–6, 465.   [64] Social Security Act 1998, s 19 (medical experts).
[65] e.g. Income Tax (Earnings and Pensions) Act 2003, ss 307, 318, 637, 677.
[66] See R. Dworkin, *Taking Rights Seriously* (London, 1977), 32–4.
[67] J. Baldwin, N. Wikeley & R. Young, *Judging Social Security. The Adjudication of Claims for Benefit in Britain* (Oxford, 1992), 209.   [68] 22–4 above.

has said that utilitarian considerations have a place and that the legislation is entitled to take the view that it is not in the public interest that an excessive proportion of the funds available for benefits and services should be consumed in administration and legal disputes.[69] While the remedies shaping our notions of contractual, property, equitable, or constitutional rights are judicial in character, in this area rights to benefits and services are enforceable initially by internal review and in tribunals rather than courts.[70] Legally this is acceptable under rule of law principles and also provisions such as Article 6 of the European Convention on Human Rights. In practice there is no reason why this difference should affect the strength of entitlement provided that internal reviewers and tribunals act in accordance with values such as openness, independence and reasoned decision making. It does mean, however, that there may be less public scrutiny unless the decision goes to appeal or judicial review. Moreover, a lack of resources may constrain the effectiveness of non-curial review.[71]

Entitlement to social rights is grounded in statute, rather than in contractual, property, equitable, or constitutional principles. Because such entitlement is sometimes expressed as an interest which it is the duty of a state or local agency to grant, rather than something which claimants have directly, it may appear more akin to an interest protected by the criminal or public, rather than the civil, law. Legally, however, its strength depends on the discretion the statute confers on the relevant agency and the extent to which its decisions are reviewable internally or by tribunals and the courts. There is no reason, in theory, why a statutory entitlement cannot be as firmly based as a traditional claim in contract, say, in that an agency cannot override it for reasons such as public economy or administrative convenience or because a particular person is thought to be undeserving. Of course social legislation may recognize the shortage of resources, as with social housing, and so require an allocation scheme ranking claims to statutory entitlement.[72]

An examination of the substantive provisions of social legislation reveals that it may not measure up to its promise of establishing social rights. With social regulation, for example, certain aspects of legislative technique become apparent. First, there may be gaps in its provisions on enforcement so that the regulated can avoid its effects.[73] Secondly, social regulation may be out of line with the present-day context of a particular problem. The simplest example is where monetary limits have not been changed so that a protective provision is rendered redundant.[74]

---

[69] *Runa Begum v Tower Hamlets LBC (First Secretary of State Intervening)* [2003] UKHL 5; [2003] 2 AC 430 para 44.   [70] N. Wikeley & A. Ogus, *op.cit.*, ch. 6.

[71] R. Thomas, 'Immigration Appeals for Family Visitors Refused Entry Clearance' [2004] *PL* 612, 641–2.

[72] Housing Act 1996, s 167(2). See R. Latham, 'Allocating Accommodation: Reconciling Choice and Need', *Legal Action*, May 2005, 12.

[73] e.g. Low Pay Commission, *National Minimum Wage* Cm 6475 (London 2005), 167–8.

[74] e.g. Landlord and Tenant Act 1985, s 8, implying a term of fitness in lettings where the rent is less than £80 pa in inner London and £52 pa elsewhere. See Law Commission, *Renting Homes*, Law Com. No. 284 (London, 2003), 78–9.

Rather than being rationally related to its ostensible goals, regulation may comprise an accretion of uneven provisions from different historical periods. A related point is that the legal approaches in the regulatory instrument may not be the most effective in achieving particular policy goals. For instance, simple criminal prohibitions are the popular instrument to back the enforcement of social regulation but are a relatively crude method of influencing behaviour compared with various types of administrative action.[75]

Similarly, any notion of social 'rights' may be belied by the substantive provisions of the social legislation conferring benefits or providing for services. In particular, there is the discretion governing the grant of benefits or services already referred to above. As with social regulation there may also be gaps in the legal framework for benefits or services, which in practice have perverse effects such as the creation of disincentives.[76] There is sometimes a complex interplay of provisions which makes unclear both entitlement and which agency is obliged to act.[77] It may be that an individual can be said to have only a right to take the benefit of a favourable agency decision, as with an offer of social housing, not a further right somehow to vet that decision for its acceptability.[78] Failure to take advantage of the decision may result in discharging the agency's obligation to provide a benefit or service, as where an applicant for social housing exceeds the offer limits (for example, rejects one or more offers).[79]

Moreover, social legislation may make the grant of a benefit or service conditional upon certain behaviour. Non-compliance leads to sanctions. Examples include the steps benefit recipients must take in respect of assisting the Child Support Agency to obtain maintenance from the other parent of their children;[80] the obligation imposed on New Deal claimants to take employment, placement and training opportunities as a condition of continuing to receive benefits;[81] and the requirements on social housing tenants not to engage in anti-social activity and generally to act as good neighbours.[82] While formulations of the rule of law emphasize form

---

[75] R. Baldwin & M. Cave, *Understanding Regulation* (Oxford, 1999), ch. 8; R. Baldwin C. Scott & C. Hood, *A Reader on Regulation* (Oxford, 1998), Parts 2–3.

[76] Cabinet Office, Social Exclusion Unit, *Preventing Social Exclusion* (London, 2001), 26.

[77] e.g. *R (Westminster CC) v National Asylum Support Service* [2002] UKHL 38; [2002] 1 WLR 2956.

[78] *R (Khatun) v Newham LBC* [2004] EWCA Civ 55; [2004] 3 WLR 417, paras 27, 32.

[79] e.g. Housing Act 1996, ss 167(1A), 193(7). See H. Pawson *et al.*, *Local Authority Policy and Practice on Allocations, Transfers and Homelessness*, Department for the Environment, Transport and the Regions (London, 2001).

[80] Child Support Act 1991, s 6(7). See *Huxley v Child Support Officer* [2000] 1 FLR 898.

[81] J. Fulbrook, 'New Labour's Welfare Reforms: Anything New?' (2001) 64 *MLR* 243, 249–50; *A New Contract for Welfare*, Cm 4101 (London, 1998), 3; *Pathways to Work. Helping People into Employment*, Cm 5690 (London, 2002), 17–18; P. Bivand, 'Rights and Duties in the New Deal', *Working Brief* [Centre for Economic and Social Inclusion], No. 136 (2002), 15.

[82] Anti-social Behaviour Act 2003, Part 2. See e.g. *New Charter Housing (North) Ltd v Ashcroft* [2004] EWCA Civ 310; cf. *Moat Housing Group South Ltd v Harris* [2005] EWCA Civ 287. A. Jones *et al.*, *Shelter Inclusion Project. Interim Evaluation Findings* (London, 2004); H. Carr, 'Anti-Social Behaviour Act 2003 and Housing', *Legal Action*, February 2004, 20; House of Commons, Home Affairs Committee, *Anti-Social Behaviour*, HC 80 (London, 2005), paras 256–269.

rather than substance, some accounts focusing on substance contend that it does not countenance such attempts to buy behaviour through such sanctions.[83] Similarly, it could be argued that under the rule of law social legislation ought not to circumscribe individual autonomy too much because that could violate the equal respect due to all in society. Although the point is not uncontroversial, there seems nothing wrong with demanding of those who receive social support and protection certain economic responsibilities and constraints on behaviour. The other side of social rights are social responsibilities.[84] These may be justified as being in the beneficiaries' own long-term interests, or as being a legitimate response to community concerns. A certain amount of paternalism goes with the territory of social legislation so long as it still accords equal respect to beneficiaries. Often the limit in practice will be effectiveness, not values: for example, there is evidence that the use of sanctions on welfare recipients with multiple disadvantage is increased social exclusion, participation in the informal economy and possibly criminality.[85] This points in the direction more of specialist support over a period, coupled with light-touch direction, rather than punitive sanctions.

Administering social legislation

Social regulation on the statute book may appear to further social rights, but its implementation may be so incomplete as to make it virtually a dead letter. The enforcement of social regulation may be entrusted to government departments or specialized agencies. In theory an advantage of the second is that a law does not have to compete with a range of other laws for enforcement. The success of the particular agency is identified with its success in implementing the relevant regulatory law. In reality, however, among the problems are that the regulator may be entrusted with limited power, endowed with insufficient resources or undermined by the regulated. Moreover, the courts may not be able to give adequate support to the implementation of the legislation. That many regard regulatory offences as morally ambiguous is one factor in this and may make it difficult to distinguish between the unscrupulous and the less serious offender. Consequently, there may be a tendency to impose uniformly low penalties, which are not a burden to the former.

Benefits and services provided for in social legislation are not accomplished social facts, whatever their juridical strength. Whether they become that depends on factors such as the commitment and resources of the social welfare agencies administering them. As well, there is the knowledge and consciousness of individuals

---

[83] T. Campbell, 'Discretionary Rights', in N. Timms & D. Watson (eds), *Philosophy in Social Work* (London, 1978), 66–7.

[84] Department for Work and Pensions, *Building on New Deal* (London, 2004), 15; P. Dwyer, *Welfare Rights and Responsibilities* (Bristol, 2000); K. Stanley, L. Lohde & S. White, *Sanctions and Sweeteners*, IPPR (London, 2004). cf. H. Dean, 'Human Rights and Welfare Rights', in H. Dean (ed.), *The Ethics of Welfare* (Bristol, 2004), 15–19.

[85] Social Exclusion Unit, *Jobs and Enterprise in Deprived Areas* (London, 2004), 76.

as to the existence of their rights and their subjective feelings about, and behaviour in relation to, them.[86] Individuals have to know and feel that they have a right, equal to others in the same position, and how they can assert that right. The reason is the passivity of social administration, that the state or local social welfare agencies, administering the benefits or services, are not generally obligated to uncover eligible claimants or to assist them pursue any entitlements. As a result, some of those eligible do not claim welfare benefits or services because they lack the knowledge, capacity, or motivation to do so (the 'take-up' problem), or because of the perceived disadvantages of doing so.[87]

The complexities of welfare benefits and services, compounded by administrative failings, may also discourage claims. A particular complexity is that the receipt of some benefits and services is a disqualification for others. Consequently, there needs to be a careful calculation if a person is to be in the best position overall. Because of the specialization of functions, administrators of particular welfare benefits and services often have a less than full understanding of others and may not be kept fully informed about changes to them.[88] A particular administrative failing is if application forms and procedures are unnecessarily complicated. Unlike universal benefits and services, means-tested benefits and services involve a scrutiny of a claimant's affairs which some are reluctant to undergo. In addition, it cannot be neglected that a stigma is still thought to attach to the receipt of some benefits and services. The low potential gain which would come of applying, or the fear of being rebuffed, may possibly deter some potential beneficiaries. So those administering social legislation must not only be under a legal duty to grant a benefit or service, but must facilitate and respect those applying for it in practice.

Dispassionate treatment by state agencies is the hallmark of equality before the law—citizens are to be treated with equal respect and according to established rules and procedures, applied in an impersonal and relatively fixed manner, rather than according to personal friendship, prejudice, or arbitrariness. In practice, this official model of bureaucracy is modified somewhat for social welfare agencies. As we have seen, discretionary language is inevitable in the legislation conferring benefits and services so that its precisely equal application is not always possible. Objectionable, however, may be other deviations from the ideal. Because of an ambiguous mandate a social welfare agency may stereotype its clientele—what has been called moral typification—aided by the fact that they are generally more deprived than the population as a whole.[89] The notion of welfare administrators as self-interested knaves, and of welfare recipients as passive recipients of a benefit

[86] P. Leonard, *Promoting Welfare? Government Information Policy and Social Citizenship* (Bristol, 2003).

[87] National Audit Office, *Tackling Pensioner Poverty. Encouraging Take-up of Entitlements*, HC 37 (London, 2002); House of Commons Work and Pensions Committee, *Pension Credit*, HC 43-1 (London, 2005), 34–42.

[88] Better Regulation Task Force, *Housing Benefit. A Case Study of Lone Parents* (London, 2001), 32.

[89] J. Wilson, *Bureaucracy* (Cambridge, MA, 1989), 336–8; J. Handler, *Social Citizenship and Workfare in the United States and Western Europe* (Cambridge, 2004), 83–5.

or service—'pawns'—only partially captures the type of undesirable moral attitudes which can arise.[90] Another example is that if a social welfare agency treats claimants as having individual problems with treatment tailored to their needs, it can lead to unfairness, or the perception of that, because it cannot easily and publicly be demonstrated that like cases are being treated alike.

A characteristic of social welfare agencies, shared by many bureaucracies, is that relatively junior officers have the power to settle simple cases, and to make crucial decisions in the more complicated. Front-line staff—those officers with whom claimants first come in contact—have a key role in social welfare, and their behaviour may well result in the rationing of a benefit or service available whatever the legal entitlement.[91] As the first point of contact in social welfare agencies, front-line staff can create an impression as to whether an application is welcome, determine whether a claimant obtains correct information as to eligibility and influence the fate of an application by presenting it to others in the agency in a certain way. Their behaviour in these respects can turn on factors such as their workload, the agency milieu, and societal values. In some situations a social welfare agency will have to rely heavily on front-line staff to deliver its policy. A contemporary example is the role of the 'personal adviser' in building a work-focused culture and supporting recipients of welfare benefits into employment.[92] The individually tailored, more personalized method of delivering public services in this way is said to be the most effective way to combat social exclusion.[93]

Social welfare officials can be expected to take an 'investigative stance', in which they do not accept an applicant's story at face value, but treat it as a collection of claims which have to be substantiated.[94] Facts for social welfare agencies must be established in certain ways—a claimant's statements alone will often not suffice—such as through documentation (for example, birth certificates, wage records, crime reference numbers for crisis loans in respect of stolen property), inquiries by officials (for example home visits, telephone calls to employers) or expert evidence. Whereas an applicant's claims are open to doubt, this sort of evidence from others may be assumed to be reliable from the outset. This may not be justified as a matter of law. Putting the onus on claimants raises obstacles to their success because they may face problems in substantiating a claim. In *Kerr*, the House of Lords held that where a matter requiring proof is within the knowledge of the social welfare agency, but not the claimant, the onus is on it to ask the relevant questions of the applicant so as to be able to determine the claim. Moreover, where

---

[90] J. LeGrand, *Motivation, Agency and Public Policy* (Oxford, 2003), 2, 25–6, 46–7.

[91] National Audit Office, *Helping Those in Financial Hardship: The Running of the Social Fund*, HC 179 (London, 2005), 20; S. Wright, 'The Street-Level Implementation of Unemployment Policy', in J. Millar, *Understanding Social Security* (Bristol, 2003).

[92] National Audit Office, *Welfare to Work: Tackling the Barriers to the Employment of Older People*, HC 1026 (London, 2004), 34–5, 37. See B. Stafford, 'Service Delivery and the User', in J. Millar (ed.), *op.cit.*, 221–3.   [93] Social Exclusion Unit, *Breaking the Cycle* (London, 2005), 103–5.

[94] D.H. Zimmerman, 'Fact as a Practical Accomplishment', in R. Turner (ed.), *Ethnomethodology* (Harmondsworth, 1974).

in effect a benefit or service is available to a claimant subject to exclusions, it is up to the agency to prove that it is within an exclusion if it seeks to rely on it.[95] However, the fact remains that claimants may not regard it as important to keep certain documents or may lose documents because, not having a permanent home, they move from place to place. Without the resources to obtain their own expert evidence, they may find it hard to counter that evidence obtained by social welfare agencies from doctors, employers, inspectors, valuers, planners, and so on.

Once an agency has developed a strategy, drawn to varying extents from its legislative mandate, it needs to establish effective operating procedures which shape its organizational structure and direct its daily activities. Strong operating procedures ensure that social legislation is properly implemented—moneys are spent for the purposes intended, value for money is secured, officials make decisions in accordance with law, policy and rules, and overall social rights are conferred as intended.[96] The quality of decision making then turns on the knowledge and judgment of officials, which comes from internal training, mentoring, job-shadowing and team discussions. Part of their guidance on decision making will be the legislation, decision-digests and case studies, updated by bulletins and the intranet, and possibly supplemented by advice lines to agency experts. An agency's performance measurement from inspectorates may involve a sample check on initial decisions and other internal checks, with feedback to correct identified errors.[97]

Routines develop in regulatory and social welfare agencies as they construct conventional ways of interpreting rules and handling ordinary cases. Bureaucratic behaviour is of necessity determined by routine since the average officer cannot know all the rules and does not have the time to determine what course the rules set for every claim. In fact routinization is one of the virtues of bureaucracy for it contributes to equal treatment, reliability, continuity, efficiency, and impartiality. Because of the large volume of rules which officers would otherwise have to assimilate, and because of the many claims which have to be handled, routinization is especially important in social welfare agencies.

To allow routine processing agencies must 'standardise' claims by fitting them into categories, and in doing this may ignore the complexity of particular cases. Unless routinization is coupled with an adequate assessment procedure, relevant information may be disregarded and officials may overlook the consequences of their action for particular individuals. In the social welfare context this may possibly lead to a failure to explore a claimant's full legal entitlements, for example, whether they qualify for additional benefits. It may also lead to injustice through

---

[95] *Kerr v Department for Social Development* [2004] UKHL 23; [2004] 1 WLR 1372. cf. *Hinchy v Secretary of State for Work and Pensions* [2005] UKHL 16; [2005] 2 All ER 129.

[96] National Audit Office, *An Early Progress Report on the New Deal for Communities Programme*, HC 309 (London, 2004), 5, 10, Part 3.

[97] e.g. National Audit Office, *Getting It Rights, Putting It Right: Improving the Quality of Decision-Making for Social Security Benefits*, HC 1142 (London, 2003).

inflexibility: that requires procedures clearly recognizing the need, for example, to enlarge the search in relation to some claims, rather than simply relying on an agency culture that this will occur.[98] Another consequence of routinisation is that it may take some time for new developments (for example judicial decisions) to penetrate the daily practices of social welfare agencies, because of a delay in incorporating them into manuals and other documentation. In itself routinization does not have to lead to the disadvantages of over-simplification and time-lags. Much depends on the human and financial resources available to social welfare agencies and the way they are managed. These define the boundaries to the amount of search officers can engage in and the point at which they must decide that an answer is reasonably satisfactory, despite the fact that additional factors could be considered.

Overall, then, the operation of regulatory and social welfare agencies turns on factors such as their internal organization, the information they make available to the public, the routines they operate and the adequacy of their financial and human resources. Societal perceptions of social legislation may feed into the judgments which officials exercise at the point of delivery of social rights. In the case of social regulation this may be an attitude that its breach is hardly a crime and thus the approach in administering the ordinary criminal law is not appropriate. Bureaucratic procedures within social welfare agencies and societal perceptions of the benefit or service for which it is responsible may mean that even if claimants 'take up' benefits and services, they can face obstacles in securing their entitlement—a relative lack of information, rationing, or channelling at the point of intake or as their claims are being processed; the apparent indifference, and in some cases unhelpfulness, of officials; or simply administrative ineptitude. Any of this can have fatal consequences for social rights.

Conclusion

What society claims is a right may be contradicted by its substance or administration. So for example, it is illusory to say that there is a 'right' to a social welfare benefit or service because it is recognized in law if that right is not palpable to eligible claimants, if they do not expect to receive it, and if the officials who administer it do not feel under any obligation to grant it. Making social 'rights' effective in practice may face formidable obstacles if at base social and economic inequalities and negative attitudes are involved. The effects of structural factors of this nature are not always capable of significant amelioration by changes in legal form and procedure. For example, changes to social welfare administration in the direction of reducing discretion by rule-making and of developing mechanisms for external review, while consistent with the rule of law, may not in the particular

---

[98] cf. *R (Refugee Legal Centre) v Secretary of State for the Home Department* [2004] EWCA Civ 1481.

circumstances advantage applicants for the social welfare benefit or service. The rules drawn up may be mean, and the sophisticated system of external review may require enormous energy to negotiate.[99] None of this should lead to the conclusion which some draw, that what liberal democratic societies proclaim as rights are a worthless abstraction which legitimize inequalities and militate against social change. Merely because there are shortcomings in practice does not mean that 'rights' are illusory or that competing notions are more desirable; social 'rights' are worth striving for as basic standards. The prominent position which such rights occupy in liberal democratic societies may be used as an argument to close the gaps between the reality and the ideal. Public disquiet that these rights are denied in practice can be a powerful force which may be tapped, not only to remedy the defects uncovered in practice but to effect real social reform.

[99] E. Sparer, 'Fundamental Human Rights, Legal Entitlements, and the Social Struggle' (1984) 36 *Stan.LR* 509, 560–1.

8

Civil Rights and Social Wrongs:
the Australian Aboriginals

Follow the Rabbit-Proof Fence is the study of how three Aboriginal girls, Molly, Gracie, and Daisy, trekked a thousand miles in 1931, from the Moore River Native Settlement, just north of Perth, to Jigalong, a small reserve in remote inland Western Australia.[1] They had been taken to Moore River as part of government policy to assimilate into the white population Aboriginals of mixed descent. At Moore River they would be trained for white society, for example for domestic work, with the expectation that they would eventually marry white men, so that their Aboriginal traits would be lost in subsequent generations. The title of the book comes from the rabbit-proof fence, which was built in the early part of the twentieth century to prevent the westward migration of rabbits, introduced by the Europeans and quickly considered a pest as they grew exponentially in number. The fence ran well over 1,000 miles from the Southern Ocean to Eighty Mile Beach in north-west Australia. The rabbit-proof fence ran through Jigalong, so the girls knew that if they could get to the fence from Moore River, they need only to follow it north to their home at Jigalong.

The account of the trek, without provisions or maps, is a powerful one. At a general level, it is about the triumph of the human spirit over tremendous odds. It is also one part of the story of Aboriginal–white relations and of the ramifications of nineteenth and twentieth century government policy regarding Aboriginals. That story is still being written. It is both historically and politically controversial. Historians have uncovered the dark side of the story, such as the alienation of Aboriginal land, the confinement of Aboriginals in missions and reserves and the official removal of Aboriginal children such as the three girls in furtherance of the assimilation policy. Doing justice to this story requires an appreciation of the complexities and the context. The assimilation policy was in line with the principles of eugenics espoused at the time in Britain and the United States by some leading socialists and others.[2] It was not universal: for example, its implementation was

---

[1] Doris Pilkington (whose Aboriginal name is Nugi Garimara), *Follow the Rabbit-Proof Fence* (St Lucia, 2002). Pilkington/Garimara is the daughter of one of the girls. The book is the basis of a Miramax film, released in 2002, and directed by Phillip Noyce.

[2] e.g. M. Thompson, *The Problem of Mental Deficiency* (Oxford, 1998), 61n, 63, 182–3. In the United States there was Holmes J's judgment in *Buck v Bell*, 274 US 200 (1927). Indeed, the

partial in some parts of Australia and where it was pursued it was fiercely opposed by some Australians.[3] Distorting the story of Aboriginal–white conflict benefits no one. There is no doubt that many Aboriginals were appallingly murdered by whites—the Myall Creek and Coniston massacres are examples[4]—but credible evidence of hundreds of massacres, and tens of thousands of Aboriginals poisoned or violently killed, is so far lacking.[5]

None of this diminishes the enormity of the wrongs done to individual Aboriginals and the destructive impact of the Europeans on Aboriginal society. One example is the removal policy dealt with in *Follow the Rabbit-Proof Fence*. In 1997 the Australian Human Rights and Equal Opportunity Commission produced a report on the Aboriginal children removed from their families and communities like the girls in the book.[6] It concluded that between 1910 and 1970 approximately one in ten Aboriginal children were forcibly removed in furtherance of the assimilation policy; in certain regions and in certain periods the number was greater.[7] Profound psychological damage was suffered by parents who lost their children and by the children who were separated from their families and culture, and in some cases exploited and abused by institution staff or foster parents. (There is a resonance here with the psychological damage suffered by the children, sometimes orphans, often of unmarried or separated parents, who were sent from Britain to institutions and foster parents in Australia in the mid-twentieth century.[8]) In the case of Aboriginal children, the Commission concluded that the emotional damage was such that many Aboriginals were less able to learn social skills, with other consequences such as low educational achievement, unemployment, and poverty.[9] It is no doubt an explanatory factor in the plight of many Aboriginal people today.

complexities are evident in those associated with *Follow the Rabbit-Proof Fence*. After returning to Jigalong, Molly had two daughters, the book's author, Doris, and Annabelle. The three were removed to the Moore River settlement in 1940, Molly absconded again, but because she could cope with only one child took eighteen-month-old Annabelle with her. Three years later Annabelle was taken south to another settlement (p. 132). Doris stayed at Moore River and eventually trained as a journalist; in middle age she tracked down her mother. According to press reports, when Annabelle was finally traced at the time of the film she was unwilling to embrace Doris, Molly, or her Aboriginality.

   [3] e.g., F. Paisley, 'Race and Remembrance: Contesting Aboriginal Child Removal in the Inter-War Years' *Australian Humanities Review*, Issue 8, November 1997–January 1998.

   [4] 242 below. On the Coniston Massacre, see *Findings and Evidence of the Board of Inquiry concerning the Killing of Natives in Central Australia by Police Parties and Others* (Canberra, 1929).

   [5] Compare e.g. H. Reynolds, *Frontier*, 2nd edn (Sydney, 1996), Part 1 with K. Windschuttle, *The Fabrication of Aboriginal History* (Paddington, Sydney, 2002), vol. 1. There is a burgeoning literature on this.

   [6] *Bringing them Home. Report of the National Inquiry into the Separation of Aboriginal and Torres Strait Islander Children from their Families*, Parliamentary Paper No. 128 of 1997. The Commission was chaired at the time by Sir Ronald Wilson, a former judge of the High Court of Australia.

   [7] *ibid.*, 37.

   [8] House of Commons, Health Select Committee, *The Welfare of Former British Children Migrants*, Session 1997–98, 3rd Report, HC 755; M. Humphreys, *Empty Cradles* (London, 1994).

   [9] *Bringing them Home. Report of the National Inquiry into the Separation of Aboriginal and Torres Strait Islander Children from their Families*, Parliamentary Paper No. 128 of 1997, 178.

The law played a crucial role in the interaction between Aboriginals and white society. From the outset the law conferred on Aboriginals the privilege of being British subjects. That meant, with some exceptions, and in the absence of statute, they had the same civil rights as the whites. Yet at the same time the law legitimated the deprivation of their land and remained aloof while their society was being destroyed. Later, the law enshrined the policy of confining Aboriginals of full descent to areas of land in reserves with which they had no traditional relationship, and deprived them of the civil rights they supposedly had as British subjects. Aboriginals of mixed descent, as we have seen, might as children be lawfully removed as part of the assimilation policy. In providing an overview of law's role in white–Aboriginal relations during the period since 1788, this chapter first focuses on the status the courts accorded the Aboriginals and on the implication of this for matters such as their civil and land rights. Then the chapter turns to the destructive public policies enshrined in legislation, such as the protective-segregative policies for Aboriginals of full descent, and the assimilation policies for those of mixed descent.[10] Finally, an attempt is made to draw these themes together with some observations on the role in recent decades of the law in Aboriginal affairs.

Status and Land

From the outset of white settlement in 1788 until the early 1990s, Australia was destined to be regarded, in legal nomenclature, as a settled, rather than as a conquered or ceded colony.[11] The rationale was that Australia was *res nullius* and that the Aboriginals, as nomadic food gatherers and hunters, lacked ostensible institutions, an easily recognizable relationship with the land, and persons with

---

[10] The following legislation is abbreviated by jurisdiction and year: N.S.W.: Aborigines Protection Act 1909–1963; Aborigines Act 1969. Victoria: Aboriginal Affairs Act 1967–1970. Queensland: Aboriginals Preservation and Restriction of the Sale of Opium Act 1897–1934; Aboriginals Preservation and Protection Acts 1939–1946; Aborigines' and Torres Strait Islanders Affairs Acts 1965–1967; Aborigines Act 1971. South Australia: Aborigines Act 1911; Aborigines Act 1936–1939; Aboriginal Affairs Act 1962–1968. Western Australia: Aborigines Protection Act 1886; Native Welfare Act 1905–1960; Native Welfare Act 1963. Northern Territory: Aboriginals' Ordinance 1918–2953; Welfare Ordinance 1953–1963; Social Welfare Ordinance 1963–1972. Other abbreviations are: *Historical Records of New South Wales*—H.R.N.S.W.; formerly—'f'; repealed—'r'. Most of the legislation referred to below (and additional State, Federal and Colonial legislation not pertinent to the matters discussed) is conveniently gathered in C. Brockwell, *Aborigines and the Law: A Bibliography* (Canberra, 1979). In addition, an excellent bibliography of the case law has been compiled by J. McCorquodale, 'An Annotated Bibliography', in P. Hanks and B. Keon-Cohen (eds), *Aborigines and the Law* (Sydney, 1984) ch. 10.

[11] *Blackstone's Commentaries on the Laws of England*, 1765, vol. 1, 107–8. See A. Castles, *An Introduction to Australian Legal History* (Sydney, 1971) chs 1–2; R. Lumb, 'Aboriginal Land Rights: Judicial Approaches in Perspective' (1988) 62 *Aust.LJ* 273; J. Hookey, 'Settlement and Sovereignty', in P. Hanks and B. Keon-Cohen (eds), *Aborigines and the Law* (Sydney, 1984). The case law never conclusively decided the issue: see *Cooper v Stuart* (1889) 14 App. Cas 286; *Coe v Commonwealth of Australia* (1979) 53 ALJR 403; 24 ALR 118.

greater material wealth or obvious control with whom treaties of cession might be concluded.[12] Moreover, since the Aboriginals were unable to offer more than sporadic resistance to the settlers, there was never any need for them to be 'conquered'. The fact that Australia was regarded as a settled colony had two direct legal consequences. First, Aboriginals were legally deprived of any rights in relation to the land, because colonization by settlement meant that all land was regarded as ultimately belonging to the Crown. Hence, when a citizen, John Batman, sought to purchase land by treaty directly from Aboriginal tribes, the New South Wales government issued a proclamation to the effect that his action amounted to a trespass against the Crown.[13] Soon afterwards, in a case involving title to land, the Supreme Court of New South Wales confirmed that the doctrine of the ultimate lordship of the Crown applied to Australia and that all land not granted in possession to a subject was in the legal possession of, and was owned by, the Crown.[14]

If Aboriginals were deprived of the ultimate ownership of their land, it was not inevitable that they should be without all land rights. In North America, some recognition was given to the principle that the indigenous people had a right to retain possession of, or be compensated for, the loss of their land.[15] The Supreme Court of the United States held that native Americans had a right of occupancy of land, although title had passed to the state, on the basis that they had held the land from time immemorial.[16] When the matter was considered by the courts in Australia, however, it was held that Australian law did not recognize native communal title (whereby the Aboriginals might have subordinate rights under native law and custom to land owned by the Crown) since throughout the history of European settlement, neither executive, legislative nor judicial recognition had been given to the doctrine.[17] Not only were Aboriginals denied the land, but they might be deprived of their rights to hunt and fish in areas given over to grazing and pastoral interests.[18]

Then in *Mabo* in 1992, the High Court of Australia held that the common law recognized a form of native title, which when it had not been extinguished by law reflected the entitlements of Aboriginals to their traditional lands, in accordance

---

[12] C. Rowley, *The Destruction of Aboriginal Society* (Ringwood, 1972) 5, 13–14, 21–3, 54–5. Throughout I am greatly indebted to this and Rowley's other great books, *The Remote Aborigines* (Ringwood, 1972) and *Outcasts in a White Australia* (Ringwood, 1972).

[13] H.R.A., Ser.I, Vol.18, at 154, 379, 811; E. Foxcroft, *Australian Native Policy* (1941) 32–5.

[14] *Attorney-General v Brown* (1847) 2 SCR (NSW) App. 30.

[15] See K. McNeil, *Common Law Aboriginal Title* (Oxford, 1989). For Canada see K. McNeil, 'Aboriginal Title and Aboriginal Rights' (1997) 36 *Alberta LR* 117; J. Borrows, 'Sovereignty's Alchemy: An Analysis of *Delgamuukw v British Columbia*' (1999) *Osgoode Hall LJ* 537.

[16] e.g. *Johnson v M'Intosh*, 21 US 240 (1823); *Tee-Hit-Ton Indians v United States*, 348 US 272 (1958); H. Berman, 'The Concept of Aboriginal Rights in the Early Legal History of the United States' (1978) 27 *Buffalo LR* 637; F. Cohen, 'Original Indian Title' (1947) 32 *Minnesota LR* 28.

[17] *Milirrpum v Nabalco Pty Ltd* (1971) 17 FLR 141. See D. Ritter, 'The "Rejection of Terra Nullius" in *Mabo*: A Critical Analysis' (1996) 18 *Syd.LR* 5, 13–20; B. Hocking, 'Aboriginal Law Does Now Run in Australia' (1993) 15 *Syd.LR* 187.

[18] Land Act 1933 (WA), s 106(2). cf. Pastoral Act 1936 (SA), Sch 1.

with their laws and customs.[19] Aboriginals thus had legally enforceable rights to land, which they inherited from previous generations, of a type which their ancestors had when the Crown acquired sovereignty over Australia. Since native title is not a form of common law tenure, but derives from the traditional laws and customs governing the relationship between a community of Aboriginal people and the land, it can vary around Australia. Native title can be extinguished by the Crown, although it may survive the grant of certain tenures. Alienation can only occur within the local native title system; native title is not fee simple. However, since the courts declare the common law of native title from time to time, there is potential for its further development.[20] So far the High Court has not adopted the approach of the North American courts to native title where, for example, so long as a group can establish occupation of land by their ancestors at the time of the coming of the Europeans, subsequent assimilation with their society will not defeat a claim.

Legislation now regulates how claims for this common law native title are to be made.[21] In addition, there is parallel legislation in the various Australian jurisdictions providing for a separate system of Aboriginal land rights.[22] The legislation may recognize as a basis for claiming an economic or cultural viability—in other words, that granting the claim under this legislation would assist in self-development or cultural integrity—which is beyond what can be used to found a claim to common law native title. Unlike common law native title, a successful claim can result in a fee simple title, that title being inalienable and held in trust for the relevant Aboriginals. Although the legislation on Aboriginal land rights is clearer about how Aboriginals establish a claim than with native title, the land potentially claimable under it is limited to what the respective governments are prepared to make available. The upshot is that native title claims have assumed a greater significance than those under the separate land rights legislation.[23]

The second consequence for Aboriginals of Australia being treated as colonized by settlement concerned their legal status. For some time, this point was uncertain. Instructions from the British government directed the early governors to educate

---

[19] *Mabo v Queensland (No.2)* (1992) 175 CLR 1. The case has spawned an enormous literature: e.g. *Essays on the Mabo Decision* (Sydney, 1993); M. Stephenson (ed.), *Mabo: The Native Title Legislation* (St Lucia, 1995); B. Attwood (ed.), *In the Age of Mabo* (Sydney, 1996); B. Horrigan & S. Young (eds), *Commercial Implications of Native Title* (Sydney, 1997). Subsequent leading cases on native title include *Western Australia v Commonwealth* (1995) 183 CLR 373; *Wik Peoples v Queensland* (1996) 187 CLR 12; *Fejo v Northern Territory* (1998) 195 CLR 96.

[20] L. Strelein, 'Conceptualising Native Title' (1999) 23 *Syd.LR* 95; R. French & P. Lane, 'The Common Law of Native Title in Australia' (2002) 2 *Oxford U.Commonwealth LJ* 15. Both refer to important contributions to the debate by Noel Pearson.

[21] e.g. Native Title Act 1993 (Commonwealth), as amended.

[22] Starting with the Aboriginal Land Rights (Northern Territory) Act 1976. Leading cases on the legislation include *R v Toohey, ex p Attorney-General for the Northern Territory* (1980) 145 CLR 374; *R v Toohey, ex p Northern Land Council* (1981) 151 CLR 170; *R v Toohey, ex p Meneling Station Pty Ltd* (1982) 158 CLR 327.

[23] G. Neate, 'Indigenous Land Rights and Native Title in Queensland' (2002) 11 *Griffith LR* 90, 136.

and Christianize the Aboriginals, to protect their persons and the enjoyment of their possessions, to prevent and restrain violence and injustices toward them, and to punish 'any of our subjects' who harmed them.[24] Governor Hunter took this to mean that the Aboriginals were under the protection of the British government, but later Governor Macquairie proposed that Aboriginals should only be regarded as under the mantle of British protection if they applied for certificates, and conducted themselves in a peaceful, inoffensive, and honest manner.[25] By the 1830s, the situation had clarified. The proclamation of Western Australia conferred the protection of the law on Aboriginals as equals of 'other of His Majesty's subjects'.[26] Then, following a report of a Select Committee of the House of Commons, which said that the Aboriginals of Australia 'must be considered as within the allegiance of the Queen and as entitled to her protection',[27] the Aboriginals were granted the protection and rights of British subjects on the foundation of South Australia.[28] It became accepted that Aboriginals were British subjects from the outset of white settlement.[29] In 1948, when an Australian citizenship was created, Aboriginals became Australian citizens along with other persons born in Australia.[30]

Equality before the Law

The most important consequence of Aboriginals being British subjects was that theoretically they were equal before the law with white settlers. A proclamation of Governor King put the matter clearly as regards crimes against the Aboriginals: white settlers were prohibited from any act of injustice or wanton cruelty towards the Aboriginals 'on pain of being dealt with in the same manner as if such act or injustice or wanton cruelty should be committed against the persons and estates of any of His Majesty's subjects'.[31] As early as 1799, a group of whites was tried for the murder of two Aboriginals, and there are similar instances in the following years, including the infamous Myall Creek massacre, where seven whites were executed for their part in the slaughter of twenty-eight Aboriginals, including children.[32] By the same token, equality before the law meant that Aboriginals

[24] H.R.N.S.W., Vol.7, at 135.

[25] H.R.N.S.W., Vol.4, at 2; H.R.A., Ser.1, Vol.9, at 143; B. Bridges, 'The Aborigines and the Law: New South Wales 1788–1855' (1970) 4 *Teaching History* 40, 43.

[26] Quoted in H. Schapper, *Aboriginal Advancement to Integration: Conditions and Plans for Western Australia* (1970), 11.

[27] *Report from the Select Committee on Aborigines (British Settlements)*, Parliamentary Paper (House of Commons) No. 425 (1837), 83.

[28] Quoted in F. Gale, *A Study in Assimilation: Part-Aborigines in South Australia* (1964), 63–4.

[29] *Report from the Select Committee on Voting Rights of Aborigines* (House of Representatives), Commonwealth Parliamentary Paper No. 1 of 1961, 37.

[30] Nationality and Citizenship Act 1948 (Commonwealth), s. 10.

[31] H.R.A., Ser.I, Vol. 3, 592.   [32] H.R.A., Ser.I, Vol. 2, 403; Vol. 12, 632; Vol. 19, 701.

accused of crimes had to be dealt with as British subjects. The documents contain reports of Aboriginals being tried and executed for murder. For example, when fifteen people of the shipwrecked *Maria* were killed in 1839, two Aboriginals thought to be responsible were tried and executed.[33] The Colonial Office condemned the military execution of two Aboriginals in South Australia for the murder of a number of whites as itself murder, not being in accordance with law after a judge had declined jurisdiction to try the case.[34]

The legal implications of disputes solely among Aboriginals remained uncertain for some time. In *R v Murrell*,[35] a case involving the murder of one Aboriginal by another, two arguments were advanced to support the contention that British law was not binding. First, counsel submitted that Australia was neither a settled colony (because the land had not been populated) nor a conquered colony (since the government had never been at war with the inhabitants), but instead was a country having a population with its own manners and customs so that, strictly speaking, the British were bound by Aboriginal law. Although avoiding a direct determination of Australia's position as a settled colony, the court held that the Aboriginals were not strong enough to be regarded as free and independent peoples, and that therefore they were without sovereignty and an independent legal status. Counsel's second argument was more subtle, and is such an eloquent exposition of the Aboriginal plight that it deserves to be quoted in full.

The reason why subjects of Great Britain are bound by the laws of their own country is that they are protected by them; the natives are not protected by these laws; they are not admitted as witnesses in courts of justice, they cannot claim any civil rights, they cannot obtain recovery of, or compensation for, those lands which have been torn from them, and which they have probably held for centuries. They are not therefore bound by laws which afford them no protection.

The court dismissed the submission. Offences committed in the colony against Aboriginal persons, it said, were liable to punishment as a protection of their civil rights. If the offence had been committed on a white it was clearly answerable, and there was 'no distinction between that case and where the offence had been committed upon one of his own tribe'.

But doubts persisted. On at least two occasions after 1836 judicial attitude was inconsistent with the principle that Aboriginals, or at least those not in contact with white society, were subject to the application of British law in disputes

---

[33] F. Gale, *op.cit.*, 85. See also B. Bridges, *op.cit.*, 50, 52.

[34] S. Lendrum, 'The Coorong Massacre: Martial Law and Aborigines at First Settlement' (1977) 6 *Adelaide LR* 26.

[35] (1836) 1 Legge (N.S.W.) 72. See G. Nettheim, 'Indigenous Rights, Human Rights and Australia' (1987) 61 *Aust.LJ* 291, 292–3; B. Kercher, 'Recognition of Indigenous Legal Autonomy in Nineteenth Century New South Wales' (1998) 4(13) *Indigenous Law Bull.* 7; B. Bridges, 'The Extension of English Law to the Aborigines for Offences Committed Inter Se, 1829–1842' (1973) 59 *Journal of the Royal Australian Historical Society* 264, 264–5; and H. Reynolds, *Aboriginal Sovereignty* (Sydney, 1996), 72–3.

involving only Aboriginals. Chief Justice Cooper of the South Australian Supreme Court expressed the view that murder of one tribal Aboriginal by another was not a crime against the law of that colony on the ground that, claiming no protection of the law, the Aboriginals owed it no allegiance.[36] The following year, Willis J, the resident judge of the Port Phillip Bay settlement, expressed doubt as to the competency of the court to try one Aboriginal for the murder of another. Willis J's judgment provoked Governor Gibbs to take the opinion of the judges of the Supreme Court of New South Wales, which was transmitted in a letter by the Chief Justice, Sir James Dowling. The Chief Justice's letter strongly disapproved Willis J's opinion, and in the event, Gibbs decided that declaratory legislation would be unnecessary to clarify the situation.[37]

Any lingering doubts were finally dispelled by two Victorian cases in 1860. In the first, an Aboriginal was charged with killing his wife. Although no evidence was adduced on whether he had changed his habits so as to be regarded as having voluntarily subjected himself to British law, the court held that its jurisdiction extended to all persons within the colony, including the accused.[38] Three months later, the point was more extensively considered.[39] In argument before the court, reference was made to American decisions for the proposition that, in some British colonies, the government had sanctioned continuation of the indigenous law. Although conceding the possibility, the court could find no evidence of an intention to continue Aboriginal law, and it therefore concluded that British legal authority was supreme throughout the colony and applied to all persons in it.

Thus, since 1860, it has been generally accepted that the courts must treat Aboriginals equally with other citizens in the absence of statutory provision. Only limited incursions have been made on this principle First, some courts have accepted a lower standard of self-control from Aboriginals where provocation has been advanced as a defence.[40] In addition, many courts have made allowances for the Aboriginal background of an accused person when sentencing.[41] This is unobjectionable in principle, since it recognizes the disadvantages in terms of education, employment, and so on experienced by many Aboriginals.

For a short time there was a threat that the industrial courts would adversely discriminate against Aboriginals. In 1932, the Chief Justice of the Federal Court of Conciliation and Arbitration laconically stated that, since award conditions were inapplicable, Aboriginals were excluded from the application of the pastoral

---

[36] *Milirrpum v Nabalco Pty Ltd* (1971) 17 FLR 141, 261.

[37] H.R.A., Ser.I, Vol.21, at 653–7. See also Australian Law Reform Commission, *The Recognition of Aboriginal Customary Laws* (Canberra, 1986), vol. I, paras 40–6.

[38] *R v Peter*, *Argus* (Melbourne), 29 June 1860.

[39] *R v Jemmy*, *Argus*, 7 September 1860. See also S. Cooke, 'Arguments for the Survival of Aboriginal Customary Law in Victoria' (1999) 5 *Australian Journal of Legal History* 201.

[40] Veen v R (1979) 143 CLR 458, *per* Jacobs, Murphy JJ; *R v Rankin* [1966] QWN 10; contra: *R v Young* [1957] Qd. R 599; *R v Callope* [1965] Qd R 456. For unreported decisions in Northern Territory, see C. Howard, 'What Colour is the Reasonable Man?' [1961] *Crim LR* 41, 43–6.

[41] e.g. J. McCorquodale, 'Judicial Racism in Australia? Aboriginals in Civil and Criminal Cases', in K. Hazlehurst (ed.), *Ivory Scales: Black Australia and the Law* (Sydney, 1987), 48–9.

industry award.[42] No reasons were given, which was surprising since the Commonwealth Conciliation and Arbitration Act governing industrial awards did not exclude Aboriginals from its operation. The judgment obviously reflected the prejudices of the time for, when the award was later reconsidered, its continued non-applicability to Aboriginals was justified on the grounds that Aboriginals were incapable of, or disinclined to, compete with Europeans or Asians in the economy; that they neither needed nor desired the ordinary standard of living prevailing throughout the country; that they were adequately provided for by the government; and that they were not being exploited or harshly treated by their station-owning employers.[43] In 1962, a 'slow workers' clause was inserted in the Aluminium Industry Award so that Aboriginals working on bauxite mining projects in northern Australia could be paid rates of pay lower than those paid to white workers.[44] Finally, in 1965, the Full Bench of the Commonwealth Conciliation and Arbitration Commission held that the exclusion of Aboriginals from the normal operation of an industrial award was invalid.[45] The Commission, though expressing the view that Aboriginals did not fully understand the meaning of work, concluded that the employers had

...not discharged the heavy burden of persuading us that we should depart from standards and principles which have been part of the Australian arbitration scheme since its inception... There must be one industrial law, similarly applied to all Australians, Aboriginal or not.[46]

State industrial courts quickly adopted the decision and deleted clauses excluding Aboriginals from state industrial awards.[47]

Another area where incursions were made on equality before the law was with evidence. In 1805, the senior legal officer in the colony, Judge-Advocate Atkins, opined that Aborigines were not bound by any moral or religious obligation to tell the truth, and that therefore their testimony could not be admitted by the courts.[48] This conclusion was universally accepted. In the result, whites were able to commit crimes against Aboriginals with impunity when the only eyewitnesses were other Aboriginals who could not be sworn to give evidence. The rule excluding Aboriginal evidence was strictly applied. Thus, in *R v Paddy*[49] the two principal

---

[42] *Graziers' Association of New South Wales v Australian Workers' Union* (1932) 31 CAR 710, 715. The award regulated employment in the pastoral industry in northern Australia.

[43] *Australian Workers' Union v Abbey* (1944) 53 CAR 212, 213; *Graziers' Association of New South Wales v Australian Workers' Union* (1948) 61 CAR 237, 249–50.

[44] *Australian Workers' Union v Alcoa of Australia Pty Ltd* (1963) 104 CAR 626.

[45] *Re the Cattle Station Industry (Northern Territory) Award 1951* (1966) 113 CAR 651. See generally W Stanner, 'Industrial Justice in the Never-Never', *Australian Quarterly*, March 1967, 38; F. Stevens, *Equal Wages for Aborigines* (1968); J. McCorquodale, 'The Myth of Mateship: Aborigines and Employment' (1985) 26 *J.Indus.Relations* 3.   [46] (1966) 113 CAR 651, 669.

[47] *Australian Workers' Union v Graziers' Association of New South Wales* (1967) 121 CAR 454, 458; *Station Hands' Award-State*, 63 *Queensl.Ind.Gaz.* 41 (23 June 1968).

[48] H.R.A., Ser.I, Vol.5, 502.

[49] (1876) 14 SCR (NSW) 440. cf. *R v Smith* (1872) 11 SCR (NSW) 69.

witnesses, who were Aboriginals, gave some indication of a belief that they would be punished for speaking falsely. Nevertheless, the court held that they did not have a sufficient belief in the future state of rewards and punishments to imply a belief in a supreme being, nor had they performed any ceremony considered binding on their consciences. Consequently, their evidence was rejected. Early attempts in New South Wales to remedy this situation failed when the Legislative Council rejected government-sponsored legislation. It was not until witnesses were able to affirm rather than swear that Aboriginal evidence became admissible in the courts.[50] Meanwhile, in other colonies, special laws to allow Aboriginals to give evidence were introduced[51] but later these were succeeded by general provisions, similar to the New South Wales enactment, for those unwilling or unable to give evidence on oath.

Evidential problems arose in other contexts. As late as 1958, Kriewaldt J of the Supreme Court of the Northern Territory excluded from evidence the dying declaration of an Aboriginal by taking judicial notice of the fact that Aboriginals did not have the requisite religious belief in the hereafter to guarantee the truth of their final statements.[52] Much earlier, a problem had arisen in trials of Aboriginals where prospective female Aboriginal witnesses were the wives of the accused according to customary law. Did the ordinary common law rule apply so that these women were incompetent to give evidence against their husbands? Australian courts refused to recognize Aboriginal marriages, and so held that Aboriginal wives were able to give evidence against their husbands.[53] Legislative provision was made in Queensland to correct the effects of this anomaly, so that where a male and female Aboriginal were cohabiting in accordance with recognized tradition, the female was not a compellable witness against the male.[54]

Inevitably injustices arose when the common law was applied to Aboriginals who were ignorant of its tenets and who were motivated by traditional values. On one hand, as Kriewaldt J pointed out, the system did not punish persons regarded as culpable according to customary law, either because the act committed did not

---

[50] See Windeyer J's illuminating judgment in *Da Costa v The Queen* (1968) 118 CLR 186, 198.

[51] e.g. S.A.: *An Ordinance to Facilitate the Admission of the Unsworn Testimony of the Aboriginal Inhabitants*, No. 3 of 1848. See R. Smandych, 'Contemplating the Testimony of "Others"' (2004) 8 Aust. J. Leg. History 237.

[52] *R v Wadderwarri* [1958] NT 53, 101 (the unreported decisions of Kriewaldt J, cited N.T., are in the Darwin Supreme Court). See P. Brazil, 'A Matter of Theology' (1960) 34 *Aust.LJ.* 195; R. O'Regan, 'Aborigines, Melanesians and Dying Declarations' (1972) 21 *Int'l & Comp. LQ 176;* E. Eggleston, *Fear, Favour or Affection: Aborigines and the Criminal Law in Victoria, South Australia and Western Australia* (Canberra, 1976) 163–4; G. Neate, 'Dying Declarations and Customary Marriages of Australian Aborigines and Rules of Criminal Evidence' (ANU, LLB Hons Dissertation, 1979).

[53] *R v Neddy Monkey* (1861) 1 Wyatt & Webb (Vict.) 40; *R v Cobby* (1883) 4 LR (NSW) 355. See ALRC Reference on Aboriginal Customary Law, *Research Paper No. 3: The Recognition of Aboriginal Tribal Marriage—Areas of Functional Recognition* (Canberra, 1982), 48–51. Similar unreported decisions exist in the Northern Territory: Kriewaldt J, 'Application of the Criminal Law to the Aborigines of the Northern Territory of Australia' (1960) 5 *Univ. of W.Aust.L.Rev.* 1, 20.

[54] Qld. 1971, s 48; f. Qld. 1965–1967, s 41; f Qld. 1939–1946, s 34(1)(b).

fall into existing categories of crimes, or because the law was set in motion by persons insufficiently appreciative of an act's ramifications.[55] On the other hand, European law punished acts which were venial, even required, according to custom. For example, in 1966, an Aboriginal elder was convicted by a Northern Territory court of spearing a fellow member of the tribe. The elder was acting in conformity with customary law, for the victim had insulted him to the extent that he would have lost face if retribution had not been taken. The dilemma of the courts in dealing with this type of situation was expressed by Blackburn J in passing sentence:[56]

I am faced with the difficulty that on the one hand I have to enforce the law on an Aboriginal living a relatively primitive life. On the other hand, I must recognize that such Aborigines have moral standards of their own to uphold which are not necessarily the same as ours. I think in the circumstances a relatively light sentence will mark disapproval of the law both for him and other Aboriginal members of the community.

For a short period between 1939 and 1954, Western Australia legislated for the establishment of Courts of Native Affairs, which were to take into account custom in the mitigation of sentences.[57] The courts were to be composed of a magistrate, acting with the assistance of an elder of the tribe of the accused. In 1939, the criminal law of the Northern Terrtory was amended so that regard could be had to customary influence in sentences, but that provision was never proclaimed.[58]

In the period following World War II, when government policy was the assimilation of Aboriginals into white society, the prevailing opinion was against recognizing customary influences. In some jurisdictions, if customary influences could be proved to have motivated the offence, the court might take that into account in fixing penalties, despite the absence of specific statutory authority.[59] However, the courts seemed generally sceptical of the influence of custom on the criminal behaviour of Aboriginals, except in the case of Aboriginals in the remoter parts of Australia.[60] From the late 1960s and early 1970s, however, judicial and administrative practices began to respond more regularly to Aboriginal customs and traditions, in matters such as sentencing, so the likelihood of traditional punishment (pay-back) would be taken into account in fixing the penalty.[61] Against that general background of the increasing recognition of Aboriginal customs, the Australian Law Reform Commission reported in 1986 that the way forward might be to build on the best aspects of existing practice, so as to take into account

---

[55] Kriewaldt, *op.cit.*, 14. See H. Douglas, 'Justice Kriewaldt, Aboriginal Identity and the Criminal Law' (2002) 26 *Crim LJ* 204.   [56] *R v Guragi, Australian* 1 December 1966, 3, col. 2.

[57] W.A. 1905–1954, s 64 (r 1954).

[58] N.T.: Criminal Law Amendment Ordinance 1939, s 8 (r 1953).

[59] E. Eggleston, 'Aborigines and the Administration of the Criminal Law', in F. Stevens (ed.), *Racism: The Australian Experience* (Sydney, 1972), vol. 2, 92.

[60] e.g. *Williams v Porter* [1959] NT 311.

[61] e.g. *Jabaltjari v Hammersley* (1977) 15 ALR 94; *R v Jungarai* (1981) 9 NTR 30; *R v Williams* (1976) 14 SASR 1.

continuing Aboriginal adherence to various forms of customary law and tradition.[62] In the context of civil law this approach was given a considerable boost by the recognition of native title in *Mabo*. It is not, however, unproblematic in criminal law if, say, custom and tradition can be used as a cover for unacceptable practices such as the sexual abuse by older men of girls or young women.[63]

The equal application of the common law to Aboriginals also created practical problems in the administration of justice. In several early trials, accused Aboriginals had to be discharged when competent interpreters could not be found.[64] But in most cases, Aboriginals were not so fortunate. Their ignorance of the law meant that they were disadvantaged from the outset. As Starke J once put it, in a case involving the conviction of an Aboriginal for murder:[65]

It is manifest that the trial of the prisoner was attended with great difficulties, and indeed was almost impossible. He lived under the law in force in Australia, but had no conceptions of its standards. Yet by that law he had to be tried. He understood little or nothing of the proceedings or their consequences to him.

Thus Aboriginals, with their sense of communal responsibility, were often unaware that they had no responsibility for acts unless they were immediate actors or accessories.[66] Racism pervaded the system. Although indifferent to crimes committed among Aboriginals, white juries were too lenient if the accused was white and the victim Aboriginal, but manifestly harsh if the situation was reversed.[67] The administration of justice on reserves—discussed below—was also highly irregular. Officials assumed power over offences outside their jurisdiction, treated all offences summarily, imposed uneven and excessive sentences, disregarded established procedures, and punished acts such as adultery and intercourse when these were not offences outside the reserves.[68] In remote areas of Australia, justices of the peace could be biased so that judgments on Aboriginals were without firm foundation and sentences imposed were sometimes excessive.[69]

A major difficulty arose with statements by Aboriginals before or during their trials for criminal offences. The position of inferiority to which Aboriginals were

[62] Australian Law Reform Commission, *The Recognition of Aboriginal Customary Laws* (Canberra, 1986), vol. I, paras 40–46.

[63] See e.g. *Guardian* (London), 30 December 2002, 12.

[64] *R v Willie* (1885) 7 QLJ (NC) 1208; P. Corris, *Aborigines and Europeans in Western Victoria* (Australian Institute of Aboriginal Studies, Occasional Papers No. 12, 1968) 103 and the cases there incited.   [65] *Tuckiar v The King* (1934) 52 CLR 335, 349.

[66] *Bolton v Neilson* (1951) 53 WALR 48, 51.

[67] P. Hasluck, *Black Australians: A Survey of Native Policy in Western Australia 1829–1897* 2nd ed. (1970), 125; e.g. *R v Pompey* (1924) 18 QJPR 59.

[68] C. Tatz, 'Queensland's Aborigines: Natural Justice and the Rule of Law', *Australian Quarterly*, September 1963, 33; G. Nettheim (ed.), *Aborigines, Human Rights and the Law* (Sydney, 1974), 16–21.

[69] In *R v Justices of Rankine River ex P Sydney; ex P Pluto* (1962) 3 FLR 215, one JP was manager of the station on which the defendants were employed, and the second JP made racist remarks in the vicinity of the court. The case is discussed further in E. Eggleston, *op.cit.* 140. See also *Bolton v Neilson* (1951) 53 WALR 48; Slaughter, 'The Aboriginal Natives of North-West Western Australia and the Administration of Justice' (1901) 116 *Westminster Review* 411, 413.

reduced by white domination meant that they were often bewildered and intimidated during police interrogation or in the course of a trial.[70] The tendency of many Aboriginal accused was to tell questioners what they wanted to know in the hope that this would ensure the maintenance of the status quo.[71] Hence, Aboriginal accused appeared to be evasive or at worst guilty. In addition, sometimes Aboriginals could not understand what was happening. Translators were available, but this was not completely satisfactory, since Aboriginal languages could not always be used to express Western concepts.[72] 'The Stuart Case' epitomized the injustices inherent in the trial of an itinerant and illiterate Aboriginal, whose statements were accepted at face value. Stuart was convicted of murder, the main evidence against him being oral and written admissions to police officers in English. Although expert evidence was given that Stuart was only fluent in an Aboriginal dialect (a fact which seemed to be confirmed by his dock statement, described by the High Court of Australia as 'a few relatively inarticulate words which denied his guilt and alleged ill-treatment on the part of the police officers who had interrogated him'[73]), appeals to the Full Court in South Australia and to the High Court of Australia failed.

In some jurisdictions, attempts were made to minimize the difficulties. Thus, in the Northern Territory, an Aboriginal could not plead guilty to an offence unless an Aboriginal affairs department official had approved the plea and was present in court.[74] In Queensland and Western Australia, the judge had to be satisfied not only that the official had approved the guilty plea but also that the Aboriginal understood the nature of the accusation, was aware of the right to trial and, without duress or pressure of any kind, desired to plead guilty.[75] Some courts readily accepted the word of the official that the prerequisites had been complied with, while others were much stricter, holding that only in exceptional circumstances should a court approve a guilty plea, particularly if dubious police behaviour was involved.

In addition, limits were placed on the extent to which statements made by Aboriginals before the trial could be accepted in evidence in the case of a serious offence. In the Northern Territory, such a statement had to be made in the presence of an officer of the Aboriginal affairs department, which meant that the officer could render the admission nugatory by withdrawal from the police interrogation.[76] Then

---

[70] D. Thompson, *Recommendations of Policy in Native Affairs in the Northern Territory of Australia*, Commonwealth Parliamentary Paper No. 56 of 1937–38, 6.

[71] A. Elkin, 'Aboriginal Evidence and Justice in North Australia' (1947) 17 Oceania 173, 176, 179–87. See also Strehlow, 'Native Evidence and its Value' (1936) 6 *Oceania* 323; G. Dickinson, 'The Testimony of Aborigines in Law Courts in the Northern Territory' (1958) 19 *South Pacific* 17, 151.

[72] S. Wurm, 'Languages and the Law' (1963) 6 *Univ of W.Aust.L.Rev.* 1.

[73] *Stuart v The Queen* (1959) 101 CLR 1, 7. See *R v Stuart* [1959] SASR 144; K. Inglis, *The Stuart Case* (Melbourne, 1961, republished 2002). The case has been turned into a film, *Black and White* (2002).   [74] N.T. 1953–1963, s 82(b); f N.T. 1918–1953, s 58.

[75] Qld 1939–1946, s 34(2)–(3) (r 1965), f Qld 1934, s 20; W.A. 1905–1954, s 61(2)–(4) (r 1954).   [76] N.T. 1953–1963, s 82(4)(c) (r 1964); *Wilson v Porter* [1959] NT 311.

in 1976 Foster J enunciated what became known as the *Anunga* rules for police questioning: an interpreter was necessary if the suspect was not fluent in English, a 'prisoner's friend' should be present, care should be exercised in administering the caution, reasonable steps had to be taken to obtain legal assistance if requested, and there should be no questioning if the suspect was ill, drunk, or tired.[77] For a time, Queensland and Western Australia went further and excluded all pre-trial statements. Not only could they not be sought from any Aboriginal charged or suspected of an offence but furthermore, if obtained, they were not receivable in evidence.[78] The courts gave these sections broad effect: it was held that the exclusion applied to any statement which was incriminating in a material particular and that, although statements volunteered without previous inquiry were not barred, when these were made to police officers they were always suspect.[79] After 1946, a statement was admitted in evidence in Queensland if the judge was satisfied that the Aboriginal understood its meaning and that it was obtained voluntarily and without pressure of any sort.[80] The section was given a liberal construction. Any intimation of the accused's guilt fell within the exclusion, and pressure short of that which would ordinarily render a confession involuntary was held to invalidate a statement by an Aboriginal.[81] As a result, judges became almost completely dependent on the assertion of Aboriginals as to the voluntariness of their statements.

The Protective–Segregative Regime

As has been seen, in the early period of white settlement, the Aboriginals were regarded as being British subjects, with the same rights and duties as the white settlers. In the second period of white-Aboriginal relations, the law and administration were more concerned with subduing the 'wickedness' of the Aboriginals than with protecting their position as British subjects. Thus some discriminatory legislation was introduced, such as that curbing Aboriginal consumption of alcohol. Associated with this period was the frontier violence which lasted from the 1840s to the 1880s (to the 1930s in some areas), during which Aboriginals had their land expropriated and were sometimes indiscriminately killed. Then, in the closing decades of the nineteenth century and well into the twentieth century, protective–segregative legislation became a hallmark of Aboriginal policy. Prompted by the need to prevent the frontier violence and its consequences, this period was later associated with the policy of assimilation whereby Aboriginals, or

---

[77] *R v Anunga* (1976) 11 ALR 412. See also *R v Clevens* (1982) 37 ACTR 57.
[78] Qld 1939, s 34(1) (r 1946); W.A. 1905–1960, s 61(1) (repealed for Aboriginals except in the north of the state in 1963). See W.A. 1963, s 31(1) (r 1972).
[79] *Louis v The King* (1951) 53 WALR 81. See also *Thompson v Brockman* (1939) 42 WALR 36.
[80] Qld 1939–1946, s 34(1) (r 1965).
[81] *R v Lindsay* [1963] Qd R 386; *R v Kina* [1962] Qd R 139, 143; *R v Saunders* [1965] Qd R 409.

at least some of them, were to be forcibly tutored for entry into white society. One aspect of assimilation policy forms the basis of *Follow the Rabbit-Proof Fence*. Finally, the decades following the 1960s have seen the period in which discriminatory legislation has been repealed, and Aboriginal self-advancement assisted by a variety of special social, economic, and land programmes. Symbolic of the change from the protective–segregative era was the success of the 1967 referendum, which deleted the constitutional limitation on the power of the federal government in Aboriginal affairs.[82]

In the main, the protective–segregative legislation originated in a humanitarian concern for the plight of the Aboriginals. Initially, the emphasis was on providing Aboriginals with rations, blankets, and medicines and on preventing individual acts of cruelty toward them.[83] But it was soon thought that more drastic action was necessary. Legislation was thus designed to isolate Aboriginals from white exploitative influences and to protect them from their own innocence. Once this paternalistic policy was enacted, however, it became self-fulfilling and self-perpetuating. It was reinforced by Darwinian ideas about the extinction of lesser races. Controls were gradually increased so that, by the World War II, most Aborigines of full descent were confined to reserves, deprived of their civil rights and strictly controlled. In the result, although Aboriginals were British subjects, they were clearly deprived of the legal rights commensurate with that status and of their theoretical equality before the law. The outlook was pessimistic, static, and repressive. Aboriginals became passive recipients of institutional assistance, so that the racist assumptions justifying the policy were reinforced. Official policy was directed to suppressing individual and social characteristics of Aboriginal origin and to destroying indigenous social organization. As an aspect of this, the authorities in Queensland and Western Australia were given power to prohibit Aboriginal customs and practices.[84]

Essential to the implementation of the protective–segregative policy was the classification of persons as Aboriginals. The method of definition adopted was, as Sir Owen Dixon once said, 'artificial',[85] but basically it depended on a person's Aboriginal ancestry or 'blood'. Hence, the demeaning terms 'full blood', 'half caste' and 'quadroon' were commonly used in statutes to describe persons of varying Aboriginal descent. The first jurisdiction that purported to define Aboriginals in other than racial terms was the Northern Territory in 1953. It introduced the concept of 'wardship': a ward was to be any person accepted by the authorities as in need of special assistance.[86] But the definition remained basically racial. Wardship was linked to the franchise so that whites could not become wards and

---

[82] See generally G. Sawer, 'The Australian Constitution and the Australian Aborigines' (1966) 2 *Fed.L.Rev.* 17.

[83] e.g. An Act to provide for the Protection and Management of the Aboriginal Natives of Victoria 1869; Qld: Fishery Act 1881, s 13.

[84] Qld 1965–1967, s 60(2) (r 1971), f Qld 1939–1946, s 23, f Qld. 1897 to 1934, s 31(15); W.A. 1905–1960, s 67 (r 1964).   [85] *Dowling v Bowie* (1952) 86 CLR 136, 138.

[86] N.T. 1953–1963, s.14(1).

furthermore, the administration declared all Aboriginals of full descent to be wards en masse.[87] The arbitrary legislative classification of Aboriginals automatically resulted in a lowering of their status. Later, state legislation defined Aboriginals as those descended from the original Australians, rather than in terms of self-identification. Because the status of an Aboriginal depended on descent, it normally had an adhesive quality. Thus, in one case, it was held that a change in nationality could not affect it. [88] The courts became adept in dealing with degrees of Aboriginal descent,[89] but if official knowledge of a person's descent was absent, the courts were entitled to determine, and did determine, status by sight.[90]

Early reserves (or settlements) were primarily designed as a place to provide subsistence to Aboriginals deprived of their lands by the settlers.[91] Later, the reserves became central to the protective–segregative policy. Despite legislative phraseology that the reserves were to be set aside for the benefit of the Aboriginals,[92] there was never the slightest suggestion that their boundaries were negotiated between the parties as in the case of the Indian reservations in North America.[93] Instead, reserves were areas of Crown land, usually the most barren and inhospitable, designated by the government as areas where the 'Aboriginal problem' would be solved. State Aboriginal affairs departments were empowered to remove Aboriginals to reserves, to confine them there, and to transfer them from one reserve to another.[94] In Queensland, for a time in Western Australia, and during the depression in New South Wales, Aboriginals were systematically rounded up and confined to reserves.[95] Once most Aboriginals were within the reserves, the powers were used on a more selective basis. For example, the power of transferral became a means of discouraging Aboriginals from seeking change in the existing system. In Queensland, Palm Island became notorious as the destination of potential 'troublemakers'.

Despite the draconian nature of the powers of removal, confinement, and transferral, the courts gave the Aboriginal Affairs Departments a virtual carte blanche in their use. For example, in 1951 Fred Waters, an Aboriginal and North Australian Workers' Union activist, was taken into custody and confined to a reserve. An appeal to Fullagar J of the High Court of Australia failed.[96] The court concluded that it lacked jurisdiction to hear the appeal, but went on to hold that there was no abuse of power in the legal sense in that the power of removal could

---

[87] s *ibid.*, 14(2); *Raabe v Wellington* [1957] NT 375, 381; *Namatjira v Raabe* (1959) 100 CLR 664, 667–9. See also C. Tatz, 'Commonwealth Aboriginal Policy', *Australian Q.*, December 1964, 52.

[88] *Dempsey v Rigg* [1914] St R Qd 245.

[89] *Branch v Sceats* (1903) 20 WN (NSW) 41; *Ex p William* (1910) 27 WN (NSW) 147.

[90] *Steele v Starr* (1912) 29 WN (NSW) 82; *Amesbury v Copeland* [1921] SASR 485; *Williams v Wright* [1943] SASR 301.   [91] e.g. S.A.: Waste Lands Act 1842; Vict.: Land Act 1869, s 6.

[92] e.g. W.A. 1886, s 6(6).   [93] *Milirrpum v Nabalco Pty Ltd* (1971) 17 FLR 141, 225.

[94] Qld 1965–1967, s 34 (r 1971), f Qld 1939 to 1946, s 22, f 1987 to 1934, ss 9–10; S.A. 1934–1939, s 17 (r 1962), f S.A. 1911, s 17; W.A. 1905–1954, ss 13–14 (r 1954); N.T. 1953–1960, s 17 (r 1961), f N.T. 1918–1953, s 6(1).

[95] C. Rowley, *Outcasts in a White Australia* (Ringwood, 1972) 83, 85.

[96] *Waters v Commonwealth* (1951) 82 CLR 188.

be based not only on the welfare of the individual Aboriginal, but also on the interests of other Aborigines and, if need be, on the general interests of the community. The unsympathetic tenor of the judgment and the unquestioning acceptance of the official line can be gleaned from the court's conclusion on this point:

I think that the immediate occasion of the plaintiff's removal most probably did lie in the part taken by him in the events of the 12th February [a protest strike at Bagot Reserve near Darwin], but I think also that for some time before that date, there had been disturbances among the natives at and about Darwin, in the course of which they had been incited not to work and subjected to threats if they continued their work...I think it impossible for any court to say that there was any abuse of power here *or even that the Director's decision was unwise or unjust.* (My emphasis)

In effect, the reserves were a microcosm of totalitarian states. The almost unlimited power of reserve authorities has been adequately described elsewhere.[97] Nothing was too trivial to escape regulation. Penalties could be imposed by a court constituted by the reserve authority for insubordination, indecent behaviour, disorderly conduct, refusal to work, personal untidiness and uncleanliness, and acts subversive to good order.[98] A reserve Aboriginal could have his individuality and dignity stripped from him; for example, his mail could be examined and his home taken from him.[99] The courts refused to interfere with the exercise of these powers, asserting that the nature of the 'Aboriginal problem' required that the authorities be given wide rein to solve it.[100]

Segregation of reserve Aboriginals was guaranteed by 'prohibitive, penal and discriminatory'[101] provisions in all jurisdictions which made it unlawful for persons other than officials or Aboriginals resident on the reserve to enter the reserve without authority.[102] Authority was almost always refused to outsiders, including academics. In the result, Aboriginals were unable to visit places where they may have spent most of their lives, and reserve residents were denied contact with close relatives. *Ogilvie v Lowe*[103] is illustrative. There the defendant was the non-Aboriginal husband of an Aboriginal woman (authorized to reside on the reserve) who had come to the reserve to gather wood for winter. In holding that the defendant was unlawfully on the reserve, the court found that there was no provision in the legislation or the regulations whereby a permit could be granted for him to be on the reserve.

---

[97] C. Tatz, 'Aborigines—Equality or Inequality?' (1966) 38 *Australian Q.* 73; G. Nettheim, *Outlawed: Queensland's Aborigines and Islanders and the Rule of Law* (Sydney, 1973).
[98] e.g. Qld: Aboriginals Regulations of 1945.
[99] *Aborigines Welfare Board v Saunder* [1961] NSWR 917.
[100] e.g. *Bray v Milera* [1935] SASR 210, 215–16.
[101] *Myers v Simpson* (1965) 6 FLR 440, 442.
[102] N.S.W. 1909–1963, s 8(1) (r 1969); Qld 1965–1967, s 60 (r 1971), Qld 1939–1946, s 31(1), f Qld 1897–1934, s 11; S.A. 1962–1968, s 20(1) (r 1972), f S.A. 1934–1939, s 20, f S.A. 1911, s 20; W.A. 1963, s.20 (r 1972), f W.A. 1905–1960, s 15; N.T. 1953–1963, s 45 (r 1965), f N.T. 1918–1953, s 19.   [103] [1963] VR 225.

Other legislative provisions helped perpetuate the segregation of Aboriginals from other Australians. From an early date, whites could be declared vagrants if they associated with Aboriginals and were unable to give an adequate account of their means of support.[104] Whites were prohibited from being near a place where Aboriginals were camped or congregated,[105] although the courts construed these provisions narrowly, so that all contact between the races was not prevented.[106] The authorities also had the power to remove Aboriginals camped in the vicinity of towns, and to declare towns as areas where it was unlawful for Aboriginals to be.[107] In Western Australia, it was an offence for a non-Aboriginal to lodge with an Aboriginal.[108] Limitations were also placed on the association between white males and Aboriginal women. To an extent this may have been justified to prevent exploitation, but it was indefensible to make marriage between Aboriginals and non-Aboriginals dependent on the consent of the authorities.[109] Bureaucratically applied, such provisions caused great hardship.[110] In part the aim of such provisions was to deal with the 'problem' of mixed descent Aboriginals, to which we now turn.

Assimilation Policy and Discriminatory Legislation

The protective-segregative policy dealt with Aboriginals of full descent. It isolated them, one aim being to prevent sexual relations between Europeans and Aboriginals. However, these occurred, and the growing number of mixed race children was seen as a moral and social problem which government policy needed to address. The ultimate aim was that they would somehow merge with the rest of the population. The law furthered this assimilation policy. Officials in charge of Aboriginal affairs were made guardians of all Aboriginal children and were empowered to override the wishes of Aboriginal parents.[111] Aboriginal children

---

[104] N.S.W.: An Act for the Prevention of Vagrancy, 6 Wm. IV No 6, s 2. See also Qld: The Vagrants, Gaming and Other Offences Acts 1931–1971, s 4(1)(ii) (r 1971).

[105] Qld: 1965–1967, s 60(23) (r 1971), Qld. 1939–1946, s 30, f Qld 1901, s 16; W.A. 1905–1954, s 40 (r.1954); N.T. 1953–1963, s 51 (r 1964), N.T. 1918–1953, s 51.

[106] *Dean v Watts* (1910) 12 W A L R 190 (1910); *Hodge v Needle* (1947) 49 WALR 1 rev'd (1947) 20 ALJ 499.

[107] N.S.W. 1909–1963, s 14 (r 1969); Qld 1939–1946, s 21 (r 1965), f Qld. 1901, s 17; W.A. 1905–1954, ss 41–43 (r 1954), f W.A. 1886, s 43.

[108] W.A.: Aboriginal Affairs Planning Authority Act 1972, s 65(2).

[109] Qld 1939–1946, s 29, 19 (r 1965), f Qld. 1934, s 9; S. A. 1934–1939, s.34a (r 1962); W.A. 1905–1960, s 43 (r 1963); s 46 (r 1946); N.T. 1953–1960, ss 64, 67 (r 1961), f N.T. 1918–1953, ss 53, 45.

[110] C. Hughes, 'The Marriage of Mick and Gladys: A Discretion Without an Appeal', in B. Schaffer and D. Corbett (eds.), *Decisions:Case Studies in Australian Administration* (Sydney, 1965). See also R. Bartlett, 'Racism and the Constitutional Protection of Native Title in Australia' (1995) 25 *Univ. of W. Aust.L. Rev.* 127, 128–30.

[111] N.S.W. 1909–1936, s 13A (r 1940); Qld 1939–1946, s 18(1) (r 1965); S.A. 1934–1939, s 10(1) (r 1962), f S.A. 1911, s 10; W.A. 1905–1960, s 8 (r.1963); N.T. 1953–1960, s 24 (r 1961); f N.T. 1918–1953, s 7.

with light skins were removed from their parents and placed in institutions or with white foster parents, as in *Follow the Rabbit-Proof Fence*. After these specific provisions were repealed, the policy of removal continued until the 1960s under general child-welfare legislation.

If there was a theoretical possibility of resort to law to challenge a removal it was not invoked. When the issue was finally litigated before the Federal Court in 2002—an attempt by two of those removed to sue the federal government for the pain and suffering, including serious psychological harm, loss of enjoyment of life and loss of cultural heritage—the judges emphasized the difficulties because decades had passed since the claimants' removal.[112] Although much of the claimants' evidence was accepted, it was not possible to establish that at the relevant time there was a general policy in force in the Northern Territory of indiscriminately removing Aboriginal children, irrespective of personal circumstances. Moreover, neither claimant could establish that consent for their removal had been refused by a parent or other responsible adult. Not only were there these gaps in the evidence, but it was held that the statute of limitations barred the common law claims for breach of duty and false imprisonment, given that the Commonwealth would suffer significant prejudice in defending the case by reason of the delay in starting proceedings. As to breach of fiduciary duty, the court held that there was no basis to such a claim.

Consistent with the policy of assimilation, provision was made to exempt from the effect of the protective–segregative legislation Aboriginals considered sufficiently 'advanced' to enter white society. But the exemption was always at the discretion of the Aboriginal Affairs Department and revocable at will. In Queensland, it could even be subject to the continued management of the Aboriginal's money and property by the administration.[113] The demeaning nature of these provisions is reflected in Western Australia's Native (Citizenship Rights) Act 1944–1964.[114] Under that Act, Aboriginals seeking exemption had to satisfy a Native (Citizenship Rights) Board, whose members included at least one local dignitary that, for the previous two years, they had 'dissolved tribal and native associations' except with close relatives; that they were industrious and of good behaviour and reputation; that they were capable of managing their own affairs; that they could speak and understand English; and that they were not suffering from leprosy, syphilis, or similar diseases. These assertions had to be attested by two 'respectable' citizens.

The protective–segregative policy was accompanied by a vast array of other discriminatory provisions. Undoubtedly some measures benefited Aboriginals.

---

[112] *Cubillo v Commonwealth of Australia* [2001] FCA 1213. See J. Clarke, 'Case Note' (2001) 25 *Melb.ULR* 218; T. Hammond, 'The "Stolen Generation"—Finding a Fiduciary Duty' *Murdoch U.Electronic JL*, vol. 5, No. 2, June 1998. cf. successful criminal injuries claims when children were in institutions or foster homes: C. Cunneen & J. Grix, 'The Stolen Generations and Individual Criminal Victimisation' (2003) 14 *Current Issues in Crim.J.* 306.

[113] N.S.W. 1909–1963, s 18c (r 1969); Qld 1939–1946, s 5(3) (r 1965), f Qld 1897–1934, s 33; S.A. 1934–1939, s 11a; N.T. 1953–1963, ss 30–37 (r 1964), f N.T. 1918–1953, s 3A.

[114] Repealed 1971. See also *Re Dingle* (1962) 3 FLR 226.

Thus, persons assaulting Aboriginals were subject to summary trial;[115] authorities were able to take legal proceedings on behalf of Aboriginals;[116] whites defrauding Aboriginals by trick or misrepresentation were guilty of an offence;[117] Aboriginals were assured of a fair return for their paintings and drawings;[118] Aboriginal children were regarded as legitimate even though their parents were married according to customary law;[119] and survivors of an Aboriginal dying intestate were not prejudiced in the disposition of the estate by the absence of a formal marriage.[120]

   Two provisions of particular note concern alcohol and employment. There can be no denying that alcohol has had a catastrophic effect on many Aboriginals. Its abuse by Aboriginals resulted importantly from the intense impact to which Aboriginal society was being subjected. In view of the obvious effects, restrictions on the consumption of alcohol predated the protective–segregative period by several decades.[121] Initially, the supply of alcohol to Aboriginals was penalized, but later it became an offence for Aboriginals to possess alcohol or to be in places where alcohol was sold.[122] Heavy penalties were imposed on those, mainly white publicans, who breached the prohibitions.[123] But there seems to be no evidence that such action had any effect in alleviating the Aboriginal plight; this is not surprising, since the basic cause of the problem went untouched. Exploitation of Aboriginals by white employers was also an early legislative concern. The first legislation was passed to govern the employment of Aboriginals in the pearl-shell fishing industry and on ships.[124] These provisions were later incorporated into general legislation and extended to cover all Aboriginal employment.[125] Under them, employment could be of only limited duration and subject to conditions approved by the authorities. Protection easily became oppression; once an Aboriginal entered regulated employment it became an offence for him to leave it.[126] It was also unlawful to induce an Aboriginal to leave regulated employment: for many years, the authorities used this, and other powers, to stifle the spread of trade unionism among Aboriginals.[127]

---

[115] W.A. 1905–1947, s 63 (r.1954).   [116] W.A. 1886, s 17 (r 1905).

[117] W.A. 1905–1947, s 66 (r 1954).   [118] N.T. 1953–1963, Part VA.

[119] Qld 1971, s 49(1), f 1965–1967, s 43(1), f 1939–1946, s 19(2).

[120] e.g. N.T., Interstate Aboriginals (Distribution of Estates) Ordinance 1961–1967.

[121] e.g. N.S.W., Supply of Liquors to Aborigines Prevention Act 1867.

[122] e.g. W.A. 1905–1960, s 49(2), 50 (r 1963).

[123] *Coleman v Dodd* (1923) 23 SR (NSW) 599; *Amesbury v Copeland* [1928] SASR 485, appeal dismissed (1923) 32 CLR 616; *Brennan v Loxton* (1947) 49 WALR 95; *Wilson v Porter* [1959] NT 311; *Camfoo v McEvoy* (1962) 3 FLR 8. cf. *Dowling v Bowie* (1952) 86 CLR 136.

[124] W.A., Pearl Shell Fishery Regulation Act 1873, formerly Pearling Act 1870; Qld, Pearl-Shell and Beche-de-mer Fishery Act 1881; Native Labourers' Protection Act 1884.

[125] e.g. Qld 1939–1946, s 14 (r 1965), f Qld 1897–1934, ss 12–13, 15–16; W.A. 1905–1954, ss 19–20, 22–28, 31–32 (r 1954), f W.A. 1886, 2; N.T., Ward's Employment Ordinance 1953–1964, 4 (r 1971), f N.T. 1918–1953, Part IV. See C. Rowley, *The Remote Aborigines* (Ringwood, 1972) chs 11–12.   [126] W.A. 1905–1954, s 27 (r 1954).

[127] *McKenna v Fletcher* (1947) 20 ALJ 498. See also *Daniel v Bolton* (1969) 12 FLR 101; W. Stanner, *After the Dreaming* (Sydney, 1968), 64.

But if some of the discriminatory measures were protective in nature, others were based on nothing more than a racist belief that Aboriginals were inherently inferior in ability to other Australians. Queensland, Western Australia, and the Northern Territory denied the franchise to Aboriginals[128] and the federal government, under the misapprehension that s 41 of the Australian constitution required it, followed suit.[129] Federal social welfare benefits were not payable to Aboriginals covered by the protective–segregative statutes,[130] although in 1959 that changed and only nomadic Aboriginals were denied benefits.[131] In Queensland from 1901, reserve authorities could direct the apportionment of an Aboriginal's wages among other Aboriginals.[132] In 1939, it became mandatory for reserve authorities to undertake the management of Aboriginals' property, whereupon they lost the power to dispose of it.[133] An aspect of this was the notorious trust account scheme, whereby the earnings of Aboriginals went into a bank account to which they had access only with the consent of the authorities. Similar management could be undertaken in the Northern Territory, but in Western Australia and South Australia the power existed only with the consent of the person.[134]

A host of other discriminatory measures existed at one time or the other. Aboriginals could not possess guns except with special permission;[135] they, but not whites, could be publicly whipped;[136] their movement outside Australia was restricted;[137] they were subject to compulsory medical examination and hospitalization;[138] and in Western Australia, special courts were constituted to deal summarily with Aboriginals charged with all but the most serious offences.[139] As late as the 1970s an objectionable number of such measures remained in Queesland: Aboriginals on some reserves could be denied access to alcohol and

---

[128] Qld, Election Act 1915–1965, s.11, 11A (r.1965), f Election Acts 1885–1905, s 6; W.A., Electoral Act 1907–1957 s 18(e) (r 1962), f Constitution Act Amendment Act 1893, ss 12, 21. In the Northern Territory, Aboriginals were excluded under the Electoral Regulations.

[129] Electoral Act 1918–1961 (Commonwealth) s 39 (r 1962), f Franchise Act 1902 (Common wealth) s 4. *Report from the Select Committee on Voting Rights of Aborigines (House of Representatives)*, Commonwealth Parliamentary Paper No.1 of 1961, 38 ff.

[130] Social Services Act 1947–1958, ss 19(2), 86(3) (r 1959), f Invalid and Old Age Pensions Act 1908–1946s, s 16(1)(c), 21(1)(b); Maternity Allowance Act 1912–1944, s 6(2).

[131] Social Services Act 1947–1965, s 137A (r 1966). This had always been the position with child endowment; Social Services Act 1947–1965, s 97 (r 1966), f Child Endowment Act 1941–1942, s 15. See Joint Committee of Public Accounts, Seventy-Third Report, *The Department of Social Services*, Commonwealth Parliamentary Paper No. 221 of 1964–1965, at 61–2.   [132] Qld 1901, s 13.

[133] Qld 1939–1946, s 16. After 1965, management was appealable, Qld 1971, ss 27–29 (r 1971).

[134] N.T. 1953–1960, ss 25–26 (r 1961), f N.T. 1918–1953, s 29A; W.A. 1905–1960, s 35 (r 1964); S.A., Community Welfare Act 1972, s 91, f S.A. 1962–1968, s 29, f S.A. 1911, s 35.

[135] W.A. 1905, ss 47–50; N.T. 1918, Part V.

[136] W.A., Criminal Code, ss 670, 680 (r 1964).

[137] C., Migration Act 1958–1971, s 64 (r 1973), f Emigration Act 1910. There were also restrictions on intra- and interstate movement, e.g. W.A. 1905–1960, s 10 (r 1963).

[138] N.S.W. 1909–1963, s 14A (r 1969); Qld 1939–1946, s 20 (r 1968), f S.A. 1936–1939, ss 25–26, f S.A. 1911, ss 25, 26; W.A. 1905–1954, s 17 (r 1954).

[139] W.A. Aboriginal Offenders Act 1883–1893. See C. Tatz, 'Aborigines and Civil Law', in P. Hanks and B. Keon-Cohen (eds), *Aborigines and the Law* (Sydney, 1984), 109–111.

Aboriginals could also be employed at lower rates of pay than would normally obtain.[140] In addition, once the management of an Aboriginal's property was assumed with his or her consent it needed to be relinquished only if the authorities were satisfied that it would not be detrimental to the person or his or her family.[141]

Conclusion

The successful working of the civil law depends on individuals knowing and taking advantage of their rights. In ordinary circumstances, this is difficult enough because of the problems discussed in Part I of the book of obtaining access to justice. To have expected Aboriginals to exercise their legal rights under such a system was preposterous. Not surprisingly, the number of civil cases brought by Aboriginals was infinitesimal.[142] On the other hand, in criminal cases, where only the state, and not the accused needed to have the knowledge and initiative, Aboriginals featured prominently. Even when Aboriginal issues were before the courts there was no guarantee of an understanding hearing. In one case, the customs of Aboriginals were described as uncivilized and their laws as nugatory.[143] 'The assertion of vague rites and ceremonies' could not interfere with the application of British law, said another court.[144] As late as 1930, a frontier judge asserted that 'retributive justice was all that the savage mind could understand'.[145] In a well-known case involving the trial of an Aboriginal for the murder of a white police officer, the same judge was severely reprimanded by the High Court of Australia for denying the accused a fair trial by distorting his defence, by failing to warn the jury of the difficulties in translated Aboriginal evidence, and by transforming the trial into a vindication of the victim's character.[146] Of course, there were sympathetic judges, although their pronouncements were tinged with paternalism.[147]

To a large extent, the courts were reflecting the prejudices of the time: Aboriginals were readily assumed to be persons of lesser intelligence[148] although

---

[140] Qld 1971, s 34; Aborigines Regulations 1972, s 69. The 1971 Queensland Act is subject to detailed scrutiny in G. Nettheim, *op cit.*   [141] Qld 1971, ss 37–47.

[142] *Ex p West* (1861) II Legge 1475 was one nineteenth century example. *Waters v Commonwealth* (1951) 82 CLR 188 and *Mitchell v Australian Broadcasting Commission* (1958) 60 WALR 38 are mid-twentieth century exceptions.   [143] *R v Cobby* (1883) 4 LR (NSW) 355, 356.

[144] *R v Neddy Monkey* (1861) 1 Wyatt & Webb (Vict) 40, 41. In respect of the non-recognition of traditional marriages, see also: J. Crawford, P. Hennessy & M. Fisher, 'Aboriginal Customary Law: Proposals for Recognition', in K. Hazlehurst (ed.), *Ivory Scales: Black Australia and the Law* (Sydney, 1987), 196–7.

[145] Quoted in A. Elkin, 'Australian Aborigines and White Relations—A Personal Record' (1962) 48 *Royal Australian Historical Society, J of Proceedings*, Part 3, 208, 219.

[146] *Tuckiar v The King* (1934) 52 CLR 335. See P. Dakin, 'Murder and Mystery at the Top End' (1996) 31(5) *Australian Lawyer* 9.

[147] *Dempsey v Rigg* [1914] St R Qd 245, 248; *Australian Workers' Union v Abbey* (1944) 53 CAR 212, 215 (1944); *Bolton v Neilson* (1951) 53 WALR 48, 50. See also *Re Mathew, deceased; The Trustees Executors and Agency Co. Ltd v Mathew* [1951] VLR 226.

[148] e.g. *R v Smith* (1906) 6 SR (NSW) 85.

Aboriginals of mixed descent, because of their 'white blood', were more highly regarded.[149] As late as 1970, an appellate court considered the obscenity of the phrase 'fucking boong', which had been used in the public performances of a play. The court focused on the obscenity of the adjective and did not even make passing reference to the grossly derogatory character of the word 'boong' when used to describe Aboriginals.[150] The failure of the courts when considering Aboriginal questions stemmed also from judicial philosophy. The common law is concentrated on the notion of formal equality even where this does not produce substantive equality. Thus concessions to Aboriginal culture and background were difficult to incorporate. As has been seen, Aboriginal evidence was excluded and Aboriginal marriages went unrecognised. Sentencing was the only important instance where Aboriginal background was considered, but this was hardly an exception for sentencing has never been regarded as part of the substantive law. Furthermore, historically the common law has disapproved of judicial activism. Deference was accorded to the legislative solution of the 'Aboriginal problem'.[151] The full bench of the Commonwealth Conciliation and Arbitration Commission expressed the attitude in modern form in the decision mandating payment of equal wages for Aboriginal pastoral workers:[152]

Although what we do in the exercise of our powers may result in social changes, and may result in the Aborigines moving from one life to another, we are not social engineers nor can we deal with the whole spectrum of aboriginal life. We can do no more than to attempt to achieve a just result in an industrial situation. We will not ignore the consequences of our acts, including what may happen to aborigines employed on stations, but we cannot attempt to mould a policy of social welfare for those people in a way a government can.

Yet this approach carried over unnecessarily as well to matters of pure common law. The Gove Land Rights Case, which denied Aboriginals any land rights, demonstrated the reluctance of the courts to take a bold approach to the issue of native title.[153] Aboriginals had to wait another twenty years until *Mabo*.

As for the legislative solution, a century of effort was without beneficial result. On the contrary, it shattered Aboriginal self-confidence and society, and caused many Aboriginals to become passive recipients of institutional assistance. This, in turn, confirmed the need for the existence of the system and greater repression became justified. Aboriginal affairs bureaucracies acquired a momentum of their own, which made it more difficult for new initiatives to be taken. Again, deficiencies in legal philosophy contributed. Legislators accepted the simplistic Austinian theory of law as a command, so that change was believed to come by direction from above. In this framework, Aboriginal participation was immaterial. From

---

[149] *Ex P Willan* (1910) 27 WN (NSW) 147, 148.
[150] *Bradbury v Staines, ex p. Staines* [1970] QdR 76.
[151] e.g. *Hodge v Needle* (1947) 49 WALR 1, 9.
[152] *Re the Cattle Station Industry (Northern Territory) Award* 1951 (1966) 113 CAR 651, 656.
[153] *Milirrpum v Nabalco Pty Ltd* (1971) 17 FLR 141; see J. Hookey, 'The Gove Land Rights Case: A Judicial Dispensation for the Taking of Aboriginal Lands in Australia' (1972) 5 *Fed.L.Rev.* 85.

the 1960s, however, it became generally accepted that social change would only result from Aboriginal participation. Statutory controls were progressively repealed; Aboriginal initiative was fostered.[154] Although legislation relating to Aboriginal affairs failed in the past, statutory law now became a positive source of social change.

Statutes, as unequivocal declarations of public policy, can influence public opinion and can have a modernizing and innovative impact. The prejudiced views which Australians had of Aboriginals were undoubtedly reinforced by the protective–segregative and assimilation legislation. In the same manner, legislation from the 1960s began to have a positive effect on the outlook and behaviour of white Australians. Statutes protecting Aboriginal cave-drawings, artifacts, and sacred sites, as well as having the immediate result of deterring vandals, also led to an appreciation of Aboriginal culture.[155] So too with statutes prohibiting discrimination: public opinion was moulded by legislation which gave support to those who did not wish to discriminate but who felt compelled to do so by social pressure. Formal measures removing the remnants of the protective–segregative and assimilation period, protecting cultural objects and sacred sites, and asserting formal Aboriginal equality were, in themselves, inadequate. The more difficult task was to promote substantive equality by social and economic reforms. The federal government began making annual grants to the states for promoting Aboriginal health, education, and housing.[156] Royalties from the exploitation of minerals were in some cases paid into trust funds for Aboriginal welfare. And Aboriginal land rights were recognized. But the story of law's facilitative role, as opposed to its destructive phase, must be read elsewhere.

---

[154] e.g. Aboriginal Enterprises (Assistance) Act 1968 (Commonwealth).

[155] Vict.: Archaeological and Aboriginal Relics Preservation Act 1972; Qld: Aboriginal Relics Preservation Act 1967; S.A.: Aboriginal and Historic Relics Preservation Act 1967; N.T.: Natural and Historical Objects Preservation Ordinance 1960. These, and later statutes, are discussed in ALRC Reference on Aboriginal Customary Law, *Research Paper No. 5: Aboriginal Customary Law: Traditional and Modern Distributions of Property* (Sydney, 1982), 30–31. See also *Foster v Mountford* (1976) 14 ALR 71.   [156] States Grants (Aboriginal Advancement) Act 1968 was the first.

9

Law and Economic Development: Credit and Security in South and South-East Asia

Perhaps the most serious aftershock from Asia's 1997–98 financial crisis has been a growing burden of bad debt that threatens the region's banks and national economies. Private estimates suggest that nonperforming loans now total a staggering $2 trillion—equivalent to almost 30 percent of the region's gross domestic product. Yet governments have yet to recognize the full extent of the problem ... [M]any banks would be insolvent if their balance sheets reflected the true value of their loan portfolios.... Worse still, bad debt is dampening economic growth: capital that could be used productively is tied up in defaulted borrowers ... [S]uch banks could alleviate the sting by acting quickly, since the value of debt recovery in Asia—already low as a result of legal systems that favor borrowers—falls sharply over time.[1]

The crisis in debt recovery in many countries in the south and south-east Asia region has had profound implications for their economies and economic institutions. But it also has ramifications for the workings of the law. At a general level the crisis threatens the rule of law. Respect for law and legal institutions must suffer if the backlog of debt recovery cases leads to delays of many years in access to the courts. Nor can respect for lawful ways of doing things be enhanced if the powerful can defer their obligations to repay credit by exerting direct or indirect pressure on banks and bank officials. Coupled with the specific changes which could be made to make the law relating to credit allocation and debt recovery work better are broader changes in commercial law. These range from stronger corporate governance measures to reduce perverse influences on credit allocation and recovery decisions; more varied forms of security and their extra-judicial enforcement; and new laws on business reconstruction and insolvency. However, the solution does not lie simply in changes in the law.

Effective credit allocation and debt recovery are central to the proper functioning of an economy. Their achievement can be measured in terms of the goals of economic efficiency and social justice. Law has a role in the realization of both goals. For example, law may facilitate more economically efficient decisions about allocation by giving credit providers access to better information about potential

---

[1] L. Berger, G. Nast, & C. Raubach, 'Fixing Asia's Bad-Debt Mess', *McKinsey Q.*, 2002, No. 4, 139–40.

borrowers. Likewise it may further social justice by making it unlawful for credit providers to act unconscionably or to discriminate unjustifiably in decisions about allocation. It is with debt recovery that law has an especially crucial role: in general terms it can assist creditors to monitor loans effectively and, in the event of default, can ensure that rights to debt recovery and security (collateral) can be readily exercised.

Debt recovery is an area where there can be disagreement about goals. One aspect is the issue of how best to achieve economic efficiency. Traditionally the assumption made in many market economies has been that the most economically efficient course is for creditors to have the legal right to recover their money relatively straightforwardly when a business borrower defaults. If a creditor chooses to exercise this right, the assumption continues, the money (or at least some of it) can be recovered and allocated to another, and it is hoped more successful, borrower.[2] Arguably, however, the more economically efficient decision in the long term may be for a creditor not to seek immediate recovery on default with the very strong possibility that the borrower will have to go out of business, but rather to provide a defaulting borrower with a breathing space in which it can seek to regain its position as a viable enterprise. For this reason the law in recent years in some countries has enhanced the mechanisms for baring creditors' remedies for a period after a borrower is in difficulty to enable it to restructure its operations and in particular its debt.[3]

Another area of disagreement about goals concerns the balance between economic efficiency and social policy. For over a century in some developed economies insolvency law has given employees a preference so that they can recover their unpaid wages when a company becomes insolvent.[4] In some jurisdictions creditors' remedies are limited in the case of consumer defaulters, who must be given an opportunity to reschedule their debt.[5] But there are relatively few other instances in developed countries where social policy has been given a primacy over economic efficiency in debt recovery; the assumption is that economic efficiency is good social policy. In developing countries, as we will see, social policy has been more regularly invoked to justify controls over credit allocation and debt recovery.

Credit allocation and debt recovery are deficient in all economies. Through the decades economic recession has exposed to public gaze the allocation of credit to uses which were not economically efficient and which were difficult to justify on social grounds. Debts have had to be rescheduled or written off where enterprises

---

[2] e.g. World Bank, *Principles and Guidelines for Effective Insolvency and Creditor Rights Systems*, excerpt in (2003) 1 *World Bank LR* 627.

[3] See 11 USC §§101–1330 (1988) (Title 11 of the US Bankruptcy Code); Enterprise Act 2002 (UK); Corporate Law Reform Act (1992) (Australia); Bankruptcy & Insolvency Act RSC ch. B-3, div. 1 (amended 1992) (Canada).

[4] See, *National Westminster Bank plc* v. *Spectrum Plus Ltd.* [2005] UKHL 41. The provision was followed in common law jurisdictions. e.g. Presidency Towns Insolvency Act 1909 (India), s 49.

[5] See, e.g., I. Ramsay, *Consumer Protection* (London, 1989), 360–1; C. Scott & J. Black, *Cranston's Consumers and the Law*, 3rd edn (London, 2000), 276–83.

have been unable to repay and security has proved inadequate. The problems have been acute in developing countries. The viability of many banks and other credit providers such as development institutions has been threatened by their portfolio of bad debts. In some cases an unfortunate upshot has been that credit providers have become more risk averse and reluctant to lend because of their experiences with bad debts. Investment in government bonds is a safer bet. This coupled with the inability to lend when existing borrowers fail to repay has no doubt choked off new, advantageous investment. It probably has also inclined credit providers to lend only to those able to offer security like land, thus perpetuating social inequalities.

It could not be expected that the problems associated with credit allocation and debt recovery are applicable uniformly across the south and south-east Asian region. A socialist country in transition such as Vietnam is in a quite different position from other countries in the region.[6] Similarly, the approach in small countries such as Cambodia and Laos will vary from that in massive jurisdictions like India and Indonesia. Clearly the economically successful like Singapore do not face the difficulties of their neighbours and the spotlight is not on them. As far as the law is concerned, the differing legal traditions in the region cannot be neglected,[7] although this does not seem to weigh as heavily as might be expected in discussions of legal reform. With these caveats what follows is a tentative attempt to tie together the threads of the law relating to credit and debt in some of the countries in south and south-east Asia. As will become clear, corporate governance and insolvency are dealt with only incidentally, although they too bear heavily on the problem.

Law's Context

The first hint of morning light has not yet appeared over the western Indian state of Gujarat when Shardaben Parmar, a landless labourer, sets off to deliver her small bucket of milk to a collection centre in Zarola, a village 2 km away...

Mrs Parmar, 35, has 1.5 litres of milk, collected from her two buffalo. It is a small amount, but the 20 rupees (30p) she earns from selling her milk every morning and evening is crucial for her survival. Her husband died a few months ago, leaving her with three children to raise. Aside from the milk money, her only source of income is from working in

---

[6] J. Gillespie, 'Transplanted Company Law: An Ideological and Cultural Analysis of Market-Entry in Vietnam' (2002) 51 *ICLQ* 641, 646–9, 657 ff.

[7] The Indian sub-continent, Malaysia, and Singapore are basically common law jurisdictions, although Sri Lanka is officially a Roman–Dutch system. Thailand and Indonesia are basically civil law systems, with German influences predominant in the case of the first and Dutch in the case of the last. The civil law system in the Philippines was overlaid during the period of US rule. See, e.g., K. Redden, *Modern Legal Systems Cyclopedia: Asia* (Buffalo, 1990); Poh-Ling Tan (ed.), *Asian Legal Systems* (Sydney, 1997); A. Guterman & R. Brown (eds), *Commercial Laws of East Asia* (Hong Kong, 1997); ASEAN Law Association, *ASEAN Legal Systems* (Singapore, 1995); J. Santos, 'Common Law Elements in the Philippine Mixed Legal System' (2000) 2 *Aust.J. Asian Law* 34.

the fields during the planting and harvest seasons. 'I can get credit from the shop owner on the basis of this milk money', she says.[8]

Throughout this book it is taken as axiomatic that in any society law works against a background of social factors. Unless this context is taken into account, the workings of the law will not be properly understood and efforts at reform will be misguided. One aspect is that a problem might not lie in inadequate laws or legal procedures but in the way law is enforced or operates in a society. Thus it is well known that in Japan litigation is relatively rare and parties seek to avoid court.[9] This could mean that it is more likely that when a borrower is having difficulty repaying, a Japanese bank may not invoke the very wide powers conferred on it by the loan agreement. Rather the borrower might receive visits from the bank and find its freedom of action curtailed as the bank prescribes a remedial course. Whether this has also resulted in Japanese banks implicitly promising to rescue troubled but viable firms—the conventional wisdom now under fierce challenge— is beyond the scope of the present inquiry.[10]

Attempts have been made to characterize legal systems along a spectrum from pro-creditor to pro-debtor.[11] The same has been done for social systems.[12] The combination of the two—the extent to which a particular society is either pro-creditor or pro-debtor in either or both the law and its context—could be represented graphically, although placing particular jurisdictions with any degree of accuracy would be well nigh impossible. What, for example, is meant by 'pro-creditor'? English law is generally thought of as pro-creditor, but while this is true in relation to bank creditors, it is not the case with small trade creditors, who face many difficulties compared with large creditors. Proposals have been advanced over the years to redress the balance between the two classes of creditor.[13] The same is true with the term 'pro-debtor'. In some countries in the region a combination of legal and social factors means that a lot of borrowers avoid repayment. Yet a problem of characterization arises because it is often a certain type of debtor (notably the elite and large organizations) who primarily benefits.[14] If such qualifications are borne in mind, however, the pro-creditor/pro-debtor dimensions of a legal system and its context are a useful heuristic device. Before proceeding

[8] A. Kazmin, 'Gandhi and the Milk of Indian Self-Reliance', *Financial Times*, 24 August 2000, 15.

[9] e.g. C. Goodman, *The Rule of Law in Japan* (The Hague, 2003), 229 ff; Y. Hasebe, 'Civil Justice Reform: Access, Cost and Expedition. The Japanese Perspective', in A. Zuckerman (ed.), *Civil Justice in Crisis* (Oxford, 1999), 248–50.

[10] Y. Miwa & J. Ramseyer, 'The Myth of the Main Bank: Japan and Comparative Corporate Governance' (2002) 27 *Law & Soc. Inquiry* 401.

[11] P. Wood, *Principles of International Insolvency* (London, 1995), ch. 1, 10–12.

[12] R. La Porta, F. Lopez-de-Silanes, A. Shleifer & R. Vishny, 'Legal Determinants of External Finance' (1997) 52 *J. of Finance* 113; 'Law and Finance' (1998) 106 *J. of Pol. Econ.* 1113.

[13] e.g., *Insolvency Law and Practice* (Cork Committee), Cmnd 8558 (London, 1982).

[14] J. Von Pischke, *Finance at the Frontier* (Washington, DC, 1991), 60, 127, 155–6; S. Fos (ed.), *Seminar on Recovery Management* (Bombay, 1988), 10; C. Gonzales-Vega, 'Cheap Agricultural Credit: Redistribution in Reverse', in D. Adams, D. Graham & J. von Pischke (eds), *Undermining Rural Development with Cheap Credit* (Boulder, 1984).

further, it is worthwhile being more explicit about what is meant by the 'context' of the law relating to credit allocation and debt recovery. Context can be conveniently divided along three dimensions: the economic, the political, and the cultural.

Economic dimension

Economic factors in credit allocation and debt recovery are various. Macro-economic influences clearly affect a borrower's capacity to repay, such as higher interest rates if its loan agreements contain a floating interest rate clause. Borrowers may simply be unable to pay: in addition to the economy turning against them, they may face a substantial increase in the prices of their inputs, or other factors may adversely affect their competitiveness such as technological innovation rendering their products unattractive.[15] The Asian economic crisis 1997–8 stemmed partly from weaknesses in financial systems—inadequate supervision of the financial sector, failure properly to assess and monitor financial risk—which lead to large borrowings of overseas capital, denominated in foreign currency, often for poor quality investments. The reassessment following the crisis led to major shifts in investment portfolios and asset market stocks.[16]

At the micro-economic level there are relevant factors in the organization and behaviour of creditors. One factor is the strong relationship between banks and borrowers in many Asian countries, which means that in case of borrower difficulty banks roll over loans or give interest rate concessions.[17] Institutionally, banks have lacked separate collection departments or workout departments and have left loan officers responsible for chasing default, which 'creates a conflict of interest in a culture in which declaring a borrower in default is akin to blaming the loan officer'.[18]

On the borrower's side there will be a range of incentives and disincentives affecting the decision to repay. In general borrowers have a strong incentive to repay, first, if on default their property can be immediately seized and sold to realize the debt, i.e. if the legal system recognizes extra-judicial enforcement of security; secondly and alternatively, if they can be readily sued for outstanding amounts, with interest continually accumulating at a higher rate than what they

---

[15] K. Jayasuriya & A. Rosser, 'Economic Crisis and the Political Economy of Economic Liberalisation in South-East Asia', in G. Rodan, R. Robinson & K. Hewison (eds), *The Political Economy of South-East Asia* (Melbourne, 2001). A distinction has been drawn between defaulters with good intentions and 'real defaulters'. Among the latter are those who intend repayment but find it difficult and finally give up, those who intend default but can be pressed to repay, and those wilfully defaulting.

[16] e.g. G. Noble & J. Ravenhill (eds), *The Asian Financial Crisis and the Architecture of Global Finance* (Cambridge University Press, 2000); W. McKibbins & W. Martin, *The East Asian Crisis: Investigating Causes and Policy Responses*, World Bank Policy Research Working Papers No. 2172 (Washington, DC, 1999); G. Walker & T. Reid, 'Upgrading Corporate Governance in East Asia' [2002] *J.Int'l Bank Law* 59, 62.

[17] R. Rajan & L. Zingales, 'Which Capitalism? Lessons from the East Asian Crisis' (1998) 11 *J.App.Corp.Fin.* 40.   [18] L. Berger, G. Nast & C. Raubach, *op.cit.*, 141.

can earn by using the money, and with non-payment on judgment being quickly followed by either seizure and sale of their property to satisfy the debt and/or compulsory bankruptcy; and thirdly, in either event, if their non-payment in this instance will lead to future sources of credit drying up.

We return to the strength of each of these incentives below, although in relation to the third point it might be observed here that in parts of the Asian region defaultors have not necessarily lost the privilege of further borrowing. In India, for example, it has not been unknown for serious defaulters with one bank to approach another bank and be granted credit there.[19] Clearly if there is to be an economic incentive to repay a loan further loans must be dependent on repayment properly occurring, subject to excusable lapses. Moreover, unless it is known within a community that serious or deliberate fault will attract sanctions, default will spread because the not unnatural temptation will be for debtors generally to emulate the delinquents. A further incentive to repayment is if sanctions are imposed on the controllers of defaulting businesses. Taking personal guarantees from controllers of a borrower means that they will be exposed to liability if their business defaults. Whether in the ordinary course of events this constitutes an additional reason for their striving to make the business a success is doubtful—if honest, they will want this in any event. In theory, the personal guarantee provides an additional avenue for recovery on insolvency occurring: in practice the bankruptcy of controllers is not likely to yield the full amount.

Wilful defaulters are said to be a significant problem in some jurisdictions. But there are obvious difficulties in identifying just who are wilful defaulters, as well as due process obstacles if their names are to be published (as a stigmatizing disincentive) or they are to be banned from obtaining further credit. A more practical approach is to proceed against controllers of businesses with a history of default. A presumption can be made where default is either so serious, or is attributable to such recklessness or incompetence, that a person should not continue in control of any business. For example, under the Singapore Companies Act persons may be disqualified from being a director of, or from taking part in the management of, a company for up to five years if they have been the director of a company which was insolvent and has gone into liquidation, and if their conduct as director of that or other companies makes them unfit so to act.[20] The directors may also be held personally liable for the debts of the insolvent company. As with any sanction the effectiveness of this type of provision turns not only on its severity, but also on the certainty that in serious cases disqualifying action will actually be taken.

Political background

Politics takes various turnings with credit allocation and debt recovery. The Asian economic crisis in the second half of the 1990s uncovered the political cronyism

[19] S. Fos (ed.), *Seminar on Recovery Management* (Bombay, 1989), 64, 76, 114, 115.
[20] Companies Act, ch. 50, s 149.

which lay behind a considerable number of the decisions on credit allocation in the region.[21] Moneys went to causes being promoted by the politically powerful or connected on favourable terms, and without proper evaluation. The chickens came home to roost with economic recession. The problem persists, if not to the same extent. A senior economist in Delhi was recently reported as saying: 'A lot of these bad loans are to do with political connections—often with very murky histories. Don't expect this to disappear'.[22] More in accordance with the rule of law have been the political decisions to allocate credit to particular sectors of the economy. The Indian system of priority sectors is illustrative. One of the deficiencies it was designed to overcome was that the bulk of bank advances went to large and medium-sized businesses, partly because they could provide acceptable security, while agriculture, small-scale industries, and exports did not receive sufficient finance.[23] The mechanisms for achieving a reallocation of credit have been various: greater representation of agriculture, cooperatives and small-scale industries on the boards of the (nationalized) Indian banks; incentives in the form of refinance from the Reserve Bank of India; quantitative targets for bank advances; and the establishment by the Reserve Bank of a credit guarantee systems for loans by banks to borrowers in the priority sectors. One corollary of a system of directed credits has been that bank lending has been channelled by definition to causes which are not necessarily efficient in accordance with ordinary economic criteria. Moreover, the policy has often led to lending without a proper evaluation of the projects funded and without adequate monitoring. The impression of some borrowers has been that credit was being made available as a political handout or grant and need not be repaid.[24] The universal trend has been to mitigate policies of directed credits through deregulation.

Perhaps political factors are more notable on the other side of the coin to credit allocation—debt recovery. First are the cases where because of hard times, a government or central bank orders or exerts moral suasion on banks in favour of leniency towards debtors.[25] This is seen even in developed countries. Occasionally this policy is legalized by promulgation of a moratorium, although typically moratoria are imposed during balance of payments crises and confined to remissions to foreign creditors.[26] Moratoria on foreign payments should not affect the ability of

---

[21] M. Pomerleano, *The East Asia Crisis and Corporate Finances: The Untold Micro Story*, World Bank Policy Research Working Papers No. 1990 (Washington, DC, 1998).

[22] E. Luce & K. Merchant, 'Time Runs Out for Bad Payers as Indian Court Ruling Backs Banks', *Financial Times* (Eur.edn), 15 April 2004, 6.

[23] Reserve Bank of India, *Study Group [on] Bank Credit* (Tandon Committee) (New Delhi, 1974), paras 3.1–3.5. See K. Sen & R. Waidya, *The Process of Financial Liberalization in India* (New Delhi, 1997), ch. 1.

[24] e.g. D. Adams & R. Vogel, 'Rural Financial Markets in Low-income Countries: Recent Controversies and Lessons' (1986) 14 *World Dev.* 477, 482.

[25] e.g. in Indonesia in 1999 there were reports 'that ministers had ordered state banks to stop seizing collateral from small enterprises, in support of a government effort to boost this sector': 'Supreme Court for Blow for Indonesian Bankers', *Financial Times*, 10 February 1999.

[26] The Philippine's moratorium of 1983 gave rise to litigation before the US Supreme Court: *Citibank NA v Wells Fargo Asia Ltd.*, 495 US 660 (1990).

domestic borrowers to repay local banks in domestic currency, although it is possible to speculate that moratoria contribute to a pro-debtor culture within a country. Political influence can enter debt recovery in a more direct way. In a telling phrase there has been a class of 'untouchables' in some countries who, because of their political influence, have been able to ensure deferral of their debts.[27] (Indeed they may also have exerted an influence at the earlier point when decisions about credit allocation were made.) For India, Sarap has written that it appeared that large farmers, because of their political connections and dominant position in formal credit institutions (especially in cooperatives), 'managed to postpone repayment of loans for a long period. [T]he large farmers not only have obtained a lion's share of loans, but also have a higher percentage of debt'.[28] Kabraji has graphically described the nature of political influence in Pakistan, where with the growth of public sector financial institutions, the provision of industrial and agricultural credit became a fertile source of political patronage. Likewise, the powerful intervened in forestalling and diverting recovery proceedings.[29] Kabraji has also described a group of wilful defaulters who obtained their loans fraudulently and then were not above using threats of violence, blackmail and other Mafiosi tactics to obstruct effective recovery.[30] In Thailand it has been said that political connections mean that the restructuring following the Asian economic crisis of the 1990s benefited the enterprises with good political connections.[31]

Law has some role in combating this subversion of the orderly processes of debt recovery. At the level of rhetoric, countries espousisng the rule of law—and that includes most in the region—cannot countenance too great a violation of the equal application of the law without threatening their own legitimacy. As Professor Yash Ghai puts it: 'The ideological strength of legality comes from the appearance of even-handedness of the legal system and of the equal application of the laws to all, including top leaders.'[32] While in the past debt recovery laws may not have received the same public exposure as other laws, the banking crisis in important parts of the region put them firmly on the agenda. The rhetoric of legality therefore has some potential for correcting the lack of even-handedness in credit allocation and debt recovery administration.

More concretely, a combination of private and criminal law may strike at unlawful political interference with debt recovery. To take just one example from private law: the common law world has long imposed fiduciary and other duties

[27] O. Pena, 'Inaugural Address', Regional Symposium on Legal Issues in Debt Recovery, Credit and Security, Asian Development Bank, Manila, June 1992, 2 (hereafter Regional Symposium).
[28] K. Sarap, 'Transactions in Rural Credit Markets in Western Orissa, India' (1987) 15 *J.Peasant Stud.* 83, 90.   [29] K. Kabraji, 'Pakistan', Regional Symposium, 76, 81.
[30] *ibid.*, 77.
[31] A. Kazmin, 'Thai Banks Ready to Hand Over Burden of Bad Loans', *Financial Times*, 26 September 2001, 31.
[32] Y. Ghai, 'The Rule of Law, Legitimacy and Governance', in Y. Ghai, R. Luckham & F. Snyder (eds), *The Political Economy of Law* (Delhi, 1987), 254.

on those involved in businesses. In broad terms they must act honestly and in the interests of their business.[33] This may apply to those in financial institutions who in breach of duty succumb to political influence when making allocation and recovery decisions. There are many legal and practical obstacles to invoking this area of law successfully (for example, who may sue? can the business ratify any wrongdoing which it might well do if the wrongdoers are dominant persons in it? how is wrongdoing to be established?), but some may be dissuaded from wrong-doing if greater legal attention were to be given to the possibility. Similarly, the criminal law of bribery and corruption may be applicable. For example, s 409 of the Indian Penal Code 1860, applicable in the sub-continent and elsewhere in the region, creates the offence of criminal breach of trust by a banker. That involves the dishonest disposal of property in violation of law or contract.[34] The banker who allocates credit or delays recovery for the type of corrupt reason we have been considering could fall foul of the section. Moreover, there are provisions, such as in the Malaysian Banking and Financial Institutions Act 1989, which penalize bank officers receiving for themselves or others any sort of benefit for procuring for anyone a credit facility, permission to overdraw an account, or 'any other thing relating to the business or affairs' of the bank.[35] Arguably the latter covers the deferral or rescheduling of repayment. As with other criminal provisions, the very presence of these offences on the statute book can have a general deterrent effect; ultimately, however, their true value is based on the vigour of their enforcement.

Cultural factors

The cultural aspects of the subject are at once the most difficult and yet possibly the most important. Culture in this context means the shared understandings of a particular society or group; in particular, legal culture as a concept characterizes the range of ideas, assumptions, and practices about law and its place in the social order.[36] In relation to credit, statements made within particular countries in the region amount to saying that the culture is more pro-debtor than pro-creditor. In 1988, at a seminar on debt recovery organized by the Bankers Training College of the Reserve Bank of India, a general manager of the State Bank of India said bluntly: 'In our country, the outlook of the borrower is generally not to repay',[37] and one of his colleagues added: 'The economic, political and legal system in the country is such that it is not conducive to recovery. Judicial decisions are more in favor of the borrowers than in favor of the banks.'[38] The pro-debtor orientation of the judiciary has been referred to in other countries as well. In Malaysia a leading

---

[33] A. Singh, *Company Law*, 14th edn (Lucknow, 2004), 276.
[34] See M. George, 'Criminal Law of Trust under Malaysian Law: A Review—Part 1' (1990) 1 *Current LJ* i.   [35] Section 115(1).
[36] R. Cotterrell, 'The Concept of Legal Culture', in D. Nelken (ed.), *Comparing Legal Cultures* (Aldershot, 1997).   [37] S. Fos, *op.cit.*, 63.
[38] *ibid.*

lawyer has said that the judges view the debtor as the underdog,[39] and in Indonesia a senior partner of an Indonesian law firm has said: 'Culturally, there is a belief that Indonesian courts see their role as protecting the weaker party *from* the stronger.'[40] As we have seen, in protecting debtors, courts are not necessarily protecting weaker parties; the role of 'underdog' is sometimes occupied by big business, large landowners, or the politically powerful.

Overall culture is an extremely complex blend of factors difficult to identify separately. The historical experience is an important strand. For example, the behaviour of moneylenders in Sri Lanka in the 1930s affected mainstream legal attitudes.[41] No doubt outrages by moneylenders elsewhere have also become part of the folklore. The impression of a fire-sale of assets in the aftermath of the Asian economic crisis may have reinforced pro-debtor sentiment.[42] Fear of unemployment has been another powerful influence on the pro-debtor culture. Government-owned financial institutions in particular are under enormous social and political pressure not to pursue non-performing loans if this will put people out of work.[43] The evolution of a pro-debtor culture is thus a product of particular experiences, not all of which are necessarily still relevant to the problems of a society as it enters a new economic and social phase. Changes in the substantive and procedural law might well contribute to a change in culture. Law has an important symbolic function and on occasions can have a transformative effect on attitudes.

The Law of Borrowing and Debt Recovery

In both Thailand and Indonesia, selling cars with a device called 'retention of title' is a well-established and profitable business... The system of title registration for cars substitutes roughly for a genuine filing archive for security interest. The fact that the car operates on the public way where the 'owner-creditor' can readily find it substitutes roughly for private repossession. The fact that the police will 'cooperate' in finding a 'stolen car' provides an enforcement system. The fact that the creditor retains title permits the quick resale of the repossessed vehicle. The problem with this as a solution is that it will not work for much more than cars... the same business operator who could buy a car on credit cannot buy a forklift truck or a lathe on credit. The same farmer who could buy a truck on credit cannot buy a tractor or a pump on credit. Such bizarre distinctions... arise from antiquated laws that no longer serve Asia's economic needs.[44]

The conventional division between substantive and procedural law sometimes leads to an over-concentration on litigation, when more important is how law

---

[39] Chen Kah Leng, 'Malaysia', Regional Symposium, 5.
[40] F. Morgan, 'Indonesia', Regional Symposium, 18–19, 22.   [41] 302 below.
[42] *Secured Transactions Law Reform in Asia: Unleashing the Potential of Collateral*, Law and Policy Reform at the Asian Development Bank 2000, vol. 2, Manila, 2000, xi.
[43] M. Ahluwalia, 'Reforming India's Financial Sector', in J. Hanson & S. Kathuria (eds), *India: A Financial Sector for the Twenty First Century* (New Delhi, 1999), 44.
[44] *Secured Transactions Law Reform in Asia: Unleashing the Potential of Collateral, op.cit.*, 9.

moulds institutions and permeates practices. Certainly this wider perspective is necessary for a fuller understanding of the problems raised by credit allocation and debt recovery. Moreover, substantive and procedural law cannot be divorced from their daily use. Substantive law may appear effective in its own terms, but may be distorted or under-used in practice. Procedural law may be consonant with standards elsewhere, but its administration in the courts of a particular jurisdiction may so subvert it as to mock its very goals. Perhaps a more helpful division than between substantive and procedural law is between law and its administration: law is used in the wider sense indicated above, i.e. substantive law, taking into account context, while administration focuses on the courts, includes the rules of procedure, but extends to their operation in practice. Thus in a particular jurisdiction the substantive law on the books may be effective, with the problem being its application in practice. Procedural rules may be manipulated and litigation grossly delayed. An early recognition of the importance of law's administration came from Dean Roscoe Pound. In 1906 he urged that lawyers should pay greater attention to the administration of the courts and urged that the expeditious disposition of cases and the efficient organization of judicial records should receive the highest priority in order to bring to the courts greater effectiveness.[45] Effectiveness is used here to mean in broad terms achieving the goals set for a system. However, as indicated at the outset, this chapter is also concerned with efficiency (i.e. minimizing the time, effort, and cost in achieving certain goals) and with issues such as the quality of justice (one aspect of which is social justice).

Before proceeding further it may be useful to identify those aspects of the law and its administration which mark out a country as being pro-creditor rather than pro-debtor. Recall that in practice it will be difficult to place a country accurately; recall also that the purpose of the exercise is not to make moral judgments, but to isolate problems and then maybe to suggest possible legal reforms. In practice what will be needed is a careful and painstaking identification of the problems in a particular jurisdiction and possible legal solutions. There will be no easy answers. Sensitivity to the context of the law is essential. A blanket introduction of pro-creditor laws without taking this into account will result in yet more ineffective laws. Indeed, it could well be counterproductive; schemes, both simple and sophisticated, will be devised to avoid their impact, and in extreme cases courts will simply refuse to apply what they see as draconian laws, further undermining the rule of law. And there are also social justice issues. Nonetheless in theory it is possible to identify an optimum point where a legal system's effectiveness declines as it becomes more pro-creditor. In general terms, the main indicators of a pro-creditor jurisdiction seem to reduce to ten: a ready ability of creditors to check the bona fides of a potential borrower/guarantor; credit agreements/guarantees not to be easily upset by non-compliance with formalities; freedom of contract to agree

---

[45] Reprinted as Roscoe Pound, 'The Causes of Popular Dissatisfaction with the Administration of Justice' (1937) 20 *J.Am.Judicature Soc'y* 178, 187; (1962) 46 *J.Am. Judicature Soc'y* 55, 66.

the terms; wide powers for creditors to monitor borrowers during the currency of the credit and to take corrective action in the event of any indication of problems; a range of security devices, easily invoked; self-help remedies possible, in particular the capacity to realize security immediately and extra-judicially; ease of initiating litigation and obtaining judgment without delay; bankruptcy procedures easily invokable, once default occurs; strong incentives (for example higher interest payable on default) to the borrower or guarantor to comply with any judgment against it; and efficient enforcement of judgments.

Contracting for credit

The association between freedom of contract and economic welfare has long been a theme in the law.[46] It has been central to the economic analysis of law since the time of the Coase theorem. Parties will reach a Pareto-optimal position by free negotiation between themselves.[47] However, lawyer-economists have recognized limitations in the contracting process, for example in information deficiencies and in identifying and negotiating the various contingencies for which provision should be made.[48] Most recently, the fallacy of assuming the free and perfect enforcement of contracts through the courts has been taken into account in the economic analysis of contract.[49] Despite these blemishes, free contracting is seen as central to a market economy.

For lenders it has long been a truism that debt recovery problems are minimized by prudent contracting. One ingredient is for lenders to inform themselves of the creditworthiness and record of potential borrowers. For example, lenders can insist on seeing the profit and loss accounts and the balance sheets of a business and other financial information such as management accounts and financial projections. The adequacy of these turns partly on the obligations of a jurisdiction's company law.[50] The Asian financial crisis of the late 1990s has built up pressure for a higher degree of financial disclosure and heavier reporting requirements.[51] Interviews, visits to the client's business and possibly information from those such as valuers and others are aspects of credit appraisal. Lax lending by some banks in the region has revealed the need for stronger internal controls over the grant of credit: head offices must exercise tighter control of a branch's risk control mechanisms and the ability of its managers. Law is only indirectly relevant in this regard. More important is the availability of experienced bankers, their training and professional standards.

---

[46] P. Atiyah, *The Rise and Fall of Freedom of Contract* (Oxford, 1979).
[47] R. Coase, 'The Problem of Social Cost' (1960) 3 *J.L. & Econ.* 1.
[48] e.g. M. Trebilcock, *The Limits of Freedom of Contract* (Cambridge, MA, 1993).
[49] S. Johnson, J. McMillan & C. Woodruff, 'Courts and Relational Contracts' (2002) 18 *J.L. Econ. & Organization* 221.   [50] R. Tomasic (ed.), *Company Law in East Asia* (Abingdon, 1998).
[51] e.g. J. Coffee, 'The Rise of Dispersed Ownership', in K. Hopt & E. Wymeersch (eds), *Capital Markets and Company Law* (Oxford, 2003), 730–1; P. Brietzke, 'Governance and Companies Law in Indonesia' (2000) 2 *Aust.J.Asian Law* 193.

With the largest loans, such as those for infrastructural projects like power stations, lawyers have a role in credit appraisal, in making due diligence inquiries about matters such as the legal status, qualifications, and powers of a potential borrower; the enforceability of the loan agreement and ancillary security; whether governmental consents have been obtained for the borrowing; that the loan is in conformity with the general law and with other undertakings of the borrower; and whether the borrower is involved in materially pending or threatened legal proceedings.[52] With cross-border lending in particular, inquiries will need to be incorporated in a legal opinion and will be a condition precedent to the creditor's liability to lend. The lawyers in the region familiar with international legal practice are able to perform such due diligence without difficulty. While important, these matters are but one aspect of credit risk.

As far as legal institutions and contracting are concerned, two aspects can be highlighted, first, what can be called credit referencing; and secondly, the system of registration for security. Both facilitate the flow of information about credit-worthiness so that more effective decisions can be made about borrowers. As for credit referencing it may be informal, as lenders exchange information between themselves about particular borrowers. Moreover, in some countries a new lender might obtain a reference from the potential borrower's bank about its credit standing. Such references are likely to be vague and therefore not especially helpful. A bank providing such a reference will typically disclaim any liability for the information provided.[53]

Information about smaller borrowers may be available through credit reference agencies, which gather details from public records such as court proceedings, as well as from creditors themselves as they refer experiences with particular borrowers. Clearly public records need to be up to date if information about adverse judgments or insolvency is to be accurately reported to lenders. This is not always the case with some public registries in the region, which have been slow in recording information and have been generally inefficient. Some countries in the region have commercially established credit reference agencies, but in others it has required (or will require) government initiative.[54] An inhibition on the operation of credit reference agencies is the law of bank secrecy. The private law of bank confidentiality in common law countries may be seen as an obstacle to disclosing information to other banks and to credit reference agencies, whether it be black information about borrowers in default, or white information about borrowers who are not. Confidentiality, however, can be waived and borrowers may be obliged to do this as a condition of being considered for credit. Statutory protection for banks

---

[52] e.g. P. Wood, *International Loans, Bonds and Securities Regulation* (London, 1995); R. Cranston, *Principles of Banking Law*, 2nd edn. (Oxford, 2002), ch. 11.

[53] World Bank, *Doing Business in 2004. Understanding Regulation* (Washington, DC, 2004), 56–61, 66–8.

[54] Indian banks finally establised a Credit Information Bureau in 2004: K. Merchant, 'Indian Banks Bureau to Track Debt', *Financial Times*, 6 May 2004, 33. cf. Credit Information Bureau of Sri Lanka Act 1990 (as amended 1995).

which disclose information to credit reference agencies puts the matter beyond legal challenge.

A more serious obstacle to credit reference agencies is bank secrecy legislation, breach of which cannot be waived. It sometimes seems to be drafted without any consideration being given to its chilling effect on credit referencing.[55] Again the Asian financial crisis has had a beneficial effect. For example, to expedite the process of debt recovery in Indonesia, Law 10 of 1998 amended the law of bank secrecy by confining the obligation of confidentiality to deposit customers only. It is no longer a breach of the law to disclose information about other customers such as borrowers and their default history.[56]

A system of registration for security has two advantages for lenders: first, it enables them to check existing encumbrances and the title of a potential borrower to the property being offered as security; and secondly, lenders can obtain priority for their security once registered, despite subsequent dealings with the property. There is the further, and to an extent, overlapping advantage that registration is a form of public notice. Those dealing with a borrower can discover the security taken over its assets and make some assessment of the borrower's creditworthiness. Conversely, it is sometimes said that registration benefits a borrower by enabling it to give some sort of assurance to prospective lenders or other third parties about property with which they propose to deal.

Effective land registration gives a solid basis to land ownership, which encourages financial development and economic growth in various ways.[57] With rural land it provides an incentive for investment which improves farm productivity.[58] In both rural and urban areas, it facilitates the advance of credit as the land can be offered as security. As in rural Thailand, bankers may hold the title deeds to farmers' land as security for loans.[59] More straightforward is if a land registry enables a lender to register security over land. For this to be effective, it is essential that a land register should be accurate and up to date. Some countries in the region have experienced

[55] See e.g. A. Yusuf, 'Pakistan', in D. Campbell (ed.), *International Bank Secrecy* (London, 1992), 554; A. Yap, 'Singapore', in *ibid.*; Poh Chu Chai, *Law of Banker and Customer*, 4th edn (Singapore, 1999).

[56] R. Bastian, 'Bank Secrecy and Tax Audit', *IBA Asia Pacific Forum Newsletter*, June 2001, 13; B. Tabalugan, 'Recent Changes to Indonesian Banking Law' [1999] *BJIBFL*, 259, 260.

[57] F. Byamugisha, *The Effects of Land Registration on Financial Development and Economic Growth: A Theoretical and Conceptual Framework*, World Bank Policy Research Working Papers No. 2240, 1999; *How Land Registration Affects Financial Development and Economic Growth in Thailand*, No. 2241, 1999; L. Charlebois, 'Creating Land Registration Systems for Developing Countries', *Amicus Curiae*, Issue 21, October 1999, 8 (which contains criticism of the UN 'Draft Land Administration Guidelines with Special Reference to Countries in Transition'). There is the separate issue that registration may deprive traditional owners of their rights: R. Haverfield, 'Hak Ulayat and the State: Land Reform in Indonesia', in T. Lindsey (ed.), *Indonesia. Law and Society* (Sydney, 1999).

[58] There are claims that as many as 90 per cent of land titles in India are unclear: *India: The Growth Imperative* (McKinsey & Company, 2001), Policy Recommendations, 6.

[59] A. Siamualla *et al.*, 'The Thai Rural Credit System and Elements of a Theory', in K. Hoff, A. Braverman & J. Stiglitz (eds), *The Economics of Rural Organisation. Theory, Practice, and Policy* (Oxford, 1993).

substantial delays in their land registries which, if borrowers were fraudulent, opened the way to lenders losing the priority they would otherwise receive.[60] Apart from land registries, the other types of registries relevant to security are fragmented. They generally record security against a particular type of personal property[61] or debtor (for example companies);[62] in a very few jurisdictions they record a particular type of security interest.[63] The lack of integration, and the cost of search, are obvious drawbacks of specific registers. This is apart from any public access problems or inefficiencies which may characterize the operation of the registries.

The most sophisticated system for registering security over property which is not land is constituted under Article 9 of the Uniform Commercial Code ('secured transactions'), adopted in all parts of the United States including Louisiana.[64] Article 9 covers all types of security interests in personal property, including their functional equivalents. These interests are effective according to their terms, although for non-possessory security to be effective against third parties the creditor must take possession of the property or file a so-called financing statement in the registry. Revised in 1998, Article 9 is a Rolls Royce system, although personal property security law in the United States is still complex and much litigated. Only Canada and New Zealand have followed suit, and most registrations there seem to be in relation to motor vehicles.[65] Other developed countries which have considered the adoption of an Article 9 system have so far rejected it as unnecessary or too costly.[66] However, a Model Secured Transactions law has had considerable success in central and eastern Europe.[67] Moreover, the Asian Development Bank has set out a model for a modern registration system for movable property inspired by Article 9. A powerful argument in its favour is that developing countries can leapfrog the theoretically inadequate and practically fragmented registers of many developed countries through using electronic means.[68]

---

[60] See J. Sihombing, *National Land Code: A Commentary*, 3rd edn (Kuala Lumpur, looseleaf), 645–701. (In Malaysia, a lender can gain protection by entering a caveat.)

[61] Examples are registries for intellectual property (India); shares, aircraft, vessels, fixtures (Indonesia); aircraft, vessels, floating houses, beasts of burden, machinery (Thailand). See *Secured Transactions Law Reform in Asia: Unleashing the Potential of Collateral, op.cit.*, 57–8.

[62] e.g. in India, Companies Act 1956, s 130; Securitization and Reconstruction of Financial Assets and Enforcement of Security Interest Ordinance 2002, s 20.

[63] See the Indonesian concept of fidusia: 280 below.

[64] See J. White & R. Summers, *Uniform Commercial Code* 3rd edn (St Paul, Minn, 1988), ch. 9; J. Ziegel & D. Denomme, *Ontario Personal Property Security Act*, 2nd edn (Toronto, 2001).

[65] M. Bridge, 'How Far is Article 9 Exportable? The English Experience' (1996) *Can.Bus.LJ* 196.

[66] A. Diamond, *A Review of Security Interests in Property* (London, 1989); Law Commission, *Registration of Security Interests: Company Charges and Property Other than Land*, Consultation Paper No. 164 (London, 2002); *Company Security Interests*, Consultation Paper No. 176 (London, 2004).

[67] J-H Röver, 'An Approach to Legal Reform in Central and Eastern Europe: The European Bank's Model Law on Secured Transactions' (1999) *Eur.J.L.Reform* 119. See also UNCITRAL, *Draft Legislative Guide on Secured Transactions* (Vienna, 2003).

[68] *A Guide to Movables Registries* (Law and Policy Reform at the Asian Development Bank) (Manila, 2002).

What has been learnt in both developed and developing countries is that law reform efforts must be sensitive to context. Simply introducing foreign models, however logically consistent and appealing they might be, will achieve little unless locally there is a will for them to succeed, unless the necessary adaptations to the local environment are made, and unless the institutions are in place to implement them and so make them 'living law'.[69]

Freedom of contract is limited in all jurisdictions with respect to the granting of credit. Even the most laissez-faire system of law will render inoperative an agreement procured by fraud, misrepresentation, or extortionate behaviour. Within that boundary, however, the limits on credit contracts vary, although it is fair to say that generally speaking they do not greatly impede lenders from doing what they want. Traditionally, legal control of credit agreements has targeted interest. The best known example is Islamic law, which forbids interest-based (*riba*) transactions. The taking and giving of interest is against the Sharia, the body of legal and ethical rules for Muslims.[70] Banks in the region, including specially established Islamic banks, act in accordance with the rule against interest.[71] Several countries in the region are trying to underline their Islamic identity. So Pakistan is legally committed to a prohibition on interest in accordance with the Sharia.[72] Elsewhere, the law may empower a court to reopen a moneylending transaction if the interest rate is excessive or the transaction harsh or unconscionable.[73] Usury law, however, is generally inapplicable to lending by banks.[74]

One complaint is that bank officials are sometimes responsible for poor drafting and for the inadequate execution of loan contracts, as a result of mistake, inadequate training, or pressure to complete a deal and make disbursement. An Indian textbook lists twenty-six common mistakes committed in bank documentation, including: documents signed in blank (for example an hypothecation with a blank schedule of the goods charged); documents signed after stamping; partners signing on different dates or directors of a company witnessing the common seal on different dates; documents written in English and signed in the vernacular; and executing documents in circumstances which allow the defendant to raise

---

[69] 28–30 above.

[70] N. Saleh, *Unlawful Gain and Legitimate Profit in Islamic Law*, 2nd edn (Cambridge, 1986); A. Saeed, *Islamic Banking and Interest. A Study of the Prohibition of Riba and its Contemporary Interpretation* (Leiden, 1996).

[71] e.g. A. Saeed, 'Indonesian Islamic Banking in Historical and Legal Context', in T. Lindsey (ed.), *Indonesia. Law and Society* (Sydney, 1999); S. Murvat, 'The Legal Framework for Islamic Banking: Pakistan's Experience', in R. Effros (ed.), *Current Legal Issues Affecting Central Banks* (Washington, DC, 1992); Cheong May Fong, 'Commercial Law and Legal Culture in Malaysia', in A. Tay (ed.), *East Asia. Human Rights, Nation-Building, Trade* (Baden-Baden, 1999), 173–5.

[72] Shariat Act 1992; A. Hamid, 'Islamic Law on Interest: The 1999 Pakistan Supreme Court Decision on *Riba*' (2003) 1 *World Bank LR* 393.

[73] e.g. Dato Seri Visu Sinnadurai, *Law of Contract*, 3rd edn (Kuala Lumpur, 2003), 266–88; *Pollock & Mulla on Indian Contract and Specific Relief Acts*, 19th edn (Bombay, 1999), 234–9.

[74] *Tannan's Banking Law and Practice in India*, 19th edn (New Delhi, 1997), 422–3, 441.

claims of undue influence or unconscionability (for example, a guarantee signed at the place of the guarantor or by a spouse without independent persons present).[75] The upshot of all this is that when matters are disputed banks find the terms difficult to enforce. Formalities may need to be observed for the validity of an agreement. Thus the implications of the doctrine of *ultra vires* may need reviewing for corporate borrowing, and the company seal may be needed for the execution of documents. In some countries with civil law backgrounds, documents need to be authenticated by a notary.[76] The notary is supposed to act as an impartial adviser to all parties and if necessary to explain the legal consequences of a document. For large borrowings, there is no justification on this basis since the borrower will already have received advice on the consequences on its action. Furthermore, where notaries have a monopoly of such work, there may be a tendency to restrictive practices.

Security (collateral)

Security (collateral) is not essential for a lender. Sometimes a lender will be prepared to advance money without security because the reputation or record of a borrower sufficiently assures that the loan will be repaid. In international lending, security is often impractical (i.e. the security could never in practice be enforced in the country where the potential security is located). At the other end of the spectrum the village moneylender will not need security if the informal sanctions which can be brought to bear guarantee repayment. In many cases, however, a lender will not lend without security. It will want the assurance that if the loan turns sour it will have a direct claim against the debtor's property, which it can readily realize so as to be able to recoup itself in the case of default. With a view to protecting lending institutions, the law of some jurisdictions makes security compulsory. For example, the banking legislation of Malaysia obliges finance companies to take security except for small loans.[77] An excessive reliance on security is often associated with a failure to engage in adequate loan appraisal. Far better for borrowers to be repaying in an orderly manner than for the lender to have to proceed against the collateral.

At one level the economic justification for security is straightforward: it makes more credit available to borrowers and at cheaper rates. Resources are more efficiently allocated and economic growth fostered. A report for the Asian Development Bank, based in part on interviews with creditors, asserts:

Private creditors in all countries—common law and civil law, industrial and transitional, north and south—worry about getting their loans repaid. Everywhere, when the debtor can offer them collateral for a loan, private creditors offer larger loans, at lower interest

---

[75] A. Baran, *Documents for Bank Advances* (Bombay, 1991), 249–53.
[76] R. Weiss & R. Ibrahim, 'Notaries, Secured Interests and the Indonesian Civil Code', *IBA Asia Pacific Forum Newsletter*, December 1998, 17.   [77] Banking and Financial Institutions Act 1989, s 60.

rates, payable over longer periods of time. Compared to a debtor who cannot offer good collateral, one with such collateral can anticipate receiving six to eight times more credit, taking two to ten times longer for repayment, and paying interest rates 30 percent to 50 percent lower. Collateral is important.[78]

There are a number of plausible mechanisms by which such economically desirable results occur. Reduction of risk is the most obvious: a lender with recourse directly against property of a borrower for discharge of its debt is not exposed to the same possibility of loss as it would be as an unsecured creditor.[79] Indeed the better terms provided by secured credit may actually reduce the risk that a debtor will default. A second mechanism is because security reduces information costs: a lender needs adequate information about a debtor and its capacity to repay before granting a loan, but with security the focus need be on information about the collateral rather than the whole of a debtor's business. Reducing search costs in this way means that by taking security the lender can charge a lower interest rate than otherwise.[80] A third mechanism by which security results in more efficient and cheaper credit relates to monitoring of a borrower's behaviour.[81] In this argument debtors are tempted to divert loan moneys to higher risk activities than contemplated, or in the interest of controllers or shareholders. Thus if a loan were unsecured a lender would need to impose a higher rate of interest to compensate, or to engage in overall monitoring of the borrower through the review of a regular flow of financial information. Taking security confines monitoring more to what the borrower does with the asset given as collateral and this can be reflected in a lower cost of credit.[82]

Facilitating secured lending demands a legal and institutional framework which enables a borrower to give security in a cost-effective and straightforward manner over the range of its property, including intangible property such as leases, accounts receivable, and intellectual property rights. To prevent borrowers fraudulently raising further credit on the strength of what are already secured assets, a mechanism is also necessary to give third parties notice of existing security. A cheap and readily accessible public register is the most effective way of doing this,

---

[78] *Secured Transactions Law Reform in Asia: Unleashing the Potential of Collateral, op.cit.*, §6. The study interviewed a broad cross-section of financial firms, dealers, traders, and manufacturers acting as creditors in India, Pakistan, China, Indonesia, and Thailand: §§359–72.

[79] J. Ziegel, 'What Can Economic Analysis of Law Teach Commercial and Consumer Law Scholars?', in R. Cranston & R. Goode (eds), *Commercial and Consumer Law* (Oxford, 1993), 267–8; J. Ziegel, 'Debtor–Creditor Regimes', in *World Bank Group on Debtor–Creditor Regimes* (Washington, DC, 1999), §§4–8; S. Schwartz, 'The Easy Case for the Priority of Secured Claims in Bankruptcy' (1997) 47 *Duke LJ* 425, 441–5.

[80] H. Fleisig, 'Economic Functions of Security in a Market Economy', in J. Norton & M. Andenas (eds), *Emerging Financial Markets and Secured Transactions* (The Hague, 1998), 19.

[81] V. Finch, *Corporate Insolvency Law* (Cambridge, 2002), 89–92; R. Goode, *Legal Problems of Credit and Security*, 3rd edn (London, 2003), 1–3; T. Jackson & A. Kronman, 'Secured Financing and Priorities Among Creditors' (1979) 88 *Yale LJ* 1143, 1149–50.

[82] The argument does not hold when security is given over the whole assets of a borrower: P. Ali, *The Law of Secured Finance* (Oxford, 2002), 38.

for it can also perform the function of ordering priorities among competing interests in the collateral (for example, first to file has priority subject, say, to purchase money security interests). A further requirement is ease of enforcement: on default security holders must be able to realize the collateral promptly and efficiently, either by self-help or access to cheap and speedy judicial remedies.

Land is the most common type of security offered to lenders. Naturally this has been restricted in communist countries like Vietnam where private ownership of land has been limited, and in countries where not all land has been alienated and much remains communally held according to customary law.[83] As mentioned earlier, mortgages over land may need to be registered. Excessive reliance on land as security has caused strain within a number of Asian banking institutions, where following the financial crisis of 1997–8 the value of the land taken as security declined relative to the value of the promise to repay. Associated with the devaluation was a reduction in the circulation of land, since general economic conditions were such that the land of defaulters, taken as security, could not be sold. Possessory security over personal property (movables) seems to face no major obstacles in the laws of the region. In some circumstances pledges of goods are possible (where, for example, the property is under the control of the bank in one of its warehouses), and such pledges are released to the borrower from time to time as the need arises. 'Key loan' arrangements are genuine pledges, and a bank has a clear right to sell the property if the borrower defaults, without resorting to the courts.[84] Possessory security can also involve documents of title to goods. The best example involves imported goods, where a buyer will pledge the shipping documents to obtain finance from its bank. Often the giving of a trust receipt will be associated with this type of transaction.[85]

The problem really arises with non-possessory security over personal property—security over future property (property subsequently to be acquired or come into existence) and over intangible property. Countries with a civil law background have inherited an aversion to this sort of security, partly because of the reasoning that it gives an appearance to third parties of a false wealth on the part of the borrower. The result is that the farmer growing crops cannot give a lien over them to a creditor. If they are to obtain credit they may have to rely on more traditional moneylenders, who can invoke informal sanctions for enforcement rather than seizing collateral. The amounts are likely to be less than they want, and at a higher interest rate. It is difficult to sell or charge accounts receivable or

---

[83] M. Hiscock, 'Law and Political Change: Land Use by Foreigners in Socialist Countries of the Third World', in R. Cranston & R. Goode (eds), *Commercial and Consumer Law* (Oxford, 1993).

[84] e.g. for India, *Bank of Maharashtra v Official Liquidator*, AIR (SC) 1969 Mysore 280. See also D. Allan *et al.*, *Credit and Security: The Legal Problems of Development* (Brisbane, 1974), 80 (mentioning the 'two key' system operating in Indonesia, Singapore, and Malaysia where both bank and borrower have warehouse keys). Professors Allan and Hiscock published a number of path-breaking volumes on credit and security in Asia in the 1970s.

[85] Phang Sin Kat, 'Trust Receipts in Singapore' [1987] BJIBFL 87. cf. *Tannan's Banking Law and Practice in India, op.cit.*, 593–4.

debts.[86] To the extent that these are not acceptable as collateral, that limits the advance of credit. In particular dealers supplying goods cannot refinance themselves by using their receivables as security and this limits their activities. The upshot is that credit tends to flow to those with land or physical plant, and investment is diverted away from those who have only future or intangible property.

Common law countries in the region have inherited a more favourable attitude to security over future and intangible property. In theory, security in these jurisdictions can take the form of a fixed or floating charge over the whole of an undertaking—all the borrowing company's present and future property and assets. These assets range from its land, buildings, plant and machinery, through its work in progress and stock in trade (inventory), to its book debts, contracts, and intellectual property. The security instrument will probably define default by the borrower in very wide terms. Crucially it may also empower the lender to appoint a manager in the case of default, who can immediately enter into and take control of the company without a court order. The manager may be given power by the instrument to continue to run the business or to sell it or any property to repay the lender. However, because this type of security only applies in relation to companies, small and medium-size enterprises (SMEs) or farmers which are unincorporated are at a disadvantage.

As indicated by the quotation at the head of this part of the chapter quasi-security in the form of hire purchase, conditional sale, lease or other retention of title devices, has come to the rescue in jurisdictions such as Indonesia and Thailand but only certain goods can be repossessed without a court order.[87] In some countries there has been legislative innovation in the area of non-possessory security. For example in Indonesia fiduciary transfer evolved in the case law, as an alternative to pledge, enabling a borrower to give security over collateral still in its possession. The Fiduciary Transfer Law No. 42 of 1999 codified this case law, but required for the first time that a fiduciary transfer agreement be in the form of a notarial deed. To minimize fraud it established a national register to give notice of fiduciary transfers. The old civil law objection to a borrower being able to give an appearance of false wealth does not hold water if there is a registration system. However, a fiduciary transfer only works if the collateral is specified, and in the case of default the creditor cannot acquire the title outright but must sell it and satisfy the debt from the proceeds of sale.[88] Consequently, banks in Indonesia do not lend on the security of inventory because the law requires its specific

[86] U. Drobnig, 'Legal Principles Governing Security Interests' (1977) 8 *Yearbook of the United Nations Commission on International Trade Law* 171, 178–9.

[87] 270 above. See also R. Foster, 'Labelling the Law—Security for Credit Sales and the Classification of Legal Systems in Southeast Asia' (2001) 3 *Aust.J. Law Asian* 167; Gan Ching Chuan & Nik Ramlah Mahmood, 'Two Decades of the Law relating to Sale of Goods, Hire Purchase and Equipment Leasing', in *Developments in Malaysian Law* (Kuala Lumpur, 1992), 212, 217, 229; V. Kothari, *Lease Financing and Hire Purchase*, 2nd edn (Nagpur, 1986), 182.

[88] R. Hornick, 'Fiduciary Transfer—Indonesia's New Law on Collateral Security', *Int'l Financial LR*, July 2000, 28.

identification.[89] By its very nature inventory is constantly changing. Yet inventory forms a substantial part of the capital of modern businesses, especially SMEs.

The effectiveness of security depends on the extent it can be enforced with speed and at low cost. Self-help, where the creditor can seize the collateral and sell it to cover the debt, is most beneficial to creditors. Many jurisdictions, especially those with a civil law background, are against self-help because of the risk that the creditor will look to its own interests and not those of the debtor. Although it is a common law jurisdiction, India adopted a restrictive approach in its Transfer of Property Act 1882. Generally speaking to sell the property, or foreclose, a mortgagee must obtain a court decree.[90] Only in certain limited situations does a mortgagee have a power to sell the mortgaged property in default of payment of the mortgage money without the intervention of the court. The origin of the restriction on self-help by mortgagees derived from a concern to protect Indians from unscrupulous moneylenders who were the main purveyors of credit to non-Europeans at the time this law was enacted.[91] There is certainly a danger that since the creditor is interested in expedition it may sell quickly, not obtaining the maximum price for the property, resulting in the debtor receiving only a small surplus or in fact being liable for a deficit. There is also a fear that self-help will lead to breaches of the peace, as the security is seized. Employees of the borrower may seek to prevent a creditor from exercising its powers if they think that this will result in the close-down of a factory; in some cases banks fear that borrowers will use force to resist. The possibility that breaches of the peace may occur is also one explanation for the fact that even in countries where extra-judicial realization of security is permitted by law, creditors may prefer to proceed through the courts.[92]

Two important consequences follow from the absence, or under-utilization, of the extra-judicial realization of security. First, the fraudulent borrower can use the delays facing a lender in obtaining a court order to dispose of the collateral. A common complaint in India is when a bank finally arrives to take possession of the security, the property has been disposed of, used up or otherwise rendered valueless. Secondly, in countries where there are extensive delays in the courts, the fact that security may not be realized without a judicial order means that it is in effect worthless from the point of view of the creditor. The very object of taking security is to enable the creditor to realize its value. So long as the borrower can delay matters in the courts, even with spurious arguments, that objective is thwarted.

To circumvent the extensive delays in the courts lenders need to be able to exercise extra-judicial powers against the security they have taken. This was

---

[89] *Secured Transactions Law Reform in Asia: Unleashing the Potential of Collateral, op.cit.*, 10, 23–4, 27–8.   [90] Section 67.

[91] 'There are parts of India in which such a power would be abused by Native mortgagees...': W. Stokes, *The Anglo-Indian Codes* (Oxford, 1887), vol. 1, 733. See generally M. Jain, *Outlines of Indian Legal History* (Bombay, 1990), 533–5.

[92] *Secured Transactions Law Reform in Asia: Unleashing the Potential of Collateral, op.cit.*, 71–2.

recommended for India in 1977 by the Banking Laws Committee.[93] Following further reports by the Narasimham and Andhyarujina committees, the Securitization and Reconstruction of Financial Assets and Enforcement of Security Interest Act 2002 was finally enacted. Its constitutionality has been upheld by the Supreme Court.[94] It facilitates—in respect of the financial assets of banks and financial institutions—the securitization of financial assets, the setting up of asset reconstruction companies and the enforcement of security. In relation to security it authorizes banks and financial institutions extra-judicially to seize the assets or take over the management control of a defaulting borrower, with the assistance of law enforcement agencies if necessary.[95] Appeal is confined to the special debt tribunals, but only if the borrower has deposited 75 per cent of what is claimed.[96]

The recent trend in some common law countries is to impose limits on creditors exercising their security so as to give borrowers a breathing space in which to seek rehabilitation.[97] There are strong arguments for a limited period in which a borrower seeks to restructure. However, India had broader measures in the Sick Industrial Companies (Special Provisions) Act 1985.[98] This legislation constituted a Board for Industrial and Financial Reconstruction. The directors of an industrial company which had become sick had to refer it to the Board; the government and banks might also refer the company. The Board can then inquire into the company: if the Board decided that it was practicable for a sick industrial company to make its net worth positive within a reasonable time it had to give it a period to do so; if not, it may direct reconstruction. The important point for present purposes is that if an inquiry was pending or a scheme under consideration, all rights to security had to be stayed. There were considerable delays in proceedings by the Board and the result was to block the exercise by many creditors of their rights to security. There are new procedures under the companies (Second Amendment) Act 2002.[99]

Law's Administration

Last week, the US embassy in Jakarta criticised the Central Jakarta District Court's decision to annul an international arbitration decision ordering Pertamina [the state oil company] to pay Karaha Bodas[100] US$261 million in damages...

The dispute originated from a contract entered into between Pertamina–PLN and Karaha Bodas in 1994, for the development and channelling of thermo-electrical energy in West

[93] 104 above.
[94] *Mardia Chemicals Ltd v Union of India* [2004] INSC 247.
[95] Sections 13–14.   [96] Sections 17–18, 34.   [97] 262 above.
[98] Sick Industrial Companies (Special Provisions) Act 1985, s 22. For Pakistan: Companies (Rehabilitation of Sick Industrial Units) Rules 1999.
[99] See also Sick Industrial Companies (Special Provisions) Repeal Act 2003.
[100] Karaha Bodas owned as to 80 per cent by two US corporations; as to 10 per cent by a Japanese company; and as to the remainder by an Indonesian firm linked to a son of a former Indonesia vice-president.

Java. However, former President Suharto annulled 156 projects, including Karaha Bodas, in response to the onset of the economic crisis in mid-1997. Consequently Karaha Bodas filed a US$560 million claim against Pertamina and PLN in Switzerland, [101] which upheld Karha Bodas' claim . . .

. . . Pertamina filed a lawsuit with the Central Jakarta District Court requesting annulment of the overseas court decisions [which froze Pertamina's assets]. Chaired by Herry Swantoro, the presiding judicial panel at the Central Jakarta District Court ruled in favour of Pertamina . . .

According to international law expert Hikmahanto Juwana,[102] the Central Jakarta District Court lacks the authority to annul [an international arbitration] decision . . . [103]

Singapore has one of the most advanced judicial systems in the world: impressive buildings, electronic filing of cases, case management, modern procedural rules, and high quality decision making.[104] Towards the other end of the spectrum of judicial systems is that of Singapore's neighbour, Indonesia. *Karaha Bodas v Pertamina* is only the tip of the iceberg. Throughout its history constitutional arrangements have made judicial independence a chimera. Until 1970 the President of the Republic could intervene directly to overturn cases; subsequently, the implementation of cases could be waived in the national interest.[105] Judicial review was effectively unknown as a concept until the establishment of the Administration Court in 1991. Worst still is the widely held view that corruption is endemic in the system. Some law firms refused to litigate because that very act would implicate them in it.[106] In 1995 retiring Supreme Court judge Professor Asikin Kusumaatmadja estimated that about one half of Indonesian judges were corrupt; that figure was challenged by a senior lawyer who said the judge was probably afraid to offend his colleagues so made such a low estimate.[107]

For years international financial institutions were critical of the judicial system in Indonesia. Creditors and investors faced delaying tactics, successive appeals, and anomalous judicial decisions, and rarely prevailed in enforcement proceedings. The World Bank saw legislation it advocated, such as the new Bankruptcy Law in 1998, subverted by a lack of judicial understanding, and a failure of

---

[101] The relevant agreements provided for arbitration in Switzerland under the UNCITRAL rules.

[102] Professor of International Economic Law, University of Indonesia.

[103] Ahmad Taufik & Agus Hidayat, 'Courting Condemnation', *Tempo Magazine* Djakarta, No. 52/11, 2–9 September 2002.

[104] K. Blöchlinger, '*Primus inter pares*: Is the Singapore Judiciary First Among Equals?' (2000) 9 *Pacific Rim L. & Policy J.* 591.

[105] S. Butt, 'The *Eksekusi* of the *Negara Hukum*: Implementing Judicial Decisions in Indonesia', in T. Lindsey (ed.), *Indonesia. Law and Society* (Sydney, 1999) 247–9.

[106] A. Harding, 'The Economic Crisis and Law Reform in South East Asia' (2001) 8 *Asia Pacific Bus. R.* 49, 54.

[107] D. Bourchier, 'Magic Memos, Collusion and Judges with Attitude', in K. Jayasuriya (ed.), *Law, Capitalism and Power in Asia* (London, 1999), 239. See also D. Lev, 'Between State and Society: Professional Lawyers and Reform in Indonesia', in T. Lindsey (ed.), *op.cit.*, 236–8; G. Goodpaster, 'Reflections on Corruption in Indonesia', in T. Lindsey & H. Dick (eds), *Corruption in Asia* (Sydney, 2002).

implementation.[108] Nevertheless, foreign and domestic credit and investment continued to flow into the Indonesian economy. The risk that there was no meaningful recourse to the courts was apparently traded off in favour of high anticipated returns. In some cases informal networks and personal influence led to the resolution of disputes. Agreements with international arbitration clauses seemed to offer some hope—at least until *Karaha Bodas v Pertamina*. In recent years, just as a more democratic Indonesia has been introducing judicial independence, and its National Law Commission has been tackling problems such as corruption in the judiciary, creditors and investors drew a line. In explaining why Indonesia was no longer a good place to invest, Professor Hikmahanto Juwana was reported as saying: 'Investors in Indonesia doubt whether their rights will be preserved and about the sanctity of contracts'.[109]

This link between weak legal institutions and poor economic growth and development is a truism with international financial institutions.[110] A well-functioning legal system is seen as indispensable to a successful market economy, primarily for enforcing long-time contracts but also protecting the property rights of domestic and foreign investors and obliging governments to act in accordance with law. In the specific area of credit, what is required is the 'predictable, transparent and affordable enforcement of both unsecured and secured credit claims by efficient mechanisms outside of insolvency as well as a sound insolvency system'.[111] The upshot of the link is that international financial institutions and other bodies allocate considerable moneys for judicial reform projects in developing countries. These focus primarily on the mechanisms of dispute resolution, public prosecutors, the legal profession, and sometimes legal education. The aim is to strengthen judicial and prosecutorial independence, to speed and widen access to the courts and other dispute resolution and generally to professionalize the whole legal system (including the system of professional ethics).[112] Reform of the legal system in this way has the further merit of enhancing public confidence in access to justice. In practical terms, assistance has taken the straightforward path of financing new or refurbished court buildings, funding court libraries and the publication of judicial decisions and promoting judicial training. Despite the common sense appeal of such programmes they may not achieve a great deal in the absence of other changes.[113]

---

[108] e.g. G. Goodpaster, 'Indonesian Bankruptcy: The Case of the Phantom Creditors' (2000) 2 *Aust.J. of Asian Law* 217.

[109] A. Sipress, 'Legal System in Indonesia Scares off Investors', *International Herald-Tribune*, 30 October 2002, 1. See also World Bank, '*Indonesia. Ideas for the Future. Justice Sector Reform*', January 2005.   [110] 25–6 above.

[111] World Bank, *Principles and Guidelines for Effective Insolvency and Creditor Rights Systems*, April 2001, para. 8.

[112] World Bank, Legal Vice Presidency, *Legal and Judicial Reform* (Washington, DC, 2002) and *Initiatives in Legal and Judicial Reform* (Washington, DC, 2002); D. Garcia-Sayan, 'The Role of International Financial Institutions in Judicial Reform' (1999) 7 *Centre for the Independence of Judges and Lawyers Yearbook* (Geneva) 31.

[113] L. Hammergen, *Judicial Training and Justice Reform*, USAID Centre for Democracy and Governance Paper (Washington, DC, 1998).

Procedure

One of the central concerns of Jeremy Bentham's jurisprudence was court procedures. The judicial system, in his view, should be organized to provide cheap, simple, accessible and local public justice. This was impeded by the complexities and expenses of procedural rules and the confusing technical rules of evidence which were, he believed, attributable in part to the self-interest of lawyers who depended on fees for their income.[114] Bentham's writings have a resonance in the present-day problems facing courts in many countries. The crucial problem tends to be delay, but cost and legal formalism are also evident. A recent empirical study of legal formalism in 109 countries found that it was associated with greater delay, more corruption, less impartiality and consistency, and inferior access to justice. Transplanting Western legal procedures to developing countries has led, in the analysis, to undesirably high levels of formalism.[115]

Rules of court could, in some respects, be strengthened and streamlined For example, the rules for summary judgment in some jurisdictions are defective in being confined to claims on a bill of exchange such as cheque or for a debt or liquidated demand in money arising on a written contract, enactment, or guarantee.[116] These jurisdictions did not adopt the amended 1933 English rules for summary judgment, which removed such limitations. Among the factors identified in a World Bank Report explaining court delay in India were limited use of *ex parte* judgments, over-use of oral arguments, easy procedural avenues to adjournment, and multiple appeals.[117] From July 2002 amendments to the Indian Civil Procedure Code have sought to compress the disposal of civil cases within a year by setting time limits for the different stages of the process. Adjournments cannot exceed three; there can be no second appeal in a money claim where the value does not exceed Rs 25,000; and the general power of the courts to extend time limits prescribed in the Code is restricted to thirty days.[118]

On the whole it would seem that the rules of procedure are not the primary impediment to litigation in the region. As the Law Commission of India put it some time ago, a good deal of the criticism that the procedural law is the cause of delay when carefully analysed shows 'that justice is delayed not so much by any defects or technicalities in the prescribed procedure as by its faulty application or by failure to apply it'.[119] Delay in the courts of some developing countries is massive.[120] Delay,

---

[114] W. Twining, 'Alternative to What? Theories of Litigation, Procedure and Dispute Settlement in Anglo American Jurisprudence: Some Neglected Classics' (1993) 56 *MLR* 380, 383–5.

[115] S. Djankov, R. La Porta, F. Lopez-de-Silanes & A. Shleifer, 'Courts' (2003) 118 *QJ.Econ* 342. The authors chose proceedings on a bounced cheque and for eviction of a tenant: the former is not especially relevant in the developing world.   [116] e.g. India Code Civ.Proc., Order 37 (1908).

[117] *Indian Policies to Reduce Poverty and Accelerate Sustainable Development* (World Bank South Asia Region, Poverty Reduction and Economic Management Unit, Report 2000), 44–5.

[118] Civil Procedure (Amendment) Acts 1999 and 2002.

[119] e.g. Law Commission of India, *Reform of Judicial Administration: Fourteenth Report* (Delhi, 1958), 262.   [120] *idid.*

where it occurs, may be the result of the way that the lawyers, judges, or court officials handle a case. Responsibility for excessive delay may be peculiar to an individual lawyer, judge, or court official: as in other walks of life there are the efficient and the inefficient, the bold and the timid, the knowledgeable and the ignorant, and the conscientious and the careless. Delay may also turn on the way that lawyers in general deal with litigation. A seminal text on judicial administration in the United States posited how lawyers' work practices affect delay in the courts. It pointed out that some lawyers are more in demand than others because of their success. Successful lawyers are predisposed to retain cases, for one psychological reason or another, even though it builds up a personal backlog. The upshot is that the backlog of cases in the legal firm or advocate's chambers may become a logjam in the courts.[121] In 2002 the Chief Justice of Singapore used a similar explanation but for a converse effect: some litigation lawyers, snowed under with work, were unable to cope with the rapid pace demanded by the court system in Singapore.[122]

A further aspect of lawyers' practices leading to delay may be that they file spurious defences on behalf of clients. It is easy enough for a borrower to deny that the advance was made, to allege a miscalculation in the amount owing or that documents were signed in blank, to deny service, or to argue that the agreement is unconscionable and should not be enforced. A report of the Asian Development Bank canvassed lawyers' opinions on such practices:

293. Dilatory defenses to slow the court process were identified in several of the countries. These included, in Pakistan for example, denying notice was received, filing unnecessary applications, and calling for adjournments because lawyers are not available, witnesses would not be properly notified, or government agencies (and others) have not produced documents. These defences could delay by many months. India and Thailand reported similar tactics.

294. Fraudulent defenses were reported in Thailand and implied in Pakistan. It was common for the debtor to assert defences based on statements of fact that were not true . . .

296. Joining issue on the merits can be a very effective delaying tactic, even if the debtor expects eventually to lose. In Thailand, delays on the merits (such as failure of creditor to advance funds as agreed, so that the debtor collapsed) can take 3 to 6 years to litigate through appeal. In India, common defenses on the merits include unreasonable condition, no default, no legal obligation to pay, and unlawful debt.

297. A third party may be brought in to challenge the secured creditor's interest, in Indonesia. The third party may be the owner of the collateral, by statute, or may even be another secured creditor by court decisions.[123]

---

[121] E. Friesen, E. Gallas, & N. Gallas, *Managing the Courts* (Indianapolis, 1971), 166.

[122] 'Response of the Honorable the Chief Justice Yong Pung How', *Singapore Academy of Law Newsletter*, No. 76, Jan/Feb 2002, 11.

[123] *Secured Transactions Law Reform in Asia: Unleashing the Potential of Collateral*, *op.cit.*, 75–6 (footnotes omitted).

There may well be genuine defences, but if lawyers are party to their clients' deceptions, or if judges are too lax in testing matters, defendants will take advantage of the law's delays to gain time, even when there is no clear defence to an action. A former Chief Justice of India identified the problem of what might be termed 'weak' judges, who do not control cases firmly enough:

[C]ounsel should be heard fully, but if the point is barely arguable or the point or authority cited is irrelevant a judge should politely ask the counsel to proceed to the next point. Times have come when the time of the court must be rationed like a scarce essential commodity. The judges and counsel must keep in mind the thousands of litigants who are impatiently waiting for their cases to be heard.[124]

This point is especially apposite in applications for summary judgment.

Judges and court officials

A hardly perennial, even in developed jurisdictions, is that judicial salaries are not high enough to attract the best lawyers—successful attorneys can earn much more than judges.[125] This, of course, may have repercussions for the quality of justice and the efficiency with which the courts operate. Yet the increase in salary to bridge the gap is substantial and there is no guarantee that attracting more practising attorneys would result in a significant improvement in the way justice is administered.[126] The number and allocation of judges may have an impact on delay. A relative reduction in the number of judges in an area may lead to a greater backlog, reduce the incentive to settle, or both, whereas a more generous allocation in other areas may expedite matters, attract new business, or both. The number of judges is a starting point in any inquiry as to whether it is possible to increase the amount of available judge time and thus reduce delay. Unfavourable comparisons have been made with other countries as to the number of judges per capita and per suit.[127] However, population is, at one level, a poor yardstick for comparison because it does not take into account the variation in the amount of litigation. Consideration must also be given to other factors such as the number of other judges handling cases in other courts, such as local courts.

This outline of lawyers' practices and the position of the judiciary suggests that changes in rules and procedure will not necessarily achieve the desired aim unless the context is appreciated. The new conventional wisdom of those researching delay is that the key lies in the practices of the profession. The literature

---

124 S.M. Sikri, quoted in V. Grover, *Courts and Political Process in India* (New Delhi, 1989), 341.

125 e.g. Law Commission of India, *Seventy-Seventh Report on Delay and Arrears in Trial Courts* (New Delhi, 1978), 53–4.

126 R. Moog, *Whose Interests Are Supreme? Organizational Politics in the Civil Courts in India* (Ann Arbor, 1997), 58. See generally S. Oxner, 'The Quality of Judges' (2002) 1 *World Bank LR* 307. In the United Kingdom the salary of high court judges can be partly discounted because of the automatic knighthood.

127 Law Commission of India, *Manpower Planning in Judiciary: A Blueprint* (New Delhi, 1987); Parliament of India, Rajya Sabha, *Law's Delays: Arrears in Courts*, Eighty-fifth Report, 2002, paras 31.6–32.2. cf. R. Moog, *op.cit.*, 51–8.

sometimes describes this in terms of the importance of the 'legal culture'.[128] If the practices of the profession, or the legal culture, are important, what can be done to effect change? Since delay is a consequence of the behaviour of those like judges and lawyers, they must have incentives to behave differently. Avenues for reform in this regard are professional ethics, training, and discipline. Nor can the engine room of court registries be neglected. Opportunities for petty corruption among court functionaries in matters such as allocating dates for court hearings or tampering with court records can be partly overcome with more routine procedures and automation of court records. Legal proceedings collapse because service of documents cannot be effected or demonstrated. Service by registered post and public notification (for example in a widely distributed newspaper) are possible solutions. Overall law's efficient and honest administration demands that there be adequate resources and supervision of the machinery.

Debt recovery courts

One sort of special court is the debt recovery court in the countries of south Asia: they impose strict time limits, control the number of adjournments, and require deposits of defendants wishing to appeal.[129] The debt recovery courts are confined to cases filed by banks and financial institutions. Yet their case load is enormous. The debt recovery courts in India have suffered from a lack of funding, delays have been common and enforcement of judgments has been weak.[130] Although the courts speeded up decision making, they did not make enforcement of judgments any quicker. Amendment to the 1993 Act, and the Securitization and Reconstruction of Financial Assets and Enforcement of Security Interest Act 2002, have attempted to challenge these deficiencies.[131] More needs to be done.

The objection to the idea of such special business courts has been primarily based on the grounds that they constitute a preference for banks and financial institutions, although opposition has been intertwined with opposition to the special procedures. Possibly the strongest argument in favour of special courts is that they will create a psychological breakthrough leading to expedition of this type of case and possibly in other areas as well. Nothing could be worse for the rule of law than the massive delays in some courts. As for the funding, 'user pays' would mean that as a practical matter claimants should have to pay filing fees sufficient to fund the court. However, a major concern would be if this cost was automatically added to the defendant's burden. There are clear advantages to claimants in quicker recovery and arguably there is no injustice if they have to bear

---

[128] T. Church *et al.*, *Justice Delayed* (Williamsburg, 1978), 79–80; B. Mahoney *et al.*, *Changing Times in Trial Courts* (Williamsburg, 1988), 206–7. See 160 above.

[129] 101–3 above.

[130] J. Hanson & S. Kathuria, 'India's Financial System: Getting Ready for the Twenty-first Century: An Introduction', in J. Hanson & S. Kathuria (eds), *India: A Financial Sector for the Twenty First Century* (New Delhi, 1999), 12.   [131] 282 above.

the cost burden. In theory, filing fees for a defendant should be pitched at a level that deters spurious defences while granting them access to justice. In practice it is difficult to determine the appropriate fee to achieve this. Consequently, a possible approach is to emphasize access to the courts at first instance but requiring a substantial deposit (subject to waiver on showing just cause) if unsuccessful defendants wish to appeal.

Conclusion

The rhetoric of the rule of law is one weapon in the battle for fairer and more economically efficient credit allocation and debt recovery. A society's claim to adhere to the rule of law and equality before the law in its formal sense is hollow if bending the rules is tolerated and law's administration is subverted. Moreover, it should not be forgotten that law reform may operate in an educative way. A significant change in the law may be an important symbol of a change in public policy having as much a psychological as a practical effect. Specific changes to make the law relating to credit allocation and debt recovery economically more efficient include stronger corporate governance measures to reduce the influence of the 'untouchables' on allocation and debt recovery decisions; improvements in credit appraisal through the establishment of credit reference agencies; more varied forms of security and their extra-judicial enforcement; and improvements in the machinery of the courts. There are no easy solutions. Nor do the solutions lie simply in changes in the law. Law reform must be systematically tailored to the problem and to the society in which it is being considered. Reform in this area is not a matter of the blanket introduction of pro-creditor law. If laws become too pro-creditor they will be honoured more in the breach than in the observance. There is a need for better consumer protection laws in the region.[132] There is also a need for flexible bankruptcy laws, which enable persons to gain economic rehabilitation fairly easily. It is also worthwhile noting the innovative approaches to providing credit to the poor pioneered by the Grameen Bank in Bangladesh.[133] Microfinancing builds on the importance of social capital. The strong ties between creditor and debtor in microfinance creates a solidarity where default is unacceptable and therefore low.

---

[132] cf. S. Sothi Rachagan, 'Protection Against Unfair Trade Practices in Malaysia—Law, Enforcement, and Redress in a Developing Country' (1992) 15 *J. Consumer Pol'y* 225.

[133] M. Robinson, *The Microfinance Revolution: Sustainable Finance for the Poor* (Washington, DC, 2001); L. Hager, 'Low-end Globalization. Bringing Wealth-creation to the Poor', in J. Faundez & M. Footer & J. Norton (eds), *Governance, Development and Globalization* (London, 2000); Y. Miyashita, 'Microfinance and Poverty Alleviation: Lessons from Indonesia's Village Banking System' (2000) 10 *Pacific Rim L. & Policy J.* 147. There are some question marks over the effectiveness of microcredit in benefiting the poor; in any event it should not be unregulated: H. Weber, *The Politics of Microcredit* (London, 2003).

If law is seen in its social context, it becomes obvious that what is often needed is institution building so that existing laws are more effective in practice. One cannot underestimate the obstacles to this. Institutions where improved administration would enhance credit allocation and debt recovery include government registries (land, motor vehicles, security) and, of course, the courts. Importantly, problems within financial institutions themselves need to be addressed since it is clear that in some cases problems in credit allocation and debt recovery are attributable to the administrative processes within a bank. On average the foreign banks operating in the region have had fewer problems with debt recovery than local banks and this has been used as an argument in favour of privatizing state banks. This does not necessarily follow since foreign banks have not been subject to the same rules for directed credits and branch networks and have confined their lending to 'blue chip', often foreign, borrowers. However, the closer relationships which some foreign banks have with their customers could well be emulated since it means better credit appraisal at the outset and more effective monitoring during the currency of a loan. If privatization does contribute to more effective credit allocation and debt recovery what needs to be determined is the point at which introducing private ownership into a state bank has a significant impact on the effectiveness of credit allocation and debt recovery (for example, is sale of a minority interest enough).

As well as institution building, reform cannot neglect the human dimension. Better training of lawyers, judges, civil servants, and others is one aspect. Mention has also been made of the need for a strong and independent judiciary. The problem of suitably qualified persons to be judges is a very difficult nut to crack. The empirical evidence in countries like Singapore is that judges with a sufficient commitment to reducing delay can have a very profound effect. 'Strong' judges can expedite matters by striking out spurious defences and hurrying on trials. Lawyers, too, cannot escape scrutiny. Legal imagination can facilitate credit, by constituting new forms of security or making the enforcement of existing security more effective. There is also the issue of legal ethics: high ethical standards at the bar, it has rightly been said, can reduce in many instances the complexity of legal processes and expedite litigation.

10

Legal Transplants: The Sri Lankan Experience

In tracing the American influence on the development of Canadian commercial law, Jacob Ziegel pointed out that Canadian commercial law is a mosaic reflecting a variety of influences—English, French, and American, superimposed on an increasingly important indigenous element.[1] While American law had an influence in the nineteenth century, in areas such as banking and conditional sale, this was the period primarily of English influence, commercially and also politically. In the interwar period, the Conference of Commissioners on Uniformity of Legislation in Canada drew on the work of their US counterpart, with legislation such as the Uniform Bulk Sales Act 1920, the Conditional Sales Act 1922, and the Small Loans Act 1939. Then followed the most important period of US influence, after World War II.

> In an earlier era the United Kingdom might have been able to supply the legal resources to enable the Dominion to cope with the *congeries* of new problems. But conditions had changed. Greatly weakened by the exertions of war, the United Kingdom lay prostrate. The British Empire was rapidly being converted into a much more loosely knit association of fully autonomous Commonwealth states. The mother country was no longer the cynosure of legal developments, certainly not in the commercial sphere and possibly not others. The mantle of legal leadership had clearly fallen on Uncle Sam and Uncle Sam was ready to assume it with bold new doctrinal strokes, masterful forms of codification, and a plethora of innovative legislative measures in the corporate, commercial, and consumer areas. Canada was the most immediate and still remains the single largest beneficiary of this shift in direction.[2]

Ziegel's discussion of the Canadian borrowings of US commercial law raises the general issue of the nature and effectiveness of legal borrowings. In the area of commercial law, there are many examples of legal concepts, legislation, and legal institutions being transplanted from one society to the other. The doctrines of the commercial law of England spread throughout the common law world as part of the impositions of Empire. Although subsequently modified, in differing ways, there is still a consequent affinity—indeed in many cases a close parallel—in the

---

[1] J. Ziegel, 'The American Influence on the Development of Canadian Commercial Law' (1976) 26 *Case Western Reserve L.Rev.* 861.   [2] *ibid.*, 868.

legal concepts applied in common law countries varying greatly in their conditions and people. The courts of common law countries may still invoke English authorities, or feel it incumbent on them to explain why they may be departing from them.[3] Perhaps the most extraordinary provision was s 5(1) of the Civil Law Act of the Republic of Singapore, which until 1993 applied current English commercial law, unless there was specific Singaporean legislation to the contrary.[4] In a great many commercial situations, therefore, Singaporean lawyers and courts applied English doctrines and legislation directly.

As to the transplant of legislation, illustrative is the introduction in many common law countries of British legislation such as the Bills of Exchange Act 1882, the Sale of Goods Act 1893, and the Companies Act 1948. An irony is that while this legislation has been reformed in Britain, countries to which it has been transplanted have not always had the inclination or resources to do the same.[5] Outside the common law, there are instances of the wholesale transplant of civil law codes. A good example is the adoption by Japan of the German civil and commercial law. Not only was German jurisprudence at the height of its prestige at the turn of the century when this was done, but in addition the German codes had been recently drafted under Bismarck. It was thus thought that they were more in accordance with modern industrial society than the French Napoleonic codes.[6]

The transplant of legal institutions started with the system of courts. Even today transplants continue, as with the introduction of special commercial courts in some countries.[7] Apart from the machinery of justice the transplant of legal institutions is well illustrated by the spread of US anti-trust law and securities regulation. Introduction of these laws is inevitably accompanied by the establishment or revitalization of a bureaucracy to give effect to them. While primarily regulatory in intention, adoption of these regimes has also had implications for private law remedies. Less transplanted in practice, although the desirability of doing so has been much discussed by legal academics around the world, has been the US system for the registration of personal property security (Article 9 of the Uniform Commercial Code).[8]

One aspect of legal transplants is what they say about the relationship between law and society.[9] Unless a law, such as a commercial statute, has some correspondence with the needs of important parts of society, it seems difficult to see how it will survive as a living, working instrument. If it is not relevant, lawyers will ignore

---

[3] For a Canadian example: *Hunter Engineering Co. Inc. v Syncrude Canada Ltd* (1989) 57 DLR (4th ed) 321.   [4] Statutes of the Republic of Singapore, No. 35 of 1993.
[5] An example of the first point is the aftermath of Jacob Ziegel's Herculean efforts with the three volume *Report on Sale of Goods* (1979) for the Ontario Law Reform Commission. Lack of resources for law reform in some Asian and many African common law countries is more understandable.
[6] See H. Oda, *Japanese Law*, 2nd edn (Oxford, 1999).   [7] 102–3 above.
[8] The story of the adoption of the latter in Canada is told in J. Ziegel, *op.cit.*, 868–74; J. Ziegel & R. Cuming, 'The Modernization of Canadian Personal Property Security Law' (1981) 31 *UTLJ* 249. See also P. Ali, *The Law of Secured Finance* (Oxford, 2002), 156–71; 275 above.
[9] 28–9 above.

it or meet business needs by drafting around it in commercial contracts. A country may be divided as to the virtue of a country transplanting a law. Perhaps because of pressure from international financial institutions those operating the levers of power may favour the adoption of laws contrary to the 'culture of the lawyers'. As we will see, this was the case in Sri Lanka. Nonetheless, the transplants already mentioned give some support to the thesis that if transplanting a law is to be a success there must be a congruence with societal values. Relevant factors include the will of officials and judges implementing it; whether it is in the self-interest of lawyers to assist in implementing the law; and whether institutional arrangements provide for access to justice for those who might want the law enforced.

The present chapter explores some of these dimensions of legal transplants by outlining, in relation to Sri Lanka, one aspect of commercial law, the law of security. The story is as interesting as it is complex. Two aspects are focused on in the following account. The first is the transplant of Western commercial law in Sri Lanka and the mosaic it produced. English commercial law was transplanted to Sri Lanka as part of colonization, but it was overlaid on the Roman–Dutch law dating from the period of Dutch power. The second aspect is the relationship of this transplant to societal needs, in particular commercial needs. For some time a modern commercial law has been seen as a necessary instrument of economic development by one part of the Sri Lankan ruling elite. Yet an important part of the legal elite resisted the requisite legal changes. Despite the opposition of the lawyers, important amendments to commercial law were effected in 1990, although their efficacy was limited because of societal and institutional resistance.[10]

Law of Security (Collateral)

Like the great majority of former British colonies, Sri Lanka enacted local versions of English commercial statutes with few, if any, changes of substance. The Bills of Exchange Ordinance and the Sale of Goods Ordinance are the best examples.[11] In addition, certain English commercial law doctrines were put into statutory form in Sri Lanka. A notable example is the Trust Receipts Ordinance,[12] to which we return. The basic common law of Sri Lanka remained, however, Roman–Dutch law. That was because in constitutional theory Sri Lanka was acquired partly by conquest, so that the law in force under the previous Dutch colonizers remained.[13]

---

[10] See A. Perry, *Legal Systems as a Determinant of FDI: Lessons from Sri Lanka* (London, 2001), 98–122, who reports on investor perceptions of laws and the courts in Sri Lanka. See 269–70 above; 306–7 below.

[11] *Legislative Enactments of the Democratic Socialist Republic of Sri Lanka*, 1980, Revised Edition, 92 and 93. [12] *ibid.*, Chapter 96.

[13] See J.C.W. Pereira, *Institutes of the Laws of Ceylon* (Colombo, Government Printer, 1901), 1–2, 13; J. Mervyn Canaga Retna, 'The Legal System of Sri Lanka', in K. Redden (ed.) *Modern Legal Systems* (Buffalo, 1985), 751–4; L.J.M. Cooray, *An Introduction to the Legal System of Ceylon* (Colombo, 1972), 60, 65, 71–2. Contrast the Australian position: 239–40 above.

In this regard Sri Lanka stands with South Africa and Zimbabwe as the only jurisdictions with Roman–Dutch law as their common law. One consequence is a certain lack of vigour in some parts of the Sri Lankan legal system, since there are fewer outside reference points for change.[14] This is especially so since South African legal thinking has not been readily available for political and other reasons (for example, the cost of obtaining South African law reports, books, and journals).

Although Roman–Dutch law is the common law of Sri Lanka, English non-statutory commercial law principles were introduced 'with respect to the law of partnerships, corporations, banks and banking, principals and agents, carriers by land, life and fire insurance', in the absence of specific statutory enactment.[15] However there are several leading decisions just before Independence, where the Sri Lankan courts resisted arguments to apply English principles to commercial law. *Hong Kong and Shanghai Bank v Krishnapillai*[16] held that the law governing the conversion of cheques was the Roman–Dutch, not the English, common law for it was an issue of tort, not of 'banks and banking' as the Civil Law Ordinance requires for English law to apply. In the course of its judgment, the court said that consequently the right of a pledgee to sell security without recourse to a court of law was a matter of Roman–Dutch law. *Mitchell v Fernando*[17] held that the Roman-Dutch law of mortgage applied to a mortgage of shares in a company. This was despite the fact that the Civil Law Ordinance required that matters relating to joint stock companies be decided according to English, not Roman–Dutch, law, and that shares were things unknown to the Roman–Dutch law. The court categorized the issue as one of mortgage, not one with respect to joint stock companies, and applied the Roman–Dutch law.

The upshot is that commercial law in Sri Lanka has been a confused amalgam of Roman–Dutch law, English common law, and statute. There is evidence amongst lawyers of a preference in unclear cases for Roman–Dutch over English common law. One reason for this success of the Roman–Dutch transplant has been the natural inclination in the post-Independence era to reject legacies of the immediate colonial period. Another reason may have been the tendency as with lawyers everywhere to foster a system bolstering yet further what has been called 'professional mystery'.[18]

---

[14] cf. 'Like the common law of England, the common law of Ceylon has not remained static since 1799. In course of time it has been the subject of progressive development... as the courts of Ceylon have applied its basic principles to the solution of legal problems posed by the changing conditions of society in Ceylon': *Kodeeswaran v Attorney-General of Ceylon* [1970] AC 1111, 1118–19, PC.

[15] Civil Law Ordinance, s 3. *Legislative Enactments of the Democratic Socialist Republic of Sri Lanka*, 1980, Revised Edition, Chapter 89.   [16] (1932) 33 NLR 249.

[17] (1945) 46 NLR 265. Although he does not discuss these two cases, Cooray notes the Roman–Dutch resurgence in this period: *op.cit.*, 76.

[18] R. Dingwell & P. Lewis (eds), *The Sociology of the Professions* (London, 1983), 84.

Parate Execution

The common law of Sri Lanka, as we have seen, is Roman–Dutch law. Immovables can be mortgaged under Roman–Dutch law, but the mortgagee does not obtain a right of ownership, only the right to recover payment of the debt secured by the mortgage through legal action.[19] Extra-judicial sale—known as parate execution—was forbidden. After 1871 it was possible to mortgage movables in Sri Lanka in only two ways—by delivery (pledge) or by registered bill of sale (which, however, did not validate the mortgage or give priority to the registrant).[20] As with the mortgage of immovables, Sri Lankan lawyers have taken the view that under Roman–Dutch law the mortgagee of movables does not have a right of sale but has to obtain a judgment of the court upon the mortgage debt and then take out a writ of execution against the property. J.C.W. Pereira stated the matter of parate execution authoritatively in relation to both movables and immovables:[21]

The effect of a mortgage is not that the creditor may retain the mortgaged property for himself or sell it on his own authority. It may not even stipulate by contract for the right of forfeiture of the ownership in default of payment, but he must after obtaining judgment allow the sale to take place according to legal process, and thus recover what is due to himself [Grot. 2.48.41]. The position is stated by van der Linden thus—where the debt secured by pledge or mortgage becomes due, the creditor is not at liberty to sell the pledge or thing mortgaged without a decree of the court or a judgment to this effect ... [v.d.L.12.57].[22]

However, in Roman law a first mortgagee ultimately acquired a power of sale which could not be excluded by express agreement.[23] Moreover, the tendency of judicial decisions in South Africa has been to recognize the validity of an agreement for the extra-judicial sale of movables. In *Osry v Hirsch, Loubser & Co. Ltd*,[24] an agreement for the sale of movables by means of parate execution was held to be valid. It was a case of pledge. The court also held that it was open to the debtor in such a case to seek the protection of the court if it could show that in carrying out the agreement and effecting the sale the creditor had acted in a manner which prejudiced its rights. The case was followed in other South African cases.[25]

The result of these decisions is that parate execution—whereby a mortgagee can sell the security without the prior intervention of a court—is looked upon

[19] R.W. Lee, *An Introduction to Roman–Dutch Law*, 5th edn (Oxford, 1953), 200.

[20] See A. de Soysa, *The Law of Ceylon* (Colombo, 1963), vol. 2, 307.

[21] *The Law of Ceylon* (Colombo, 1904), vol. 2, 442–3.

[22] The references are to Grotius' *Introduction to Dutch Jurisprudence* and van der Linden's *Institutes of the Laws of Holland*.

[23] E.R.S.R. Coomaraswamy, *The Conveyancer and Property Lawyer* (Colombo, 1949), 209; R.W. Lee, *op.cit.*, 200.　　　　　　　　　　　　　　　　　　　　[24] 1922 CPD 531.

[25] e.g. *Aitken v Miller* 1951 (1) SA 153 (SR). See generally T.J. Scott & S. Scott, *Wille's Law of Mortgage and Pledge in South Africa*, 3rd edn (Cape Town, 1987) 120–4.

with disfavour by the Roman–Dutch law of Sri Lanka. The view of some Sri Lankan lawyers is that the *Hong Kong and Shanghai Bank* case was wrongly decided, because it was made in ignorance of developments in South Africa. Even if the approach of South African Roman–Dutch law were adopted, however, parate execution would only be available in the case of movables and, on one reading of the authorities, only in the case of pledge.

The Mortgage Act[26] gave full effect to the conception of a mortgage as understood in Roman–Dutch law.[27] Thus the Mortgage Act assumed that parate execution was not possible in the case of a mortgage of land, and so provided in detail for how hypothecary actions were to be conducted and their effect.[28] However, the Act permitted an approved credit agency, which was a mortgagee of shares, debentures, stock, life insurance policies, and corporeal movables deposited with the agency, to realize them without resort to the courts.[29] A mortgagor could sue for any loss or damage suffered as a result of an agency not duly exercising its powers or not following the correct procedures.[30] Section 85, dealing with corporeal movables, required that the corporeal movable be 'actually in the possession and custody of the agency'. With particular transactions, such as the import of goods, it might be possible for an agency financing them to have 'possession and custody' of the goods by a system of control over their warehousing. In many cases, however, as where the movables were the facilities and stock in trade of a business, such control was impracticable.

Generally, as we have seen, the law in Sri Lanka set itself against parate execution. Over the years, however, a number of state or state-related institutions were given the right of parate execution by specific enactment. The justification for giving these state institutions this privilege was that they were accountable to Parliament for any misuse of it, and possibly also that they had sufficient financial resources to compensate any person who suffered loss as a result. The power in the Bank of Ceylon Ordinance was illustrative. The bank was empowered to grant loans, advances or other accommodation on the security of a mortgage of any movable or immovable property. When default occurred, the board of directors of the bank could authorize a person to take possession of any immovable property or seize any movable property mortgaged to the bank and to manage and maintain such property as might have been done by the mortgagor if it had not made default.[31] Moreover, s 19 provided that the board of directors might resolve to authorize a specified person to sell by public auction any movable or immovable property mortgaged to the bank as security for any loan in respect of which default

---

[26] Act No. 6 of 1949 as amended.   [27] H. de Soysa, *op.cit*, 336–7.

[28] Especially ss 7–9, 16, 25, 33, 48, 52.

[29] Sections 73, 81, 85. To acquire the status of an approved credit agency, an institution or individual applied to the Director of Commerce, who referred the matter to a board (s 114). Banks, finance houses, and cooperative societies making loans have been approved under this provisions.

[30] Sections 78, 84, 88.

[31] Bank of Ceylon Ordinance, Chapter 397 as amended by Act No. 34 of 1968 and Law No. 10 of 1974, s 17. See also s 18 on the manager's powers.

had been made in order to recover the whole of the unpaid portion of such loan, and the interest due up to the date of the sale, together with the moneys and costs recoverable under s 18. If the mortgaged property were sold, all right, title, and interest of the borrower rested in the purchaser.[32]

Whatever the 'law in the books', the institutions entrusted by specific enactment with the power of parate execution have generally used it as a last resort. Even where the board of an institution has authorized parate execution, often a sale has not been proceeded with because a settlement has been reached. For example, the People's Bank has initiated parate proceedings fairly frequently. However, actions have not continued in most of these cases because borrowers have often responded by coming to an arrangement about repayment. A most striking example of abnegation in this area is that although the Bank of Ceylon has had the power of parate execution in relation to movable property since 1974, it has exercised it sparingly and has generally taken action against defaulters through the courts.

Opposition to the power of parate execution has been mainly on the basis that it can be 'abused'. Abuse has different meanings. One widely accepted sense of abuse is of the foreign lending institution exercising a power of parate execution ostensibly against the national economic interests of Sri Lanka by closing down a factory or project. Even without a power of parate execution, however, a foreign lender could decide on this course if the project were in difficulty. It would simply need to pull the plug on future financial assistance. As far as abuse by state banks is concerned, the evidence above suggests that it is not a phenomenon of recent times.[33] The tendency of some state banks has been to use the power only when the borrower himself agrees on a sale. While abuse of the power of parate execution is a clear possibility, there is a remarkable lack of empirical evidence of it occurring in Sri Lanka.

Independent of the law of parate execution stands the floating charge, which has long existed in Sri Lankan law. The Companies Act[34] specifically recognizes it. Indeed, it provides that nothing in s 63 of the Mortgage Act shall apply to any floating charge on the undertaking or property of a company.[35] That section of the Mortgage Act renders conventional general mortgages invalid and ineffective inasmuch as they give the mortgagee any lien, charge, claim, or priority over or in respect of any property. In other words, s 63 means that any general mortgage or assets by agreement between the parties is invalid, unless otherwise recognized by

---

[32] Section 28. See also s 29 on the purchaser's right to obtain a court order for delivery of possession of the property.

[33] In *Mendis Silva v Ceylon State Mortgage Bank* (1959) 61 NLR 385, the judges criticized the way the bank had acted. The borrower had suffered a 'cruel fate' at the hands of the bank (*per* Basnayake CJ at 386); the plaintiff 'could not have suffered as great a loss even if his creditor had been a rapacious moneylender' (*per* Pulle J at 392). Certainly the properties were sold at just under half their estimated value, but the sale had been well advertised and the borrower himself had been unable to sell them previously even after advertising widely. The borrower's 'cruel fate' appears to be simply by way of comparison with those borrowing from an institution without a power of parate execution.

[34] Act No. 17 of 1982.   [35] Section 91(10).

law. But not the floating charge which, as indicated, is fully effective as a result of s 91(10) of the Companies Act. As in other jurisdictions, the Sri Lankan Companies Act provides that a floating charge is void against the liquidator or any creditor of the company, unless it is registered with the Registrar of Companies within the twenty-one days of its creation.[36]

A crucial point about floating charges is that the instrument can provide for the appointment of a receiver without resort to the court. In other words, the general prohibition on parate execution in Sri Lanka does not apply in the case of floating charges. This is recognized in the Act itself.[37] Given that the general prohibition on parate execution does not apply to floating charges, it is surprising that so few have been created. Why has the floating charge been used so infrequently? While there are many unincorporated businesses in Sri Lanka which cannot create floating charges, there are a significant number of companies which can. One explanation for the infrequent use of the floating charge seems to lie in a combination of ignorance and a lack of expertise in its use. The view of lawyers and bankers in Sri Lanka seems to have been that it was really only appropriate for the most creditworthy and larger companies because it was not possible to follow stock in trade under a floating charge, with the result that the fraudulent borrower, or the borrower in trouble, could dissipate the assets so that there would be nothing left subject to the charge. Of course it is the essence of a floating charge that a company can continue to dispose of assets in the ordinary course of business, but a standard clause should be that the charge crystallizes as soon as the company disposes of assets otherwise than in the ordinary course of business. Another explanation is the lack of expertise. Because there are no receiverships, there are no experienced receivers, and hence a reluctance to use the device.

Hire purchase has been recognized by the law of Sri Lanka and widely used as a method of financing the purchase of goods, especially motor vehicles.[38] The right of the owner to repossess the goods on hire purchase was restricted by s 20 of the Consumer Credit Act:[39] once the hirer paid or tendered 75 per cent of the hire-purchase price, the owner could not repossess the goods but must claim what is owing by legal action. For present purposes, the point to be made is that the right of an owner to repossess goods under a hire-purchase agreement is functionally equivalent to the right of a mortgagee of goods to exercise the power of parate

---

[36] Section 91(1), (2)(f).

[37] 'Where any person obtains an order for the appointment of a receiver or manager of property of a company, *or appoints such a receiver or manager under any powers contained in any instrument . . .*' (my emphasis) s 98(1). See also s 382(1)).

[38] Some financing of motor vehicles has been by financial leasing and mortgage finance. Some banks have preferred the latter, partly because hire purchase has been thought to be disreputable, and partly because mortgage finance does not face the hire purchase barrier of blocking repossession of a vehicle once 75 per cent of the price has been paid (see below). Finance companies have been effectively confined to hire purchase and leasing because if they take a mortgage they cannot seize the motor vehicle without a court order. By contrast, banks can do this under specific legislation for the state banks or, as we will see, under the Recovery of Loans by Banks (Special Provisions) Act 1990.

[39] Act No. 29 of 1982.

execution. If goods subject to hire purchase can be seized and sold on default, why not goods subject to a mortgage?

Repossession of motor vehicles when the hirer is in default is a relatively straightforward matter in many countries. Representatives of the owner locate the vehicle through the owner's address and then, if necessary, force entry to it when it is parked unattended on the street. One reason repossession is not straightforward in Sri Lanka is that because labour is cheap vehicles are rarely left unattended. The person who can afford a vehicle can afford a driver, who also acts as a guard. A second reason is that the vehicle may not be readily located because the hirer has 'sold' it or has changed his address. There has been considerable concern in Sri Lanka with hirers fraudulently disposing of goods and then defaulting under the hire-purchase agreement. Being unable to repossess the goods, the owner has been forced to sue for arrears and loss under the agreement if the hirer can be located, but because of delays in the courts that is unattractive.[40] Thirdly, the Commissioner of Motor Vehicles has refused to register the owner as the absolute owner on repossession without giving the hirer the opportunity of objecting. This delicacy of treatment of hirers is another factor against financiers using repossession.

Law can do little about the first factor mentioned. It does have some bearing on the second. Legislation in 1982 strengthened the Consumer Credit Act in that a hirer failing without reasonable cause to provide information about the whereabouts of the goods is subject to a greater fine and ultimately to imprisonment.[41] The penalty provision on hirers fraudulently selling or disposing of goods was strengthened by introducing summary trial by a magistrate. However, there is no obligation on hirers to notify the motor vehicle registry of a change of address. Moreover, there is no right to search the motor vehicle registry, which would give a potential buyer the opportunity to check any plausible story which a hirer has given for not being able to produce the registration certificate.

The third factor—the opportunity which the Commissioner gives hirers to object to a transfer of absolute ownership when a vehicle is repossessed—was apparently motivated by a fear that unscrupulous finance companies would repossess vehicles. The Commissioner is given no such power in the Motor Traffic Act or the Consumer Credit Act 1982. It may be that the general principles of natural justice can be invoked as justification, on the grounds that hirers should be given an opportunity of being heard before their name is removed from the registration certificate. However, the principles of natural justice are the same in Sri Lanka as in other common law jurisdictions, and it has never been suggested elsewhere that

---

[40] *Report of the Committee Appointed by the Honourable the Minister of Justice Dr Hissanka Wijeyeratne to Examine and Report on the Law and Practice Relating to Debt Recovery*, Colombo, A Ministry of Justice Project, 1985 (hereinafter Debt Recovery Committee, *Report*), 15. The Committee was chaired by the late Mr D. Wimalarante, a retired judge of the Supreme Court, and had as members Mr H.L. de Silva, PC, later President of the Bar Association of Sri Lanka, and Mr N.U. Jayawardena, a former Governor of the Central Bank. In Sri Lanka as elsewhere the composition of a government committee throws important light on its findings: see 301n, 306n below. cf. repossession in Thailand and Indonesia: 280 above.   [41] New s.15.

a hirer is protected by them.[42] Giving a hirer the opportunity to object to registration of the owner as absolute owner defeats one of the advantages of hire purchase, which is to enable a financier to repossess the goods on early default by the hirer and to sell them quickly while they still have a value.[43] Of course it may be desirable to limit the rights of owners to repossess.[44] Unscrupulous financiers should certainly have their licence withdrawn. It may also be desirable to introduce machinery whereby consumer hirers can apply for time to pay. However, the practice may act to the detriment of hirers if repossessed vehicles, which cannot be sold by the financier, deteriorate greatly in value between when they are repossessed and when the legal proceedings are disposed of or settled.

Legal Change

In 1990 the Supreme Court of Sri Lanka, the country's highest court, opined:

Expeditious debt recovery is, in the long-term, beneficial to borrowers in general for at least two reasons. Firstly, expeditious repayment or recovery of debts enhances the ability of lending institutions to lend to other borrowers. Secondly, the Law's delays in respect of debt recovery, howsoever and by whomsoever caused, tend to make lending institutions much more cautious and slow in lending; by refusing some applications, by requiring higher security from some borrowers, and by insisting on more stringent terms as to interest from other borrowers. Expeditious debt recovery will thus tend to make credit available more readily and on easier terms, and will maximise the flow of money into the economy. Undoubtedly, there is a legitimate national interest in expediting the recovery of debts by lending institutions engaged in the business of providing credit, and thereby stimulating the national economy and national development.[45]

It said this in upholding, in the main, the constitutionality of one of a number of Bills introduced by the government to facilitate debt recovery in Sri Lanka. The aim of this legislation, as the Supreme Court noted, was to facilitate economic development, although it is fair to add that lenders both from within and outside the country had been pressing for change for some time. The matter has a long history and is illustrative of how law can be thought to lag behind what is thought to be economically desirable. It is also illustrative of how law, even what might be thought to be the arcane law of security, can reflect a political struggle, in this case between traditionalists, led by the lawyers and modernizers, with economists in the vanguard.

---

[42] An early discussion is R.M. Goode and J.S. Ziegel, *Hire Purchase and Conditional Sale. A Comparative Survey of Commonwealth and American Law* (London, 1967), ch. 11.

[43] The Debt Recovery Committee, *Report*, 15 recommended insertion of a provision in the Motor Traffic Act to ensure speedy registration of repossessed motor vehicles subject to a hire or lease agreement.

[44] In other countries once one third of the price has been paid, the goods cannot be repossessed, e.g. Consumer Credit Act 1974, s 90 (UK).

[45] S.C. Special Determination No. 1/90, 4 January 1990.

In 1934, the Banking Commission of Sri Lanka reported.[46] It had been established to report on existing conditions of banking and credit, and to consider feasible steps in respect of the provision of banking and credit facilities for agriculture, industry, and trade. In the course of its report, it made several suggestions as to reform of the law to increase the availability of credit by removing what were perceived to be legal handicaps.

Banks and commercial bodies have emphatically complained to us that the commercial laws of Ceylon do not help the creditor . . . The [banks] rightly urged that, if the law helped the debtors against the legitimate rights of the creditor, no one should blame the latter if he became too cautious . . . We come to the conclusion that the legal machinery of the Island is very defective from the point of view of credit and lending, and that it should be overhauled if banking is to be its legitimate business.[47]

Specifically, the Banking Commission recommended changes in the law of security. The Commission suggested that the law relating to the mortgage of immovable property should be made to conform to Indian law.[48] Consequently, a mortgagee would in some cases have been able to realize his security by sale, enter into possession or appoint a receiver, all without recourse to a court. Generally in relation to the mortgage of movables, it recommended a simpler scheme, together 'with power to the lender to sell off the security in the event of the borrower failing to repay, after giving him due notice'.[49] Significantly, the Commission concluded its discussion of legal reforms by identifying the unsuitability of the Roman–Dutch law to modern commercial and credit activities. 'This is the main reason why the mercantile legislation in Ceylon is in its infancy and out of date . . . Modernisation of the legal system of Ceylon is a necessity for the smooth running of its commercial and banking machineries.'[50] Five years later the recommendations of the Banking Commission were endorsed in part by the Sub-Committee on Commercial Legislation.[51]

The Banking Commission had recommended that the defects in the law which it had identified should be examined in depth by a special commission. This was the origin of the Mortgage Commission, appointed in November 1943. The Second Interim Report of the Committee[52] led to the Mortgage Act. In essence

---

[46] *Ceylon Sessional Papers*, No. XXII, 1934. The Commission comprised mainly bankers—Sir N. Pochkhanawala, Managing Director of the Central Bank of India Ltd, and two Sri Lankans, Sir Marcus Fernando, Chairman of the State Mortgage Bank and Dr Samuel Chelliah Paul F.R.C.S. Dr Professor B.B. Das Gupta and Mr N.U. Jayawardena, both later associated with the Central Bank of Sri Lanka, were secretary and assistant secretary respectively of the Commission.

[47] *Ceylon Sessional Papers*, No. XXII, 1934, 106.   [48] *ibid.*   [49] *ibid.*

[50] *ibid.*, 110.

[51] *Sessional Paper*, No. X, 1939. The Committee comprised government officials and a representative of the law firm E.J. & G. de Saram.

[52] *Ceylon Sessional Papers*, No. V of 1945. The Commission comprised lawyers—L.M.D. de Silva KC as Chairman (a prominent lawyer, who later sat on the Supreme Court and Privy Cuncil); G. Crossette Thambiah as the other Commissioner (later Solicitor-General); and H.N.G. Fernando as secretary (later Chief Justice). The Commission was to report generally on the law of mortgage; to make recommendations for law reform 'with a view to removing defects and supplying deficiencies in

the Report and the Act rejected the approach of the Banking Commission; instead, both clung to the Roman–Dutch principles of mortgage. The traditionalists had routed the economic rationalists. The Report begins by rejecting the recommendations of the Banking Commission in relation to the mortgage of land. The reasons given can be gathered under four broad heads: it would be a 'perilous adventure' to superimpose one part of a foreign system of law (i.e. the English law of mortgage) upon the different system of land law in Sri Lanka; the evidence about delay in enforcing mortgages and its adverse effects on the confidence of investors, was thin; the English rule, that a mortgagee should be able to sell the property on default without intervention of the court, would lead to breaches of the peace;[53] and there was a need to protect borrowers. None of these reasons was overwhelmingly persuasive, except possibly the last.

Although it hardly featured in the Report, the nature of lending in Sri Lanka, and its consequences, in the first part of the twentieth century had burnt itself into the collective consciousness of many and clearly influenced the Commission. The story, in brief, is that in colonial times the British banks would not lend to Sri Lankans, except the very wealthy or very influential. To borrow money, Sri Lankan businessmen and agriculturalists had to turn to foreign moneylenders— Afghans and the South Indian Nattukottai Chettiars. This meant that in the economic depression of the 1930s, many Sri Lankan landowners were thus in the hands of foreign moneylenders to whom they had mortgaged their lands.[54]

The world-wide depression hit Ceylon as well . . . The banks having suspended all credit to the Chettiars after [abuses and collapses in the 1920s] further tightened their lending policies. The Chettiars on their part, unable to obtain facilities from the banks, demanded the repayment of their loans from their Ceylonese borrowers. When they found that the Ceylonese were unable to pay, the Chettiars put their promissory notes in suit and foreclosed on their mortgages. The period between 1930–1936 saw a spate of litigation initiated by the Chettiars against their Ceylonese borrowers who had defaulted in payment. One has only to scan the pages of the Ceylon Law Reports of that period to see the number of law-suits filed by the Chettiars against their debtors. Many a Ceylonese landowner lent his property to the Chettiars and many a Ceylonese debtor ended up in the Insolvency Court at the instance of his Chettiar creditor.[55]

The Land Redemption Ordinance[56] resulted from the political pressure exerted by dispossessed landowners. It was to enable the government to acquire land sold

the laws which limit the availability in Ceylon of adequate facilities for agricultural, industrial and commercial purposes'; and, significantly, to report on the nature of protection for 'the ancestral and other lands of agriculturalists, and to preserve a sufficient portion thereof for the maintenance of themselves and their families'.

[53] 'We are aware that in this country attachment to land and the desire at all costs to retain possession are one of the primary causes of crime': *ibid.*, 29.

[54] H. Tambiah, *Principles of Ceylon Law* (Colombo, 1972), 485.

[55] W. Weerasooria, *The Nattukottai Chettiar Merchant Bankers in Ceylon* (Colombo, 1973), xvi. It is only fair to add in defence of the Chettiars that they made credit readily available to Sri Lankans, were not demanding about the security they took, and were very reluctant to realize their security.

[56] No. 61 of 1942.

during the depression to pay off debts. The land was then to be restored to its original owners on the payment of its value in instalments. For our purposes, however, the most important upshot of the Mortgage Commission report was that, as previously mentioned, the Mortgage Act 1949 did not change fundamentally the Roman–Dutch law on parate execution.

Then in 1985, the Debt Recovery Committee recommended that parate execution in relation to corporeal movables be extended.[57] Despite opposition from the Bar Association[58] and another government-appointed committee,[59] the Debt Recovery Committee adhered to its views in a supplementary report, 'because movables in the custody of a borrower, secured by a mortgage, provides in the main the basic security for working capital of a trade or business. The right of parate execution in this instance will contribute to easy and enlarged availability, and reduced cost, of credit against such security'.[60]

By the late 1980s, the view that the law of credit and security needed reform was shared widely by government officials, bankers and by some lawyers.[61] Change was prompted in part by a crisis in non-bank financial intermediaries. Importantly, there was significant pressure as well from outside the country, notably from the World Bank.[62] The modernizers won the day in December 1989, when the Sri Lankan Cabinet approved a series of Bills to be introduced to the Parliament. In announcing the legislation, the Ministry of Finance noted that the present laws were 'outdated and not in line with legislation governing bank loans in force in other progressive countries'.[63] Thirteen Bills were enacted by the Sri Lankan Parliament in early 1990. The Prime Minister noted the economic rationale behind the legislation. 'The banks state that the long delays and the high cost of recovery of bank debts is one of the causes for the high interest rates which are being charged by banks from borrowers. It is very desirable that interest rates

[57] Debt Recovery Committee, *Report*, 8.

[58] Bar Association of Sri Lanka, *Report of the Bar Association of Sri Lanka, Seminar on Report to . . . Examine and Report on the Law and Practice Relating to Debt Recovery* (Colombo, 1987).

[59] Central Bank Committee, *Report of the Committee Constituted to Examine and Consider Certain Aspects of Law Relating to Recovery of Debt* (Colombo, 1987).

[60] *Summary of Comments on the Debt Recovery Committee (DRC) Report and the Responses to these Comments* (Colombo, 1987). The Supplementary Report was prepared by two members of the Debt Recovery Committee, Mr H.L. de Silva PC and Mr N.J.U. Jayawardena (the chairman having died after the original report).

[61] e.g. Minister of Finance in *Hansard*, 25 November 1987, 898. See also 'If the right of the parate execution had been granted to the Finance Companies most of them would not have collapsed and the poor depositors would have been saved from being deprived of their life savings': *Legal Aid Newsletter*, vol. 4, No. 5 May 1989, 1 (Comment).

[62] I declare my role as author of the World Bank report leading to the 1990 legislation: this did not escape criticism at the time or subsequently. e.g. Nayana, 'Legal Watch. Is the Law too Drastic in Destroying Businesses?', *The Island* (Colombo), 3 June 2001.

[63] Minister of Finance—Press Communique. Debt Recovery Legislation, 21 December 1989. In Parliament the Prime Minister said: 'Modern banking laws in other countries, in developed countries like the United Kingdom as well as developing countries like Singapore, allow the right of parate execution to banking institutions'.

should be reduced to the lowest possible level in order to encourage investment and development in the country.'[64]

Among the tranche of legislation were amendments to the Civil Code to speed up debt recovery;[65] to the Mortgage Act and the Consumer Credit Act and to the Trust Receipts Ordinance and the enactment of an Inland Trust Receipts Act. The Debt Recovery (Special Provisions) Act 1990 provides a special procedure for the recovery of loans by banks and finance companies.[66] A lending institution can file a plaint in court setting out particulars of the loan in default. The court then enters a decree nisi against the debtor.[67] If the defendant fails to show sufficient cause, the court converts the decree nisi into a decree absolute.[68] Thereafter it is not necessary for the lending institution to go to court again for a writ of execution. The decree absolute itself is deemed to be a writ of execution issued to the Fiscal.

Most importantly for our purposes is the Recovery of Loans by Banks (Special Provisions) Act 1990. The Act is a very significant change in giving the commercial banks the power of parate execution hitherto reserved for the state banks. (The Act does not entrust the finance companies with the power). The right of parate execution covers all property, movable, and immovable. There is a power on default to sell mortgaged property,[69] and a power to sell in a manager where immovable property has been mortgaged or where security has been given on any plant, machinery, or other movable property of an agricultural or industrial undertaking.[70] A manager has powers to control and manage the undertaking.[71] Moreover, the holder of the security can decide to sell if, for instance, the management is not working.[72]

The reforms introduced in 1990 had several technical shortcomings, which were one factor in their under-utilization. There was also a hesitancy in invoking the new powers of parate execution. One local commercial bank used it on a number of occasions after the Act came into force. Other local commercial banks, and certainly the foreign commercial banks, were rather hesitant at being in the vanguard in this regard. Interestingly, the state banks became more willing to use their existing power of parate execution. The culture of opposition to conferring additional powers on financiers did not dissolve overnight. Pressure for change continued from outside, however, notably from the World Bank and International Monetary Fund. To accommodate these different forces, a Presidential Commission was formed to review the new laws and suggest amendments. In 1993 the Commission published a report on the subject. Its unenthusiastic

---

[64] *Hansard*, 23 January 1990, 864.   [65] Notably ss. 705A, 705B.

[66] Act No. 2 of 1990.

[67] Section 2(1), 4. The method of serving the decree nisi incorporates ss 705A and 705B of the Civil Procedure Code.

[68] Act No. 2 of 1990. Thus others are excluded, such as merchant banks, brokers and cooperative societies. Claims under the Act are limited to loans of Rs 150,000 or greater, i.e. commercial loans: s 2(2).

[69] Section 4.   [70] Section 5.   [71] Sections 5(2), 6.   [72] Section 3, proviso.

conclusion on parate execution was that it was a harsh remedy, to be used only as a last resort.

[A]fter the introduction of the new laws the private commercial banks, with a single exception, have not resorted to the power of parate execution for reasons which vary from bank to bank, but with the underlying realisation that it is after all not in the interests of the bank to resort to harsh legal measures in a highly competitive banking market. *The Commission hopes that this cautious attitude of the banks will continue to prevail in the interests of the variable economic system where the banks acknowledgedly are the principal lenders.* Indiscriminate use of these measures by banks to hasten the process of debt recovery may lead to the creation of a thriving non-institutional, non-supervised, high interest lending sector with the banking system gradually sidelined (emphasis added).[73]

Most of the committee's limited recommendations were implemented in amendments to the Debt Recovery (Special Provisions) Act in 1994.

Despite the changes to the law in the 1990s, banks continued to use the debt recovery laws as a last resort. Apart from cultural factors, technical defects were one explanation. For example, in relation to parate execution the law requires a resolution for the possession or sale of property to be passed by the board of directors of the bank. Foreign banks carrying on business in Sri Lanka through branch offices found this a practical difficulty. There is also a statutory obligation on the banks to inform the borrower that the resolution has been passed. Dishonest borrowers have taken this opportunity to make one or two repayments so that enforcement action was withdrawn but then continued to default. Another explanation had to do with institutional deficiencies. For example, debt recovery suits filed under the Debt Recovery Special Provisions Act No. 2 of 1990 probably amounted to about 700 in the first decade of its operations, less than originally anticipated. The most general but obvious reason was that lawyers and judges working outside the cities were ignorant of the new law. Moreover, some judges showed an indifference, if not an outright hostility, to the law by treating cases filed under the new law in the same manner as those filed under ordinary procedures. For example, s 6 of the Act does not permit a defendant to appear or show cause in relation to a decree nisi unless leave to do so has been first obtained from the court. The stringent requirements of this section were not taken into account by some judges.[74] With parate execution the law gives the power to lenders to take possession of secured property and manage it for the debtor until the debt is repaid. Yet typically staff have not had the skill and competence to manage a business in financial difficulties so as to revive it to profitability and enable the loans to be repaid. Elsewhere, there are qualified insolvency practitioners, part of a regulated profession, who can act as managers of businesses. In Sri Lanka the accountancy and legal professions have yet to evolve to any extent such specialized services.

---

[73] *Third Interim Report of the Committee on Debt Recovery Legislation* (Colombo, 1991), 12.
[74] S. Abeyratne, *Banking and Debt Recovery in Emerging Markets* (Aldershot, 2001), 177–80, 200–1, 221–2.

Conclusion

The transplant of commercial law into Sri Lanka was the outcome of a combination of historical circumstances. The result was a mix of systems—the Roman–Dutch law, English common law, and statutory law. Even in the colonial period, Sri Lankans had some flexibility. From the point of view of policymakers, the conflict between different strains of Sri Lankan opinion blocked legal change. Economic opinion was in favour of the abandonment of Roman–Dutch law, in particular in the area of security. That, as mentioned above, was a recommendation of the Banking Commission in the early 1930s. This change was opposed by an important strand of legal opinion, which crystallized in the report of the Mortgage Commission. The traditionalists were influenced partly by the experience of the Depression, and possibly also by a perception amongst some lawyers that the preservation of Roman–Dutch law, not being British law, was important in the anti–colonial struggle.

That conflict between economic opinion and a strand of legal opinion was played out again in Sri Lanka half a century later.[75] This time, however, economic opinion won, at least on the surface. In the 1990s a series of Bills was enacted by the Sri Lankan Parliament, notably that extending the power of parate execution to all banks. In effect common law notions of enforcing security were transplanted into Sri Lankan law. The outcome is explained partly by political changes—in 1989 there was a new president in Sri Lanka—and partly by pressures for full legal change from sources of external funding to the country.

A larger issue in the Sri Lankan story is the efficacy of law in meeting commercial needs. Clearly there has been widespread support for the changes, as being necessary for Sri Lanka to achieve desirable economic goals. Whether the law has achieved these is a different matter. One of law's functions is to represent symbolically a change in public policy, and the 1990s legislation seems to have had some effect in changing attitudes. As we have seen, however, there is a right to be sceptical about law's role in social change.[76] One factor is an underlying theme of this book, that fine laws on the books can be sabotaged in their actual working. A survey of export-oriented foreign investors in Sri Lanka, and business people, lawyers, and accountants in Sri Lanka uncovered a picture of both under-enforced and inconsistently enforced laws by government agencies. More seriously, it revealed substantial concerns that the courts were racked by delays, ignorant of modern commercial law principles and, indeed, biased against foreign investors.

It was alleged by many respondents in interviews, including lawyers with first hand experience, that many judges are incapable of impartiality towards them. This was

---

[75] And with one of the original actors—N.U. Jayawardena served as assistant secretary to the Banking Commission and was one of the members of the Debt Recovery Committee (1985).

[76] 23, 26–7 above.

attributed to the fact that, being low paid, the judiciary was an avenue pursued by the less bright and less high flying members of Sri Lanka's legal profession, and that these people tended to come from provincial areas with little experience or trust of foreign investors.[77]

None of this should mean that attempts to transform legal systems are misguided or, even worse, politically suspect. Places like Sri Lanka can now draw on the experience of economically successful countries in the region like Singapore. The problem of the poor remains; legal support for cooperative activity is just one method of giving some relief in this regard.[78] Yet it is still the case that our knowledge of the role of commercial law in facilitating economic activity is rudimentary. The gap between the law in the books and the law in action—as in other countries—reflects the limited efficacy of the law in achieving the goals of social engineers. As Ziegel has noted in another context: '[S]ocial engineering is much more difficult than mechanical engineering, and...much friction must be expected between the component parts.'[79]

[77] A. Perry, 'Is Legal Globalisation an Impossible Dream? National Implementation of International Standards', CEPMLP Internet Journal, Vol. 3, article 4, www.dundee.ac.uk/cepmlp/journal

[78] See the interesting discussion about cooperative activity in Sri Lanka in I. Bakhoum *et al.* (eds), *Banking the Unbankable* (London, 1989), 88–99. As we have seen the 1990s reforms in Sri Lanka are mainly confined to larger transactions.

[79] J.S. Ziegel, 'The Politics of the Imagination: A Life of F.R. Scott' (1989) *UTLJ* 426, 433.

11

Conclusion

A number of threads run through this book about how law works. The first concerns some fundamental values in the law, access to justice, equality before the law, and the rule of law. These values do not have the same purchase on legal claims as legal rights, although specific claims can sometimes be constructed on the back of them. Importantly they are a base for agitation for change in the civil justice system (including the legal profession), the working of public and private bureaucracies, and the allocation of public moneys. Related in particular to access to justice is the second thread, procedure. Procedure has a broad ambit, covering not just what lawyers know as the rules of procedure but also the working of the courts and the facilitation of justice more generally in society. Finally there is the thread of law in society. Understanding the working of the law cannot come from within the law alone. As Holmes put it, in the passage following his oft-quoted aphorism that the life of the law has not been logic, but experience:

The felt necessities of the time, the prevalent moral and political theories, intuitions of public policy, avowed or unconscious, even the prejudices which judges share with their fellow-men, have had a good deal more to do than the syllogism in determining the rules by which men should be governed. The law embodies the story of a nation's development... In order to know what it is, we must know what it tends to become. We must alternatively consult history and existing theories of legislation.[1]

Let us examine each of these threads—values, procedure, and context—in the light of the present study of how law works.

Access to justice, equality before the law, the rule of law—these are fundamental legal values in liberal democratic societies. Among their counterparts in the political sphere are universal suffrage, free and fair elections, and government accountability to those elected and to society. The routine of the law's working means that the beneficial impetus of these fundamental legal values can pass unnoticed and unappreciated. Casual acquaintance with situations where they are absent or inchoate brings into sharp focus their essential worth. That does not mean that their ambit, content and implications are unambiguous. Nor should it be taken to imply that these values have regular application in the daily practice of

---

[1] O.W. Holmes, Jr, *The Common Law* (London, 1882), 1.

the law.[2] But the law's specific rights and duties, and its potential, are played out against the backdrop of these fundamental values. They are represented in the ethical duties of each lawyer. They give coherence to the legal system as a whole. They thus have a significance even in its mundane working.

For our purposes we have taken access to justice to mean that there is machinery enabling individuals and groups to vindicate rights recognized by the legal order; equality before the law, that like cases are treated alike and in a wider sense, that differences in treatment in the substantive law do not violate notions of equal respect and are rationally justified; and the rule of law, that the state acts under legal authority and in accordance with law.[3] Each of these values imply institutional arrangements. Thus common features of states with the rule of law are public and general laws, an independent judiciary and legal profession, and provisions for judicial review of state action.[4] Apart from fleeting glimpses of what these values encompass, our task has not been one of jurisprudential analysis where the meaning of these values is mapped, their strengths and weaknesses exposed and their contradictions laid bare. Rather, what has been centre stage is the ordinary functioning of these values in the civil justice system, to some degree across time and to a limited extent across jurisdictions.[5]

An overriding factor in how these values work in practice, as we have seen, is that they come up against economic inequality and powerful interests. At its simplest a lack of financial resource and its common correlates like knowledge, skills, and contacts lead to unmet legal need. Unmet legal need concerns our first fundamental legal value, access to justice. Many with legal problems do not pursue them to resolution; many with legal rights do not vindicate them; and many needing the law's protection continue to be exposed to arbitrary and oppressive action.[6] Partly the answer to unmet legal need lies in publicly funded legal services, which put parties on a more equal footing. Publicly funded legal services take various forms—subsidy of private lawyers who can consequently take on clients not able to pay, employed lawyers working for state bureaux or independent law centres, and the not-for-profit sector which uses paralegals, as well as

---

[2] Examples of cases where access to justice has been invoked are at 37, n.13 above; equality before the law featured in *Gwilliam v West Hertfordshire Hospitals NHS Trust* [2002] EWCA Civ 1041; [2003] QB 443, 461B, *per* Sedley LJ; *Goodwin v United Kingdom* (2002) 35 EHRR 18, para. 74; *Stafford v United Kingdom* (2002) 35 EHRR 32, para. 68; and Lord Steyn used the rule of law in his reasoning in *R v Secretary of State for the Home Department ex p. Pierson* [1998] AC 539, 591A–F; *R (Anufrijeva) v Secretary of State for the Home Department* [2003] UKHL 36; [2004] 1 AC 604, 621H. See J. Jowell, 'The Rule of Law Today', in J. Jowell & D. Oliver (eds), *The Changing Constitution*, 5th edn. (Oxford, 2005); R. Fallon, 'The "Rule of Law" as a Concept in Constitutional Discourse' (1997) 97 *Colum.LR* 1; K. Mason, 'The Rule of Law', in P. Finn (ed.), *Essays on Law and Government* (Sydney, 1995), vol.1.   [3] See 3–4, 36–9, 217–9 above.
[4] E. Jensen, 'The Rule of Law and Judicial Reform', in E. Jensen & T. Heller (eds), *Beyond Common Knowledge* (Stanford, 2003). See 25 above.
[5] Some jurisprudential discussions of equality before the law and the rule of law incorporate what happens in practice: see R. Dworkin, *A Matter of Principle* (Cambridge, MA, 1985), 12; 221 above.
[6] 9, 38, 84, 90, 108–12 above.

lawyers, who are expert in areas of need such as social welfare and housing law. Partly the answer also lies in reforming the procedure of the ordinary courts, creating special courts such as those for small claims, and fostering alternative dispute resolution which bestows legal redress quickly and cheaply. To each of these procedural issues we return.

Even in its narrowest formulation our second value, equality before the law, demands the equal application of legal rules irrespective of endowments like power, wealth, status, and race. In other words courts by their very nature can to an extent cut through social and economic equalities in their treating of like cases alike. In practice that turns importantly on an equality of arms before the courts; in other words, effective access to justice. Treating like cases alike is clearly not confined to courts but extends to all agencies of the state in their daily application of the law. The principle must run through the administration of the whole of the law, even areas like commercial law where at first blush it does not seem especially relevant.[7] Apart from specific cases, where the absence of an equality of arms tips the scales, the substantive law itself may be moulded over a period as certain arguments acquire a natural quality because they are constantly advanced but the other side is not. It is a matter of inquiry into the extent to which this has happened historically in the common law because employers have tended to be heard, not employees, property owners, not tenants and producers, not consumers.[8] Certainly we know that substantive law can trump equality before the law in a more direct, indeed brutish, way. From the nineteenth century equality before the law led Australian courts generally to accord Aboriginals the same rights and to subject them to the same duties, as others. But equality before the law broke down completely once state power attempted forcibly to assimilate Aboriginals to, or segregate them from, mainstream society. Equality before the law in its formal sense meant little as the substantive law rendered it meaningless in so many ways.[9]

The state with its power and wealth is given no special privilege under the third fundamental value, the rule of law. It is the rule of law, not rule by law. No one is above the law and the state and its officials must obey it like everyone else.[10] As Lord Phillips MR has put it:

It is the role of the judges to preserve the rule of law . . . The common law power of the judges to review the legality of administrative action is a cornerstone of the rule of law in this country and one that the judges guard jealously.[11]

Police abuse provides some of the most egregious examples of the rule of law being violated.[12] The kowtowing by courts to powerful interests, in contravention of the

---

[7] 36–7, 216ff, 267–8 above.   [8] 223 above.   [9] Chapter 8 above.
[10] This is A.V. Dicey's most lasting contribution: *An Introduction to the Study of the Law of the Constitution*, 10th edn (London, 1965), 193–4. See T. Allan, *Constitutional Justice* (Oxford, 2001), 16–17, 42–3 and passim; C. Gearty, *Principles of Human Rights Adjudication* (Oxford, 2004), 60–8.
[11] *R (G) v Immigration Appeal Tribunal* [2004] EWCA Civ 1731; [2005] 1 WLR 1445; [2005] 2 All ER 165, paras 12–13.   [12] 84, 90, 220 above.

law, also brings one up short.[13] But it is as well to recall that there is potential for breach of the principle of legality in the quotidian functioning of the state. Broad discretion in social regulation and in the statutory framework for social benefits and services, for example, creates opportunities for state agencies to evolve their own moral ethos which they apply without clear cover of law.[14] The consequence for the beneficiaries of social legislation is that they may be denied that to which they are entitled. Definite and openly published rules, coupled with systems of external review, can bring the administration of social rights into closer harmony with the rule of law. It should also not be forgotten, as Julius Stone reminded us some time ago, that the rule of law is fruitful as a value only if it says something intelligible about the justice embodied in the law.[15]

So these fundamental legal values have some role in ameliorating economic inequalities and in restraining powerful interests. More importantly, they are a persuasive advocate for legal and social reform. Access to justice is a rallying cry supporting publicly funded legal services. It has driven procedural change and the re-design of legal institutions. Lord Woolf used access to justice as the label for his comprehensive package of procedural and other reforms for the courts of England and Wales. Equality before the law has acted as a restraint on state power and has proved a tool for sweeping away distinctions in the substantive law when these seemed to flout notions of equal respect or to incorporate distinctions which could not be rationally justified.[16] And the rule of law is now standard fare prescribed by international institutions if countries are to develop as liberal democracies and reduce poverty.[17]

Because these values are a lever for legal and social reform their implications are not accepted uncritically. Nor should they be. Too often, to take one example, ingredients of the rule of law like independence of the legal profession have been lazily invoked as a mask for restrictive practices or institutional arrangements which can no longer be justified. Moreover, lawyers too readily assume that their institutional ways are sacrosanct. Thus the Woolf Inquiry demonstrated that access to justice was ill-served by a Rolls Royce treatment of every case heard in the higher courts. Under the Civil Procedure Rules a different path is taken and proportionality is the key in allocating the court's resources. Similarly, budgetary pressures in most jurisdictions have put a great strain on publicly funded legal services. Apart from justifications derived from equality for the law, we have seen that another justification for publicly funded legal services lies in their prophylactic potential for social deprivation. To take one example: the person protected against domestic violence may not be on the homeless list, her children may stay out of care and she may still be able to keep her part-time job. In this discussion, however, the crucial point is that the case for public subsidy for legal services, at

---

[13] 282–3 above.
[14] 232 above. A classic exposition is K. Davies, *Discretionary Justice* (Westport, CT., 1969).
[15] J. Stone, *Legal System and Lawyers' Reasoning* (London, 1964), 12.
[16] 223 above.   [17] 25 above.

the expense of other public goods like schools, hospitals, and national development must be made; it cannot be assumed.

Part of the lawyer's ethical duty is to uphold the law, its institutions, and its fundamental values. Around the world bar associations have been strong defenders of the rule of law and vocal critics of governments which fail to comply with its postulates, especially when the independence of the judiciary is under attack.[18] In the result governments have sometimes moved to curb the activities of lawyers in their attempt to call state agents to account for breach of the principle of legality.[19] As well as their obligation to the rule of law, lawyers have a duty to further equality before the law in the sense of ensuring, as far as practicable, an equality of arms or level playing field between parties before the court. Whatever that duty may imply in particular cases, it certainly includes an advocacy of publicly funded legal services to further access to justice and a degree of pro bono commitment. As Sir Jack Jacob put it, not only should there be equality before the law, but equal access to law and legal services which comes, in part, from a society's determination to 'improve its system of civil justice'.[20]

That introduces the crucial role of procedure in the working of the law. In some analyses, procedure is a special kind of substantive right.[21] Certainly it can be said that procedure is sometimes the dead hand impeding justice and the realization of the fundamental values we have been considering. In 1745 Rev John Wesley, who was to lead the spiritual revival in the Church of England which ultimately became Methodism, wrote about 'that foul monster', the Chancery Bill which had been commenced against him:

A scroll it was of 42 pages in large folio to tell a story which needed not to have taken up forty lines, and stuffed with such stupid senseless improbable lies, many of them, too, quite foreign to the question . . .[22]

Chancery procedure has moved on since then, but Wesley's complaint is a salutary reminder how, by accretion, procedure can become a barrier to, not a facilitator of justice. Procedure needs constantly to be renewed in the light of its purposes and the fundamental values of the law. As we have seen Lord Woolf's access to justice reforms tried to cut through late twentieth century English procedure with his big bang reforms in the rules and administration of the courts in England and Wales.

Procedural reform is not easy. People have an attachment to the established ways. There can be genuine disagreement as to the path to be taken: one person's delay, for example, is another person's careful pursuit of justice. One person's

---

[18] e.g. S. Irwin, C. Maguire, G. Martin, & R. Martin, *The State of Justice in Zimbabwe* (London, 2004), a report by the bars of England and Wales, Scotland, Ireland, and Australia. See also the work of the International Commission of Jurists, Centre for the Independence of Judges and Lawyers, www.icj.org.   [19] 90–1 above.

[20] J. Jacob, *The Fabric of English Civil Justice* (London, 1987), 277.

[21] See L. Alexander, 'Are Procedural Rights Derivative Substantive Rights?' (1998) 17 *Law & Phil.* 19.

[22] Quoted by A. Birrell, 'Changes in Equity, Procedure and Principles', in *A Century of Law Reform* (London, 1901), 182.

attempt to reduce costs by encouraging settlement, another's denial of the public value of judgments. These days a major driver of civil justice policy in many countries is the competing demands on public resources. Even in a wealthy jurisdiction like England and Wales, not every demand for access to justice can be met by the courts. Nor can every demand for the high-class service generally available in the higher courts. The Overriding Objective of the CPR now acknowledges this: cases are to be dealt with justly, which means, so far as is practicable, allotting to each an appropriate share of the court's resources, while taking into account the need of other cases, including those still in the queue.[23] It is a world of limited public resources where the case for competing demands such as education and health are politically highly persuasive. The case for civil justice can be made, and made persuasively, not least by comparison elsewhere.[24] But public subsidy is rationed and so innovative ways must also be found to handle disputes and give effect to legal rights. Lawyers have an obligation to assist in this task.

Various avenues for reform are open. Within the existing courts procedures can be calibrated to the level of dispute. The fast track, established within the CPR as a result of the Woolf reforms, is an example. Another is the epistolary jurisdiction of the Supreme Court of India, where public interest litigation can be commenced in the most casual manner.[25] Another avenue of institutional reform is to found new courts, with truncated procedures. At one end of the spectrum are small claims courts. In some jurisdictions these are separate from the ordinary courts and prohibit appearances by lawyers. At the other end are the special courts founded in the sub-continent of India for speedy debt recovery by banks. The justification for this type of economic access is the extensive delays, and hostile environment for such claims, in the ordinary courts. Banks carry a high ratio of bad debts on their books which is a drag on their lending activities and hence growth in the economy. Yet another avenue of procedural reform embraces any number of the alternative dispute resolution procedures we have encountered, from the adoption of village procedures in the Indian sub-continent to court-annexed mediation in the United States.[26] The merit of each of these needs careful consideration in the light of factors such as the effectiveness of the courts, the resources available to them, the efficacy of the alternatives and the impact on values such as the fundamental legal values identified earlier.

Through these various procedures and institutional arrangements, coupled with the quite separate processes for legislation, law works in social life and for social ends. Although a discrete body of knowledge, often impenetrable to those

---

[23] CPR r 1.1(2)(e). See *Jones v University of Warwick* [2003] EWCA Civ 151; [2003] 1 WLR 954, para. 25; A. Zuckerman, *Civil Procedure* (London, 2003), 34–43.

[24] Even taking into account the different working of courts elsewhere in Europe, the amount spent in Britain on courts (excluding legal aid) is low by comparison, measured per capita, as a proportion of the national budget or as a percentage of the gross average salary; Council of Europe (European Commission for the Efficiency of Justice), *European Judicial Systems* 2002, CEPEJ (2004) 30 (Strasbourg, 2004), Tables 1–3. [25] 92–3 above.

[26] 96–7, 174–6 above.

without specialist training, law is moulded by social forces, is used to effect social purposes and has social consequences. It is neither autonomous nor a self-referential system. Law cannot be understood in a vacuum but only as a complex of people, practices, and institutions working in different ways across time and societies. Throwing light on how law works can derive from an appreciation of its historical and social setting, the purposes to which it is put, its distinctive institutions, its functioning in everyday life, and its consequences for government, markets, and society generally.

Little need be said about the first of these. The importance of law's historical and social setting is self-evident. So historical experiences etch themselves on the collective mind of lawyers to influence current events even if they are no longer relevant. The same legal institution in different societies can operate in different ways or even prove redundant in some because of other factors such as the functioning of other professions. Legal reforms might be successfully grafted onto some legal systems but not others because the receptive conditions are absent. Some legal institutions thrive in a society, while others, performing very similar functions, prove sluggish. Across time the same legal rules apply differently because major users adopt a new policy or the subject matter of their application undergoes significant change. The quality of a jurisdiction's judiciary, court staff, and legal profession, indeed, its legal culture, cast a long shadow over how its legal system works. We have encountered each of these and other examples of the role of history and social setting.[27]

Law is an institutional framework for guiding and managing society. As an important form for the expression of public policy it seeks to effect a huge range of purposes. Those purposes represent the outcome, or part of a continuing process, of social and political movement, possibly a conflict of ideas but often a conflict over resources. Past injustices may drive change. In some instances law proceeds to effect its purposes by big bang, rather than incremental, change. Sometimes it performs important symbolic functions by broadcasting that public policy has changed or is moving in a particular direction. In these circumstances the immediate effectiveness of the law is secondary. Sometimes the law will represent a second-best solution—for example rougher justice for small claims in the civil justice system—because other priorities demand resources. Achieving change is not only or even primarily a matter of technical expertise but a matter of leadership— building support, collaboration, appealing to fundamental values, education, and campaigning. Supportive social research may be a factor in successful change. Especially when the purpose is social engineering on an ambitious scale, such as reforming the civil justice system, advancing minority rights or using law to further economic development, proponents of change are likely to be in for a long haul.[28]

---

[27] e.g. 302–5, 100, 279–8, 298–9, 46, 48–9, 114, 120 above.
[28] See R. Cranston, *Law, Government and Public Policy* (Melbourne, 1987) for one discussion of these issues.

Dispute resolution is generally conceived of as the quintessential function of courts, although other social arrangements such as tribunals, mediators, ombudsmen, and community organizations perform this function, with differing levels of formality. A great many of the grievances, disagreements, and conflicts in society never get near a court. Societies vary in their propensity to litigate.[29] One reason is that other social organizations may handle disputes. Even if individuals and groups proceed to courts with their disputes, these must be cast in legal terms. Many disputes are abandoned or settled, and are never subject to formal resolution. There is an accretion of matters through the civil justice system as this occurs.

While courts are oriented to adjudicating disputes that is only part of their functioning. First, they contribute to dispute settlement outside courts by the so-called radiating effects of those they do adjudicate. At its simplest parties settle disputes in the light of how litigated cases have been decided, which underlines the need for a regular flow of decisions in all parts of the civil law. Moreover, courts have a radiating effect with the values to which they give effect in their reasoned decision making. Common law courts do not have the same scope as constitutional courts to give meaning and expression to public values, although there are still important opportunities with the values in the common law itself and in statutory law,[30] and occasionally with the fundamental values of access to justice, equality before the law, and the rule of law.

Courts may be a limited vehicle for influencing public policy and forcing social change. Even when litigation fails, it sometimes attracts publicity to an issue and acts as a catalyst for change through the political system. Public interest litigation in places like the United States and India has been facilitated by a written constitution and bill of rights, an activist judiciary and a perception that political avenues are blocked. In the US courts have directed school desegregation and the reform of prisons through the use of injunctions and court-appointed masters.[31] That, however, is a fading vision in an age when the watchword is judicial restraint in who is appointed to many US courts. In India those acting for the marginalized and under-represented have used legal advocacy to advance their interests in public interest cases. But there has been considerable disappointment that court orders to institutions to transform their practices in accordance with constitutional values have not always sustained change over a period.[32]

With more liberal rules of standing and an expansive public law the English courts have been attracting some public interest litigation. The advent of the Human Rights Act 1998 has accentuated this. Non-government organizations

---

[29] 112 above.

[30] In Britain the Human Rights Act 1998 is especially important. See also P. Finn, 'Statutes and the Common Law' (1992) 22 *U. W. Aust. L. R.* 7; J. Beatson, 'Has the Common Law a Future?' (1997) 56 *Camb. LJ* 291. See also 15 above.

[31] M. Feeley, 'Implementing Court Orders in the United States: Judges as Executioners', in M. Hertogh & S. Halliday (eds), *Judicial Review and Bureaucratic Impact* (Cambridge, 2004).

[32] 93 above.

(NGOs) have used litigation strategically as part of a campaign to effect or block social change.[33] Yet public interest litigation has never taken off in Britain. That has turned partly on it not being possible to characterize many issues in legal terms in the absence of a written constitution or bill of rights. Partly also is that courts are rightly not seen as the same political resource as in the United States. For social reformers government, not the courts, is the pathway to a better society. Legislators are in a better position than judges to give expression to public values. Social change is a matter of political activity, campaigning for change, generating a public awareness about issues, and using the machinery of the state for beneficial purposes. Quite apart from other factors this acknowledges the courts' institutional limitations such as the inability in complex cases to see all the consequences of tampering with an issue and that judicial law-making is incremental, with breakthroughs like *Donoghue v Stevenson*[34] being the exception. Perhaps most importantly, it also recognizes that too grand a vision for the courts threatens to diminish their legitimacy.

Outside the courts law permeates daily activity. This is not just, or even mainly, dispute resolution by other means. It is individuals, groups, and institutions invoking law to contract, incorporate, form partnerships, take security, and enter any other number of legal arrangements.[35] It is lawyers serving their clients in their daily business, their behaviour moulded not only by the necessities of this and the law but by the network of ethical rules for their profession. It is the bank official making a loan to a customer using standard forms drawn in the light of the law, and in accordance with manuals and procedures designed to comply with legal requirements. It is the enforcement of regulatory law by government agencies operating with an institutional memory of how best to ensure compliance by the regulated with legal requirements.[36] It is the social welfare agency authorized by law to administer welfare benefits and services but sometimes with perceptions of its beneficiaries and values driven by public policy and community mores.

Most of this activity, although governed by law, will never be seen by a lawyer, certainly not by a court. Disputes may occur in relation to any of these matters, which can take a legal turn. A feature of government agencies, for example, is that often for the best of motives they develop their own agendas. Some of these are not authorized by, and may even be in breach of, the law. External review of their performance by inspectorates, and to a limited extent of their individual decisions by tribunals, ombudsmen and exceptionally courts, is a means of keeping them on the right track. While external review has an important role, what is essential is the ethos of the agency and integrating lawful behaviour within their everyday practices. Transparency and accountability can be keys to guaranteeing this.

It is a sociological truism that the law in the books does not always coincide with the law in action. Partly that is because of the factors we have been considering.

---

[33] 120 above.   [34] [1932] AC 562.
[35] H. Collins, *Regulating Contracts* (Oxford, 1999), 149 ff.
[36] e.g. K. Hawkins, *Law as Last Resort* (Oxford, 2003).

Even assuming people are legally conscious and competent, there can be all sorts of reasons that they do not mobilize the law when things go wrong. Or to take another example, law fails to trigger behavioural change because those entrusted with implementing social regulation fall short in the task. As for the courts, they have only an intermittent impact even in areas where there is a steady stream of litigation. The administrative machinery thrown up by some US and Indian courts following public interest litigation is quite exceptional. In some instances, however, law can mould opinion and guide behaviour if it captures the public mood or operates in a sustained manner. For the reasons we have identified courts are generally incapable of this, except on a limited scale. Legislation, supported by executive action, is what is needed. That raises a whole set of other issues. One is that a law can have unintended consequences, some of which may be beneficial but others which may eat away at its very purpose. Another is the obvious point that social change is not always beneficial. We have seen one example where the upshot of public policy enshrined in law was the destruction of the whole way of life of a people.[37]

Overall, then, the working out in practice of legal norms and institutions needs to be seen against the backdrop of social life. Even if the focus were legal concepts and rules alone, our understanding would be enhanced by an exploration of their historical development, location in values, customs or commercial practice, or operation comparatively. When the subject, as here, has been practical working of the law, the need for the broader canvas of history, public policy, social organization, and market setting is almost self-evident. How else can we understand issues such as why fundamental values such as access to justice, equality before the law, and the rule of law fall short in their operation; the forces behind successful legal reform in areas such as procedure, social rights, and emerging markets; and how the direction of legal change is conditioned in different societies?

That does not mean that the task of understanding the working of the law in these broader contexts is easy. There is no grand theory or master idea which, however attractive on the page, does not break down when tested against reality. At most there are a number of frameworks for thinking about issues. Some of these have been deployed, along with the findings of social research. Social research is important because it highlights the run of the mill, rather than the vivid, possibly atypical individual case which lawyers often use in argument to identify problems and suggest solutions. So in this manner the book has offered a combination of specific studies into the machinery and impact of the law, tied together with the threads of values, procedure, and social context. Bacon once observed that the eye of understanding is like the eye of sense: just as great objects can be seen through small holes, so far-reaching axioms can be seen through small and maybe unimpressive instances. This is the premise of *How Law Works*.

---

[37] Chapter 8.

Index